Sons of the Reich

The History of II SS Panzer Corps
in
Normandy, Arnhem, The Ardennes
and on The Eastern Front

SONS OF THE REICH

THE HISTORY OF II SS PANZER CORPS
in
NORMANDY, ARNHEM, THE ARDENNES
AND ON THE EASTERN FRONT

by

Michael Reynolds

SPELLMOUNT
Staplehurst

British Library Cataloguing in Publication Data:
A catalogue record for this book is available
from the British Library

Copyright © Michael Reynolds 2002
Maps copyright © Jay Karamales 2002

ISBN 1-86227-146-1

First published in the UK in 2002 by
Spellmount Limited
The Old Rectory
Staplehurst
Kent TN12 0AZ

1 3 5 7 9 8 6 4 2

Typeset in Palatino by Rowland Phototypesetting Limited
Bury St Edmunds, Suffolk
Printed in Great Britain by
TJ International Limited, Padstow, Cornwall

Contents

CONTENTS

List of Maps

(between pages 361–96)

Publisher's Note

It is regretted that for commercial reasons it has been impossible to include coloured or pull-out maps in this book; however, for those purists who enjoy knowing the exact location of the places mentioned and their relationship to one another, it is suggested that they photocopy and enlarge the maps provided and have them to hand when reading. This will also enable them to insert thrust and defence lines etc., which particularly interest them.

Acknowledgements

In the course of studying history one makes many acquaintances and I have been constantly cheered by the generous way in which so many of my fellow researchers have been prepared to share with me their particular knowledge or expertise. Often these relationships have developed into rewarding and lasting friendships and I have been delighted to find that in writing this my fourth book that my circle of friends has widened yet again.

Every author needs a good publisher and I am particularly fortunate that mine, Jamie Wilson, is not only that, but a good friend as well. He and a team of other stalwarts have assisted me through two more years of research and writing and I am most grateful to them all. I list them below in no particular order of priority:

American

Jay Karamales for my Maps and Appendices and carrying out research for me in the US National Archives.

Bill Warnock for providing photographs from his personal collection and detailed information originating in the Berlin Document Centre relating to certain characters in this book.

Doug McCabe, the archivist of the Ryan Collection at Ohio University for help in obtaining rare photographs.

Canadian

John Fedorowicz and Mike Olive, President and Vice President respectively of Fedorowicz Publishing Inc., for allowing me to quote freely from their excellent publications.

Belgian

Edouard and Marie-Berthe de Harenne for having me to stay over and over again in their beautiful Château during my many visits to the Ardennes.

Georges and Susie Balaes, Joseph and Madeleine Dejardin-Nyst and Marie-France Grégoire and Ben for their hospitality, friendship and help in innumerable ways.

British

Tony Baxter for proof reading and suggesting useful amendments to my first drafts.

Vanessa and John Hampson for translating documents in the German language.

Gordon Cantley, a former Royal Engineer and veteran of Operation MARKET GARDEN, for his personal story and advice on engineer matters.

Mike Chilcott for translating documents in the Russian language and for providing other information from French sources.

Charles Dick for the provision of Soviet documents and advice on the Red Army.

Jack Francis for the provision of information from the British Army's Tactical Doctrine Retrieval Cell.

Mike Wood for never failing to come up with accurate information from the US and German National Archives concerning German equipment holdings and for the loan of numerous important books.

Charles Markuss for advice on military equipment.

Martin Middlebrook for permission to use three maps of Arnhem and Oosterbeek, slightly amended, from his book *Arnhem 1944 The Airborne Battle*.

Dutch

Adrian Groeneweg, a Trustee of the Hartenstein Museum in Oosterbeek, for his advice and guidance concerning MARKET GARDEN.

Frank van den Bergh, historian of the National Liberation Museum 1944–1945, Groesbeek, for his advice concerning MARKET GARDEN.

I would also like to thank most sincerely all those who have kindly allowed me to quote from their writings. Their books and publications are listed in the Bibliography.

Most of the photographs in this book are from my personal collection, built up over a number of years from American and German National Archives and the private collections of generous American and German friends. Precise attributions are shown where known. Photographs show-ing German officers and equipment were usually taken by uniformed German cameramen and photographers and are available in the Bundes-archiv in Koblenz. I am most grateful to all those, named and unnamed, who have enabled me to publish this particular set of photographs.

And finally, I must once again thank my wife Anne – for all those cups of coffee, for her generosity in allowing me to 'do my own thing' and for an unfailing ability to upset my computer every time she looked at it!

MFR
Sussex, England
March 2002

Preface

'This is not the end. This is not even the beginning of the end. But it is, perhaps, the end of the beginning.' – Winston Churchill, in an address to the British people, 11 November 1942. But in fact it *was* the beginning of the end, for British Commonwealth troops had just penetrated the Axis defences at El Alamein and a month later the Red Army launched its first major counter-offensives on the Eastern Front. For the first time in its history, Nazi Germany was being forced on to the defensive and it would soon be facing the military nightmare of a war on three fronts.

Hitler's response was predictable and inevitable – he ordered the formation of more divisions and an increase in the number of armoured formations. It was no less surprising that Heinrich Himmler, the Reichsführer SS, ensured that the Waffen (armed) SS was included in this expansion – an increase which suited the Führer for two reasons. First, he saw it as a counter-balance to the Army which he never trusted completely and, second, in the event of unrest at home the Waffen-SS, rather than the Army, was to be the designated instrument of law and order.

The three new Waffen-SS Panzer-Grenadier Divisions raised during 1943 were the 9th and 10th, which started forming early in the year, and the 12th SS Hitlerjugend which came into existence under a Führer Order dated 24 June. They joined the existing 1st SS Leibstandarte Adolf Hitler, 2nd SS Das Reich, 3rd SS Totenkopf, and 5th SS Wiking Panzer-Grenadier Divisions. By the end of the year they had all been restructured and retitled as Panzer Divisions.

This increase in the number of Waffen-SS armoured formations was also accompanied by an organisational change which was unique to the force. For more than two centuries it has been, and still is, normal military practice to group divisions of all types, and independent brigades, into Corps for specific tasks or operations. For example, on D-Day the Americans planned to land one armoured and three infantry divisions on OMAHA Beach under the command of their V Corps, and the British and Canadians grouped three armoured brigades and three infantry divisions under the British I Corps for use on JUNO and SWORD Beaches. As the European campaign progressed, however, the composition of both these Corps changed many times and their divisions moved to different Corps as the need arose. A prime example is the US 82nd Airborne Division which operated under ten different Corps during WWII.

The German Army operated in much the same way as the Allies. The

Waffen-SS, as in so many other matters, did not. Its first Corps was formed in June 1942 at Bergen-Belsen, near the infamous Concentration Camp, under the command of SS General Paul Hausser. It comprised the Leibstandarte Adolf Hitler, Das Reich and Totenkopf Divisions. After a short period in France, this SS Panzer Corps was sent to the Eastern Front in February 1943 where it fought with distinction in the battles of Kharkov and Kursk. By the December of that year, however, following the formation of the new Waffen-SS divisions, Hausser's Corps had been broken up. The 1st SS Panzer Division Leibstandarte Adolf Hitler and 12th SS Panzer Division Hitlerjugend formed a new I SS Panzer Corps, commanded by Sepp Dietrich, and Hausser's Corps was demoted and renamed II SS Panzer Corps. The latter was to be given the 9th Hohenstaufen and 10th Frundsberg SS Panzer Divisions which, like the Hitlerjugend, had yet to see action. A third SS Panzer Corps was also authorised, comprising two more SS Panzer Divisions, the 3rd Totenkopf and 5th Wiking. Only the 2nd Das Reich remained outside this triple Corps structure and even it became absorbed in the last months of the war.

Whilst it is true that Army and Luftwaffe divisions were sometimes placed under the command of these Waffen-SS Panzer Corps, and that their designated SS Panzer Divisions were sometimes detached to other corps for short periods, the basic composition of the SS Panzer Corps remained more or less constant: the Leibstandarte and Hitlerjugend in I SS Panzer Corps, the Hohenstaufen and Frundsberg in II and Totenkopf and Wiking in IV SS Panzer Corps. Thus, even as the war reached its climax, six of the seven Waffen-SS Panzer Divisions were still grouped under these three Corps, making them unique in military history.

This is the story is of one of these Corps – II SS Panzer. By the time it was activated in early 1944, North Africa and Sicily had already fallen to the Western Allies, the sieges of Leningrad and Stalingrad had been raised and virtually the whole of the Soviet Union to the east of the river Dnieper had been cleared of German forces. This threat from the East demanded the deployment of more and more German divisions, which resulted in France being denuded of troops at a time when it was clearly about to be invaded by the Western Allies. Consequently, II SS Panzer Corps, with its two constituent Divisions, was created specifically to act as an armoured reserve in France.

The history of II SS Panzer Corps is short, violent, and more complicated than that of I SS Panzer Corps. The veteran 2nd SS Das Panzer Division Das Reich replaced the designated 10th SS Panzer Division on one important occasion during the Normandy campaign, and permanently from mid-December 1944. This account will therefore describe fundamentally the actions of the 9th and 10th SS Panzer Divisions from activation until October 1944 and the 2nd and 9th SS Panzer Divisions from December 1944 until the end of the war. In doing so it will cover critical parts of the Battle of Normandy, the escape from the Falaise Pocket, the MARKET GARDEN episode, the 1944 Ardennes Offensive, the last offensives on the Eastern Front and the final surrender of these famous Divisions, including the 10th SS Panzer Division.

Before beginning this history, it is important to correct a popular misconception. It is often contended that the whole of the Waffen-SS was a volunteer force of fanatics who enjoyed fighting and were totally dedicated to Nazi philosophies. Whilst this is certainly true of many of the early members of the organisation which eventually grew to a strength of some 900,000, it is not true of the majority of the members of the first component Divisions of II SS Panzer Corps – the 9th and 10th Panzer Divisions. Far from being volunteers, most of their soldiers were conscripts and, as casualties mounted, their replacements were almost all non-volunteers. From this point of view, therefore, they were no different from the majority of American and British divisions. And, just as the men of the two Allied countries – one already the strongest industrial country in the world and the other with the largest empire in the world – considered themselves better than all others, so did these German soldiers. But there was a difference! Members of the SS, whether volunteers or conscripts, whether soldiers or otherwise, had been *taught* that they were superior to all others and, more importantly, they knew that they could expect no mercy in the event of defeat. The Allied declaration of 'Unconditional Surrender', fully exploited by the Nazi propaganda machine, merely stiffened their resolve to fight on – to protect their Homeland from what they had been brainwashed into believing were sub-human hordes advancing from the East; and in the hope that their Führer, who had raised the Fatherland to a position of prominence in the world, could deliver just one more 'miracle'.

Guide to Abbreviations and Terms

AA	Anti-aircraft
AAA	Anti aircraft artillery
AAR	After Action Report
Abn	Airborne
AEAF	Allied Expeditionary Air Forces
Appx	Appendix
Armd	Armoured/Armored
Arty	Artillery
Aslt	Assault
ATAF	Allied Tactical Air Force
A/Tk or a/tk	anti-tank
Bazooka	US hand held rocket launcher
Bde	Brigade
Bn	Battalion
Brig	Brigadier
Bty	Battery
Capt	Captain
CCA/B/R	Combat Command A/B/R
Cdn	Canadian
CinC	Commander-in-Chief
Col	Colonel
Coy	Company
CP	Command Post
Cpl	Corporal
CT	Combat Team
D	Deutschland Regiment
DF	Der Führer Regiment
Div	Division
DR	Das Reich (2nd SS Pz Div)
DZ	drop zone
Engr	Engineer
ETHINT	European Theatre Historical Interrogations
F	Frundsberg (10th SS Pz Div)
FA	field artillery
Fd	field
FBB	Führer Begleit Brigade
Flak	anti-aircraft

FSD	Parachute Division
Gds	Guards
Gen	General
GI	US infantryman
Gp	Group
H	Hohenstaufen (9th SS Pz Div)
Heer	German Army
H-Hour	time of an attack
HJ	Hitlerjugend (12th SS Div)
HMG	heavy machine-gun
How	howitzer
HQ	Headquarters
Hy	heavy
Indep	Independent
Inf	Infantry
IVMV	Istoriya Vtoroi Mirovoi voiny (Soviet Official History 1939–1945)
IVOVSS	Istoriya Velikoi Otechestvennoi voiny Sovetskovo Soyuza (Soviet Official History 1941–1945)
IWM	Imperial War Museum
JgPz	Jagdpanzer (tank hunter)
KG	Kampfgruppe (Battle Group)
km	kilometre
LAA	light anti-aircraft
LAH	Leibstandarte Adolf Hitler (1st SS Pz Div)
Lt	Lieutenant or light
Lt Col or LTC	Lieutenant Colonel
LZ	landing zone
m	metre(s)
Maj	Major
Med	medium or medical
MG	machine-gun
Mk	Mark
mm	millimetre(s)
MMG	medium machine-gun
Mor	mortar
Mot	motorized
MP	Military Police
Ms	Manuscript
NCO	Non Commissioned Officer
OKH	Supreme Headquarters of the German Army
OKW	Supreme Headquarters of the German Armed Forces
Op	Operation
Pdr	pounder

PIAT	Projector Infantry Anti-tank
Pl	Platoon
Pnr	Pioneer (German engineer)
POW or PW	prisoner of War
PRO	Public Record Office
Pz	Panzer
Pz-Gren	Panzer-Grenadier (armoured infantry)
PzJg	Panzerjäger (tank hunter)
RASC	Royal Army Service Corps
RCE	Royal Canadian Engineers
RCT	Regimental Combat Team
RE	Royal Engineers
Recce	reconnaissance
Regt	Regiment
G-3	US Operations Branch
G-4	US Supply Branch
Sgt	Sergeant
SHAEF	Supreme Headquarters Allied Expeditionary Force
Sigs	Signals
SP	self-propelled
Spitze	vanguard
SPW	open-topped, German half track
Sqn	Squadron
SS-VT	SS-Verfügungstruppe
STAVKA	Soviet Supreme Command
StuG	armoured assault gun
TD	tank destroyer
TF	Task Force
Tk	tank
Tp	Troop
Tpt	transport
V1/V2	German rocket weapon
VGD	Volks-Grenadier Division
Wehrmacht	German Armed Forces
Werfer	German mortar
WWI	World War I
WWII	World War II
XO	Executive Officer

CHAPTER I

Beginnings and First Campaign: December 1942 – June 1944

Formation

(Map 1)

Although the formation of the 9th and 10th SS Panzer-Grenadier Divisions started in December 1942, it was to be another fifteen months before they were considered ready for combat and allocation to Waffen-SS General Hausser's II SS Panzer Corps. By then they had been reorganised as Panzer Divisions and given their honorary titles – the 9th SS Panzer Division Hohenstaufen[1] and 10th SS Panzer Division Frundsberg.[2] The Corps became the reserve Panzer Group of the Commander-in-Chief (CinC) West, Field Marshal Gerd von Rundstedt.

Paul Hausser had served on both Fronts in WWI and had retired from the Reichswehr as a Lieutenant General in 1932. In 1934, however, at the age of 54, he joined the SS in the rank of Colonel and two years later, after establishing and commanding the SS Officers' School at Braunschweig, he was promoted SS Brigadier General and made Head of the Inspectorate of the SS-Verfügungstruppe (SS-VT) – Hitler's Special Purpose Troops. The SS-VT developed later into the Waffen-SS. Hausser went on to command the first Waffen-SS Division, known as the SS-V-Division, in the 1940 campaigns in Holland, France and Yugoslavia. He earned a Knight's Cross in Russia in 1941 but shortly after being promoted to SS Lieutenant General in the same year, he was severely wounded. Despite the loss of his right eye, Hausser then distinguished himself in 1943 as the commander of the first SS Panzer Corps on the Eastern Front. Known affectionately to his men as 'Papa Hausser', he became CinC Army Group 'G' in 1945. This made him the senior Waffen-SS field commander; however, after a furious argument with Hitler in the April of that year, he was placed on the reserve. Following Hitler's suicide, he ended the war on Field Marshal Kesselring's staff.

The two new Waffen-SS Divisions began receiving their first personnel drafts in February 1943: the 9th at Mailly-le-Camp near Reims, under the command of SS Major General Wilhelm Bittrich; and the 10th in the Saintes area of western France, under SS Major General Lothar Debes. We shall hear much more of Willi Bittrich. Born in 1894, he served in

1

WWI as a fighter pilot and afterwards joined the Reichswehr. Germany was forbidden aircraft under the Treaty of Versailles but Bittrich obtained further experience as a pilot in Russia. He joined the SS-VT in 1934, earned the Iron Cross 2nd Class with the Leibstandarte Adolf Hitler in the 1939 Polish campaign as Sepp Dietrich's Headquarters Adjutant and went on to command the SS Regiment Deutschland in France in 1940, winning the Iron Cross 1st Class. When Hausser was wounded on the Eastern Front in 1941, he took command of the SS Division Das Reich and was awarded the Knight's Cross in the December of that year. Then, after a five- month illness at the beginning of 1942, he was given command of the SS Cavalry Brigade and told to expand it to Divisional strength. He earned a German Cross in Gold whilst commanding the Division and, after taking command of the Hohenstaufen, was promoted SS Lieutenant General on 1 May 1943. Bittrich's pedigree as a Waffen-SS commander could hardly have been bettered.

Officers and senior NCOs for the two new formations, the majority of them veterans, came from the existing Waffen-SS Divisions; however, the provision of the required number of soldiers proved a major problem. Already under extreme pressure to find enough men to replace the losses in the existing Divisions, there was simply no way the Waffen-SS Replacement Bureau could find enough volunteers for the new formations. Of the first 27,000 men, nearly 14,000 were conscripts[3], in the main Volksdeutsch (expatriate Germans) from the conquered south-eastern or allied territories, and mostly aged 17 or 18. Despite these manpower difficulties, by the end of December 1943 the Hohenstaufen numbered 485 officers, 2,685 NCOs and 16,455 men and the Frundsberg 487 officers, 2,722 NCOs and 16,104 men.[4] There were also major shortages of equipment with most of the initial issues of anti-tank and infantry guns being made from captured Soviet stocks.

In view of the predicted Allied invasion of France and to provide both Divisions with better training facilities, they were moved a number of times during 1943 and early 1944. The 9th Hohenstaufen moved initially to the Maria ter Heide military training grounds near Courtrai in Belgium, thence to the Amiens sector of northern France at the end of June and finally, in February 1944, to the Nîmes–Avignon area of southern France. The 10th Frundsberg Division moved to the Marseille region of southern France in August and then in October to the Bernay sector of Normandy, south-west of Rouen – an area they would see again in very different circumstances in less than a year. It was whilst the Division was in Normandy that SS Lieutenant General Karl von Treuenfeld took over command from Major General Debes. Aged 59, von Treuenfeld was much older than most of his contemporaries. Although he had been in the Waffen-SS since May 1939 and had reached the rank of Major General by January 1944, a recommendation for him to receive the Knight's Cross was rejected by Himmler and the award reduced to a German Cross in Gold. This was almost certainly because his origins lay in the elite pre-WWI German Officer Corps.[5]

The French Resistance caused numerous problems during this work-up period and inflicted several casualties on the Hohenstaufen. Men of both Divisions had to be diverted from their training to protect the railway network and on at least one occasion the Hohenstaufen was used in a raid on a suspected resistance centre, as a result of which some ten members of the Resistance were handed over to the Gestapo together with captured weapons, gold and supplies. Those handed over were later hanged from a bridge in Nîmes. After the war Bittrich was brought before a War Crimes Court in Marseille but was acquitted on the grounds that no one in the Hohenstaufen knew about the executions until *after* they had happened.

By the end of March 1944 the 9th and 10th SS Panzer Divisions were considered ready for operational service and allocation to II SS Panzer Corps. Their organisation was based on that of a standard Waffen-SS Panzer division (see Appendix II) but neither Division had a Panzerjäger (anti-tank) battalion and the Frundsberg lacked one of its two authorised Panzer Battalions. Although all elements were motorized, only one Panzer-Grenadier Battalion[6] in each Division was equipped with armoured personnel carriers (SPWs); similarly, only one of the Pioneer companies in each Pioneer Battalion had SPWs. In addition, each Division had a Divisional Escort Company. The Hohenstaufen's Regiments and Battalions were all prefixed with the number 9, except for its Panzer-Grenadier Regiments which were numbered 19 and 20. In the same way the Frundberg's were prefixed with a 10, except for its Panzer-Grenadier Regiments which were numbered 21 and 22.

As well as designated Panzer Divisions, II SS Panzer Corps had a number of important specialised units under command. All initially numbered '102', these units included a Heavy Panzer Battalion with Tiger I tanks, Heavy Artillery and Werfer Battalions, a Flak Company and various administration units. They were all manned by Waffen-SS personnel.

First Campaign: 2 April – 12 June 1944
(Maps 2 & 3)

Author's Note

Since even the most reputable modern atlases and guide books fail to agree on the correct spelling of many place names in the Ukraine, and Ukrainian maps are difficult to obtain outside that country, 1944 place names have been used throughout this chapter and on Maps 2 and 3.

However, to assist those who may wish to visit the area, current international boundaries are shown. It should also be noted that today's roads tend to by-pass most villages; in 1944 they usually followed the valley floors and connected the villages.

By mid-March 1944, a major Soviet offensive between the Pripet Marshes and the Dniester river was causing consternation in Berlin. A huge wedge had been driven between Rowno and Schepetowka, separating the German Army Groups Centre and South, and General Hube's First Panzer Army of some 200,000 men, part of Field Marshal von Manstein's Army Group South, had been surrounded in the area of Kamenez Podolsk. Part of Marshal Zhukov's First Ukrainian Front[7] had advanced south-west through Buczacz to the Dniester in its rear and troops of General Konev's Second Ukrainian Front had broken through to Mogilev Podolcsk near the Dniester in the south. The encirclement became known as 'The Hube Pocket'. Although it had no great strategic significance, Hitler declared Tarnopol, in the northern part of the pocket, a 'fortress'. This meant it had to be defended to the last man. It was into this crisis situation that, on 24 March 1944, Hausser's II SS Panzer Corps was ordered to move from France to the Eastern Front. Trains would be provided at a rate of seventy-two per day for each Division.

On 2 April Field Marshal Walter Model relieved von Manstein and Army Group South was renamed Army Group North Ukraine. The same day the first elements of the Frundsberg and Hohenstaufen Divisions detrained at Lemberg. The Frundsberg had suffered its first casualties from an air attack during the move from Normandy. It has to be pointed out, however, that at the time of the move the 1st Battalion of each Panzer Regiment was still awaiting the issue of its seventy-six Panther tanks and had to be left behind at Mailly-le-Camp in France. Also, because of an overall shortage of Mark (Mk) IV tanks, the 2nd Panzer Battalion of the Hohenstaufen Division had only forty-nine Mk IVs, organised into two Companies, whilst the other two Companies had a total of forty-four SP assault guns (StuGs). The StuG looked like a tank but its gun had a very limited traverse. The Frundsberg was similarly organised with forty-six Mk IVs and forty-four StuGs. Lack of equipment had also prevented the Panzerjäger Battalions of each Division moving east. A simple guide to German and Allied equipments is provided at Appendix X.

Snowstorms, slush and 'bottomless' roads greeted these young, inexperienced soldiers of the Waffen-SS – a far cry from the relative luxury of their French billets and, in the case of those of the Hohenstaufen, the sun of the Riviera. It was fortunate for many of them that most of their leaders were battle-hardened veterans of the Eastern Front.

II SS Panzer Corps was placed under the command of General Raus's Fourth Panzer Army. His orders, issued on 3 April, were simple (Map

3). In a preliminary operation, two Army Divisions, the 100th Jäger and 367th Infantry, were to secure a forward assembly area for Hausser's men in the region of Rohatyn and Brzenany. Once that had been achieved, all four Divisions were to attack south-east in the general direction of Buczacz and break through to the First Panzer Army.

The approach march for the attack could not have been more difficult – ice, snow drifts, slush and the few roads and relevant tracks choked with traffic. The whole area soon became a sea of mud and made the movement of all but tracked vehicles virtually impossible. A thaw on the 5th merely compounded the problems. To add to these difficulties, whenever the weather permitted, Soviet aircraft launched numerous strafing attacks. Nevertheless, the Army Divisions attacked as planned on 4 April and, as the fifty-seven trains carrying the Frundsberg and thirty-five with the Hohenstaufen arrived in the Lemberg area, units were despatched immediately towards the Divisional assembly areas.

The first sub-units of II SS Panzer Corps to see action were those of the Frundsberg's 10th SS Reconnaissance Battalion which detrained farther east at Zloczow. On 5 April three platoons of the 2nd and 3rd Companies, under the command of SS Lieutenant Hinze, advanced south-east; by 2100 hours they had reached the Strypa river at Osowce, 10km north of Buczacz, and established a small bridgehead. Adverse ground conditions prevented the rest of the Reconnaissance Battalion reinforcing them.

Following up on the right flank, the Mk IVs and StuGs of SS Major Reinhold's 2nd SS Panzer Battalion, led by SS Captain Franke's 6th Company, reached Kowalowka, 15km from Buczacz, by last light. Franke was wounded during the day but his men had overcome strong Soviet anti-tank forces and appalling ground conditions. After dark they were joined by advance elements of the 21st SS Panzer-Grenadier Regiment. It had been a successful day for the men of the Frundsberg.

Those of the Hohenstaufen had little or no success on this day. With most of its units arriving after those of its sister Division, the few that did move off from the Lemberg area became 'completely mired on bottomless roads'.[8] The only unit to see action was SS Major Hagenlocher's 1st Battalion of the 19th SS Panzer-Grenadier Regiment (1st/19th). This advanced detachment was placed under the command of the 367th Infantry Division and was successful in pushing back the Soviets on the southern flank of the Corps front at Horozanka near the Dniester.

During the night 5/6 April the rest of the Frundsberg's 21st SS Panzer-Grenadier Regiment closed up to its leading elements and was ready to move off towards Buczacz around midday. Under the direction of SS Lieutenant Colonel Kleffner, the commander of the 10th SS Panzer Regiment, the 6th SS Panzer Company continued the advance. Its commander, SS Captain Franke, had been wounded in the previous day's fighting, but despite strong opposition and for the loss of only two tanks, the

Company burst into Buczacz at 1700 hours, and fifteen minutes later the eighteen Mk IVs met the leading elements of the 6th Panzer Division withdrawing from the east – the link between the First and Fourth Panzer Armies, severed fourteen days earlier, had been restored. Nevertheless, without infantry support the tanks were highly vulnerable and they waited in vain for the arrival of the Grenadiers of the 21st Regiment. They, led by the rest of Reinhold's 2nd SS Panzer Battalion, had advanced on the right flank but had soon run into strong Soviet forces in front of Monasterzyska as well as difficult ground conditions. SS Major Laubscheer's 1st/21st (SPW) Panzer-Grenadier Battalion was forced to dismount, and when the commander of the 3rd/21st Battalion, SS Major Molt, was wounded the advance came to a halt. The Regimental commander, SS Lieutenant Colonel Diesenhofer, called for support from Stuka aircraft and by 1600 hours SS Captain Maurer's 2nd Battalion had managed to storm the village. Even so, it would be the following day before the 21st Regiment reached Buczacz.

Meanwhile, the bulk of the Frundsberg's 10th SS Reconnaissance Battalion had found it impossible to link up with its 3rd Company at Osowce and during the night the small bridgehead over the Strypa was evacuated. The Soviets wasted no time in establishing strong positions along that part of the river.

On 7 April the 367th Infantry Division, on the right flank of II SS Panzer Corps, advanced towards the junction of the Strypa and Dniester rivers and linked up with the Frundsberg's 21st SS Panzer-Grenadier Regiment on its left. The same day the 100th Jäger Division, with an Army Tiger Battalion under command, fought off strong Soviet attacks against the slender bridgehead it had managed to secure on the east bank of the Strypa at Zlotniki in the north of the Corps sector.

By now most of the First Panzer Army had managed to withdraw to the line of the Seret river, 25km to the east of the Strypa, but its chances of being reinforced and re-supplied were slender unless the Frundsberg could close up and expand the bridgehead at Buczacz, and the Hohenstaufen, most of which was still back in the area of Brzezany, brought into action. Although a few Grenadier reinforcements had reached the Frundsberg's 6th SS Panzer Company in the Buczacz bridgehead on the 7th, the mass of the Division was still north-west of Monasterzyska.

It was on this day that German Intelligence began to suspect that the Soviets were concentrating strong forces, including their X Guards Tank Corps (equivalent of a Waffen-SS Panzer division, see Appendix III), opposite the 25km gap which had developed between the right-hand elements of the 100th Jäger Division at Zlotniki and the weak Frundsberg force at Buczacz. The only Germans operating in this gap were those of SS Major Brinkmann's 10th SS Reconnaissance Battalion and if the Soviets succeeded in crossing the Strypa and turning south, they would once more encircle the First Panzer Army – *and* the 10th Frundsberg Division. Not surprisingly, Fourth Panzer Army issued new orders at 2035 hours that night. The Hohenstaufen, which since 4 April had been trying to advance south to come in on the right or southern flank of the Frundsberg, was now to attack due east through Kosowa and cross the Strypa to the north of Zlotniki. At the same time the Frundsberg was to strike north-east out of the Buczacz bridgehead and link up.

During the night 7/8 April SS Major Wild's 1st/22nd SS Panzer-Grenadier Battalion caught up with the leading elements of the Frundsberg Division at Buczacz and soon after first light it joined the 2nd Panzer Battalion in an attack to the north-east. After destroying fourteen anti-tank guns and an assault gun[9], they consolidated in a position 5km to the north-east of Buczacz. The 2nd Battalion of the 22nd Regiment also crossed the Strypa and made contact, thus strengthening the bridgehead. On the same day the 367th Infantry Division secured a line running 30km from Buczacz south-west to the Dniester river.

Meanwhile, the 100th Jäger Division had secured the west bank of the Strypa to a point 5km south of Zlotniki and this provided flank protection for the 2nd/20th and 3rd/20th SS Panzer-Grenadier Battalions of the Hohenstaufen to cross the river into the Jäger Division's bridgehead. This provided a strong base for operations planned for the 9th towards Tarnopol, where the 1,500 survivors of an original garrison of over 4,700 men were defending Hitler's 'fortress'.

During the afternoon of 8 April, Field Marshal Model and the commander of the First Panzer Army, General Hube, met in Buczacz. Hube was ordered to set up a firm defensive line on the Seret as far south as its junction with the Dniester and told that Hausser's II SS Panzer Corps would extend this line by relieving Tarnopol. Having done so, it would then come under Hube's command. The whole of Luftflotte (Air Fleet) 4 would support this thrust. However, at 2145 hours that evening, strong Soviet armoured forces were reported approaching the Seret in the Trembowla sector, 35km south of Tarnopol, and orders were issued immediately by Fourth Panzer Army for the Hohenstaufen, 100th Jäger and Frundsberg Divisions to bring this force to battle and destroy it.

The following day dawned sunny and mild but the ground was still a morass with cross-country movement impossible for anything other than tracked vehicles and even they faced severe difficulties. It was a day which brought significant, albeit temporary, changes to the structure of II SS Panzer Corps. Despite the directive for the Corps to attack eastwards towards the Soviet force in the Trembowla region, the slow progress of the Hohenstaufen towards the assembly area for the attack precluded any chance of it being launched on the 9th. All that could be achieved was an expansion of the small bridgehead at Zlotniki by the 20th Regiment and units of the 100th Jäger Division. Meanwhile, the

2nd/9th SS Panzer Battalion, the 19th SS Panzer-Grenadier Regiment and the Divisional artillery struggled to reach the assembly area for the attack east of the Strypa. The Soviets, realising the importance of this bridge-head, launched heavy attacks during the evening, supported by armour, but these were fought off. The Frundsberg Division limited its activities to local actions as it waited for the Hohenstaufen.

During the same day German Intelligence identified the X Guards Tank Corps, the VI and IX Mechanised Corps (the equivalent of three Waffen-SS Panzer divisions) and several Rifle divisions (see Appendix IV) in the Trembowla sector. In the face of such a force and knowing that another Tank Corps had penetrated into the gap between the Carpathian Mountains and the Dniester immediately to his south, General Hube realised that he had no chance of holding the Seret line. Even if the II SS Panzer Corps was successful in its attack, he believed it would be too late to help him establish a position that far east. He therefore asked Model for permission to pull back to the Strypa. A withdrawal of this magnitude could not possibly be authorised without permission from Berlin (Hitler), but to everyone's relief this was granted – with the proviso that the garrison at Tarnopol be brought out.[10]   At 2000 hours Hube's First Panzer Army was formally ordered to set up a new defensive line on the Strypa north of Buczacz. Hausser's II SS Panzer Corps, less the Hohenstaufen, was placed under command. Bittrich's 9th SS Panzer Division Hohenstaufen, less those units already in the bridgehead to the east of the Strypa, was to prepare for a new mission on 11 April under the command of General Balck's XLVIII Panzer Corps. Balck's mission was to break through to Tarnopol and bring out the surviving garrison.

The 10th of April saw the two SS Panzer-Grenadier Regiments of the Frundsberg, supported by the Division's 2nd SS Panzer Battalion, engaged in vicious fighting to expand the German bridgehead north-east of Buczacz. Unless this could be achieved Hube's Panzer Army had no chance of being resupplied and withdrawing behind the Strypa. In what was later described and used as a 'textbook' operation, the SS men suc-ceeded in pushing the bridgehead perimeter out to a total distance of 10km by last light.

On this same day the operation to break through to Tarnopol was discussed in detail by the commanders of the Fourth Panzer Army, XLVIII Corps and SS Lieutenant General Wilhelm (Willi) Bittrich of the Hohenstaufen. A previous attempt at the end of March by a Kampfgruppe (KG) of one Panzer and two SPW battalions of the 8th Panzer Division under the command of a Colonel Friebe had already failed. This time the plan saw the Hohenstaufen thrusting across a northern tributary of the Strypa called the Wosuszka, and then turning north-east through Chodaczkow towards Tarnopol, whilst KG Friebe, with twenty-four Pan-thers, nine Tigers and over 100 SPWs, launched an attack due east across the same stream with the same objective. The guns of two infantry div-isions[11] were to provide additional artillery support. There were, how-ever, two major drawbacks to this plan: first, the Soviet forces between Tarnopol and the Strypa were considerably stronger than they had been at the time of the previous attack and second, the Hohenstaufen Division was still spread out between Brzezany and Kozawa and there was no way it could possibly assemble its units in time for a successful attack. Indeed, on the evening of the 10th, only SS Major Frank's 2nd/20th SS Panzer-Grenadier Battalion and the Pioneer Company of the 20th Regi-ment had arrived in the forward assembly area.

KG Friebe launched its attack as planned on 11 April, but by last light this was judged to have failed. The 9th SS Panzer Division Hohenstaufen did little better. Its attack was launched, near Plolgcza, at about the same time, but as the first StuGs of the still arriving 9th SS Panzer Regiment and Pioneer platoons moved forward, the leading Company of the 1st/19th SS Panzer-Grenadier Battalion was only just reaching the assembly area. The next unit to arrive was the 1st Battalion of the 9th SS Artillery Regiment with its eighteen SP 105mm guns, but they still had to register their targets before they could come into effective action. Nevertheless, the attack went ahead. The Pioneers, using their rubber boats, crossed the Wosuszka and attempted to capture the only serviceable wooden bridge in the area, supported by fire from the few StuGs. Their valiant efforts were in vain for the Russians managed to blow the bridge and, despite the arrival of SS Major Hagenlocher's 1st SS Panzer-Grenadier Battalion, the Soviet defence line could not be broken. This was hardly surprising since the Grenadiers had been thrown into battle without the benefit of either reconnaissance or proper briefings. By the end of the day the Battalion had suffered a total of 50% casualties.

SS Major Frank's 2nd Battalion of the 20th Regiment achieved the only slight success of the day. Shortly before first light his men succeeded in wading the stream 2km farther south, but as daylight came they were bombed in error by German Stukas and suffered eighty casualties. Despite the inevitable chaos this air attack caused, the Battalion still managed to push ahead and capture a dominant hill on the east side of the stream. Unfortunately the ground conditions, made even worse by a cloudburst during the afternoon, precluded any chance of building a bridge over the stream in order to get tanks and other vehicles across. Attempts to drag the bridging equipment forward with StuGs came to nothing and, although the 1st SS Panzer-Grenadier Battalion joined Frank's depleted 2nd Battalion in the small bridgehead during the night, the chances of further success seemed minimal. Frank himself was killed leading a coun-ter-attack during the early hours of the 13th. He was awarded a post-humous Knight's Cross.

During this same night SS Major Gruber's 3rd SS Panzer-Grenadier

Battalion caught up and was thrown in on the left flank, together with units of KG Friebe, but without success. And then, just when everything seemed hopeless, a Pioneer reconnaissance party found another potential bridging site within the bridgehead. Despite heavy Soviet harassing fire, the 9th SS Pioneer Battalion managed to construct a tank bridge before dawn and at 0600 hours on 14 April the first StuGs crossed, supported by Grenadiers of the 2nd Battalion of the 19th Regiment. By the end of the day the bridgehead had been expanded to a depth of 3km and a width of 9km and the three Grenadier Battalions had been joined by thirty Mk IVs, thirty StuGs of the 9th SS Panzer Regiment and a battery of the 9th SS Flak Battalion.[12] It seemed that the relief of Tarnopol might at last be on the cards. In fact it was too late – on the same day Tarnopol was overrun by units of the Soviet IV Guards Tank Corps (equivalent of a Waffen-SS Panzer division) and XV and XIX Rifle Corps. That night the 1,500 survivors of the German garrison broke out to the west, leaving behind their dead commander, General von Neindorff, and some 700 wounded. It fell to Bittrich's Division and KG Friebe to rescue these exhausted men.

Early on 15 April, KG Friebe and the 3rd/20th SS Panzer-Grenadier Battalion reinforced the German bridgehead but the advance could not be continued owing to fuel shortages. After an aerial resupply, the attack was renewed at 1000 hours with the Hohenstaufen's Mk IVs and StuGs under SS Lieutenant Colonel Otto Meyer on the right, and Friebe's Tigers and Panthers on the left. The 2nd and 3rd SS Grenadier Battalions of the 19th Regiment followed up with the twelve Wespe 105mm and six 150mm Hummel SP guns of the 9th SS Artillery Regiment in support, as was the Luftwaffe which flew several sorties during the day. The Divisional commander, Willi Bittrich, accompanied the attack throughout the day by riding in Otto Meyer's command tank. Resistance from units of the Soviet 52nd Guards Tank Brigade (the equivalent of a German Panzer battalion), and two Rifle Divisions[13] was stubborn, but by last light ten Soviet tanks had been knocked out and the Germans were in possession of Chodaczkow.

Heavy fighting continued on the 16th with the German bridgehead being extended another 3km to the east and to the north. But Soviet counter-attacks were increasing in intensity and, when only fifty-five survivors of the Tarnopol garrison reached German lines during the day, it was realised that further efforts were likely to be costly and futile. That evening Fourth Panzer Army ordered Balck's XLVIII Corps to salvage as many vehicles as possible from the bridgehead and bring the Hohenstaufen and KG Friebe back behind the original main line of resistance – i.e., the Strypa. Field Marshal Model gave further orders that Bittrich's Division was to be placed in Army Group reserve from noon on the 20th. By the time this order was given the bulk of the Hohenstaufen was in the bridgehead. The Division and KG Friebe claimed seventy-four Soviet tanks, eighty-four SP assault guns, twenty-one anti-tank guns and twelve mortars during the fighting on the 15th, 16th and 17th.[14] Otto Meyer was awarded the Knight's Cross for the performance of his 2nd SS Panzer Battalion. At last light on the 17th he had only eighteen Mk IVs and six StuGs fit for action (combat-ready) and KG Friebe had been reduced to six serviceable Tigers and twenty Panthers.[15] The whole relief operation had cost XLVIII Corps 1,200 dead.[16] In the meantime, between 11 and 15 April, the Frundsberg's 21st and 22nd SS Panzer-Grenadier Regiments had continued to defend their bridgehead north-east of Buczacz against frequent Soviet counter-attacks. The commander of the 22nd Regiment, SS Lieutenant Colonel Schtüzeck, and the commander of its 1st Battalion, SS Major Wild, were both seriously wounded in this fighting. Since the Division's 10th SS Panzer Regiment had only one Battalion under command, SS Lieutenant Colonel Kleffner moved across and took over the 22nd Regiment.

During this same period the Frundsberg's 10th SS Reconnaissance Battalion had been engaged in bitter fighting against a Soviet bridgehead which had been established across the Strypa at Osowce, 12km north of Buczacz. It will be recalled that the Battalion was the only German unit in the gap which had developed between the Frundsberg and the 100th Jäger Division near Zlotniki to its north, and it was obvious that unless this bridgehead could be eliminated quickly, the Soviets would use it for another attempt to envelop First Panzer Army.

On 14 and 15 April units of the 7th Panzer Division relieved the Frundsberg's 21st SS Panzer-Grenadier Regiment in the Buczacz bridgehead so that it could be brought into action alongside the 22nd Regiment in an attack on the east side of the Strypa aimed at destroying the Soviet bridgehead. In conjunction with this thrust, a strong force comprising the 3rd/21st SS Panzer-Grenadier Battalion, units of an Army Panzer-Grenadier Regiment and twenty Tigers of the 506th Heavy Panzer Battalion were to strike north on the west side of the river, whilst elements of the 100th Jäger Division were to attack from the north and the 10th SS Reconnaissance Battalion from the west. The attack went in on the 16th and by 1900 hours it was all over – the Soviet bridgehead had been eliminated and the Germans were firm on the line of the Strypa and were still holding their own Buczacz bridgehead.

By the morning of 20 April the First Panzer Army had been saved and was safely behind the Strypa, and within two days the Hohenstaufen had been withdrawn into reserve to the east of Lemberg. On the 25th two Army Divisions relieved the Frundsberg and LIX Army Corps took over the II SS Panzer Corps' sector. Thus the Corps' first campaign was virtually at an end. The Hohenstaufen had suffered 1,011 casualties, of which 216 were dead and ninety missing[17], and the Frundsberg 2,076, including 577 killed or died of wounds.[18]

Although it would appear that both the Hohenstaufen and Frundsberg Divisions had 'won their spurs', the Hohenstaufen came in for strong criticism after the war in a book, *Fester Platz Tarnopol* by Gert Fricke. He alleged that the War Diaries of the Army Group, Fourth Panzer Army and Balck's XLVIII Corps contained severe criticisms of Bittrich's leadership and the performance of his soldiers. The counter-argument by Wilhelm Tieke, in his *In the Firestorm of the Last Years of the War*, is that Fricke produced a biased account, based on Balck's version of events, and that no attempt was made to hear or present Bittrich's side of the story. He goes on to allege that Balck, who as we shall see later was no friend of the Waffen-SS, tried to put the blame for the failure of the Tarnopol relief operation – an operation for which he was responsible – on to Bittrich and the Hohenstaufen. In doing so, he hoped to influence the opinions of his superiors at Army and Army Group levels and protect himself from the Führer's anger. The reader will no doubt judge for himself the Hohenstaufen's performance. What is certainly clear is that, after arriving piecemeal and late in the theatre of operations, Bittrich's Division was given numerous missions, all of which were complicated and frustrated by atrocious ground conditions. It seems doubtful that any other division, German or Allied, could have done any better in similar circumstances. It is also clear that the Tarnopol operation was launched far too late for it to have had any real chance of success.

Respite

On 27 April 37-year-old SS Colonel Heinz Harmel took over command of the Frundsberg Division from von Treuenfeld who was moved to another Waffen-SS command. Harmel, who had already won the Knight's Cross with the Deutschland Regiment of the 2nd SS Panzer Division Das Reich in March 1943, was destined to lead the Frundsberg for the rest of the war. Like many Waffen-SS officers, he had come up through the ranks and well understood the needs of his soldiers. For this he was much respected.

The rest of April and the whole of May saw II SS Panzer Corps, with the Hohenstaufen and Frundsberg Divisions back under command, in Army Group reserve in the Lemberg area. The main task of the Corps was to be prepared to confront an expected Soviet offensive in that sector between Army Groups Centre and North Ukraine. To this end numerous alarm exercises were carried out and blocking positions prepared. Neither Division undertook any specific offensive operations during this period, but the 9th SS Reconnaissance Battalion was engaged in anti-partisan

actions in the first half of May and both Divisions gave occasional assistance to other formations.

In fact, unknown to Hitler and the Headquarters of the German Armed
Forces (OKW), the Soviet offensive had been postponed until the end of
June so that it could take advantage of the forthcoming Allied invasion
of France, and Hausser's Corps was left in peace for the last time in its
history. Then, on 6 June, came the momentous news of the landings in
Normandy and within six days II SS Panzer Corps was ordered to move
to the Western Front – it was to undertake the task for which it had been
formed – to throw the Allies back into the sea.

On leaving the Ukraine, Field Marshal Model issued the following
Order of the Day to the men of II SS Panzer Corps:

> The Corps has ... played a major role in strengthening the front at a
> very difficult time and in establishing a shield for the ... Homeland.
> With the relief attack at Tarnopol and in re-establishing contact with
> First Panzer Army at Buczacz, you, men of the 9th and 10th SS Panzer
> Divisions, have helped to erect this shield in a very critical situation. ...
> I give you my thanks and recognition! ... The Führer's order calls you
> to new missions. I am certain that you will accomplish these in the
> spirit of our motto, 'No soldier in the world is better than the soldiers
> of Adolf Hitler!'

NOTES

1. The German Hohenstaufen dynasty, founded by Count Friedrich who died
   in 1105, ruled the Holy Roman Empire from 1138 to 1208 and 1212 to 1254.
2. Georg von Frundsberg, who died in 1528, was a soldier and devoted servant
   of the Habsburgs. He fought on behalf of the Holy Roman Emperors Maximil-
   ian I and Charles V.
3. Tieke, *In the Firestorm of the Last Years of the War*, p. 3.
4. Ibid., pp. 7 & 11.
5. He allegedly committed suicide whilst a Soviet prisoner in 1946.
6. 3/19 SS Pz-Gren Regt Hohenstaufen & 1/21 SS Pz-Gren Regt Frundsberg.
7. A Front was the equivalent of a British or American Army Group.
8. Fourth Pz Army War Diary.
9. Tieke, op. cit., p. 34.
10. Gen Hube had already commanded corps with distinction at Stalingrad, in
    Sicily and at Salerno in Italy. He was promoted and awarded Diamonds to
    his Knight's Cross for this campaign but later killed when his aircraft was
    shot down on a flight to Berlin.
11. 357 & 359 Inf Divs.
12. Tieke, op. cit., p. 54.
13. 68 Guards (Gds) Rifle & 302 Rifle Divs.
14. Tieke, op. cit., p. 57.
15. Ibid., p. 58.
16. Ibid., p. 59.

17. Based on strength returns dated 1 Apr and 1 Jun for 9th SS. Not all of these would have been battle casualties.
18. Tieke, op. cit., p, 476.

CHAPTER II
The Situation in Normandy: 25 June 1944

(Map 4)

By the time II SS Panzer Corps arrived in Normandy in late June 1944 the Allied invasion plan was seriously behind schedule and in some disarray. Although the D-Day landings had been successful, the planned expansion of the bridgehead had failed to materialise. The Americans, after their bloody landing on OMAHA, had managed to push over 20km inland and capture the critical ridge at Caumont, but two weeks later they were becoming entangled in what became known as the 'Battle of the Hedgerows'[1] and were a long way from securing their primary objective, and the hinge of their planned breakout – St Lô. British and Canadian attempts to capture or envelop Caen, a D-Day objective and variously called the bastion, anvil and pivot of the Normandy campaign, had all failed. And the whole administrative build-up had been delayed by the 'Great Storm' in the English Channel between 19 and 21 June.

Montgomery's demands that 'armoured columns must penetrate deep inland, and quickly, on D-Day'[2] had come to nothing and his overall plan of getting 'control of the main enemy lateral Granville–Vire–Argentan–Falaise–Caen' and having 'the area within it firmly in our possession' seemed as far away as ever.[3] In the corridors of power in London and Washington, the lack of progress and knowledge that the Allies had already suffered over 30,000 casualties began to cause alarm; the fear that the campaign might bog down into a costly war of attrition returned to haunt the planners.

There was no agreed German plan for countering the Allied invasion. The arguments between Field Marshal von Rundstedt, Commander-in-Chief (CinC) West, and General Geyr von Schweppenburg, Commander Panzer Group West, on the one hand, and Field Marshal Erwin Rommel, Commander Army Group 'B' on the other, are well known and have been described in most books written about the Normandy campaign. Von Rundstedt was senior to Rommel but he did not have Hitler's confidence and could not overrule the latter's views. Rommel, with his experience of Allied air superiority, wanted all available armoured forces positioned as close as possible to likely landing areas. He knew that the

14

Luftwaffe would be incapable of protecting his armoured columns moving to the battle areas in daylight and that the very short summer hours of darkness would be insufficient for any long-distance movement. He reasoned that the Germans would lose the battle of the build-up. Von Rundstedt and von Schweppenburg, correct in theory but wrong in the circumstances, wanted to hold the armour well back from the coasts until they could see where the main threat was developing and then launch coordinated counter-thrusts against it. It would seem that the views of General Friedrich Dollmann, the commander of the Seventh Army and the man charged with the defence of the Normandy coast, were not sought.

The result of all this argument was a disastrous compromise; and to compound matters further, the command system designed to put the strategy into operation was also complicated and inefficient. This was in some ways deliberate on the part of Hitler who, as well as mistrusting his army generals, wished to retain supreme command and have the opportunity to intervene at all levels.

The combination of all these factors led to overall confusion on the German side and a failure to throw the Allies back into the sea before the landings could be consolidated. Hitler remained unconvinced that Normandy was the main thrust and refused to release the necessary forces, with the result that Panzer Divisions[4] had already been committed in defensive actions and were therefore unavailable for a coordinated counter-attack. By the evening of 9 June Rommel gave instructions that:

> There should be a return to the defensive in the sector between the Vire and the Orne and the counter-attack should be postponed until all preparations have been completed.[5]

He had decided to await the arrival of II Parachute Corps from Brittany so that his existing armoured forces could be extracted and reinforced by others en route for Normandy – these included Hausser's II SS Panzer Corps from the Ukraine. Nevertheless, despite the German failure to throw the Allies back into the sea, Rommel's forces had prevented the planned expansion of the Allied bridgehead and they still held the vital high ground running from south of Caen more or less due west to St Lô and Périers.

It was in these circumstances that Montgomery decided to deliver a single, sledgehammer blow on the west side of Caen. His previous attempt to outflank the city and rip open the German left flank had failed when the veteran British 7th Armoured Division was brought to an ignominious halt just to the east of Villers-Bocage on 13 June and then forced to withdraw. Monty's vision of this thrust being 'the turning point in the battle [of Normandy]' had come to nothing. His new operation was originally scheduled for 23 June, but the 'Big Storm' caused the main attack to be postponed until the 26th – the day the vital port of Cherbourg fell to the Americans. Code-named EPSOM, the coming battle was to be II SS Panzer Corps' first major engagement in the West.

NOTES

1. It took four US Corps, totalling twelve divisions, to fight their way through the 'bocage' in their sector of Normandy. The bocage consisted of numerous small fields, surrounded by steep banks carrying hedges and trees. Sunken lanes further restricted movement.
2. On 15 May, at St Paul's School in London, before Churchill, Eisenhower and all the senior Allied commanders. Montgomery was the overall land force commander.
3. Ibid.
4. 21, 12 SS & Pz Lehr.
5. Seventh Army telephone log, 1730 hrs.

CHAPTER III
The Move to Normandy
(Map 1)

Between 12 and 23 June Headquarters of II SS Panzer Corps and the Hohenstaufen and Frundsberg SS Panzer Divisions moved by train from the Eastern Front to eastern France. Under normal circumstances this move should have taken no more than two and a half days; but these were not normal circumstances, and whilst the journeys through the Greater German Reich went reasonably well, the farther west the trains rolled the greater the delays caused by air attacks and damaged tracks. After passing through Cologne (Köln), Frankfurt am Main and Strasbourg, the Divisions detrained in their initial assembly areas – the Hohenstaufen near Epinal and the Frundsberg near Nancy and Bar-le-Duc. It was only then that the real difficulties started.

On 23 June, as the trains bringing the last Regiment of the Frundsberg finally arrived in Nancy, the first armoured elements of the Division were leaving for Dreux, 70km west of Paris. From there on they had to complete a journey of over 100km on their tracks, reducing, as we shall see, their serviceable life by many hours. Meanwhile, the motorized units faced a drive of over 500km through Troyes and Chartres to the Divisional concentration area in the sector south of Falaise. This had to be carried out mainly at night due to the air threat and in the face of the French Resistance. One SS corporal in the Division said of the move:

> We are now 30 kilometres behind the front after a nightmare journey across France which has taken a fortnight under the most frightening conditions on account of enemy planes. . . . I have hardly slept at all and have forgotten how many times the enemy has strafed us. We have suffered many casualties in men and vehicles but our Luftwaffe has not ventured to put in an appearance. There was nothing like this in Russia.

The 1st SS Panzer Battalion of the Division, which readers will recall had been left at Mailly-le-Camp awaiting the issue of its Panthers, had received its first ten tanks whilst the Division was still in the Ukraine. But then, to everyone's disappointment, it had been ordered to hand them over to the Panzer Lehr Division, already in Normandy. The Battalion was due for a long wait before it would see any more.

The Hohenstaufen was more fortunate. Its 1st SS Panzer Battalion, under the command of SS Major Bollert, at Mailly-le-Camp was now fully equipped with Panthers and they joined the rest of the tracked vehicles of the Division as they reached Paris by rail. From there, they were forced to make a dangerously long road march to the new concentration area west of Falaise. Some 50% of the tanks broke down on the way[1], creating major problems for the repair and supply units. The motorized units had to take an even longer route through Troyes, Orléans and Alençon.

It was at this time that II SS Panzer Corps received an important addition to its strength – the 102nd SS Heavy Panzer Battalion. Formed in Holland during the Spring of 1944 and commanded by SS Major Weiss, a former member of the 2nd SS Panzer Division Das Reich, the Battalion was manned mainly by Volksdeutsche from Rumania.[2] On 1 June, just before it moved to a position near St Pol south of Calais, it had forty-five Tiger Is on strength but only twenty-eight were combat-ready. On 14 June the Battalion started its move by rail to the grounds of the palace of Versailles from where, after a short rest, it continued its laborious move to Normandy. It would be too late to join in the initial actions of its parent Corps.

On arrival in its concentration area, the Hohenstaufen's newly joined 1st SS Panzer Battalion had seventy-nine Panthers, and its 2nd SS Panzer Battalion had forty-eight Mk IV tanks in its 5th and 6th Companies and forty StuGs in the 7th and 8th. The Frundsberg's 2nd SS Panzer Battalion was organised in the same way with thirty-nine Mk IVs, thirty-eight StuGs and three Mk III command tanks. The Hohenstaufen was suffering from a serious shortage in transport capacity[3] and we can assume the Frundsberg was no better off.

NOTES

1. Fürbringer, *La Hohenstaufen*, p. 309.
2. Tieke, *In the Firestorm of the Last Years of the War*, p. 83.
3. Zetterling, *Normandy 1944*, p. 336.

CHAPTER IV

EPSOM: 25 June – 1 July

(Maps 4 & 5)

Montgomery's plan for EPSOM involved the use of three Corps. Its aim was to cross the Odon and Orne rivers and capture the high ground astride the Caen–Falaise road, thus isolating, and then capturing, Caen and exposing the whole German right flank in Normandy. The attack was to be in two Phases. Phase I, code-named MARTLET, was to begin on 25 June with XXX Corps capturing the commanding ground around Rauray and then, after taking Noyers, exploiting south to Aunay-sur-Odon. With its right flank thus protected, the recently landed VIII Corps was then, in Phase II, to carry out the main thrust, EPSOM, on 26 June. As the operation progressed, I Corps was to eliminate the Germans to the north of Caen and, after capturing Carpiquet airfield, clear the city itself. There was to be a concurrent thrust out of the airborne bridgehead east of the Orne.

The scale of EPSOM was obvious to all the senior Allied commanders, and although there can be no doubt that it was an essential part of Monty's strategy to draw as much German armour as possible on to the British sector and away from the planned American breakout on the western flank, there is also no doubt that EPSOM was seen by everyone as a major effort to break through the German defences in the east.

Before EPSOM was launched, Montgomery had written to Eisenhower:

I shall put 8 Corps through in a blitz attack supported by great air power as at El Hamma.[1]

In fact, EPSOM turned out to be the very antithesis of Blitzkrieg.

25 June

Unaware of the impending British attack, the Germans went ahead with preparations for their own counter-stroke and Hausser issued orders for reconnaissances to be carried out for his part in the Panzer Group West counter-attack[2] towards Bayeux, from a line drawn roughly between Villers-Bocage and Caumont. The aim of this strike was to split the American and British Armies, and then destroy the US eastern wing at Balleroy before turning on the British. Further orders were issued that night for the armoured units of the Hohenstaufen and Frundsberg Divisions to begin their moves to the assembly area, which was west of the Orne river and south of a line drawn from Condé sur Noireau to Tinchebray. The motorized units were to move the following night. Allied air power precluded any attempt to do this in daylight.

At 0415 hours on 25 June, 250 Allied guns heralded the beginning of Phase I[3] of the British attack. Behind the 'wall of fire' produced by this barrage, the 49th (West Riding) Infantry Division (see Appendix V), with the 8th Armoured Brigade under command, advanced into the thick ground mist which came with the dawn and reduced visibility to a few metres. Most of the soldiers, like those of the II SS Panzer Corps in the Ukraine, were entering battle for the first time; and like their German counterparts, they were a mixture of volunteers and conscripts. It was to be a bloody initiation – their enemy was the much feared 12th SS Panzer Division Hitlerjugend.[4]

The day did not go well for the British. In the confusion caused by the mist, the supporting tanks halted, and although the infantry plodded on without them, few knew where they were. Monty's hope of using 'great air power' was out of the question. Although some objectives, like the Tessel Woods, were secured with heavy losses on the western flank of the attack, at the end of the day the Hitlerjugend still held all the vital ground, in particular the high ground around Rauray. This meant that Phase II, the main assault by VIII Corps, would have to be launched with an open and highly vulnerable flank.

26 June

General Sir Richard O'Connor's VIII Corps comprised just over 60,000 men and 800 tanks and could call on the supporting fire of over 700 guns, three naval cruisers, a monitor (a heavily armed, shallow-draught warship) and the fighter-bombers of the Second Allied Tactical Air Force. The opening barrage of Operation EPSOM[5] commenced at 0730 hours on 26 June and was fired by 344 field and medium guns. Even the British soldiers approaching their Start Line found it awesome. But once again

19

air support was severely restricted by low cloud and ground mist and none of the aircraft based in England was able to take off. As the day wore on torrential rain put an end to flying altogether.

The artillery barrage, which advanced 90m every three minutes, soon left the foot soldiers behind and the lack of efficient communications between tanks and infantry led to confusion and disorder. The young, but well trained Waffen-SS soldiers of the Hitlerjugend, in their cleverly camouflaged and carefully prepared positions, allowed the creeping barrage and first lines of British infantry to pass over them. Then they opened fire, causing havoc amongst their attackers as they delayed their advance to deal with them. Equally carefully laid minefields delayed and then halted the British armour and, to intensify the nightmare, the whole undulating and sodden battlefield was swept by fire from SS tanks on the high ground at Rauray and from SS Panzer-Grenadiers in the small villages and woods to the north of the Odon. German artillery was also very effective.

By nightfall the limit of the British advance was only 6km from their Start Line and the Odon had not even been reached, let alone crossed. The Germans[6] still held the high ground south of Cheux and at Rauray and had claimed fifty British tanks knocked out during the day.

The men of II SS Panzer Corps had no knowledge of the bitter fighting taking place 30km away to their north. Nor did they know that they, and elements of the Leibstandarte Adolf Hitler (LAH), were about to be called upon to assist their hard-pressed comrades in the Hitlerjugend (HJ) and Das Reich (DR) Divisions. Thus, units of five of Hitler's seven elite Waffen-SS Panzer Divisions were about to be involved in the same battle.

27 June

On 27 June the British were more successful. On the western flank, they captured the Rauray heights, although they failed to reach Brettevillette or cross the Odon north of Gavrus. In the east, however, they secured the bridge at Tourmauville and by last light four battalions of infantry were across the river and tanks had reached the northern slopes of the strategically vital Hill 112.[7] This strike into the heart of the German defences forced the Hitlerjugend commander, Kurt 'Panzer' Meyer, to order a withdrawal from Marcelet to the western edge of Carpiquet airfield on his right flank. Although he was still holding the flanks of the British thrust at Mouen and Grainville, his line now ran from the airfield to Haut de Verson, on to Fontaine-Etoupefour, Hill 112, Esquay, Gavrus and Grainville, and finally to Brettevillette.

During the night of the 27th/28th, SS Lieutenant Colonel Albert Frey, with two Battalions of his 1st SS Panzer-Grenadier Regiment LAH, arrived in the Venoix area of Caen and came under Meyer's command. He received orders to attack as soon as possible – down the line of the Caen–Villers-Bocage road to cut off the British salient south of the Odon and link up with the HJ forces at Grainville. It is also of note that during the 27th a KG Weidinger[8] took up positions at Brettevillette and Haut des Forges, to the north and east of Noyers, on the HJ's left flank. This KG, with a strength of about 2,500 men, was part of the 2nd SS Panzer Division Das Reich, which had arrived in the St Lô area from the south of France on 23 June. Its journey had been seriously delayed by the actions of the Allied air forces and the French Resistance. KG Weidinger was placed initially under the command of the Panzer Lehr Division, but was destined to become part of II SS Panzer Corps on the 29th. It contained the officers and men[9] who had been responsible for the infamous massacre of 642 men, women and children at Oradour-sur-Glane (Map 1), seventeen days earlier.

28 June

The attack by the two Battalions of Frey's 1st SS Panzer-Grenadier Regiment, supported by five Mk IVs from the 21st Panzer Division, was launched at 0600 hours on 28 June. It did not go well and, although the advance reached Mouen and Tourville, a counter-attack by the British, coming south from Cheux, resulted in heavy and confused fighting which went on into the night. There was no question of linking up with KG Weidinger which had spent the day resisting attempts by the 49th Infantry Division to move south from Rauray.

Meanwhile, the lack of really aggressive action on the part of the British on 28 June was greeted with incredulity and delight by the few senior German commanders in the immediate vicinity of the bridgehead over the Odon – men like Sepp Dietrich, commander I SS Panzer Corps, and Kurt Meyer of the HJ. This lack of aggressiveness resulted mainly from almost total congestion in the middle of the narrow salient around Cheux, caused by minefields, isolated pockets of resistance and general destruction. No one seemed capable of solving the problem and so the vast majority of the British tanks and other vehicles remained immobile throughout the day. The only offensive actions ordered were the capture of Hill 112 and the seizure of the bridges over the Odon at Gavrus.

Hausser knew that if the British were ever to cross the Orne they had to capture Hill 112, which he had described as 'the key to the backdoor of Caen'. From its summit, you can see Caen, 9km to the north-east, Carpiquet airfield, Cheux, Point 213 near Villers-Bocage, Mont Pinçon, 18km to the south-west, and the Bourguébus ridge to the south-east of Caen. Lying between the Odon and the Orne, it is in reality the eastern height at the end of a 2km-wide ridge, which runs from Evrecy in the west, almost to Maltot in the east. In 1944, as now, it was completely open with some standing cornfields and a small wood near its summit surrounded by hedgerows. Since it was clearly vital to both sides, it was destined to become the scene of some of the fiercest fighting in the whole campaign.

All British efforts to secure the summit of Hill 112 on the 28th failed. Those tanks that did struggle up the northern slopes, not more than twenty-five[10], with their accompanying infantry[11] came under sustained fire from HJ Panthers and Mk IVs in the area of Fontaine-Etoupefour and its associated Château. Casualties soon reached an unacceptable level and the group withdrew back to the Baron area. A German counter-attack at about 1700 hours was beaten off – neither side being able to evict the other from this bitterly disputed ground.

The only real success on the 28th came when a Battalion of Scottish infantry[12] secured the bridges over the two arms of the river near Gavrus, but even this success was jeopardised when the unit became isolated.

The British bridgehead over the Odon[13], and in particular the fact that enemy armour had reached the northern slopes of Hill 112, was a matter of serious concern at Seventh Army Headquarters. It was obvious that until this probe had been eliminated and the Odon line re-established, there could be no question of launching the pre-planned counter-attack towards Bayeux. General Dollmann, already reeling from the loss of Cherbourg two days before and fearing the worst from Hitler's ordered investigation into the reasons for its loss, panicked. At 0810 hours he ordered Hausser's II SS Panzer Corps 'to attack immediately in order to clear out the breach south of Cheux'. Hausser replied that since many of his units had yet to reach the combat area, no counter-attack was possible before the 29th. Nevertheless, he told his senior commanders to reconnoitre the area between Villers-Bocage and Evrecy.

One of the most extraordinary things about the German command system on 28 June was that, at this most critical time in the campaign, there was no one senior to Dollmann left in Normandy – Hitler had called both von Rundstedt and Rommel back to Berchtesgaden in southern Germany. Having given his order and been told by Hausser that it could not be carried out, Dollmann committed suicide. The Headquarters of CinC West, Army Group 'B' and Seventh Army were therefore all without their commanders.

At 1300 hours Hausser advised the Chief of Staff of Seventh Army that, although he would prefer to use the next day to fight a containing action whilst he organised his Corps for the required counter-attack, he could, if really necessary, launch it on the 29th. At 1500 hours Headquarters Army Group 'B' informed Seventh Army that Hitler had appointed Hausser to replace Dollmann and, pending the return of

Rommel, he was also to assume supreme command in the invasion sector. He was thus the first Waffen-SS officer to command an Army.

Lieutenant General Pemsel, the Seventh Army Chief of Staff, advised Hausser to stay with his Corps to organise the counter-attack, at least until the following morning. But this extraordinary decision by Hitler, to remove a Corps commander just before a vital counter-attack, inevitably set off a chain reaction which did nothing to help the success of the forthcoming operation. In particular, one of the commanders of the two Divisions due to carry out the attack, Willi Bittrich, had to give up the Hohenstaufen in order to take over II SS Panzer Corps. He was replaced temporarily by the commander of the 20th SS Panzer-Grenadier Regiment, SS Colonel Thomas Müller. Nicknamed 'Cigars', for obvious reasons, Müller held the Iron Cross 1st and 2nd Class and the Infantry Assault Badge. He was to end the war commanding the 27th SS Freiwilligen Grenadier Division, Langemarck.

At 1700 hours the Seventh Army operational sector was split. General Geyr von Schweppenburg[14] became responsible for the invasion front from the Seine to a line drawn roughly between Caumont and Bayeux, whilst Hausser continued to look after the area to the west of that line. This meant that II SS Panzer Corps, along with I SS and XLVII Panzer and LXXXVI Infantry Corps were all transferred to the new command.

Von Schweppenburg wasted no time in confirming the order for the II SS Panzer Corps counter-attack. It was to be launched from a line running from Noyers to Evrecy and the Corps mission was to capture Grainville, Mouen and Cheux, to the north of the Odon and Gavrus, Baron and Hill 112 to the south. KG Weidinger was to come under command of the Hohenstaufen for this operation and was ordered to join in the attack as 9th SS reached the vicinity of Noyers.

29 June

The weather, which had improved considerably on the 28th, now favoured the Allies and ground attack aircraft were able to roam freely over the battlefield. Nevertheless, this major asset was not used to support any offensive actions on the fourth day of EPSOM. Through ULTRA (the British decrypting organisation) intercepts, Lieutenant General Miles Dempsey, commander Second Army, knew of the moves of II SS Panzer Corps and the planned German counter-attack and he was only too pleased to give his approval to the VIII Corps commander's new orders, issued at 1000 hours. O'Connor, although not privy to ULTRA, was also aware of the German build-up from aerial reconnaissance and felt his Corps to be over-exposed. He decided therefore to strengthen his bridgehead by ordering his infantry Divisions to clear the ground between Cheux and the Odon and coordinate their anti-tank defences with the two armoured Brigades in the salient. He went on to order the 11th Armoured Division not to attempt any further crossings of the Odon.

The assembly areas for II SS Panzer Corps' attack, which had been ordered for 0600 hours on 29 June, were in the areas of Monts and Tournay for the Hohenstaufen and Neuilly, St Honorine and Maizet for the Frundsberg. Neither was ideal: the Hohenstaufen's was covered with hedgerows which made the movement of armoured vehicles difficult; whilst the Frundsberg's was bounded in the east by the Orne, which could only be crossed on the few bridges available, and in the west by streams, hedges and thick undergrowth which again restricted the movement of vehicles. These problems, aggravated by delays caused by Allied artillery fire and low level air attacks, meant that the H-Hour for the attack had to be postponed until 1400 hours and it was this delay which allowed the British to strike first with their 15th (Scottish) and 43rd (Wessex) Infantry Divisions. These formations had been ordered to clear and enlarge the salient astride the Odon. In furtherance of this directive, an infantry Battalion of the 44th (Lowland) Brigade[15] moved in on the northern flank of two other Battalions of the 15th Scottish Division in Grainville[16] and le Valtru[17], and secured the wood around the Château north of Grainville. All three of these Battalions, plus another[18] in Mondrainville, were therefore right in the path of the Hohenstaufen's attack. Similarly, another unit[19] holding the two bridges just north of Gavrus, and tanks with more infantry[20] attempting to advance on Evrecy via Hill 113 would find themselves lying across the main axis of the Frundsberg's counter-attack.

Before describing the II SS Panzer Corps' counter-attack, it is important to mention other British actions which, although they failed to win any significant ground, had a very detrimental effect on the German plan. On the eastern flank of the salient, infantry of the 43rd (Wessex) Infantry Division, with strong artillery and tank support[21], captured Mouen by 1100 hours and went on to take Baron by the early evening, so forcing KG Frey of the LAH to pull back to Verson and Fontaine-Etoupefour. Meanwhile, at 0800 hours, two companies of another Battalion of infantry[22] had re-occupied the small wooded area 300m east of the summit of Hill 112; but when tanks[23] tried to support this move they became engaged in a fierce duel with HJ tanks positioned around Eterville and the nearby Château de Fontaine. A similar attempt by armour[24] to advance towards Esquay was stopped by Tiger Is of the 101st SS Heavy Panzer Battalion, part of I SS Panzer Corps. Six British tanks were destroyed. It will be appreciated therefore that substantial elements of the 1st and 12th SS Panzer Divisions[25], which were meant to support the II SS Panzer Corps attack by themselves attacking from the south and east, were instead fully involved resisting the various assaults just described.

The Hohenstaufen attack was violent and lasted over six hours.[26] It began at 1400 hours with heavy artillery concentrations on Grainville and le Valtru. The 20th SS Panzer-Grenadier Regiment advanced from just south of Noyers, towards the Château north of Grainville and the hamlet of le Haut du Bosq, with Cheux as its objective. At the same time the 19th Regiment moved across the completely open ground on the right flank, south of the Caen road, through Missy and Haut des Forges, towards Grainville and le Valtru. Panthers, Mk IVs and StuGs of the 9th SS Panzer Regiment supported both Regiments.[27] Dealing with the right-hand advance first, tanks and Grenadiers of the 19th SS Panzer-Grenadier Regiment soon overran a company of infantry[28] just to the west of le Valtru and then went on to attack the village itself. Anti-tank weapons knocked out four German tanks when they attempted to drive down the village street and intense artillery fire forced the accompanying Grenadiers to pull back. Six of the defending unit's officers were killed and four wounded in this vicious fighting.

The fighting in the Grainville area was no less intense. The Germans managed to capture the wood around the Château, only to lose it again to an immediate counter-attack.[29] They claim also to have captured the village itself[30], but British accounts deny this. Certainly by last light, after confused hand-to-hand fighting, the British[31] were still in control.

The biggest crisis for the British in this sector came at 1830 hours when tanks of the 9th SS Panzer Regiment, with supporting groups of 19th SS Regiment Panzer-Grenadiers, attacked again in the area of the Château wood. This happened as one British unit was relieving another[32] and in the ensuing chaos the Germans infiltrated between the forward defences. When however, the Panthers and Mk IVs ran into tanks and SP guns[33] which had been positioned in depth as an emergency measure, and strong defensive artillery fire denied them their intimate infantry support, they had no hope of making further progress. Those that tried to penetrate deeper were knocked out. A single vignette will give a small impression of the fighting:

Under SS Senior Sergeant Holte, we drove with one platoon of the 2nd Battalion, 9th SS Panzer Regiment, in an attack in the area of Grainville and struggled with British tanks all around us. In the course of the fight our Panther took a direct hit on the ball mount [mounting for hull machine-gun]. The phosphorus shell penetrated and our Panzer was immediately in flames. Holte yelled 'Bail out!'. He, the gunner and myself, the loader, made it out of the turret, but the radio operator, Gödtke, and the driver, Appel, were severely wounded and did not get out. From outside we tried to open the driver's and radio operator's hatches, but to no avail. The heat was unbearable. The ammunition exploded inside the Panzer. We ran back 30m, threw ourselves into a shell crater and had to watch as our Panzer burned out. It was a coffin for Appel and Gödtke and we could do nothing to help them.[34]

Farther south, a similar penetration by tanks and Grenadiers of the 19th Regiment between Grainville and le Valtru towards Mondrainville was eventually beaten back by British tanks and infantry[35] with heavy artillery support.

On the left flank, the Hohenstaufen attack met with no success at all. The 1st/20th and 2nd/20th SS Panzer-Grenadier Battalions moved into Brettevillette in preparation for the main assault on Cheux by Panthers of SS Major Bollert's 1st SS Panzer Battalion and Grenadiers of the 3rd/ 20th Battalion in their SPWs. This assault was meant to follow the axis of the road leading north-east from Noyers but it never developed. According to Wilhelm Tieke's *In the Firestorm of the Last Years of the War*, and Herbert Fürbringer's *La Hohenstaufen*, the group was subjected to 'carpet bombing' by about a hundred Lancaster heavy bombers whilst it was forming up around Noyers, and this ended any hope of the attack proceeding as planned. These accounts claim the Grenadiers lost sixty men, including twenty killed, and suffered 20% vehicle casualties.[36] It is of interest that the British archives have no record of any such raid during the afternoon and neither H G Martin's *History of the 15th Scottish Division* nor any of the British unit records make any mention of it. This author believes the story of the heavy bomber raid is fictitious and that the real reason for the attack being cancelled was disruption caused by artillery and naval gunfire, together with the realisation that it was likely to be suicidal. The attack was, after all, due to be carried out across open ground, with British troops and tanks at Rauray[37], only a few hundred metres away on the left flank, and with an objective, also strongly held, in 'dead' ground. This is not to say the casualties were fictitious – but they were almost certainly caused by the naval gunfire and heavy artillery fire just mentioned, and possibly by ground attack aircraft.[38] Nor is a raid by heavy bombers in this general area fictitious. At 2030 hours that evening, 256 RAF heavy bombers dropped 1,100 tons on Villers-Bocage, 8km from Noyers, in the mistaken belief that it was a major assembly area for an impending German counter-attack. There were no Germans in the small town, which was obliterated.

It will be remembered that KG Weidinger of the 2nd SS Panzer Division DR was also under Bittrich's command for this counter-attack and was due to join in as the 20th SS Panzer-Grenadier Regiment KG came into line in the Brettevillette area. In his book, *Comrades to the End*, Otto Weidinger himself says little about the events of this day, except to speak of the intense British artillery fire which, in his opinion, precluded any chance of the German attack being successful. It is of interest that he confuses the 9th and 10th SS Panzer Division sectors in his description of the battle.

By 2300 hours the 15th Scottish Division could justly claim that it had fought off the 9th SS Panzer Division's counter-attack. It has to be added though, that Weidinger's statements about the overwhelming weight of British artillery and naval gunfire are significant and there is no doubt that this firepower[39] played a major part in defeating the Hohenstaufen's attack.

The designated H-Hour for the Frundsberg's attack was the same as the Hohenstaufen's, but since only the 1st/21st SS Panzer-Grenadier Battalion had arrived in the assembly area by 1400 hours, the whole Divisional attack was delayed for half an hour. It will be recalled that the Division's objectives were Gavrus, Baron and Hill 112.

A major obstacle in the path of the 10th SS Panzer Division's advance was a small tributary of the Orne river which ran just to the north of Avenay and Evrecy and covered the approaches to Hills 112 and 113. SS Colonel Harmel decided therefore to put the main weight of his attack on his western flank – between this stream and the Odon. Here the Grenadiers of the 22nd SS Panzer-Grenadier Regiment advanced from their assembly area around Neuilly into the close country near the Odon, with the StuGs of the 7th and 8th Companies of the 2nd/10th SS Panzer Battalion moving across the open rolling ground on their right flank. Their combined advance took them towards Bougy, which stands on a hill with deep valleys on either side, and Gavrus. A Battalion of infantry with only three companies[40] held the latter village as well as the two bridges a couple of hundred metres to its north. Wilhelm Tieke claims that the 22nd Grenadiers took the village late in the afternoon, only to lose it after a short time to a counter-attack, preceded by heavy artillery fire. The British reports[41] differ slightly, saying that at 2000 hours, after five hours of confused and heavy fighting, they were still in firm possession of the bridges. The Commanding Officer of the defending Battalion wrote later, 'If ever there was a platoon and section commanders' battle this was. Observation over 100 yards was seldom possible.' The reports make no mention of the counter-attack on the village, merely saying the enemy 'drew off'. It seems likely that intense artillery fire caused this German withdrawal and that the village became a 'no man's land'.

On the eastern flank, SS Colonel Diesenhofer's similarly reinforced 21st SS Panzer-Grenadier Regiment had the more difficult task of advancing across open ground from the St Honorine–Maizet area, crossing the Evrecy stream and capturing Hills 113 and 112. The whole operation was further complicated by the late arrival of important sub-units of his Regiment. The 2nd Grenadier Battalion, after being delayed initially by heavy artillery fire, soon ran into tanks and infantry[42] in the eastern part

of Evrecy. Although these were forced to withdraw, it took the Mk IV
tanks of the 2nd/10th SS Panzer Battalion the remaining hours of daylight
to secure Hill 113. Twenty-eight British tanks were claimed during this
fighting, although the British figure of twelve seems more realistic.

It was obvious to Bittrich and his Divisional commanders that the
major reasons for their lack of real success on the 29th had been the
overwhelming weight of Allied artillery and naval gunfire and the freedom with which Allied fighters and fighter-bombers had ranged over
the battlefield. It was decided therefore that both Divisions should launch
night attacks in a desperate effort to obtain their objectives and eradicate
the British salient across the Odon. Little did they realise that Generals
Dempsey and O'Connor, influenced partly by captured documents[43] and
aerial reconnaissance, were convinced that they had yet to receive the
main German counter-attack and, at 2030 hours, had ordered all British
armour to withdraw to the north bank of the Odon. Only an infantry
bridgehead was to be left on the south side of the stream. All thought
of continuing the advance towards the Orne had been abandoned – at
least for the present. At 2100 hours a rainstorm lasting five hours turned
the ground into a quagmire, making life a misery for the foot soldiers
and movement treacherous for vehicles. It was in these conditions that
the renewed German counter-attacks were to be launched.

30 June – 1 July

The Frundsberg, with a total strength of strength of 13,552[44], began its
attack at 0120 hours. The 1st/21st and 3rd/21st SS Panzer-Grenadier
Battalions secured Avenay and crossings over the Orne tributary between
there and Vieux, and the Mk IV companies of SS Major Reinhold's 2nd
SS Panzer Battalion soon moved into their assembly area for the assault
on Hill 112. Then, at dawn, following an intense barrage by the guns and
massed mortars[45] of both the Frundsberg and Hitlerjugend Divisions,
supplemented by those of II SS Panzer Corps and the 7th and 8th Werfer
Brigades[46], the main attack on Hill 112 began. In a complicated, three-
pronged operation, the 2nd/21st SS Panzer-Grenadier Battalion Group
from Hill 113 advanced from the south-west, the remainder of the 21st
Regiment and Reinhold's Mk IVs from the south and KG Wünsche[47] of
the Hitlerjugend Division from the east and south-east. By 0730 hours
the combined German force reached the crest of Hill 112 and by noon
the northern slopes were secured. A young Hitlerjugend officer described
the attack as follows:

> Early in the morning rockets from our launchers, trailing veils of
> smoke, howled into the English positions . . . These launchers decided
> the success of the attack during the morning. This was our fourth

attack on Hill 112, and it was crowned by the capture of the square wood and the hill. As we drove up, we saw numerous destroyed vehicles, among them knocked out Sherman tanks.[48]

And a member of the 6th SS Panzer Company HJ later wrote:

The rocket launchers were firing right above us toward the hill. The Grenadiers reported the 'Tommies' were on the run ... When we reached the top, it was all over. Some tank engines were still running, but no one could be seen inside. Grenadiers from Frundsberg were already coming up the other side. Some hours later they came under a heavy artillery barrage and suffered heavy losses.[49]

Accounts of the fighting to the north of Hills 113 and 112 differ. The Germans say the 22nd SS Panzer-Grenadier Regiment was involved in heavy fighting in Gavrus[50] before dawn on the 30th and that their enemy[51] was driven out soon after daylight. This account goes on to say that initial attempts to advance on Baron were defeated by intense artillery fire; but later in the day assault troops penetrated into gardens in the south of the village and houses on the west side. British counter-attacks soon forced them 'back to their jump-off positions'. The British version of events is very different.[52] It claims that the night was quiet, but at noon the Germans put down a heavy artillery and mortar barrage in the Gavrus area and at 1500 hours launched a strong attack. The barrage caused some confusion north of the Odon, but the three companies on the south side were largely unaffected and, with the help of artillery, the attack was easily repulsed. Later, at about 2130 hours, the companies were withdrawn back across the stream and on through le Valtru to the north.[53]

But what of the Hohenstaufen[54] and KG Weidinger on the 30th? The attack against le Valtru was renewed at 0130 hours but the defenders were not to be moved. Later in the day, around 1500 hours, the 19th SS Panzer-Grenadier Group managed to penetrate between the two Battalions[55] defending the Grainville and le Valtru sector but it could not sustain this success and withdrew with further losses. The Regimental commander, SS Lieutenant Colonel Woith was wounded in this fighting and SS Major Zollhöfer took over. On the left flank of the Hohenstaufen sector the way through Rauray and le Haut du Bosq to Cheux was firmly blocked by the 70th and 44th Infantry Brigades[56], reinforced with 17-pounder anti-tank guns.

The daylight hours of 30 June saw the continuation of the devastating artillery and mortar duel between the two sides. Amongst the many casualties on the German side was the commander of the 1st SS Panzer-Grenadier Battalion of the Der Führer Regiment (KG Weidinger), SS

Major Diekmann, killed by shell splinters somewhere to the north of Noyers. He was the officer who had been in command of the Das Reich troops in Oradour-sur-Glane on 10 June and had given the order to shoot the men of the village and set fire to the church containing the women and children. The commander of the Company involved in this massacre, SS Captain Kahn, had already been seriously wounded by shellfire, losing an arm and an eye. He was evacuated – never to be seen again!

During the evening of the 30th, Paul Hausser sent the following message to Rommel's Headquarters:

> The counter-offensive by I and II SS Panzer Corps has had to be temporarily suspended in the face of intensive enemy artillery fire and supporting fire of unprecedented ferocity from naval units. . . . The tenacious enemy resistance will prevent our counter-offensive from having any appreciable effect.

In fact, Bittrich had ordered both his Divisions to renew their attacks. He was unaware that the VIII Corps bridgehead south of the Odon had virtually ceased to exist and that as far as the British were concerned EPSOM was over.

Heavy preparatory mortar and artillery barrages were fired at 0330 hours on 1 July and half an hour later the Frundsberg assault began. By 0500 hours it had failed. British patrols later found an estimated 300–400 German dead on the northern slopes of Hill 112.[57]

The Hohenstaufen attack towards le Haut du Bosq, through the Rauray and Château Grainville sector, initially fared rather better. Following a heavy mortar and artillery barrage, tanks of Otto Meyer's 9th SS Panzer Regiment, together with Hohenstaufen and Der Führer Panzer-Grenadiers, advanced soon after 0600 hours behind a smoke screen. After some four hours of heavy fighting, they managed to penetrate into and between some of the positions of the defending British infantry and anti-tank guns[58], before being halted in front of Rauray and the commanding high ground to its south-east. British reports speak of a further four attacks during the day, with the last two being broken up by artillery fire – the final one even before it could be properly launched. British casualties were heavy – one Battalion alone lost 132 men during the day.[59] One source[60] says ten field and two medium artillery battalions (272 guns), firing an average of ninety rounds each, were used to break up the German attacks. A counter-attack in the early evening, which included Shermans[61] and flame-throwing Churchills, restored the original British line. By then, the commander of the 1st/20th SS Panzer-Grenadier Battalion, SS Major Lederer, had been wounded, the 20th Regiment as a whole had lost 328 men, including fifty-one killed[62] and KG Weidinger had suffered 642 casualties, including 108 killed.[63] Its commander complained later that the squads that had advanced the farthest were forced to disengage in daylight, with consequently heavy casualties.

The following day, the German Divisional commanders were ordered to consolidate the ground so far gained. Their line ran from Verson to Eterville, to Hill 112, on to a point 200m south-east of Tourmauville, west to the northern edge of Gavrus and then west of le Valtru to Tessel-Bretteville. The same day, British patrols reported the Germans digging in to the south of the Odon bridgehead. Aerial photographs taken two days later showed large numbers of newly dug weapon pits and by 8 July these gradually took shape as a line extending right across the front.

EPSOM had failed and there is no doubt that this was partly due to the II SS Panzer Corps counter-attack. Many historians have dismissed this attack as a failure; but without it there is a strong possibility that the British would have secured 'the key to the back door of Caen' and then reached and even crossed the Orne. On the other hand, if Montgomery had not launched this costly operation[64], Hitler's strategy of driving a wedge between the Americans and the British with his Panzer Corps, and then pushing each Army into the sea, might well have succeeded. As it was, Hitler himself seemed encouraged by the outcome of the battle since it had proved that the Allies, despite their overwhelming firepower and mobility, could still be prevented from breaking out of their slender bridgehead. Of course, any chance of evicting the Allies from that bridgehead had long since disappeared. Some idea of the rate of the Allied build-up can be gauged by the fact that, despite the casualties suffered, VIII Corps was 22,735 men stronger on 30 June than it had been at the beginning of Operation EPSOM.[65]

NOTES

1. Monty had turned the Mareth Line at El Hamma in Tunisia on 23 Mar 43.
2. I & II SS and XLVII Pz Corps.
3. Full details of Operation MARTLET can be read in the author's book, *Steel Inferno – I SS Panzer Corps in Normandy*.
4. Part of I SS Pz Corps.
5. As Note 3 for Operation EPSOM.
6. The HJ suffered 730 casualties on this day.
7. 11 Armd Div.
8. The Der Führer (DF) SS Pz-Gren Regt under the command of SS Maj Otto Weidinger, but with only one of its own inf Bns (the 1st) and the 1st Bn of the Deutschland Regt. It also comprised motor-cycle recce, inf gun (150mm), Pnr and Flak coys.
9. SS Maj Diekmann, SS Capt Kahn and the 3rd Coy, 1st Bn, Der Führer Regt.
10. 23rd Hussars (23 H), later relieved by 3rd Bn, Royal Tank Regt (3 RTR).
11. 8th Bn, The Rifle Bde (8 RB).
12. 2nd Bn, The Argyll & Sutherland Highlanders (2 Argylls).

13. By last light on 28 Jun, there were 152 combat-ready tanks of 29 Armd Bde, a tank bn of 4 Armd Bde and four bns of inf south of the Odon.
14. On 10 Jun, as a result of an ULTRA intercept, Schweppenburg's HQ had been destroyed in an attack by four sqns of rocket-firing Typhoons and seventy-one med bombers. Schweppenburg was slightly wounded and his Chief of Staff and sixteen others killed.
15. 8th Bn, The Royal Scots (8 RS).
16. 9th Bn, The Cameronians (9 Cameronians).
17. 7th Bn, The Seaforth Highlanders (7 Seaforth).
18. 2nd Bn, The Glasgow Highlanders (2 Glasgow Hldrs).
19. 2 Argylls.
20. 44 RTR & 2nd Bn, The Kings Royal Rifle Corps (2 KRRC).
21. 7 RTR.
22. 8 RB with support from 3 RTR.
23. 2nd Regt, The Fife and Forfar Yeomanry (2 F&F Yeo).
24. 44 RTR.
25. 12 SS Pz &12 SS Arty Regts, 12 SS Recce Bn, 3/26 SS Pz-Gren Regt, a coy of the 101 Hy SS Pz Bn, KG Frey & 83 Werfer Bn.
26. Readers who visit the area should be aware that the old Noyers – Caen railway line is today a motorway.
27. A POW, taken by 4 Armd Grenadier Guards (Gren Gds) in Aug 44, stated that 6/2/9 SS Pz Bn had only seven serviceable Mk IVs for this attack.
28. 7 Seaforth.
29. By 8 RS.
30. Tieke, *In the Firestorm of the Last Years of the War*, p. 89.
31. 9 Cameronians.
32. 6th Bn, The Royal Scots Fusiliers (6 RSF) was relieving 8 RS.
33. From 4 Armd Bde & 91 A/Tk Regt.
34. Tieke, op. cit., p. 103.
35. 7 RTR and 2 Glasgow Hldrs.
36. Tieke, op. cit., p. 89.
37. Rauray had been captured by 11th Bn, The Durham Light Infantry (11 DLI) and tks of 8 Armd Bde on 27 Jun from the 1/12 SS Pz & 3/26 SS Pz-Gren Bns HJ.
38. Over 1,000 sorties were flown by 2 ATAF on this day. Despite Allied air superiority, 151 Typhoon pilots were killed during the Normandy campaign. They are commemorated by name on a memorial in Noyers.
39. As well as the guns of VIII Corps, those of I & XXX Corps joined in when required.
40. 2 Argylls.
41. Martin, *History of the 15th Scottish Division 1939–1945*, pp. 49–50.
42. 44 RTR & 2 KRRC.
43. A map and notebook showing the German plan had been found on a captured officer of 19 SS Pz-Gren Regt, Frundsberg.
44. Tieke, op. cit., p. 473.
45. German mortars allegedly accounted for 70% of British casualties in Normandy.
46. A Werfer bde comprised two regts of three bns; each bn had between fifteen and twenty-two Nebelwerfers; two bns had 150mm and one had 210 or 300mm – Zetterling, *Normandy 1944*, pp. 142–4.
47. 2/12 SS Pz Bn & 3/26 SS Pz-Gren Bn HJ.
48. Meyer, *The History of the 12th SS Panzer Division Hitlerjugend*, p. 128.

49. Ibid.
50. Tieke, op. cit., p. 92.
51. 2 Argylls.
52. Martin, op. cit., pp. 52–3.
53. 2 Argylls suffered 245 casualties during EPSOM.
54. According to Tieke, op. cit., p. 473, its strength on this day was 15,898.
55. 7 Seaforth & 9 Cameronians.
56. Of 49 and 15 Inf Divs respectively.
57. Jackson, *Operations of Eighth Corps*, p. 58. This small but valuable book is firmly based on the VIII Corps War Diaries.
58. 6th Bn, The King's Own Scottish Borderers (6 KOSB), 1st Bn, The Tyneside Scottish, 11 DLI, 4th Bn, The Lincolnshire Regiment (4 Lincolns) & 17-pdrs of the 55 & 97 A/Tk Regts.
59. 1 Tyneside Scottish.
60. Jackson, op. cit., p. 58.
61. 24th Lancers (24 L).
62. Fürbringer, *La Hohenstaufen*, pp. 287 & 289.
63. Zetterling, op. cit., p. 323.
64. According to Jackson, (op. cit.), the Corps suffered 4,078 casualties between 26 Jun and 1 Jul. The Germans claimed sixty-two British tanks knocked out.
65. Ibid., p. 52.

CHAPTER V

A Relatively Peaceful Time: 2 – 9 July

(Map 5)

EPSOM may have been costly for the British, but it also caused 'grievous losses' to the Germans.[1] We have already heard that KG Weidinger suffered 642 casualties and a report for the period 1200 hours 29 June to 1900 hours 2 July shows the Hohenstaufen had lost 1,145 men, six Panthers, sixteen Mk IVs and ten StuGs.[2] A CinC West report[3] gives a casualty figure of 571 for the Frundsberg. This may not seem too serious but some idea of its combat state can be gauged by the fact that on 6 July the strength of its 2nd/22nd SS Panzer-Grenadier Battalion was only 303 men.[4]

In the case of combat-ready armour, strength returns dated 7 July show the Hohenstaufen with only forty-three Panthers, fifteen Mk IVs and twenty-three StuGs and the Frundsberg with twenty-seven Mk IVs and twenty-five StuGs. This is a total of thirty-six Panthers, forty-five Mk IVs and twenty-two StuGs fewer than when they arrived in Normandy. However, some of this shortfall was due to mechanical breakdown and many of the battle casualties were not write-offs but were undergoing short or long-term repair. By 10 July the Tigers of the Corps' 102nd SS

Heavy Panzer Battalion were still not complete in their designated assembly area 3km to the south-west of Evrecy. Their progress from the Versailles area had been badly disrupted by massive Allied air interdiction.

There were political as well as battle casualties. On 30 June Field Marshals von Rundstedt and Rommel returned from their meeting with Hitler. Although they both believed a withdrawal to the line of the Seine (Map 4) to be the only sensible course of action, they had reluctantly agreed to continue a policy of aggressive and unyielding defence. Waiting for Rommel on his return was a new appreciation of the situation prepared by the commander of Panzer Group West, von Schweppenburg, and endorsed by Hausser of the Seventh Army. It stated that the Panzer Divisions were being so seriously worn down that a withdrawal was essential, to a new line drawn south of the Orne from Caen to Bully, then north-west to Hills 112 and 113, and then west again to Villers-Bocage and the high ground around Caumont. As well as calling Hill 112 the 'key to the back door of Caen', Hausser had said, 'He who holds Hill 112 holds Normandy', and this new line included 112 and all the strategically important ground to its west for a distance of 30km. Rommel forwarded the report to von Rundstedt with his concurrence and later that night the latter informed OKW of its contents and authorised Rommel to begin the limited withdrawal. The reaction from Berlin was swift. Von Rundstedt received a Führer Order at 1730 hours on 1 July halting all preparations for the planned withdrawal. Rommel transmitted von Schweppenburg's response to von Rundstedt:

> If the requested straightening of the front does not occur within a few days, the 9th SS, 10th SS, 12th SS and Panzer Lehr Divisions will burn out to the extent they will no longer be useable. We are not talking here about running away, but rather about a sensible and methodical removal from the fire of ships' artillery for which the men are helpless targets at the present time.[5]

That night von Rundstedt, in answer to the question from Keitel, Chief of the OKW, 'What shall we do?' made his famous reply, 'Make peace, you fools!'

The following morning, 2 July, one of Hitler's adjutants arrived at von Rundstedt's Headquarters with another decoration for the ageing Field Marshal, and more importantly, a letter from the Führer relieving him of his command. Field Marshal Günter von Kluge was already on his way to take over. On the same day von Schweppenburg was told by Rommel that he was to be replaced by the 48-year-old General Heinrich Eberbach, Inspector of the Panzerwaffe, and that his Panzer Group West would henceforth come under the direct command of CinC West. Rommel added the fateful words, 'I'm next on the list!'.

Montgomery's strategy had always involved holding as many Panzer Divisions as possible on the eastern flank in Normandy in order to facilitate the planned American breakout in the west. He therefore ordered further operations in the Caen sector – the capture of Carpiquet airfield by the Canadians on 4 July and Caen itself by the British I Corps on the 8th. In the meantime, pressure was to be kept up to the south-west of Caen against II SS Panzer Corps.

On 2 July KG Weidinger was relieved by units of the 277th Infantry Division and reverted to the command of its parent Division, 2nd SS Panzer DR. At the same time, the Hohenstaufen's 9th SS Pioneer Battalion took over in the Gavrus sector, releasing units of the Frundsberg's 22nd Regiment to form a reserve. The Hohenstaufen's Panzer-Grenadier Regiments continued to occupy positions to the east of Missy and north of Haut des Forges to Brettevillette and Vendes; the 3rd/20th SPW Battalion and two SS Panzer Battalions were withdrawn into reserve. On the left of the Division, the newly arrived 276th Infantry Division came into the line.

Apart from constant heavy shelling, the period 3 to 10 July turned out to be a relatively quiet one for the Hohenstaufen and it was during this time that it was gradually relieved by the 277th Infantry Division. The first units were pulled back on the 6th and 7th, and on the 8th the Frundsberg took over the Gavrus sector again. On the 9th and 10th the relief was completed and the Division went into reserve in an area west of the Orne and south of a line drawn from Amayé to Aunay. During this period it also welcomed its new commander – SS Colonel Sylvester Stadler. He had moved across from the Das Reich Division to replace Thomas Müller. Stadler was 33 years old and already the holder of the Iron Cross, 1st and 2nd Class, and a Knight's Cross with Oakleaves, won on the Eastern Front. His arrival meant that the three senior commanders in II SS Panzer Corps were former Das Reich officers – Bittrich, Harmel and now Stadler.

According to one German report[6], the first few days of July were very different for the Frundsberg Division. It says the British launched a holding attack in the Maltot sector on the 3rd, which necessitated not only the deployment of the Divisional reserve, the 2nd/22nd SS Panzer-Grenadier Battalion, into the Château de Fontaine but, at 1300 hours, a full scale counter-attack by the right wing of the 21st Regiment and 1st Battalion of the 22nd Regiment. By 1500 hours Maltot had been recaptured. It goes on to say that attacks against Hill 112 were beaten off by the 1st/21st SS Panzer-Grenadier Battalion and tanks of the 2nd/10th SS Panzer Battalion. This had to be followed by a night attack by SS Pioneers to evict British infantrymen who had penetrated into the small wood on the east side of the summit. The following day, as the Canadians launched their attack on Carpiquet airfield (Operation WINDSOR), the Frundsberg front apparently quietened down. The author can find no corroborating reports of these actions on the British side.

WINDSOR was seen by Montgomery and Dempsey as a prerequisite for the capture of Caen, but despite massive fire support only the village of Carpiquet and the northern part of the airfield were secured. Kurt 'Panzer' Meyer's Hitlerjugend remained in control of the vital southern hangars and the area of the control tower. The failure of this operation was to have serious consequences for the people of Caen – it convinced the commander of Second Army that it would be impossible to take the city quickly and without unacceptable casualties, unless he was assisted by Bomber Command.

Operation CHARNWOOD, the assault on Caen by the 115,000-strong British and Canadian I Corps, was preceded by an artillery and naval bombardment on the evening of the 7th, followed by 467 Lancaster and Halifax heavy bombers dropping 6,000 bombs (2,500 tons) on the city. Several hundred French civilians were killed and most of the built-up area obliterated but the Germans, whose defences lay on the northern outskirts, suffered only minimal casualties. Further raids lasting two hours by 250 medium bombers of the Ninth US Air Force followed on the 8th. The British and Canadian attack was, not surprisingly, successful in that it secured what was left of the city north of the Orne, but it took two days and cost 3,817 casualties and at least eighty tanks.[7]

In conjunction with CHARNWOOD, the VIII British Corps was required to be at twenty-four hours notice to launch another attack with its 43rd Wessex Infantry Division, designed to reach the Orne in the region of St André-sur-Orne. This attack, code-named JUPITER, would involve the capture of Hill 112 and would confront II SS Panzer Corps. H-Hour was set for 0500 hours on 10 July.

NOTES

1. Von Rundstedt's situation report for 30 Jun.
2. Zetterling, *Normandy 1944*, p. 338.
3. Zetterling, op. cit., p. 345.
4. Tieke, *In the Firestorm of the Last Years of the War*, p. 473.
5. Meyer, *The History of the 12th SS Panzer Division Hitlerjugend*, p. 133.
6. Tieke, op. cit., pp. 101–2.
7. Ellis, *Victory in the West, Vol I*, p. 316.

CHAPTER VI

JUPITER: 10 – 11 July

(Map 5)

Montgomery's aim in Operation JUPITER was to seize the high ground between the Odon and the Orne in the general area of Hill 112 and Maltot and then advance to the Orne at May and St André. Major General Ivor (Butcher) Thomas's 43rd (Wessex) Division was given the task and reinforced with two tank Brigades and an infantry Brigade, bringing his total strength to five tank and thirteen infantry Battalions.

Thomas's wildly optimistic plan required two of his own infantry Brigades, with support from the Churchills of the 31st Tank Brigade, to take Maltot and the crest of Hill 112 in one and a quarter hours[1] and then for the 4th Armoured Brigade and his reserve Brigade to exploit to the Orne. The additional infantry Brigade[2] was to secure the eastern flank of the assault. In addition to his own three artillery Battalions, Thomas was to have the support of two Army Groups Royal Artillery[3], the guns of the 11th Armoured and 15th Scottish Divisions (a total of over 300 guns) and on-call ground attack aircraft. The commander of the 4th Armoured Brigade, Brigadier (later Field Marshal) Michael Carver, wrote after the war:

> The only stipulation I insisted on was that, before launching my lead-ing regiment over the crest of Hill 112, the square wood on its reverse slope must be firmly in our hands. If it were not, my tanks would be shot up from the rear as they went forward. After further heated argument and objections from the infantry, it was agreed.[4]

It is difficult to imagine a similar argument amongst senior German officers!

How were the Germans deployed to meet the British onslaught? In the eastern part of the sector, running from le Mesnil to the south-east of Maltot, there were some thirty tanks of the 12th SS Panzer Regiment HJ and forty-one StuGs of the 1st SS StuG Battalion LAH, backing up the Leibstandarte's 1st SS Panzer-Grenadier Regiment. This whole group was under the command of Kurt Meyer's 12th SS Panzer Division. The three LAH Panzer-Grenadier Battalions were responsible for the front from le Mesnil, through Eterville, to Maltot. To the west of this line, SS Captain Hauck's 2nd/22nd SS Panzer-Grenadier Battalion held the Château de Fontaine and the other two Battalions defended Hill 112. Hill

113 was the responsibility of the 21st SS Panzer-Grenadier Regiment. The Mk IVs and StuGs of the Frundsberg's 2nd SS Panzer Battalion were positioned behind the long ridge line, centred on Esquay, with the StuGs of the 5th Company just south of the small wood mentioned by Michael Carver. The Division's 10th SS Reconnaissance Battalion had been pulled back to an area 12km north-west of Falaise and placed in Army Group reserve.

During the night of 9/10 July, the first elements of the recently promoted SS Lieutenant Colonel Weiss's 102nd SS Heavy Panzer Battalion began to arrive in the St Martin area. Only twenty-five of its forty-five Tiger Is were operational but its arrival could not have been more opportune.

The almost totally bare slopes of Hills 112 and 113 offered virtually no cover for either defender or attacker. The Frundsberg's SS Panzer-Grenadiers therefore occupied the reverse slopes, with only observation posts and a platoon of Mk IVs from the 5th SS Panzer Company in forward outpost positions. The defence was organised in great depth, with only one third of the Grenadiers in the first line. SS Captain Karl Keck's 16th SS Pioneer Company occupied the small wood near the crest, which became known to the Germans as 'The Wood of the Half-Trees' and the British as 'The Crown of Thorns'.

10 July

The opening of JUPITER was heralded at 0455 hours by a devastating barrage from more than 300 guns and mortars. Behind it the British infantry advanced on their feet, together with their equally slow moving Churchill tanks, including flame-throwers.

The attack against Hill 112 was carried out by two infantry Battalion groups[5] from the 129th Brigade advancing from the woods north of Baron towards the summit and a third Battalion[6] directed on Esquay. Despite constant artillery and mortar fire, including the 88mm guns of the 10th SS Flak Battalion and the Nebelwerfers of the 8th Werfer Brigade[7], the British reached the line of the Eterville road by 0900 hours, only to be faced with the impossible task of clearing the four-hectare (10-acre) bare plateau in front of it. Although Keck's 16th SS Pioneer Company was forced out of the infamous Wood of the Half-Trees and the three Mk IVs of the outpost platoon knocked out, their stubborn resistance and a holding action by SS Captain Hauser's 5th Mk IV Company allowed time for two counter-attacks to be organised. A maximum of twenty Tigers of Weiss's 2nd and 3rd Companies took up positions south-east of Hill 112 while the Mk IVs and StuGs of SS Major Reinhold's remaining three Companies, accompanied by Grenadiers of Laubscheer's 1st (SPW) Battalion of the 21st Regiment, came forward for a counter-attack between

Hills 113 and 112. Both attacks[8] were launched with great ferocity and by midday most of the British tanks had been knocked out[9] and the Wood of the Half-Trees recaptured. An officer from Carver's 4th Armoured Brigade, waiting to take part in the planned exploitation phase to the Orne, described the scene on Hill 112:

> The skyline was dominated by Churchill tanks 'brewing up', not a pretty sight. They had all gone just too far over the ridge and were knocked out like ninepins by the enemy who were in extremely good positions ... there were dead and wounded men lying all over the ground in the long grass, rifles stuck in the ground marking the positions of their owners – a gruesome sight ... Tank crews who had managed to escape from their flaming vehicles were crawling back, their clothing and all exposed parts of their bodies burnt, black all over from smoke, oil and cordite fumes.[10]

But, just as the British could not survive on the crest or the southern side of 112, so the Germans could not clear the northern slopes where the British survivors had dug in. Seventy Grenadiers, three invaluable Tigers and a number of Mk IVs, StuGs and SPWs were lost in these attacks.

Michael Carver again:

> I reported [to Thomas's senior staff officer] that I would not order my leading regiment over the crest towards the river Orne until the wood [of the Half-Trees] had been cleared of the enemy, as had been agreed. Thomas came on the set [radio] himself and said that his information from his infantry brigades was that all the objectives had been secured and that I must start my forward thrust. I said I was on the spot, as his infantry brigadiers were not, and that if he did not believe me, he could come and see for himself.... Finally, he accepted my arguments.[11]

Again, it is difficult to envisage a Waffen-SS Regimental commander arguing this way with Harmel or Stadler. Nevertheless, that evening fourteen Churchills and a Battalion of infantry[12] from the reserve Brigade, *not* Carver's, were ordered to relieve the pressure on their comrades[13] near the crest of Hill 112 and make a final attempt to secure the summit. Aided by a curtain of friendly artillery fire, the infantrymen took the same route as their predecessors and advanced in spitting rain through the carnage of the previous fighting and the hulks of the British and German tanks knocked out in the previous two weeks. Despite crippling casualties from artillery and mortar fire and machine-guns which swept the whole area, part of the Battalion managed to dig in along the line of a hedge which bisected the Wood of the Half-Trees. The Frundsberg

Grenadiers had been forced to abandon the northern part of the wood, but they too were dug in only 100m or so away on its southern edge. At last light, in accordance with British practice, the surviving Churchills withdrew, leaving the infantry to face the night and their enemy unsupported.

A German counter-attack was launched soon after dark by the Tigers of the 2nd Company and Grenadiers of the 21st Regiment. SS Second Lieutenant Schroif, who had taken over the 2nd Company from SS Captain Endemann who was 'missing in action', remembered:

> I saw Panzer-Grenadiers coming back down the slope and I knew that the British must have attacked again and that we would be sent to drive them back. It was almost dark when the order came. . . . My objective was the square wood. We got to within 300m of it. I halted the Company and we opened fire. We couldn't have been more than 100m away. We fired with machine-guns and sent high explosive into the treetops. Machine-gun fire rattled on the armour and we could see the muzzle flashes of the anti-tank guns.[14]

The situation near the crest of Hill 112 soon degenerated into one of total confusion. The incessant artillery fire held back the Grenadiers and separated them from the Tigers which then became too vulnerable to remain in the forward area, and the British infantry were too reduced in numbers to clear either the wood or their enemy just beyond it. Both sides were exhausted and needed time to reorganise and bring up fresh troops.

On the eastern side of Operation JUPITER, one Battalion[15] of the 130th Infantry Brigade reached the Château de Fontaine by 0615 hours. There it became engaged in confused fighting and, although the British claimed success, they later found to their cost that Hauck's 2nd Battalion of the Frundsberg had not given up. Nevertheless, the claim of success was the signal for another Battalion group to advance[16] and less than two hours later Eterville was secured. At 0955 hours the third Battalion group[17] of the Brigade reported that it had taken Maltot but that its attempt to dig in on the higher ground 400 yards south of the village had been prevented by tank fire. At 1035 hours the Battalion said that twelve of its supporting Churchills[18] had been knocked out and that Tiger tanks were entering the village. These were seven Tigers of Weiss's 1st Company, commanded by SS Lieutenant Kalls, supported by Grenadiers from the 11th Company of the Leibstandarte's 3rd Battalion.[19] Their commander, SS Lieutenant Hasse, was awarded a Knight's Cross for his bravery on this day. The British troops at the Château de Fontaine tried to move forward across the open ground to make contact with their comrades near Maltot but failed in the face of the Tigers and Grenadiers, and by 1400 hours the

Germans had retaken the Maltot sector. At 1620 another British Battalion group[20] was sent forward towards the village. After suffering terrible losses[21] from artillery and mortar fire and from the tanks and Grenadiers defending Maltot and its surrounding woods, the attackers were then mistakenly attacked by a squadron of RAF Typhoons. Not surprisingly, the dazed survivors had no chance when the German tanks and Panzer-Grenadiers counter-attacked later that evening. Many never received the order to withdraw, and the ground in, and to the north-west of, Maltot became a Wessex graveyard.[22]

As the day ended, the British line ran from Eterville, through Fontaine-Etoupefour and its Château, to the line of the Eterville–Esquay road near the summit of 112. It had been a costly day for them – forty-three tanks and well over a thousand men. As far as Bittrich was concerned though, it was clearly time to use his reserves and re-establish his main defence line. That evening the commander of the 9th SS Panzer Division Hohenstaufen, SS Colonel Stadler, carried out a reconnaissance of the forward area and, at 2200 hours, sent a message to his Chief of Staff ordering Bollert's 1st/9th SS Panzer Battalion and Hagenlocher's 1st/19th SS Panzer-Grenadier Battalion to be prepared to lead the Regimental attack against Hill 112. Gruber's 20th Regiment was to recapture Eterville. Soon after this two of his artillery Battalions arrived and were in action before midnight.

11 July

The overall task given to the Hohenstaufen on 11 July was to clear the British from the northern slopes of Hills 112 and 113 – particularly 112 – and to recapture the Château de Fontaine and Eterville. The commander of Panzer Group West, General Eberbach, had made this very clear to Bittrich:

> On no account must Hill 112 be given up; it is the pivot for the whole front. We might be able to do without Eterville, but we must hang on to Hill 112.

Stadler was directed to exploit as far as Baron in the west and Fontaine-Etoupefour in the east.

During the early part of the night, as both sides continued to drench Hill 112 and its immediate environs with artillery and mortar fire, the Hohenstaufen's Grenadier Regiments arrived in the forward area. By 0200 hours, however, had become obvious that Bollert's Panther Battalion would not be in a position to attack before dawn at the earliest.

Soon after dawn fifteen Shermans[23] joined the remnants of the proud Battalion[24] that had occupied the summit of Hill 112 the previous evening.

The combined force did not have to wait long for the German response. At 0615 hours Grenadiers from both the Hohenstaufen and the Frundsberg went into action. The 3rd Battalion of the 22nd Regiment attacked from the south-east with Tigers of Schroif's 2nd Company, whilst the 1st Battalion of the 19th Regiment advanced from the south-west with more Tigers from the 3rd Company. Five Shermans were soon knocked out and under the weight of the combined assault, the British group was forced to withdraw down the northern slopes to the relative security of their comrades in the woods of the Odon valley. But the Germans too were decimated and exhausted. Stadler ordered his men to consolidate the ground they had gained but to leave the minimum number possible in the forward area. One of the Tiger crewmen said afterwards that the British defensive fire was: 'such as [even] we East Fronters had never known'. Once more the summit of Hill 112 became a no-man's land.

Meanwhile on the eastern flank, Grenadiers of SS Major Gruber's 20th Regiment, having secured Maltot during the night, went on to wrest Eterville from the Scottish Battalion[25] which had taken over that sector the previous evening. By 0720 hours they were within 500m of the village and, although the SS men later broke into the defences and inflicted heavy casualties in what was described as a 'dog fight', they failed to take their objective. A further attack was launched later in the day and again it failed – this time in the face of strong supporting fire from British tanks. Eterville remained in Scottish hands.[26]

Meanwhile on Hill 112, the same British Battalion[27] that had been forced off the summit earlier in the day, was reorganised and sent back up to the Wood of the Half-Trees. Again it did not take long for the Germans to react and at 1500 hours six Tigers of Kalls' 1st Company, with StuGs of the 2nd/9th SS Panzer Battalion and Panzer-Grenadiers of SS Major Gruber's 20th Regiment had to leave the protection of the Maltot woods and launch yet another counter-attack. One of the Grenadiers described the scene:

> The sight was beyond all imagination. The dead, friend and foe, lay in masses on the open ground right up to the little wood. . . . The air was putrid with the smell of decomposing corpses.

Three of the StuGs were knocked out and three others hit, but the British could not withstand such an attack. When they evacuated the Hill, they left behind ninety-three bodies.

So ended JUPITER. As far as Major General Thomas and the men of his Division were concerned, it was a bloody and costly failure.[28] Their only compensation – and few would view it this way – was that their sacrifice had held the 9th and 10th SS Panzer Divisions, as well as significant elements of 1st and 12th SS on the eastern flank, away from the planned American breakout from the Cotentin peninsula for another few, but vital, days. And the losses of II SS Panzer Corps were now reaching very serious levels. In two weeks' fighting the Hohenstaufen had lost 1,891 men and the Frundsberg 2,289. In terms of armour, the 102nd SS Heavy Panzer Battalion had been reduced to only fourteen operational Tigers by 11 July, with another twelve in short-term repair. Strength returns indicate losses, for one reason or another[29], of fifteen Panthers, eight Mk IVs and sixteen StuGs for the 9th SS Panzer Regiment and seven Mk IVs and twelve StuGs for the 10th.

This author has not attempted to describe the full horror of the carnage and misery on and around Hill 112 in mid-1944. For readers interested in the full details of the battle, particularly from the British point of view, it is recommended that they read Major J J How's excellent book, *Hill 112 – Cornerstone of the Normandy Campaign*.

NOTES

1. Jackson, *Operations of Eighth Corps*, p. 62.
2. 46 Highland Bde.
3. 3rd & 8th.
4. Carver, *Out of Step*, p. 193.
5. 4th Bn, The Somerset Light Infantry (4 SLI) with C Sqn 7 RTR & 4th Bn, The Wiltshire Regt (4 Wilts) with A Sqn 7 RTR.
6. 5 Wilts.
7. This Bde supported II SS Pz Corps from 28 Jun until at least 15 Aug 44.
8. Against 4 Wilts and 4 SLI on the right flank and 5 Wilts on the left.
9. The Germans claimed twenty-five.
10. Carver, *Second to None*, p. 115.
11. Carver, *Out of Step*, p. 194.
12. 5th Bn, The Duke of Cornwall's Light Infantry (5 DCLI) with four 17-pdr guns of 59 A/Tk Regt & med MGs of the 8th Bn, The Middlesex Regt (8 MX), and A Sqn 7 RTR.
13. 4 SLI.
14. The British had eight 6-pdr and four 17-pdr a/tk guns with them.
15. 5th Bn, The Dorset Regt (5 Dorset).
16. 4 Dorset with B Sqn 9 RTR.
17. 7th Bn The Hampshire Regt (7 Hamps) with A Sqn 9 RTR.
18. From 9 RTR.
19. There are conflicting claims over who took part in the recapture of Maltot on 10 Jul. As well as the LAH force mentioned here, the Frundsberg commander, Heinz Harmel, later claimed that his 1/21 SS (SPW) Pz-Gren and 10 SS Recce Bns participated, and Wilhelm Tieke, in his *In the Firestorm of the Last Years of the War*, p. 110, says parts of the Hohenstaufen's 20 SS Pz-Gren Regt recaptured the village. In this author's view, all these claims have to be questioned and Tieke's is the most unlikely.
20. 4 Dorset & C Sqn of 9 RTR.
21. A further twelve tanks were lost in this fighting.

22. 7 Hamps suffered 226 casualties.
23. A sqn of the Royal Scots Greys (Scots Greys)
24. 5 DCLI
25. 9 Cameronians.
26. As a matter of interest, the Chief of Staff of the Hohenstaufen in his post-war interview, Harzer MS # P – 162, erroneously describes this, and the 19th Regt's attack on Hill 112, as happening on 3/4 Jul.
27. 5 DCLI.
28. The Official British History admits to 2,000 casualties. As examples: 5 DCLI lost 254 men; 5 Dorset 208 and 4 SLI 189. In less than twelve hours in Eterville on 11 Jul, after it relieved the 9 Cameronians, 2 Glasgow Hldrs suffered eighty-five casualties from mortar fire alone.
29. Ground or air action, arty fire or mechanical failure.

CHAPTER VII
GREENLINE to GOODWOOD: 12 – 18 July

(Map 5)

JUPITER may have ended, but Hills 112 and 113 remained as important as ever for British and Germans alike and the fighting between the Odon and Orne was far from over. Both sides, however, were now suffering a manpower crisis. In only two weeks' fighting the British I and VIII Corps had lost nearly 10,000 men and the Canadians, an all-volunteer force, over 4,000. II SS Panzer Corps had also lost nearly 4,000 by this time and I SS Panzer Corps reduced in strength by a comparable figure.[1] Inevitably and tragically, 80% of all these casualties had occurred amongst the infantry and neither side had enough trained replacements. Montgomery and Dempsey had already been warned that if their 'infantry casualties continued at the recent rate it would be impossible to replace them and [the British would] have to "cannibalise" – to break up some divisions in order to maintain the rest'.[2] Their answer to this problem was to attack with armour, of which there was a surplus. This had the added advantage that the Germans, rather than risk a breakthrough by massed tanks, would be forced to move their reserves to meet it. The way in which the Germans overcame their manpower problem will become clear as this narrative unfolds.

The commander of Panzer Group West, General Eberbach, visited SS Colonel Harmel on 13 July and told him that, despite his heavy losses[3], the Frundsberg Division would remain responsible for the vital sector between the two rivers until units of the 271st and 272nd Infantry Divisions could be brought forward to relieve it. Their advanced elements were not expected before the night of 15/16 July at the earliest. The relief of his sister Division, the Hohenstaufen, was already underway. It had begun the night before when the 3rd Battalion of SS Colonel Diesenhofer's 21st Regiment and a company of Frundsberg Pioneers had taken over from the 19th SS Panzer-Grenadier Regiment in the area of Hill 112. The remainder of the 10th SS Pioneer Battalion had been given the task of preparing the rail and bridges over the Orne for demolition as far south as Brieux, and preparing a ford near Grimbosq. The significance of these preparations was not lost on Harmel.

During the night of 15/16 July the Frundsberg was given responsibility for the whole II SS Panzer Corps sector and the remaining units of the Hohenstaufen pulled back into Panzer Group reserve. This was a huge task for a single, already weakened, Division. Diesenhofer's 21st SS Panzer-Grenadier Regiment, less its 1st SPW Battalion, held the left part of the front to as far west as Hill 113 and the 22nd Regiment was behind and to the east of Hill 112 in deeply dug defences. Harmel kept the 1st SPW Battalion as an immediate reserve near St Honorine. It was to operate as a counter-attack force with his armour which comprised the 2nd/10th SS Panzer Battalion, with only nine Mk IVs and seven StuGs[4], and the Corps' 102nd SS Heavy Panzer Battalion. Because of the risk of air attack and artillery fire, SS Lieutenant Colonel Weiss left only one tank forward in an observation role and kept his remaining eighteen Tigers under whatever cover they could find in and around St Martin.[5] Harmel's 10th SS Reconnaissance Battalion, which would normally have acted as an additional reserve, was right back at Hamars, 5km north-west of Thury-Harcourt, and it seems likely that Bittrich had placed it in Corps reserve.

On the Frundsberg's left flank the 277th Infantry Division had come into position with units as far forward as Gavrus and, during this same night, elements of the 272nd Infantry Division began to relieve the Frundsberg's 22nd Regiment on the eastern side of Hill 112 and elements of the LAH in the Maltot sector.

Despite the failure to break through to the Orne in Operation JUPITER, Montgomery knew he had to keep up the pressure on his eastern flank. He could not afford to let the Panzer Divisions get away to confront the planned US breakout in the west and the recent arrival of four German infantry divisions in Normandy presaged exactly that move.

By mid-July Monty was facing criticism from all quarters. The way to the Falaise Plain was still blocked south-east of Caen, insufficient ground had been captured for the necessary airfields to be constructed, Cherbourg was not yet operational and the Americans had failed to achieve their breakout. He decided therefore to launch a strong armoured thrust on the east side of Caen on 18 July – Operation GOODWOOD. As he put it in a letter the Field Marshal Alan Brooke on the 14th:

> The Second Army is now very strong . . . and can get no stronger [a reference to the infantry replacement problem]. So I have decided that the time has come for a real 'showdown' on the eastern flank, and to loose a Corps of three armoured divisions [877 tanks] into the open country about the Caen–Falaise road.[6]

This was to be followed by the breakout (Operation COBRA) by Omar Bradley's First US Army around St Lô (Map 4) on the 20th.

Montgomery knew that as well as the three infantry divisions in the path of his planned attack on the east side of Caen, there were certainly two[7], and potentially three Panzer Divisions[8], facing his armoured forces east of Caen. This suited him because one of his main aims in GOODWOOD was: 'to engage the German armour in battle and write it down to such an extent that it is of no further value to the Germans as a basis of the battle'.

Montgomery knew also that, just to the west of the Orne, on and to the south of Hill 112, there were two more Panzer Divisions – the Hohenstaufen and Frundsberg. These had to be held on the eastern flank as well and 'written down' in the same way. He therefore resolved to launch subsidiary attacks between Caen and Tilly-sur-Seulles with his newly arrived XII Corps and veteran XXX Corps in an Operation code-named GREENLINE. XII Corps was to attack south towards the Orne on the night of the 15th/16th, with XXX Corps thrusting towards Noyers on the morning of the 16th and then exploiting to the high ground north-east of Villers-Bocage – the infamous Point 213.[9] The details of this latter attack need not concern us. The junior participants in both these attacks were, for obvious reasons, unaware that GREENLINE was a subsidiary operation to GOODWOOD, and thought their job was to capture important ground. In fact, their real mission was to hold the Hohenstaufen and Frundsberg Panzer Divisions on the eastern flank.

The official task given to XII Corps was to secure a corridor to the Orne through Bougy, Evrecy and Maizet. The attack was to be led by II SS Panzer Corps' old enemy – the 15th Scottish Infantry Division. It was reinforced with an extra Infantry Brigade and the 34th Tank Brigade[10], and given the task of capturing Evrecy and the dominating ground 2km to its south-east before moving on to Maizet. On the Scottish Division's left flank the other old enemy, Ivor Thomas's 43rd Wessex Division, was to 'dominate' the Germans on Hill 112. The third Division in XII Corps, the 53rd Welsh, was to secure the start lines for these attacks, cover the right flank and provide the extra Brigade for the 15th Scottish. Over 450 guns were in support.[11] It will not have escaped the reader's notice that the main weight of the XII Corps attack would thus hit the Frundsberg sector.

The XII Corps plan in GREENLINE involved the 15th Scottish Division advancing from Baron and les Vilains initially in a south-westerly direction. After securing Esquay, Hill 113, Gavrus and Bougy, it was then to turn south and capture Evrecy. The 43rd Wessex Division's main task in the operation was to occupy the attention of the Germans on the reverse slopes of Hill 112 and so prevent them from interfering with this advance.

The attack by the 15th Scottish Division began at 2130 hours on 15 July. It had been a hot and hazy day and for the first time in Normandy the British used 'artificial moonlight' to help them find their way. This involved bouncing searchlight beams off clouds in order to light up the area beneath. The initial advance went well and, with the help of Churchill flame-throwers, one Battalion[12] advancing from the woods north of Baron soon secured le Bon Repos just to the north of Esquay. Fifty Grenadiers from the 21st Regiment were captured in this area. Two more Battalions[13] advanced from Baron and les Vilains at 2330 hours and, although they met only light opposition, heavy German artillery and mortar fire soon disrupted their progress and put one of the Brigade commanders and his tactical Headquarters out of action. Nevertheless, by 0230 hours on the 16th, the British were in control of the western part of Hill 113; however, one of their Battalions[14] had veered to the east of the Hill where the 15th Company of the 21st Regiment, although being surrounded for a time, continued to hold out. Counter-attacks by armour of the 2nd/10th SS Panzer Battalion and Grenadiers of the 1st/21st Battalion in SPWs managed to seal off this penetration and restore the tenuous German line between the two vital Hills.

With the coming of daylight, the left flank of the British attack was exposed to fire from the reverse slopes of Hill 112 where, despite heavy casualties but with help from the Corps' Tigers, Major Bünning's 3rd Battalion of the 22nd Regiment was still firmly in position. The British attack now began to break down in chaos. The follow-up Battalions[15], which had already been heavily shelled in their assembly areas, were due to advance through their comrades on Hill 113, but they found it unsecured and their way impeded by other British units:

Harassed by mortar fire, this whole densely packed column of infantry and supporting Churchills, Crocodiles [flame-throwers], AVREs [assault engineer vehicles] and machine-guns slowly progressed by fits and starts . . . .When dawn came it found all three Battalions[16] of the 227th Brigade with their supporting arms in an area less than a thousand yards deep and three hundred yards wide[17] . . . on a forward slope under the direct observation of the Germans on Hill 112 and beyond the river Orne.[18]

In view of this confused situation, the planned attack on Evrecy and the isolated farm complex, known as the Ferme de Mondeville, on the high ground to its south-east had to be cancelled and the follow-up Battalions withdrawn. But even this did not go well:

> Some of our accompanying tanks got into difficulties while withdrawing through the badly marked minefield and blocked the gap. The whole Brigade was therefore obliged to remain for several hours exposed on that forward slope while our Gunners fired a great quantity of smoke-shells to blind the enemy's vision.[19]

Without ever being in direct contact with their enemy, just one of the Battalions in this Brigade suffered seventy-one casualties.[20]

But all was not well on the German side either. The Frundberg's thinly held sector was under great pressure and over on the left flank, the 277th Division, despite knocking out twenty-six British tanks, had lost both Gavrus and Bougy[21] by 1000 hours. It was clearly time for intervention by the II SS Panzer Corps' reserve Division – the Hohenstaufen. At this time it had thirty-eight Panthers, nineteen Mk IVs and sixteen StuGs ready for action.

SS Colonel Stadler's orders were to counter-attack and restore the situation between Gavrus and Hill 113. Having been told he could use part of the 277th Infantry Division, he resolved to advance with one Battalion of SS Lieutenant Colonel Zollhöfer's 19th SS Panzer-Grenadier Regiment and the Fusilier Battalion of the 277th, supported by twenty Panthers of the 1st/9th SS Panzer Battalion, against Hill 113; and another, with support from part of the 2nd/9th SS Panzer Battalion, in the Odon valley against Bougy. The attacks went in at 1100 hours from a start-line running from Nouilly to Evrecy, with strong support being provided by the 9th SS Panzer Artillery Regiment.

The fighting in the Odon valley was confused and vicious. The British group[22] at Bougy was heavily attacked by StuGs of the 7th and 8th Companies of the 2nd/9th SS Panzer Battalion and 19th Regiment Grenadiers; part of their positions were overrun and eighteen Churchills lost before they managed to withdraw to Gavrus at about 1400 hours. Even there the Germans got into the outskirts of the village and it was 1800 hours before they were finally evicted and the situation restored.

The first attacks against the British on Hill 113 were unsuccessful. In one, at about midday, the unit[23] positioned a kilometre to the north-east of the summit claimed five tanks knocked out. However, later in the afternoon, heavier assaults by Grenadiers of SS Major Gruber's 20th Regiment, with tank support, succeeded in penetrating some 500m on to the northern slopes, only to be pushed back by a British counter-attack at about 1830 hours.

The British Battalion[24] that had penetrated into Esquay during the night and then pulled back on to the higher ground around le Bon Repos was in a difficult position. Its companies were deployed:

> as it were, round the rim of a saucer[25], with Esquay, unoccupied below them at the bottom, and the enemy in position above them on the rim, both at Hill 112 to the eastward, only 600 yards away, and, to the westward, on the slopes of Hill 113.[26]

It reported repeated attacks on the axis of the Evrecy road throughout the afternoon and evening. Nevertheless, with the aid of intimate artillery support, it held its positions, claiming two German tanks.

In the fighting on and around Hill 113, the Hohenstaufen claimed a further eight Churchills. The commander of its 1st/9th SS Panzer Battalion, SS Major Bollert, was severely wounded on the 16th and the Division's tank state shows twenty-five Panthers, thirteen Mk IVs and fifteen StuGs still combat-ready after the fighting. This indicates thirteen Panthers, six Mk IVs and a StuG either knocked out or at least immobilised. The 19th Regiment lost 15% of its combat strength on this day, with the result that Zollhöfer decided to disband his 3rd Battalion and distribute the men amongst the other two Battalions. Since this had already happened in the 20th Regiment, the Hohenstaufen was now reduced to only four Panzer-Grenadier Battalions.

The Corps Tiger Battalion appears to have suffered no losses in this fighting but the 2nd/10th SS Panzer Battalion had four Mk IVs and three StuGs put out of action or immobilised on 16 July.

The 9th SS Panzer Reconnaissance Battalion was detached at this time to the 277th Infantry Division on the Hohenstaufen's left flank. Panzer Reconnaissance Battalions were very powerful units, comprising nearly 1,000 men, and they were often used as independent KGs in this way. The Battalion arrived west of Noyers, which had been captured by XXX Corps, at around 1730 hours on the 16th and was used in a successful counter-attack that night along the axis of the Caen road. The Battalion commander, SS Captain Gräbner, was later awarded the Knight's Cross for his part in this operation.

The first attempt to take Evrecy having failed, the commander of the 15th Scottish Division[27] decided to use his reserve Brigade[28] for another attempt during the night of 16 July. At 2330 hours, after a delay caused by the supporting tanks having to negotiate a badly recorded minefield[29], the Brigade advanced towards Evrecy and between Hill 113 and Esquay, in total darkness and into a heavy mist which was compounded by smoke rounds fired by the Hohenstaufen. The attack on Evrecy by one Battalion[30] failed with heavy losses, but the other Battalions reached a stream running across their front between Evrecy and Avenay (the Guigne) and some elements managed to cross and continue the advance towards the Ferme de Mondeville. But the supporting anti-tank guns were unable to cross and, in the confusion caused by the thick mist, the attack broke down. Soon after dawn the British commander gave orders that his men were not to advance beyond the range of their anti-tank guns and they were subsequently ordered to withdraw[31] – only to be exposed, as the mist lifted from the bare slopes of Hill 113, to machine-gun and mortar fire. At 2115 hours that evening two of the Battalions[32] were ordered to try again – this time with support from Churchill tanks, but the Grenadiers and dug-in tanks of II SS Panzer Corps would not give way and the assault did not get beyond the Evrecy–Caen road. GREENLINE was over. No significant ground had been gained but the sacrifices of the men of XII Corps[33] had not been in vain. They had held the Hohenstaufen and Frundsberg Divisions in the Caen sector. As Montgomery said later: 'The fighting had been severe, [but] above all we were attaining our object by pulling the enemy armour back into the line.' From his point of view, and perhaps that of the Americans, that was all that mattered. The following morning he would launch Operation GOODWOOD.

The night before GOODWOOD, the 271st Infantry Division came under the command of Bittrich's II SS Panzer Corps and two infantry battalions, together with Pioneer and artillery units of the 271st Infantry Division, arrived in the rear of the Frundsberg's area. The following two nights, the 18th and 19th, one Battalion took over the Maltot sector on the Division's right flank and the other was inserted north of Esquay to relieve the 3rd/22nd SS Panzer-Grenadier Battalion. Some idea of the severity of the Division's losses during the previous nineteen days of almost continuous combat can be gauged by the fact that SS Major Bünning brought out a mere forty-five men. He was the only surviving officer. The Frundsberg's losses now amounted to 2,289 killed, wounded and missing and the Hohenstaufen's 1,891.[34]

NOTES

1. 12 SS Pz Div HJ had lost a minimum of 2,988 men by 11 Jul.
2. Dempsey Diaries, PRO, WO 285/10.
3. Gen Eberbach's Special Missions officer reported that on 13 Jul 22 SS Pz-Gren Regt had a combat strength of only 400 men, but that 114 reinforcements had arrived that day – MS # B-840.
4. A further ten Mk IVs and ten StuGs were in short-term repair on 16 Jul.
5. A further ten Tigers were being repaired and ten more were in transit to the Bn.
6. Directive No. M 511.
7. 1 SS Pz and 21 Pz.
8. 12 SS Pz Div had been ordered to the Lisieux area, 40km east of Caen, on 16

Jul. Part was already there and the remainder, to the north of Falaise, was preparing to follow on.

9. 7 Armd Div (Desert Rats) had lost its leading Combat Team here on 13 Jun to the Waffen SS's greatest Panzer ace – Michael Wittmann.
10. 107, 147 & 153 Regts, Royal Armoured Corps (RAC).
11. Appx C to 15 Inf Div Orders for Op GREENLINE.
12. 2 Glasgow Hldrs.
13. 2nd Bn, The Gordon Highlanders (2 Gordons) & 6 KOSB.
14. 2 Gordons.
15. 2 Argylls & 10th Bn, The Highland Light Infantry (10 HLI).
16. 10 HLI, 2 Gordons & 2 Argylls.
17. Martin, *History of the 15th Scottish Division 1939–1945*, p. 71.
18. Graham, *Ponder Anew*, p. 69.
19. Ibid.
20. 2 Argylls.
21. To 8 RS and 153 Regt, RAC.
22. 2 Gordons.
23. 2 Gordons.
24. 2 Glasgow Hldrs.
25. By coincidence 'Saucer' was the British code-name for Esquay.
26. Martin, op. cit., p. 74.
27. Maj Gen G MacMillan
28. 158 Inf Bde with 4th, 6th & 7th Bns, The Royal Welsh Fusiliers (RWF).
29. Appx B to XII Corps War Diary for Jul 44.
30. 4 RWF.
31. 53 Inf Div War Diary, 17 Jul 44.
32. 4 & 6 RWF.
33. According to Ellis, *Victory in the West*, Vol I, p. 334, the British suffered 3,500 casualties.
34. Zetterling, *Normandy 1944*, pp. 338 & 345.

CHAPTER VIII

East and West of the Orne: 19 July – 2 August

(Map 5)

By 19 July Operation GOODWOOD, the British onslaught east of Caen, was causing great consternation in the Headquarters Army Group 'B'. Montgomery's plan was working. That night CinC West sought permission to bring forward the 116th Panzer Division from the Fifteenth Army north of the Seine, and General Eberbach, the commander of Panzer Group West, ordered the Hohenstaufen to move with all speed to a reserve position under the cover of the Forests of Grimbosq and Cinglais, on the east side of the Orne. On arrival it was to come under command of Sepp Dietrich's I SS Panzer Corps fighting south-east of Caen. The Hohenstaufen's Reconnaissance, Pioneer and 1st SS Artillery Battalions were to remain behind with the Frundsberg and its 7th SS Panzer (StuG) Company in support of the 277th Infantry Division. At the same time, the Frundsberg's 10th SS Reconnaissance Battalion was also sent to join I SS Panzer Corps.

Meanwhile, in the Hill 112 sector the agony continued for the Frundsberg and the 102nd SS Heavy Tiger Battalion. The gradual relief by the 271st Infantry Division continued during the last week of July but, coincident with this, local actions took place which constantly sapped the strengths of the already weak Panzer-Grenadier companies. As the Division's units were relieved they were immediately placed in reserve and remained in the forward area north of the Evrecy–Amayé road.

One such local action occurred on the night of the 21st when the 1st and 2nd Battalions of the 21st Regiment, whose combined strength totalled fewer than 150 men, launched a successful attack in the le Bon Repos area. Sixty-seven prisoners were taken and the commander of the 2nd Battalion, SS Captain Bastian was awarded a Knight's Cross for his part in the action. The War Diary of the British XII Corps reported as follows:

> Enemy attack by approx two companies of infantry supported by six tanks ... Enemy tanks withdrew at 2330 hours after losing one of their number, but infantry fighting continued for several hours. Under heavy enemy pressure, 1st/5th Welch [an infantry battalion] were compelled to withdraw and take up new positions north of the road at Le Bon Repos.

The following day a British attack against Hill 112 was held; however, an infantry company of the 271st Division was forced out of Maltot[1] and at 1800 hours Frundsberg reserve units with the 2nd Tiger Company had to be deployed to set up a new defensive line 500m south of the village. The British attack, aimed at securing the Orne bridges at St André and May, continued early on the 23rd but was halted with the loss of six tanks – all claimed by the Tiger Company.

On the 31st the relief of the Frundsberg by the 271st Infantry Division was finally completed. By this time it had lost only seven Mk IVs and three StuGs as total write-offs.[2] Its combat-ready strength on this day was twenty of each. A day later II SS Panzer Corps was ordered to move west – the British were threatening a breakthrough west of Villers-Bocage and the Americans had already achieved one at St Lô.

But what of the Hohenstaufen? Its move to the new concentration area was carried out successfully. Rain and low cloud on the 22nd and 23rd prevented interference by the Allied air forces and, by using side roads and tracks and crossing the vulnerable bridge at Thury-Harcourt in small groups, the Division was safely under cover by the morning of the 24th. The 19th SS Panzer-Grenadier and 9th SS Panzer Regiments were located in the Grimbosq Forest and the 20th Regiment in the Cinglais Forest. On the 24th Gräbner's 9th SS Reconnaissance Battalion returned from the west side of the Orne and Brinkmann's 10th SS Reconnaissance Battalion passed back to the Frundsberg. According to Wilhelm Tieke's *In the Firestorm of the Last Years of the War*, the latter had taken part in a major action on the 22nd as part of a KG Koch to recapture May, St Martin and St André. The KG was meant to comprise units of the 272nd Infantry Division and tanks and Panzer-Grenadiers from the Hohenstaufen, but the latter was still on its way from the west side of the Orne and only three Panthers arrived in time for the attack. Nevertheless, Brinkmann's men launched their assault at 0600 hours and allegedly fought their way into May. Tieke's account of the fighting[3] claims they were unable to clear the village – even after a couple of Panthers joined them. Surprisingly, no mention of this action is made by the Canadians who attacked in this sector on the 20th and captured St André[4], but not St Martin or May.

By 24 July Stadler realised that his Panzer-Grenadier Regiments were no longer viable and he ordered a reorganisation. The 1st/20th SS Panzer-Grenadier Battalion joined the two remaining Battalions of Zollhöfer's 19th, to form SS Panzer-Grenadier Regiment Hohenstaufen, and the 3rd/20th SS (SPW) Battalion was allocated permanently to Otto Meyer's 9th SS Panzer Regiment. The specialist companies of the 19th and 20th Regiments were also amalgamated to produce an infantry gun Company with twelve 150mm howitzers, a Flak Company with twelve 20mm guns, a Mortar Company with twelve 120mm mortars, a Pioneer company partly equipped with SPWs and a Headquarters Company with Signals, Motor-Cycle, and SPW platoons.

It was towards the end of July that Bittrich received an important addition to his armoury. The 102nd SS Werfer Battalion, which had originally been intended as a II SS Panzer Corps unit but up to that time had been operating with Das Reich, was finally allocated to his command. Under SS Major des Coudres, its ten remaining 150mm Nebelwerfers were to fire their first salvoes in the Gavrus area on 1 August.[5]

GOODWOOD, which ended on 20 July, had been extremely costly for the British and Canadians[6], and it had neither 'written down' the German armour[7], as Monty had demanded, nor gained any significant ground. On the other hand, it had achieved one of Montgomery's major aims in that it had held the German armour on the eastern flank. But, with the American breakout (Operation COBRA) due to start on the 25th, there could be no respite for Dempsey's Second Army. A further operation was necessary to keep the Panzer Divisions in place. Accordingly, Operation SPRING was ordered for the same day as COBRA. The aim of this operation was outlined in a letter sent by Montgomery to Eisenhower on 24 July, in which he set out his overall intentions. The II Canadian Corps, reinforced by two British Armoured Divisions[8] (see Appendix VI), was to capture the high ground on the Caen–Falaise road, 10km southeast of Caen, and then XII Corps was to attack again west of the Orne to capture Evrecy and Amayé. Even so, these operations were, in Montgomery's mind, 'preliminary to a very large scale operation by three or four armoured divisions' towards Falaise – in other words, a re-run of GOODWOOD.

Facing SPRING, the Germans had the 272nd Infantry Division on the western flank, the 1st SS Panzer Division LAH covering the centre, including the Caen–Falaise road, and the Hitlerjugend on the eastern flank. The Hohenstaufen was in reserve to the left rear.

A full account of Operation SPRING, as it affected I SS Panzer Corps, can be read in this author's book, Steel Inferno – I SS Panzer Corps in Normandy. For the purposes of this narrative, however, we need consider only the attack by the 2nd Canadian Infantry Division between the Caen–Falaise road and the river Orne. Its task was to secure May and Verrières.

On the evening of 24 July, sixty Allied medium bombers took part in an air attack on the 272nd Infantry Division's positions in the St Martin area, but due to very effective German flak only fifteen aircraft succeeded in finding their targets. Then, at 0330 hours on the 25th, the Canadians advanced. They were met, on the west side of the Caen–Falaise road, by the three SS Panzer-Grenadier Companies of the LAH's 1st Regiment in prepared positions on the northern edge of Verrières, supported by two Heavy Companies and the 5th SS Panzer and 1st SS StuG Companies. A further three Grenadier Companies were in a perfect reverse slope blocking position 400m south of the village. Despite this strong opposition, the Canadians[9] took Verrières by 0750 hours and forced the LAH armour to withdraw. Shortly after this, Canadian infantry and British tanks[10] moved through this force in an attempt to take Rocquancourt, but they soon ran into the fire of some thirty German tanks hull-down behind a ridge between Verrières and their objective. By midday the advance had bogged down.

On the western flank of the Canadian assault things did not go at all well. The leading Battalion[11] eventually managed to fight its way up the open slope into May, but before long it was forced to withdraw back to St André. Even there, pockets of enemy resistance were still holding out. This failure to secure both St André and May spelled disaster for the Battalion[12] tasked with attacking Fontenay. Although it made a valiant attempt to advance up the ridge towards its objective, the Battalion was decimated – only some fifteen of the 300 men committed returned to friendly lines.[13] A further attack against May in the early evening by another unit[14] also failed.

By midday it was clear that on the west side of the Caen–Falaise road, SPRING had failed. In fact, this was also true on the east side, where the 3rd Canadian Infantry Division had failed to secure the vital village of Tilly-la-Campagne. While the failure of the Operation may have been clear to the Canadians, it was certainly not to the staff of Headquarters I SS Panzer Corps. At 1200 hours Sepp Dietrich's Chief of Staff, Fritz Kraemer, called his opposite number at Bittrich's Headquarters, SS Colonel Harzer, and told him that the 'Tommies' had broken through in the 272nd Infantry Division's sector and that immediate counter-attacks by the Hohenstaufen had been authorised by CinC West.

Stadler organised his Division into two KGs for this attack. KG Meyer, under Otto Meyer, consisted of his own Panzer Regiment, the 3rd/20th SS Panzer-Grenadier Battalion and 3rd SS Pioneer Company in SPWs and the 4th SS Flak Company. On this day the 9th SS Panzer Regiment had twenty-three Panthers and twenty-one Mk IVs combat-ready. The other KG, under SS Major Zollhöfer, was made up of the three Battalions of the, just formed, SS Panzer-Grenadier Regiment Hohenstaufen, and fourteen StuGs. KG Meyer was to advance north-east from Bretteville, along the axis of the Fontenay to Ifs road, and secure Rocquancourt and Hill 88, while KG Zollhöfer was to move north from Clinchamp, along the N 162 (today 562), and recapture May, St Martin and St André. Both KGs moved off just after 1300 hours with the 9th SS Artillery Regiment in support and Weiss's 102nd Battalion Tigers able to give fire support from the west side of the Orne.

The single available bridge over the Laize river caused serious delays for KG Meyer, but by 1800 hours his tanks were within 800m of Hill 88. This feature dominates the entire area and the British had established strong defensive positions there, backed by tanks and anti-tank guns. The Canadian Official History mentions a 'formidable' German tank attack at Verrières at this time, in which eight tanks penetrated right into the Canadian positions. There are no references to such an attack in *The Leibstandarte IV/1* by Rudolf Lehmann and Ralf Tiemann, so we can assume these were Hohenstaufen tanks. Certainly, an attack by twelve Typhoons[15], firing ninety-six rockets between 1840 and 1940 hours at German tanks a few hundred metres south-east of Verrières, was said to have been very effective. The pilots claimed three tanks destroyed. The Germans make no mention of this, but interestingly a strength return dated two days later shows the Hohenstaufen with three fewer Mk IVs and three fewer StuGs. At 2110 hours Meyer told his Divisional commander that he had no chance of taking Hill 88 from the south and that he intended to attack again in a left flanking movement via St Martin.

Meanwhile, KG Zollhöfer managed to fight its way through to the northern outskirts of May by early evening and, by last light, a firm German line had been re-established from May in the west, through Fontenay, to some 800m south of Hill 88. That evening the Canadian commander[16] decided to suspend Operation SPRING.[17]

Whilst it is clear that the defensive battle on 25 July was won by the men of the 272nd Infantry Division and the Leibstandarte, it is equally clear that the presence of the Hohenstaufen in this sector, and in particular its counter-attack that evening, were major factors in the Canadian commander's decision to call off his attack.

The Allies may have decided to terminate SPRING, but as far as Stadler and the Hohenstaufen were concerned, their counter-attack had still not achieved its planned objectives. On 26 July, despite intense Allied aerial activity, the attack was renewed. KG Zollhöfer's assault was led by SS Captain Borchers' 1st/19th SS Panzer-Grenadier Battalion and after four hours his Grenadiers had fought their way into, and beyond, St André. Borchers was awarded the Knight's Cross for his actions in this fighting. On the right flank, KG Meyer took all day to secure Hill 88 but, as darkness fell, the Hohenstaufen could be content with its achievements – it had restored the 272nd Infantry Division's original defence line.

The following day the 272nd Division was withdrawn and the Hohenstaufen took over its sector. This ran from the Orne, through St André, to a point just to the west of Verrières. During the night of the 28th, this frontage was extended to the east as far as the Caen–Falaise road. Stadler therefore deployed his Division with the 3rd/20th SS (SPW) Panzer-Grenadier and 2nd/9th SS Panzer Battalions on the right, to the south of Verrières, where they occupied the former positions of the Leibstandarte, and with Zollhöfer's three SS Panzer-Grenadier Battalions on the left in the St Martin sector. The 2nd/9th SS Panzer Battalion now had twenty-two Mk IVs and twenty-two StuGs combat-ready. The 1st/9th SS Panzer Battalion, with twenty-six combat-ready Panthers, was held in reserve near Bretteville.

By the 29th the operational tank strength of the Hohenstaufen had increased to a total of seventy-eight – three more Panthers and five more StuGs. But this good news was marred when the Divisional commander, who had only a few days previously been promoted to the rank of senior SS Colonel, was wounded by artillery fire. Senior SS Colonel Wilhelm Bock, the II SS Panzer Corps artillery commander, took over. He had won the Knight's Cross in 1943 at Leningrad whilst serving with the SS Polizei Division.

In the afternoon of 1 August the Hohenstaufen's new commander received bad news – as well as the Americans breaking through at St Lô, the British had launched a major attack to the west of Villers-Bocage. His Division was to be relieved by the Leibstandarte during the next twenty-four hours, so that it could rejoin II SS Panzer Crops and take part in a major counter-attack to the south of Caumont. The Corps' 102nd SS Heavy Panzer Battalion, then comprising thirty Tigers in positions south of Maltot and Hill 112, was to be placed under his command for this operation. KG Meyer, with its two Panzer Battalions of thirty-one Panthers, seventeen Mk IVs and twenty-eight StuGs, and the 3rd/20th SS (SPW) Panzer-Grenadier Battalion moved out that evening and by 0600 hours on the 2nd the rest of the Hohenstaufen was moving west.[18] The Tigers, with the Divisional Escort Company and part of the 9th SS Reconnaissance Battalion providing close protection, had already begun their move under the cover of darkness during the night of the 1st.

NOTES

1. By 5 Wilts with support from 7 RTR.
2. Zetterling, *Normandy 1944*, p. 345.
3. Tieke, *In the Firestorm of the Last Years of the War*, p. 134.
4. By the Cameron Hldrs of Canada.
5. Zetterling, op. cit., p. 147.
6. The British and Canadians suffered nearly 5,500 casualties and VIII Corps alone lost 253 tanks; for details, see Reynolds, *Steel Inferno – I SS Panzer Corps in Normandy*, pp. 186–7.
7. I SS Pz Corps lost only 20% of its armour; for details, see Reynolds, op. cit., p. 187.
8. 1 Gds & 7 Armd.
9. The Royal Hamilton Light Infantry (RHLI).
10. Royal Regt of Canada & two tps of 1 RTR.
11. The Calgary Hldrs.
12. The Black Watch (BW) of Canada with elements of the 1st Canadian Hussars.
13. Stacey, *The Official History of the Canadian Army in the Second World War*, Vol III, p. 190.
14. Le Régt de Maisonneuve.
15. 181 and 182 Sqns, RAF.
16. Gen Guy Simonds.
17. According to the Canadian Official History, p. 194, some 1,500 casualties were suffered on 25 Jul, of which about 450 were fatal.
18. By 31 Jul twenty Panthers, thirteen Mk IVs and fourteen StuGs were total write-offs – Zetterling, op. cit., p. 339.

CHAPTER IX

BLUECOAT: 2 – 15 August

(Map 4)

By the end of July 1944, Montgomery's overall strategy of holding the bulk of the German armour in the east and breaking out in the west had achieved its aim. The Americans were opposed by nine hotchpotch divisions, of which only two were armoured with a total of just over one hundred tanks, whilst the British and Canadians were facing fourteen divisions, of which seven were armoured with 600 tanks. To the delight of the 21st Army Group commander, the Germans still believed the main Allied effort would be made towards Falaise on the eastern flank. As General Eberbach, the commander of Panzer Group West, put it:

> The favourable terrain between Caen and Falaise ought to attract him now as ever. In the comparatively open terrain of that sector, he could fully deploy his superior material. If he achieves a breakthrough, Paris beckons as a magnificent reward. Since the bridges across the Seine have been demolished below Paris, the river offers effective flank cover to the advancing British forces. If, in addition, the German forces could be pushed back away from the Seine towards the south, their supply problems would become acute and their annihilation possible.[1]

Nevertheless, despite the success of his overall strategy, the failure of Operation SPRING led Montgomery to modify the plans he had outlined to Eisenhower in his letter of 24 July (Chapter VIII, page 54). On the 27th he issued a new Directive, M515, which, whilst it contained no significant changes to the plans for the American front, ordered a new British offensive to the west of the Orne. The Directive was very clear:

> There are no Panzer or SS formations to the west of Noyers, and therefore the situation is favourable for a very heavy blow to be delivered by the right wing of the Second British Army in the Caumont area. . . . The armies on the eastern flank must now keep up the pressure in the Caen area; and Second British Army must hurl itself into the fight in the Caumont area so as to make easier the task of the American armies fighting hard on the western flank.

Eisenhower could not have been more pleased with the new plan and the next day encouraged Monty to launch the attack sooner rather than later: 'I feel very strongly that a three-division attack now on Second Army's right flank will be worth more than a six-division attack in five days' time.'

(Map 6)

Operation BLUECOAT, with two Corps of six Divisions, was launched two days later.[2] The basic concept was for XXX Corps, with one armoured and two infantry Divisions, to advance generally south-east through Villers-Bocage and Aunay, towards Mont Pinçon and the Orne, whilst VIII Corps on its right flank would advance towards Condé and Flers with two armoured Divisions and a single infantry Division. Opposing the British were less than two divisions – the 326th Infantry and elements of the 276th – backed up by some thirty 88mm self-propelled anti-tank guns. However, extensive minefields had been laid, the ground over which the advance was to be made was the most rugged and dense in the whole Normandy bocage and the attackers had first to capture a number of significant hill features, particularly Hill 309 and Mont Pinçon, and then cross a series of east-west ridgelines.

Both sides generally hated and feared the bocage; senior SS Sergeant Major Ernst Streng of the 102nd SS Heavy Panzer Battalion wrote later:

> The bocage was a cruel area. Every road, every little field and meadow, was surrounded by thick hedges two or three metres in height. It was full of frightening opportunities ... The fighting was confused and difficult.

On the other hand, following their painful experiences in Operation GOOD-WOOD, some British troops viewed it differently:

> The close country of which we had once been so apprehensive proved far more friendly than the open expanses of the Caen plain.[3]

On the day BLUECOAT was launched, 30 July, General George Patton's Third Army became operational and by nightfall on 1 August his leading elements had crossed the river at Pontaubault (Map 4) and entered Brittany. On the same day Bradley assumed command of the US 12th Army Group, General Courtney Hodges took over First US Army and von Kluge warned OKW, 'The left flank has collapsed.'

By the afternoon of 1 August, when II SS Panzer Corps received the order to move west, the British BLUECOAT offensive had created a significant wedge between Eberbach's Panzer Group West and Hausser's Seventh Army. Progress had been slow on the eastern flank, but on the VIII Corps' front, an infantry Division[4], with a tank Brigade[5] under command, had seized Hill 309 and the reconnaissance unit[6] of one of the armoured Divisions[7] had found the vulnerable and unprotected seam between the 326th Infantry and 3rd Parachute Divisions and, after advancing through the Fôret l'Eveque, had exploited south to le Bény-Bocage. Following this spectacular success, the same unit had then pushed on towards Vire, finding only light opposition. It was obvious to the Germans that if this vital road centre fell, and it was virtually undefended at this time, all their forces holding the eastern flank of the American breakthrough, from Tessy to Percy to Villedieu (Map 4), were likely to be cut off. It was this thrust therefore that Bittrich's II SS Panzer Corps, with its own Hohenstaufen and Frundsberg Divisions and the depleted 21st Panzer Division[8] under Lieutenant General Edgar Feuchtinger, was first to halt, and then eliminate. There remained, however, a problem of time; as Eberbach put it:

> II SS Panzer Corps could not cover the distance of the approach march, carry out all the attack preparations and establish contact with the enemy before the afternoon of 2 August. The enemy therefore had at least 24 hours of complete liberty of action. But it was our luck that the British, in general, stood still during this period.[9]

The first KG of the Frundsberg reached Aunay during the afternoon of 1 August. It was under the command of SS Lieutenant Colonel Paetsch, the commander of the 10th SS Panzer Regiment, and comprised Brinkmann's 10th SS Reconnaissance Battalion, Reinhold's 2nd/10th SS Panzer Battalion with twenty Mk IVs and fifteen StuGs, and a company of the 10th SS Pioneer Battalion. Aunay was blocked by bomb damage caused by a raid on 30 July and before the KG could move through the Pioneers had to clear a way. A British Guards officer who passed through the town in late August described it as 'nothing but rubble with not a whole house standing'. Paetsch used the waiting time to report to the commander of the LXXIV Corps, whose Headquarters was in the Château de Courvandon, 4km east of Aunay, and under whose command he had temporarily been placed. There he learned that Panzer Group von Oppeln of the 21st Panzer Division, with forty-two operational Mk IVs, and the 503rd Heavy Panzer Battalion with thirteen operational Tigers[10], had already arrived in the sector and were trying to hold some sort of line from Coulvain to Bremoy. Its first counter-attack had been repulsed and it had insufficient troops to extend this line south to le Bény-Bocage.[11] Paetsch was ordered to secure the area Aunay–Ondefontaine for the rest of the Frundsberg and then advance towards the Jurques–Bremoy part of the 21st Panzer Division line. By first light on 2 August, the northern and western edges of the Bois de Buron had been occupied, with Brinkmann's Reconnaissance Battalion on the vital high ground just east of la

Bigne and Reinhold's tanks holding Hill 301 and covering the Caen–Vire road south of Jurques.

During 2 August, the day the Americans captured Mortain (Map 4), one battlegroup of the British XXX Corps[12], advancing towards Ondefontaine, took the villages of Jurques and la Bigne, while another[13] penetrated onto Hill 188. There, however, the advance petered out. KG Paetsch held its ground and claimed twenty British tanks destroyed, but 21st Panzer lost both Bremoy and Hill 321. The same day Bittrich established his II SS Corps Headquarters in le Huan and ordered Harmel to attack Hill 188 and secure the area to its north-west. This was impossible because the bulk of his Division had not arrived and would not do so until later that night.

Despite the fact that the critical road centre of Vire was known to be only lightly held, on the morning of 2 August General Dempsey ordered VIII Corps to ignore it and swing south-east towards Flers. His reason for doing so was simple – Vire lay on the American side of the boundary of the First and Second Armies and was one of General Omar Bradley's objectives. Sadly, no one at Headquarters 21st Army Group noticed what was happening and a great Allied opportunity was wasted. This decision was to have serious consequences – not least for the Hohenstaufen Division and 102nd SS Heavy Panzer Battalion, both of which were now on a collision course with the British VIII Corps.

Early on the same day, the leading elements of KG Meyer of the Hohenstaufen, after moving via Thury-Harcourt, arrived in the area just to the east of le Bény-Bocage. There they took up positions from Arclais in the north, through Montchauvet (called Montcharivel in 1944) to Montchamp in the south. The main body of the Division, following on, was heavily interdicted between Thury-Harcourt and Condé by air strikes. 83 Group of the RAF flew 923 fighter-bomber and rocket-firing Typhoon sorties between 1430 hours and dusk on 2 August, and claimed to have destroyed ten tanks and fifty motor vehicles, and damaged thirteen tanks and seventy-six wheeled vehicles.[14] These figures, unlike many other air force claims, will be shown to be reasonably accurate.

SS Lieutenant Colonel Weiss's Corps Tiger Battalion, which it will be recalled was now under command of the Hohenstaufen, also arrived that morning at Roucamps, having moved through Hamars and Campandré. With these new armoured forces, Bittrich was able to make a plan for halting the British thrust. He ordered the Frundsberg to attack as soon as possible in the Ondefontaine sector, 21st Panzer to attack north of Bremoy, and the Hohenstaufen to close the gap between Panzer Group West and Seventh Army by recapturing le Bény-Bocage. The latter was to do this by attacking with KG Meyer from the east and, at the same time by launching another attack from the direction of Vire with a new KG commanded by SS Lieutenant Colonel Weiss. This KG was made up of Weiss's 102nd SS Tiger Battalion, the Hohenstaufen Divisional Escort

Company and most of the 9th SS Reconnaissance Battalion. This extraordinary order, which involved the Tigers moving some 50km, first of all south-west through Estry, Viessoix and Vire, and then attacking north-east, was issued in the hope that, even if the attack on le Bény-Bocage failed, it would at least establish a strong force in, or covering, Vire.

Frundsberg: 3 – 5 August

The Frundsberg attacks were launched on the morning of 3 August. Following a concentrated artillery barrage, Grenadiers of Diesenhofer's 21st SS Panzer-Grenadier Regiment, reinforced by tanks of the 2nd/ 10th SS Panzer Regiment and a LXXIV Corps Jagdpanther Battalion, counter-attacked the British troops advancing from the area of Hill 188. The enemy was successfully halted and Hill 188 captured. In heavy fighting on the left flank of the Divisional area, KG Paetsch eventually took la Bigne and, with elements of the 21st Panzer Division and the 503rd Tiger Battalion, held Hill 301. The British say five dug-in Tigers held them up.[15] 21st Panzer managed to recapture Hill 321 on the same day.

Throughout the 4th, KGs Paetsch and Diesenhofer continued to defend their thinly held line from Hill 301, through la Bigne to Hill 188, strongly supported by the 10th SS Artillery Regiment. In spite of this, British reconnaissance troops and elements of an infantry Battalion penetrated into Ondefontaine during the day and a strong counter-attack was required to evict them.[16] Harmel's plan for a major counter-attack on the 5th came to nought when he received orders from Bittrich to disengage during the night and move his Division to the Vassy area. He was not yet aware of it but the 10th SS Panzer Division Frundsberg was to take part in Hitler's great counter-attack in the direction of Avranches (Map 4) – better known as the Mortain counter-attack. In the meantime, his Division would be required to go to the assistance of its running mate, the Hohenstaufen. The disengagement was carried out under heavy pressure, with some elements having to fight their way through Ondefontaine which the British[17] found virtually undefended early on the 5th. Despite intense Allied air interdiction, the first units of the Division arrived east of Chênedollé (Map 6a) that evening. The new inter-Divisional boundary between the Hohenstaufen and 21st Panzer ran north-west, just to the north of Montchauvet.

Hohenstaufen: 2 – 5 August

On 2 August the Hohenstaufen's main actions were against the British Guards Armoured Division. In the north, KG Meyer, which it will be recalled comprised the Panthers of the 1st/9th SS Panzer Battalion, the 7th StuG Company of the 2nd/9th SS Panzer Battalion and the 3rd/20th

SS (SPW) Panzer-Grenadier Battalion, spent the day resisting a thrust[18] towards Montchauvet. Jackson's *Operations of Eighth Corps* describes events in this sector as follows:

> The enemy entrenched on the plateau south of Montamy and Arclais, countered with a thrust by several Tiger tanks[19], which caused a temporary withdrawal of the Guards, since tanks had not been able to support their attack up the steep heavily wooded slopes. Several more enemy sorties were made from this area during the day and no further progress was made.

SS Lieutenant Fröhlich's 7th SS Panzer Company, which provided right-flank security and fought with a remnant KG of the 326th Infantry Division, was able to hold the high ground near Arclais throughout the day. From there it could cover the main Vire–Villers-Bocage road, but by last light the risk of being surrounded became too great and it withdrew to Montchauvet. The mixed force claimed seven Cromwell tanks knocked out during the day.

KG Zollhöfer, comprising the Hohenstaufen Panzer-Grenadier Regiment and the rest of the Mk IVs and StuGs of the 2nd/9th SS Panzer Battalion, arriving later in the day, took up positions on the high ground to the west of Montchamp, covering the main road leading into Estry. This KG, by launching its own counter-attack, halted a British thrust[20] moving east through St Charles de Percy towards Montchamp. Interestingly, the 32nd Guards Brigade War Diary correctly identified the 2nd/19th, part of the 1st/19th SS Panzer-Grenadier Battalions and Mk IVs of the 2nd/9th SS Panzer Battalion as the units taking part in this attack. The only real British success in this sector on 2 August seems to have been achieved by the Guards Armoured Reconnaissance Battalion, which outflanked the opposition and reached a point some 3km west-north-west of Estry. Fortunately for the Hohenstaufen, however, it was ordered to remain there, inactive, for the next two days and nights.[21]

(Map 6a)

Meanwhile, on this same day at 1500 hours, a battlegroup of the British 11th Armoured Division[22] moving on the right flank of the Guards ran into part of KG Weiss near Chênedollé. This KG, with its 102nd SS Heavy Panzer Battalion and Divisional Escort and 9th SS Reconnaissance Companies, was at the time moving south-west from Estry towards Vire. Leaving the Tigers of SS Captain Kall's 1st/102nd Company to deal with the situation, the rest of the KG pushed on to Vire, which they reached at 2030 hours, making contact with the troops of the 3rd Parachute Division now defending the town. The clash near Chênedollé was soon over and the British were able to enter the unoccupied village; to their surprise, however, at about 1800 hours a mixed force of SS Panzer-Grenadiers and Panthers suddenly appeared on the scene and forced the British to withdraw to the Perrier spur, a kilometre to the north-west, where they lost five tanks in a further attack at 2000 hours.[23] By 2230 hours other units of the 11th Armoured Division reached Etouvy on the western flank[24] and the le Busq area[25], just to the west of Estry, thus creating a dangerous salient between KGs Weiss and Zollhöfer. Although the British lost a further three tanks in the le Busq area at about 2000 hours, they had 114 Shermans on the Perrier spur and the high ground to the north of Presles by last light on 2 August.[26] Little did they realise that they had virtually no enemy between them and their objective of Flers.

Although the Hohenstaufen had fought well on 2 August and halted two British armoured Divisions, it was obviously being dangerously out-flanked to its south. During the night Zollhöfer was told to withdraw his 2nd SS Panzer-Grenadier Battalion from the Montchamp area and strengthen the Estry sector. The only reserve available to the Division was the 9th SS Pioneer Battalion and this was positioned just to the north-east of the town. But if Bock's Hohenstaufen Division had its prob-lems, so did the British. The commander of VIII Corps, General Sir Richard O'Connor, alarmed that his eastern flank was exposed, ordered a halt to allow time for more infantry to be brought forward to cover it. In the event, as we shall see, most of the additional infantry were used to relieve rather than reinforce those in place, or to protect supply lines. With hindsight, it is clear that XXX Corps' failure[27] to take its objectives of Villers-Bocage and Aunay (Map 6), thus exposing VIII Corps' flank, should not have been allowed to squander the golden opportunity to break through the weak and over-stretched German forces and take Flers on 3 August. Sadly, Dempsey failed to overrule his subordinate and the caution, for which the British were becoming renowned, prevailed. In a later report[28] it was claimed that, 'as a result of its long advance VIII Corps was not suitably disposed for defence in that it was inevitably strung out and thin along the front'. This was surely a more appropriate descrip-tion for II SS Panzer Corps? In an unbelievable failure of intelligence, the British believed that the 9th Hohenstaufen and 10th Frundsberg Divisions had 'been heavily reinforced' and that:

> The revived enemy strength was brought about by the newly arrived presence of 9 SS Panzer Division. . . . Guards Armoured Division was in contact with a vastly strengthened enemy.[29]

In reality, nearly 500 tanks of VIII Corps' armoured Divisions had been facing just seventy-two Hohenstaufen Panthers, Mk IVs and StuGs and a maximum of thirty Tigers of Weiss's 102nd SS Heavy Panzer Battalion.

By 3 August, after the British commanders had ordered a halt to their advance, the Hohenstaufen had been reduced to only thirty-four combat-ready tanks and StuGs. Reliable figures for the 102nd Tiger Battalion are not available but some casualties and breakdowns must certainly have occurred. This indicates overall losses of at least thirteen Panthers, ten Mk IVs and nineteen StuGs on the 1st and 2nd, many of which would have been caused by the air attacks already mentioned.

During the night of 2 August, SS Colonel Bock ordered a reorganisation of his Division. The 1st/19th and 2nd/19th SS Panzer-Grenadier Battalions were detached from SS Major Zollhöfer's KG, leaving him only the 1st/20th Grenadiers. The 1st/19th Battalion was allocated a few tanks from the 2nd/9th SS Panzer Battalion to form a new small KG, whilst the 2nd Battalion joined KG Meyer to give it two Grenadier Battalions. By then deploying his only reserve, the 9th SS Pioneer Battalion, Bock had five KGs for use on the 3rd. All were told to attack. One cannot but admire the tactical thinking behind the overall plan to hold the leading units of the Guards and to cut off and destroy those of the 11th Armoured Division.

It is important to understand the tactics used against the British in this fighting. The War Diary of the Guards Armoured Division states that no attempt was made by the Germans to occupy permanently the numerous obstacles, hamlets and dominating features; instead, they used them tactically as needed. Small groups of single, or sometimes up to five tanks, with accompanying SS Panzer-Grenadiers, would infiltrate between the British units and cut lines of communication. It was 'like having a rabble of snipers loose in the battalion area', one Guards unit said. Others described how their re-supply columns were shot up in the area between Montchamp and the Perrier spur. In fact, the situation became so serious that a substantial part of the additional infantry Brigade[30] allotted to the 11th Armoured Division, instead of being used to strengthen its positions, was employed protecting its supply lines.[31]

In the northern part of the Hohenstaufen sector (Map 6), the small 1st/19th KG, after a heavy artillery and mortar bombardment, 'debouched from the woods west of Montchamp' on 3 August and captured Hill 176 from the 5th Guards Armoured Brigade by 1100 hours. The Guards claimed three tanks knocked out. The remainder of KG Zollhöfer attacked from west of Montchauvet in the direction of le Bény-Bocage, but was halted on the Vire–Villers-Bocage road in front of Hill 266 by devastating artillery fire. More successful was KG Meyer which, attacking from the line Estry to Pierres, succeeded in capturing Presles[32] by 1330 hours, only to give it up without a fight during the night. Nevertheless, this success had serious implications for the British 11th Armoured Division because its leading elements, to the south-east of a line drawn between Estry and Burcy, were to all intents and purposes cut off. As it was reported later:

Though leading units, like 23 Hussars and 2 Fife and Forfar Yeomanry [and 8 RB], were placed in a precarious and unhappy position for some days, General Roberts [the Divisional commander] accepted the risk entailed in maintaining these positions.[33]

Farther south, Bock threw in SS Major Monich's 9th SS Pioneer Battalion at Burcy in an attempt to link up with KG Weiss on its left flank on the Vire–le Bény-Bocage road. Unfortunately, none of the Divisional artillery was within range to give support and the advance soon ran into trouble. British tanks[34] produced heavy flanking fire and, after the SPW-mounted 3rd Pioneer Company became mired in a swampy valley, the other two Companies were thrown back. To make matters worse, Allied ground attack aircraft then appeared above the battlefield and the attack had to be called off. The commander of the 3rd SPW Company, SS Captain von Cölln, was killed in this fighting.

Meanwhile, KG Weiss had advanced north-east from Vire up the Villers-Bocage road. Its orders were to seize Hill 119, a kilometre north of la Bistière, and to make contact with the 3rd Parachute Division farther to the west at la Graverie. SS Second Lieutenant Schroif's 2nd/102nd Tiger Company led the way, with dismounted squads of the 3rd/9th SS Reconnaissance Battalion on each flank. SS Captain Kalls' 1st Company followed, with the 2nd Company of SS Captain Gräbner's 9th SS Reconnaissance Battalion in support. It is not known where Weiss's 3rd/102nd Tiger Company was operating but it would be reasonable to assume that it remained in defence in Vire – always supposing that there were enough operational tanks for three viable Companies on this day.

Cromwell tanks of the 11th Armoured Division's Reconnaissance Regiment were encountered at the first major road fork, 3km north of Vire, but the leading Tiger soon disposed of three of them and the remainder withdrew – no doubt surprised by the direction of the German advance. Kalls' 1st Company group turned north-west at this point and soon reached la Graverie where, after linking up with the 3rd Division paratroopers, it took up excellent fire positions. The 2nd Company had a more difficult time. The terrain on each side of the main Villers-Bocage road was very broken and the many hedgerows and ravines meant that men on their feet had to investigate each potential enemy position before the Tigers could proceed. Nevertheless, soon after 1300 hours, the combined force reached la Bistière and a short time later, after the loss of seven more tanks, the British withdrew to the north and the Tigers occupied Hill 119. Once there they fought off a series of counter-attacks in which they claimed a further seven British tanks, two anti-tank guns and two armoured cars. German losses for the day were one Tiger, hit seven times and set on fire and another disabled but subsequently repaired. As darkness fell, the remaining seven organised themselves for defence, relying heavily on their Reconnaissance Battalion comrades for protection – they need not have worried, the British rarely attacked at night and, up to this time at least, never with armour. KG Weiss had achieved its mission, but sadly for II SS Panzer Corps, the other Hohenstaufen KGs had failed to link up and complete the encirclement of much of VIII Corps' armour. Their exhausted and depleted ranks were simply not strong enough. To add to their problems, it was on this same day that the British placed an additional infantry Brigade[35] from the 15th Scottish, II SS Panzer Corps' old adversary, and an armoured Brigade[36] in support of the Guards Armoured Division and provided, as we have heard, another infantry Brigade[37] to back up the 11th Armoured Division.

(Map 4)

The 4th of August was a momentous day for the Allies and Germans alike. On the Allied side, George Patton's Third US Army entered Rennes, 100km to the south-west of Vire, and after its 4th Armored Division went on to seal off the Brittany peninsula, Montgomery issued a new directive which ended, 'The broad strategy of the Allied Armies is to swing the right flank towards Paris and force the enemy back to the Seine.' If this strategy worked it would spell the end for most of the German troops in Normandy. On the German side, Hitler issued an order that was destined to hasten just such a catastrophe. Thanks to II SS Panzer Corps, Hausser's Seventh Army was still more or less intact from Mont Pinçon to Vire and then south to Barenton, and so the Führer directed von Kluge to launch a counter-offensive from the Vire–Mortain area, aimed first at Avranches, with the aim of cutting off all American forces to the south of that line, and then north-east to the Channel coast to drive the Allies back into the sea. The counter-offensive, code-named LÜTTICH, became better known as the Mortain counter-attack. As usual with Hitler it was a highly imaginative plan, calling for the use of eight of the nine Panzer divisions in Normandy (for obvious reasons only the Hohenstaufen was excepted), and the entire reserves of the Luftwaffe. Of course, both von Kluge and Hausser knew that it would be impossible to assemble these forces before the collapse of the entire front to the west of the Orne – but they also knew that there was no point in arguing.

(Map 6)

By the end of 3 August Bittrich knew that his Corps had no chance of pushing the British VIII Corps back behind the Vire–Caen road. The Hohenstaufen was down to eighteen Panthers, seven MK IVs, nine StuGs and fewer than thirty Tigers, and the Panzer-Grenadier Battalions amounted to little more than companies. The best he could do was to pull back to a good defensive line and continue his forlorn attempt to destroy the British armour in the salient.

During the night of the 3rd, the Hohenstaufen KGs withdrew to a new line running roughly from Montchauvet, south-west to Hill 175, 2km west of Montchamp, and on to Sieurmoux. On the Division's northern flank, parts of the 21st Panzer and 326th Infantry Division were still holding a front on the high ground between Montchauvet and Ondefontaine and in the Bois de Buron. South-west of Sieurmoix, on the left flank, there was a tenuous link to KG Weiss on Hill 119 and at la Graverie, but the attempted encirclement of the British forward elements was by no means complete. They were able to continue re-supplying their units, albeit at times with great difficulty, in the salient south and south-east of the Estry–Presles road (Map 6a), the latter village having been reoccupied during the night of the 3rd/4th.

The Hohenstaufen withdrawal was carried out without too many problems except in the case of SS Captain Borchers' small 1st/19th SS Panzer-Grenadier Battalion KG, which had to fight its way back from the Arclais area.[38] The only good news Bittrich received at this time was that his Corps was to be reinforced that night by a Hitlerjugend KG, under the command of SS Major Erich Olboeter, and the 600th (Army) Pioneer Battalion. KG Olboeter consisted of the HJ's 2nd SS Panzer Company with thirteen Panthers, 9th SS (SPW) Panzer-Grenadier Company, six 105mm SP Wespe artillery pieces, and six armoured cars from the Leibstandarte's 1st SS Reconnaissance Battalion. He resolved to use both units at the apex of the British salient.

During the early morning of 4 August, both Montchauvet and the high ground 2km north-west of Montchamp fell to the British.[39] Montchamp itself was a different matter – around 1800 hours a mixed battlegroup[40], after entering the village, was counter-attacked by either the 1st/19th or 1st/20th SS Panzer-Grenadier Battalion with, according to the British, six Panthers. The War Diary goes on to say that the supporting tanks were unable to support the Guardsmen who, at 2200 hours and after suffering 115 casualties, were forced to withdraw. 'No. 2 Company was cut in half . . . the Prince of Wales' Company was completely overrun.' It adds that one SS Panzer-Grenadier was singing the 'Horst Wessel' as he died! What is puzzling about the British activity in this sector, or rather the lack of it, is that, according to their War Diaries, two tank Battalions and one infantry Battalion[41] were sitting less than 4km to the west of Montchamp at this time doing nothing.

To the south of Montchamp, the Guards were also in trouble from pockets of resistance which had been bypassed on the 3rd, and other groups which had infiltrated during the night. One battlegroup[42], just south-east of Sieurnoux, was unable to evacuate its wounded and had its re-supply columns shot up. The 2nd Armoured Irish Guards War Diary describes how it lost two tanks to a single 'sniping' Panther and how one of its Fireflys (Sherman with a 17-pounder gun) had to hit a Tiger four times before the crew bailed out. It goes on to say that fifty of its wounded were eventually evacuated in six trucks flying Red Crosses. They were not fired upon.[43]

A clear indication of the growing crisis for the Germans was the fact that on the 4th XXX Corps finally entered Villers-Bocage and XII Corps took Evrecy and advanced to the Orne near Amaye (Map 5). The threat to the rear of II SS Panzer Corps was obvious.

(Map 6a)

Despite the threat from the rear, Bittrich continued his efforts to eliminate the 11th Armoured Division force on the Perrier spur. The Hohenstaufen and Army Pioneer units, together with KG Olboeter, held the apex of the salient whilst the batteries of the 9th SS Artillery Regiment and Nebelwerfers of the 8th Werfer Brigade forced the British to abandon the villages of Chênedollé and Presles which they had occupied during the night. The Germans claimed thirty-six tanks knocked out, despite which Burcy and the Perrier spur remained firmly in British hands. At the end of the day, they still had 131 tanks in the salient.[44]

To the north-west, KG Weiss came under heavy pressure from artillery and both ground and air attack. By 2030 hours Hill 119 had been given up and the seven Tigers of the 2nd/102nd SS Panzer Company and 3rd/9th SS Reconnaissance Company were back in la Bistière. A further withdrawal was made at 2230 and an hour later a new position had been taken up in the northern outskirts of Vire. Kall's 1st/102nd SS Tiger Company and its accompanying SS Reconnaissance Company pulled back from la Graverie at the same time.

During the night of the 4th, KG Weiss pulled out of Vire and by first light on the 5th its remaining Tigers and Gräbner's 9th SS Reconnaissance Battalion were in position on the northern edge of Chênedollé and at Pierres. However, with Montchamp lost at 1800 hours, and Burcy and Presles also in British hands and further reinforcements arriving, the difficulties for the 11th Armoured Division were nearing their end. By the evening its units captured Chênedollé and Viessoix and counter-attacks by the 9th SS Reconnaissance and Pioneer Battalions, supported by a few Tigers, failed in the face of devastating tank and artillery fire. Throughout the day, however, the Germans continued their tactics of infiltration and short, sharp attacks. The War Diaries of the 11th Armoured Division and 1st Armoured Coldstream Guards variously describe an attack on an ammunition column by four tanks and about thirty Panzer-Grenadiers, and another during the night by four StuGs and accompanying infantry just to the south-west of Montchamp. The Guards' Diary says all four StuGs were knocked out.

Farther north, whilst KGs Meyer and Zollhöfer were still covering Estry and the main road immediately to its north-east, a British infantry Brigade[45] reached the same road 3km to the east of Montchauvet (Map 6). This new thrust to the south-east, combined with another[46] moving south towards Mont Pinçon (Aunay had been found empty of enemy), emphasised the threat to the Hohenstaufen. Its tank strength was now down to just eleven Panthers, eight Mk IVs, eight StuGs and twenty Tigers. Amazingly, the 5th Guards Armoured Brigade was told that 'no move was imminent' on this day; one of its strongest battlegroups[47], and the Divisional Armoured Reconnaissance Battalion were in fact to remain unused in the St Charles de Percy area for another four days!

As the day ended, Eberbach's Panzer Group West was renamed Fifth Panzer Army and the boundary with Hausser's Seventh Army moved to a line running through Viessoix. More significantly for the men of the Hohenstaufen, it saw the arrival in the Vassy area of their comrades of the 10th SS Panzer Division Frundsberg. At the same time, the 102nd Tiger Battalion reverted to the command of II SS Panzer Corps.

It is appropriate now to examine the reason why, at this critical stage of the Normandy campaign, the British Second Army, and VIII Corps in particular, did not launch a major breakthrough attempt against the weak German front east of Vire. VIII Corps had, after all, four Divisions and an armoured Brigade[48] available to throw in against the remnants of the Hohenstaufen, the 326th Infantry Division and the 21st Panzer KG. The reason is comparatively simple – Montgomery's strategy. VIII and XXX Corps had done, and were doing, their job – they had held, and were holding, substantial elements of the German armour away from the western flank where the Americans had broken out. There was no point in risking further casualties in costly attacks in thick bocage country. Just as JUPITER had been launched as a holding operation, so BLUECOAT had now developed into one. The deflection of the Frundsberg from its role in the Mortain counter-attack was confirmation that the strategy was intact and fully effective.

6 August

The VIII Corps report of the Frundsberg's attack on 6 August states:

> Two more days [following its relief in the Ondefontaine sector] were spent in preparation and survey, and finally a heavy attack was launched . . . on 6th August against the apex of the Corps salient.[49]

As readers will be aware, nothing could be further from the truth. Recall that the Frundsberg had been heavily engaged until late on the 4th and that some elements even had to fight their way back to the east on the 5th in order make the move south to Vassy. As had happened so many times before, the men of II SS Panzer Corps, who had been fighting almost continuously since their arrival in Normandy in late June, were required to go into action on unfamiliar ground and with little or no time for briefing or preparation. On nearly every occasion, and this is the latest example, they were merely given an objective and told to attack it. Indications of enemy strengths were rarely available, the situation on the flanks often unknown and any idea of attacking other than frontally usually dismissed. Amazingly, many of these attacks were successful; but then, these men were no ordinary soldiers – they were extraordinary.

There are few details of the Frundsberg's attack from the German side. All that is known is that the assault was made by two mixed KGs towards British positions north of Chênedollé, on the Perrier spur and in the Sourdeval (spelt Sourdevalle in 1944) area. After heavy fighting, Hill 242 and then Sourdeval and Hill 224 were captured, but intense artillery fire and attacks by close support aircraft brought the attack to a halt and enabled the defenders to recapture their lost positions. The Division began the day with twenty Mk IVs and StuGs and ended it with half that number.

British War Diaries[50] say that after an intense twenty-minute artillery and mortar barrage, the Frundsberg attack was launched at 1400 hours. Tanks and infantry managed to penetrate into the positions of one infantry Battalion[51] on the Perrier spur, inflicting heavy casualties, and an associated attack caused chaos and equally heavy casualties in the Sourdeval sector where one infantry Battalion was in the process of relieving another.[52] German tanks even managed to reach a British armoured unit sited in depth, knocking out a number of tanks. Another tank Battalion[53] lost five Shermans during the day, reducing its total strength to only twenty-five. The fighting lasted some four hours before devastating artillery and tank fire forced the Germans to call off their attack. One British report[54] says that the Germans used more than fifty tanks, including a battalion of tanks from the 116th Panzer Division, Tigers of the 102nd SS Heavy Panzer Battalion and a Battalion of engineers. Whilst there is no confirmation of the unit from 116th Panzer, it seems quite logical that either the Hohenstaufen or 600th Pioneers would have supported the attack and it is certain that Tigers of Kalls' 1st/102nd Company did so.

In Estry on this day two Battalions of the 227th Highland Brigade with two squadrons of tanks[55], advancing down the Aunay road (Map 6) at 0930 hours and believing their enemy 'to be in full retreat', ran into well positioned units of KG Zollhöfer:

It soon became clear that the 9th SS Panzer Division had turned Estry into a strong-point, which it meant to hold at all costs. Two or three companies of an SS Regiment, a dug-in tank, 88mm guns, bazookas [Panzerfausts], mortars, Nebelwerfers, machine-gun nests, mines – all were there, and the garrison had a call on powerful artillery farther back.[56]

Although part of the attacking force managed to get as far as the orchards in the north-eastern part of Estry, by 2200 hours it had suffered 'heavy casualties' (the Battalion in question suffered forty-six casualties and one of the tank squadrons lost eleven Churchills), and in order 'to avoid piecemeal destruction', the attack was called off.[57]

Just to the south-west of Estry a Guards Battalion took le Busq by 1400 hours but found the forward slope on the south side of the hamlet untenable due to German fire.[58]

The 6th of August was also an important day at the strategic level. As Patton's tanks approached Le Mans (Map 4), 100km to the south-east of Vire and only 170km from Paris and the Seine, von Kluge began to panic. Despite the fact that the attack force was far from complete, he ordered the Mortain counter-attack to be launched that night – in clear defiance of Hitler's order that it should not be made before 'every tank, gun and plane was assembled'.

7 – 15 August

On 7 August Vire fell to the Americans. That morning the 10th SS Panzer Division Frundsberg received orders to pull out of the II SS Panzer Corps sector and move as rapidly as possible – 50km – to an area just to the east of Mortain (Map 4), where it was to come under Seventh Army command. Recall that it was to be part of Hitler's great counter-offensive, Operation LÜTTICH. With the 3rd Parachute Division on its left flank, the Hohenstaufen was left holding the line from a point 2km west of Chêne-dollé to just north-east of Estry. Two Tigers of Schroif's 2nd/102nd Company, the 9th SS Pioneer and Reconnaissance Battalions, KG Olboeter of the Hitlerjugend with seven Panthers and the 600th Army Pioneer Battalion continued to hold the apex of the British salient at Chênedollé, while KGs Meyer and Zollhöfer, with seven Panthers[59], nine Mk IVs and seven StuGs, remained responsible for the Pierres and Estry sectors respectively. Kalls' 1st Tiger Company was pulled back into reserve at Vassy.

One of the most extraordinary events on this day was the destruction of an entire company of British tanks[60] by a single Tiger just to the north of Chênedollé. A planned German attack by Monich's 9th SS Pioneer and Kalls' 1st/102nd Tiger Company was cancelled early in the day, only to be replaced by a British attack in the same area. The Tiger in question was commanded by SS Sergeant, later Captain in the post-war West German Army, Will Fey. Readers particularly interested in this episode should read Fey's own account in his book *Armor Battles of the Waffen-SS 1943–45*.

There are no detailed reports of the fighting on KG Meyer's front on the 7th but:

> Estry remained a very hot spot. Enemy machine-guns and 88s commanded the crossroads. Spandaus swept the roads; artillery exchanges were incessant; our mortars plastered the enemy defences concentrated round the church; enemy mortars plastered the orchards and the road from la Caverie [leading in from the north-east].[61]

Apart from one tank squadron involved at Estry, the War Diary of the 6th Guards Tank Brigade reported 'the whole Brigade resting' (nearly 200 tanks).

During the night of the 7th, the left wing of the Hohenstaufen pulled back from the Chênedollé ridge and, in conformity with the 3rd Parachute Division on its left flank, took up new positions on the ridge south of the Vire–Vassy road. The inter-Divisional boundary ran north-west some 3km west of Vassy. At the same time, KG Olboeter was returned to the Hitlerjugend and the 600th Army Pioneer placed in Divisional reserve near Vassy. An important loss to Bittrich's Corps at this time was the removal of the thirteen remaining operational Tigers of Weiss's 102nd Battalion. On 9 August they were sent east to join the remnants of the 12th SS Panzer Division Hitlerjugend, part of Sepp Dietrich's I SS Panzer Corps, struggling to hold the Canadian assault on Falaise (Map 4).

The period 8 to 10 August saw further British attacks against the Hohenstaufen at Estry. They were all repulsed. Two examples will suffice to paint the picture:

> The 44th Brigade [of 15th Scottish Division] attacked at noon [on the 8th]. . . . A squadron of Grenadiers [tanks] and a large contingent of Crocodiles [flame-throwing tanks] and AVREs [assault engineer armoured vehicles] were in support. The first job of the infantry and the Churchill tanks was to manoeuvre the Crocodiles and AVREs into position where they could blast and burn the garrison [the 1st/20th SS Panzer-Grenadier Battalion with a few Mk IVs]. Once more, however, the banks and narrow sunken lanes round Estry proved impassable obstacles; so much so that not one of these 'funnies' got near enough to use its weapon. . . . At about 1 p.m. German infantry, led by three Mk IV tanks, counter-attacked and pushed the RSF back

over the cross-roads. . . . By 3 p.m. the attack was entirely held up everywhere. Casualties had been heavy.[62]

> A number of wounded men were left out in the open . . . The stretcher-bearers could not reach them, so Major Moreton of 'C' Company went out with a Red Cross flag to where they lay. Almost immediately a German officer joined him; they arranged a half-hour's suspension of hostilities; the wounded were brought in.[63]

Elsewhere the front remained reasonably quiet except for constant artillery exchanges and Allied air attacks. The lull was because of British preparations for Operation GROUSE. This involved the Guards Armoured Division taking over from the 11th Armoured, which was to go into reserve, and then advancing on Flers, with the 3rd Infantry Division on its right flank aimed at Tinchebray (Map 6).

At 0900 hours on 11 August, the Guards Armoured and 3rd Infantry Divisions began their drive, keeping north and south respectively of the Vire–Flers railway line. They immediately ran into heavy resistance. In an opening attack, it took two Battalions of the 32nd Guards Brigade just to secure Chênedollé. 'The tanks that ventured forward were all knocked out and the two leading companies suffered 70% casualties.' The Hohenstaufen was far from being a spent force. A British officer wrote in his diary, 'We are fighting some of the best troops the Germans have, they seem to hang on till the end'; and his description of the Sourdeval area two days after the fighting ended on the 14th gives a horrifying picture of this Normandy battlefield:

> I find it hard to describe the horror and chaos in this place. Most of our own dead have been or are being buried with the exception of the knocked out tank crews who are still inside the tanks. The German dead are everywhere in grotesque attitudes, blown up to twice their size in some cases and black from the hot sun. The result of three battles, the corpses are in all stages of decomposition with rats and maggots in charge . . . A guardsman learnt a smart lesson today. He was removing a leather belt from a German corpse when the corpse suddenly emitted a series of deep groans. It was escaping gases but the Irishman dropped the belt and fled.[64]

At Viessoix, two battlegroups were held up with heavy casualties – the 5th Guards Armoured Brigade War Diary reported: 'It was a very disappointing day and achieved little.' On the right flank, the leading infantry Battalion of the leading Brigade, with tank support, found little initial opposition but the picture soon changed and by 1400 hours it had only reached a point 3km south-west of Viessoix. The day's objective was still

2km away and it would be another twenty-four hours before it was captured.

The fighting continued on the 12th but little progress was made. The British War Diaries do not reflect the intensity of the combat but a German report shows that it was as bitter as ever:

We all knew the Tommies would attack again the next day, August 12th. For the entire night armored vehicles clattered around bringing up reserves. With the break of day heavy enemy weapons cover our lines with shellfire. Ground fog lies over the terrain and blinds us. We are tense. When will they come? And then they are here, with tanks and infantry. Their artillery lifts to the rear and hits the roads and staffs in their little farms. Our Company is pulled back to the next prepared positions ... Every rise in the ground, every farm is contested. A deep penetration is cut off and ironed out by SS Major Monich [commanding officer 9th SS Pioneer Battalion] with the reserves, a platoon each from the 2nd and 3rd Companies. The losses in the Battalion are high, the situation remains critical. The ambulances can no longer make it through and the wounded are collected in the sheep pens of a farm. . . . Many casualties result from machine-gun and rocket attacks from the Jabos [ground attack aircraft]. . . . With the fall of darkness the battles of attack and defence which have broken up into many individual struggles, come to an end. . . . Then wounded are finally collected.[65]

The following night the Hohenstaufen began its long overdue withdrawal to the east. Hitler's great counter-offensive had failed and the nightmare long expected by the German generals in Normandy had materialised – their Armies were being surrounded and were facing annihilation.[66]

While Monich's battered 9th SS Pioneers held the left flank, KGs Meyer and Zollhöfer withdrew without the British being aware of it. 'On the morning of 13th August, the Royal Scots found that the enemy had gone, whereupon they occupied Estry.'[67] The same day the 6th Guards Tank Brigade, operating with the 3rd Infantry Division, reported the first signs of a 'universal withdrawal', but that the 'pursuit [was] being limited to an infantry operation so far'. Interestingly, the Supreme Allied Commander, General Dwight D Eisenhower, had issued a special message on this day:

I make my present appeal to you more urgent than ever before. I request every soldier to go forward to his assigned objective with the determination that the enemy can survive only through surrender. Let no foot of ground once gained be relinquished, nor a German soldier escape through a line once established.

That night the 9th SS Pioneers pulled back, but with the non-arrival of any relieving infantry units, the rest of the Hohenstaufen was forced to stay in position. It hardly mattered – they were not under any real threat. On 14 August the 11th Armoured Division was placed under Lieutenant General Horrocks' XXX Corps and nominated to carry out the pursuit 'as it appears likely the enemy is pulling out'. 'A series of conferences were held' which resulted in Operation KITTEN.[68] The War Diary of the same day for the 6th Guards Tank Brigade says, 'little for tanks to do in this advance apart from giving extra fire support . . . and holding temporary defensive positions'. The following day the Diary says, 'General Eisenhower has called on all the Allied forces to make this the most momentous week in the history of war'. Yet, two days later and despite the exhortation, the Brigade had, 'Nothing to report. Whole day spent in rest and maintenance.' A platoon commander in the 32nd Guards Brigade wrote:

> My platoon was up to strength, so we spent ten days out of the line doing drill in the mornings, PT in the afternoons and between times checking weapons and equipment.[69]

The War Diary of the 29th Armoured Brigade for 14 August is even more revealing:

> Orders to units were that it is NOT the intention to push on as quickly as possible, but to mop up every position as they are discovered and put as much equipment etc as possible in the bag. [At 2300 hrs] GOC [general officer commanding] phones to say 'form for tomorrow is "soft pedal" – maintain contact, follow up if enemy withdraws but units not to get involved'.

On the 14th what was left of the Hohenstaufen was ordered to withdraw that night, through Vassy and Condé, and get back across the one remaining bridge over the Orne at Putanges (Map 4). Due to fuel shortages, however, this was easier said than done and by dawn on the 15th the Hohenstaufen was still west of the Orne. Allied air activity prevented further movement in daylight and, after another day spent under cover in the woods south-east of Condé, the Division finally crossed the Putanges bridge during the night of the 15th. By dawn the next day, its sad remnants were under the cover of the Forêt de Gouffern, north of Argentan.

For the British, BLUECOAT was over. Again, it had been a costly operation. VIII Corps alone had lost 5,114 men[70] plus some 135 tanks to the Hohenstaufen and its attached 102nd SS Heavy Panzer Battalion. Nevertheless, it had achieved Montgomery's aim of attracting German armour which otherwise would have been used against the American breakout in the west. The Hohenstaufen and Frundsberg Divisions had suffered serious casualties but they remained dangerous adversaries with a combined combat-ready strength of fifteen Panthers, thirty-eight Mk IVs and forty-four StuGs. Exact personnel figures for the Hohenstaufen are unavailable but the Frundsberg still had a combat strength of 4,136.[71]

As a postscript to this Chapter it is worth noting that a major adversary of II SS Panzer Corps, the 15th Scottish Infantry Division, had by 14 August spent thirty-seven days in action or in contact with the enemy, and the famous 'Desert Rats' 7th Armoured Division forty days. By comparison, the Hohenstaufen and Frundsberg had each spent forty-seven days in continuous action and, unlike their enemies, had been under the constant threat of, or actual, air attack. There was one other major difference. In the case of the British troops:

> The Brigade's thoroughly earned rest was well organised. Many visited the Army and Corps rest camps on the beach; baths and ENSA shows (including George Formby) were available. . . . The weather was gloriously fine and the rest most enjoyable.[72]

In the case of the Hohenstaufen and Frundsberg there was to be no rest – just the hell of the Falaise Pocket.

NOTES

1. Eberbach, MS # B-840.
2. XII Corps, on the eastern flank, was also required to advance and secure a bridgehead over the Orne north of Thury-Harcourt; however, since its operations did not affect II SS Pz Corps at this stage of the campaign, they will not be discussed.
3. 11 Armd Div War Diary, 29 Jul 44.
4. 15 Scottish Div.
5. 6 Gds Tk Bde.
6. 2 Household Cavalry Regt (2 HCR).
7. 11 Armd Div. This Div had reorganised its two Bdes so that each comprised two tk and two inf bns. The Armd Recce Bn became the fourth tk bn. The Guards Armd Div had reorganised in a similar way.
8. 21 Pz Div had been fighting in the Caen sector since D-Day.
9. Eberbach, MS # B-840.
10. 10 The total number of Mk IVs and Tigers in these units was sixty-nine and twenty-nine respectively, but the balance were under repair.
11. Eberbach (MS # B-840) blamed von Oppeln for the failure of the counter-attack, saying he lost time by waiting for the rest of 21 Pz Div to arrive.
12. 4 Dorset of 130 Inf Bde & tks of 8 Armd Bde – part of 43 Inf Div.
13. 214 Inf Bde & tks of 8 Armd Bde – part of 43 Inf Div.
14. Wilmot, *The Struggle for Europe*, p. 398, and PRO London.
15. 130 Inf Bde War Diary, 3 Aug 44.

16. 43 Recce Regt & 4 Dorset.
17. 4 Dorset, part of 130 Inf Bde.
18. 1st Bn Grenadier Gds (Gren Gds) & 2 Armd Gren Gds from 5 Gds Armd Bde.
19. There were no Tigers with KGs Meyer or Zollhöfer.
20. 5 Coldstream Guards (Coldm Gds) & 2 Armd Irish Guards (IG) from 5 Gds Armd Bde.
21. 2 Armd Recce Welsh Gds (WG) War Diary.
22. 23 H & 8 RB of 29 Armd Bde.
23. 29 Armd Bde, 23 H & 8 RB War Diaries, 2 Aug 44.
24. 2 Northamptonshire Yeomanry (Northamps Yeo).
25. 3 RTR & 4 KSLI.
26. 29 Armd Bde & 3 RTR War Diaries, 2 Aug 44.
27. 50 Inf & 7 Armd Divs respectively. The commanders of XXX Corps, 7 Armd Div & 22 Armd Bde were sacked on 2 & 3 Aug.
28. Jackson, *Operations of Eighth Corps*, p. 137.
29. Jackson, op. cit., p. 136.
30. 185 Inf Bde of 3 Inf Div.
31. 11 Armd Div & 159 Inf Bde War Diaries, 3 Aug 44.
32. 8 RB War Diary, 3 Aug 44.
33. Jackson, op. cit., p. 137.
34. Probably from 3 RTR. Its War Diary mentions an enemy attack at 1300 hours.
35. 44 Lowland Bde plus 7 Seaforth.
36. 4 Armd Bde.
37. 185 Inf Bde.
38. Against 6 RSF & a sqn of 4 Armd Gren Gds.
39. To 6 RSF & 4 Armd Gren Gds.
40. 1 WG & 3 Sqn 1 Armd Coldm Gds
41. 4 Armd Coldm & 3 Armd Scots Gds (SG) & 1 Gren Gds.
42. 5 Coldm & 2 Armd IG.
43. The War Diary of 5 Coldm Gds describes a similar or the same incident, but says it happened on 5 Aug.
44. 29 Armd Bde War Diary, 4 Aug 44.
45. 227 Inf Bde of 15 Scottish Div.
46. 43 Wessex Inf Div.
47. 1 Gren & 2 Armd Gren Gds.
48. Gds & 11 Armd, 3 & 15 Inf Divs & 6 Gds Tk Bde.
49. Jackson, op. cit., p. 138.
50. 11 Armd Div, 185 Inf Bde, 23 H, 2 F&F Yeo, 1 Royal Norfolk (R Norfolk), 2 Royal Warwickshire (Warwicks), 3 Monmouthshire (Monmouth) War Diaries, 6 Aug 44.
51. 2 Warwicks; this Bn suffered 202 casualties in the period 2–8 Aug 44.
52. 1 R Norfolk was relieving 3 Monmouths. They were reduced to a composite Bn of four coys nick-named the 'Normons'.
53. 23 H and 2 F&F Yeo.
54. Jackson, op. cit., p. 138.
55. 2 Gordons & 10 HLI with a sqn (coy) of 4 Gren Gds & 3 SG each respectively.
56. Martin, *History of the 15th Scottish Division 1939–1945*, p. 99.
57. 6 Gds Tk Bde, 3 Armd SG & 10 HLI War Diaries, 6 Aug 44. It is of note that 3 Armd SG numbered amongst its officers at this time: a future Archbishop of Canterbury, a future Chancellor of the Exchequer, a future Marshal of the Diplomatic Corps and five future generals.

58. 5 Coldm Gds War Diary, 6 Aug 44.
59. It is possible that the Panthers reported are those of KG Olboeter.
60. Of the 23 H.
61. Martin, op. cit., p. 101.
62. Ibid., pp. 102–3.
63. Ibid., p. 101.
64. Cooper, *Dangerous Liaison*, pp. 35–6.
65. Tieke, op. cit., p. 175.
66. Full details of the Mortain counter-attack and its results can be read in the author's book, *Steel Inferno – I SS Panzer Corps in Normandy*.
67. Martin, op. cit., p. 105 & *Steel Inferno – I SS Panzer Corps in Normandy*.
68. XXX Corps War Diary, 14 Aug 44.
69. Wilson, *The Ever Open Eye*, p. 52.
70. Jackson, op. cit., p. 142.
71. Zetterling, *Normandy 1944*, pp. 340, 346–7.
72. 131 Inf Bde of 7 Armd Div.

CHAPTER X

Mortain to the Falaise Pocket: 16 – 21 August

Hohenstaufen

(Map 7)

By 16 August the decision had already been made to extract what was left of the 9th SS Hohenstaufen and 2nd SS Das Reich Panzer Divisions from west of the Dives river, for use as a counter-attack force. That day SS Senior Colonel Bock received orders to move his Division through the Trun sector of the Dives to the Vimoutiers area where, as part of II SS Panzer Corps, it would go into Army Group reserve. He was warned that enemy armoured forces were already south of Falaise. In fact that same afternoon Montgomery telephoned the commander of the First Canadian Army, General Crerar, and warned him that the German divisions west of Argentan would try to break out between there and Trun and that it was vital for him to seize Trun and close the gap between his troops and the US Third Army.

On 17 August the main Divisional march group, including some twenty to twenty-five tanks and StuGs, set out from the Forêt de Gouffern on the main Argentan–Trun–Vimoutiers road, with a flank protection force under the command of SS Major Hagenlocher, commander of the 1st/19th SS Panzer-Grenadier Battalion, moving through Nécy, Bierre and Merri (Map 8). At Bierre, Hagenlocher's group was allegedly attacked by 'enemy tanks' moving south-east[1] and forced to set up a holding position to enable the main force to cross the Dives at Trun, where some guns of the 4th/9th SS Flak Battalion provided minimal air defence. Fortunately for Bock's men, the pedantic approach of the leading Canadian units[2] meant that Trun did not fall until the 18th and although they suffered from incessant air attacks[3], most members of the Division got through. But even after crossing the river their problems did not end. With reports of Allied units already across the Trun–Vimoutiers road, SS Major Monich's 9th SS Pioneer Battalion, with the support of two tanks and a StuG, was given the task of clearing the way forward. The armour led, whilst the 3rd SPW Company brought up the rear. Although the timings do not match exactly, it would appear that the Monich group clashed with elements of the 1st Polish Armoured Division[4] advancing during the night of the 18th/19th towards Chambois. The clash occurred near the hamlet of Hordouseaux, 5km north-east of Trun. The Germans claim that, after two hours' fighting, the Polish units were pushed back and the road cleared.[5] The Poles say there was a short sharp engagement in which the Germans suffered badly, before they continued their advance. After successfully reaching Vimoutiers, Monich himself apparently set out once more for Trun in order to show other units the way, but was never seen again. The main body of the Hohenstaufen, described as about 30% of its authorised strength,[6] reached Vimoutiers over the course of the 18th.

Frundsberg

We left the Frundsberg as long ago as the night of 7 August, hurrying to join in Hitler's great Avranches counter-offensive. It was expected to act as a reserve for General Freiherr Hans von Funck's XLVII Panzer Corps, which was already attacking towards Avranches (Map 4) with the 1st SS, 2nd SS, 2nd, 116th and Panzer Lehr Panzer Divisions and a KG of the 17th SS Panzer-Grenadier Division Götz von Berlichingen. However, by the time the first units of the Frundsberg arrived in the new assembly area south of St Clement and Ger on 8 August the attack had, to all intents and purposes, already failed.

After conferring with the commander of the 2nd SS Panzer Division Das Reich, Heinz Lammerding, Harmel ordered patrols from Brinkmann's 10th SS Reconnaissance Battalion to investigate what he believed might well be an open flank to the south of a line from Mortain to Domfront. Sure enough, they reported that the Americans had taken Barenton late on the 7th and were now advancing along the road towards Domfront. To add to this already alarming news, Harmel was now ordered to relieve units of the 275th Infantry Division in the Barenton area but at the same time to keep the bulk of his Division in an assembly area near Ger for use in the still active counter-attack towards Avranches. He therefore ordered his first units to arrive – Brinkmann's 10th SS Reconnaissance and the 1st/21st SS (SPW) Panzer-Grenadier Battalions – to take up defensive positions in the hills north of Barenton and to block any movement towards his Divisional assembly area at Ger.

According to Wilhelm Tieke's *In the Firestorm of the Last Years of the War*[7], the situation worsened during the 9th. He claims that as the Frundsberg formed up to advance out of its assembly area at Ger, the Americans turned north and threatened its temporary blocking line on Hill 266 in the Forêt de Mortain, 3km north-east of Barenton and on two other adjacent features. As the Grenadier Companies of the 22nd Regiment and Pioneers of the 10th SS Pioneer Battalion arrived in sector, they too had to be used to thicken up the defensive line. In spite of these problems, Tieke claims that, on the morning of the 10th, Harmel's Division went into the attack and established positions on the southern edge of the Forêt de Mortain barely 3km north of the Mortain–Barenton–Domfront road. Schultze's 22nd SS Panzer-Grenadier Regiment was on the right, Diesenhofer's 21st Regiment on the left and SS Major Tröbinger's 10th SS Pioneer Battalion in the centre, in possession of the village of Bousentier, just south of Hill 266. 'No more than ten combat-ready Mk IVs and StuGs' supported the attack and 'enemy artillery and ground attack planes exacted substantial casualties', after which 'the exhausted companies went over to the defence'.

The situation remained much the same on the 10th and 11th, with the Americans engaging in a series of holding attacks. Harmel, quite rightly, began to realise that his enemy was intent on advancing east rather than north, and that their efforts against his Division were designed principally to prevent him interfering with that advance. By the 12th, when the Frundsberg received the order to withdraw, it was, according to Tieke, down to eight serviceable tanks, its 21st Regiment numbered only 500 men, the 22nd Regiment a mere 250, the Pioneer and Reconnaissance Battalions, 150 and 350 respectively and the 10th SS Artillery Regiment could field only twenty-five guns, eight of which were self-propelled. The 10th SS Flak Battalion had nine 88mm guns and one each in the 37mm and 20mm categories.

During the period 13 to 17 August, Harmel's men withdrew, first to positions north of Domfront (which fell to the Americans on the 14th), then to a front covering Lonlay and Briouze, and finally to Fromentel. They were on the flanks of the main American advance and constantly involved in fighting off American probes. Details of these actions are sketchy, though of minor importance, for their enemy was far more intent on reaching Argentan and closing the pincers with the Canadians and Poles than on turning north. Alençon fell to the Americans on the 12th and the German force which had been intended for a major counter-attack, included in which was the Frundsberg, had to be committed instead to the defence of Argentan. During the night of the 17th, the remnants of the Frundsberg finally crossed the Orne at Putanges and went into an assembly area near Habloville. All serviceable administrative vehicles were sent on to the east without a pause and most managed to escape the carnage of the Pocket. It is of interest that the British 11th Armoured Division, which had reached Flers the previous night, might well have presented Frundsberg and other important Divisions, such as the Leib-standarte, with a major problem at Putanges had it not halted each night[8] instead of pushing on hard for the Orne crossing. Similarly, if the Guards Armoured Division had not been placed in Army Reserve where the tasks of its fine soldiers:

> were of the most menial. The sappers [engineers] were indeed fully employed on mine-lifting and bridge building in order to open the main roads to traffic but, apart from the few men required to give them local protection in these tasks, the activities of the remainder of the Division were largely confined to the disposal of dead and rotting cows, of which there were many hundreds in the district.[9]

Again, perhaps if the 5th Guards Armoured Brigade had not spent the 18th and 19th attending an investiture parade, listening to a speech by Monty, and then 'resting and sightseeing'[10], more Germans might have been killed or captured.

By the afternoon of the 18th it was too late to think of using the Frundsberg for the defence of Argentan and so the Division was ordered to move east again, this time to the area of Villedieu les Bailleul. Field Marshal Model, who had replaced von Kluge as CinC West the night before[11], had in fact already issued orders that morning for a new front to be established west of the Seine (Map 4). Hausser's Seventh Army, with Panzer Group Eberbach[12] under command, was to make an initial stand in the Trun area and then at Vimoutiers – it was to be behind the Dives river by 20 August and the Touques (Map 8), 5km to the east of Vimoutiers, by the 22nd. II SS Panzer Corps was to use the 2nd Das Reich and 9th Hohenstaufen Panzer Divisions, which were already across the Dives and re-organising to the south-west of Vimoutiers, to launch a counter-attack towards Trun and Chambois with the aim of securing the escape routes. Meanwhile, what was left of the Hitlerjugend and 21st Panzer Divisions would protect the northern flank of the Pocket, while XLVII Panzer Corps, with the 2nd and 116th Panzer Divisions, would continue to hold the south side. The Leibstandarte and Frundsberg were not to be involved in this operation and were to move initially to l'Aigle and then to Mantes on the Seine (Map 9); nor were Panzer Lehr or the 17th

SS Panzer-Grenadier Divisions, whose remnants were to start moving at once to a refitting area east of Paris.

It took until midday on the 19th for the Frundsberg to reach the centre of the chaotic Falaise Pocket. Allied air activity was intense – on the 18th their attack aircraft flew 3,057 sorties, and on the 19th 2,535.[13] On arrival, it became part of the morass of Divisions which had once formed the Fifth and Seventh Armies; and there its men found their Waffen-SS comrades of the Leibstandarte, Das Reich, Hohenstaufen, Hitlerjugend and Götz von Berlichingen Divisions. Contact with II SS Panzer Corps had of course been severed as long ago as 7 August, but at 1430 hours at Villedieu les Bailleul, Harmel was briefed on the overall situation by the commander of the Seventh Army himself, General Paul Hausser. He was not the only important Waffen-SS commander to be briefed by Hausser that day – Teddy Wisch of the Leibstandarte and Kurt 'Panzer-Meyer' of the Hitlerjugend were also there. By then, however, the situation had worsened radically from that pertaining when Model had issued his orders twenty-four hours previously. There was now no chance of making a stand in the Trun area and the planned II SS Panzer Corps counter-attack, of which we shall hear much more later, could not take place until the following day, the 20th. In the meantime, SS Colonel Harmel was to report to the commander of the LXXXIV Corps, Lieutenant General Elfeldt, who would give him orders for a breakout from the Pocket that night by individual KGs.

Harmel met with the Operations staffs of the Leibstandarte and Hitlerjugend Divisions in the forest of Bailleul and made plans for the breakout.

It is difficult to comprehend the hell of the Falaise Pocket at this time. Perhaps three small vignettes will enable the reader to form some sort of picture – the first through English eyes and the other two through German:

> The floor of the valley was seen to be alive ... men marching, cycling and running, columns of horse-drawn transport, motor transport, and as the sun got up, so more targets came to light. ... It was a gunner's paradise and everybody took advantage of it. ... Away on our left was the famous killing ground, and all day the roar of Typhoons went on and fresh columns of smoke obscured the horizon ... We could just see one short section of the Argentan–Trun road, some 200 yards in all, on which sector at one time was crowded the whole miniature picture of an army in rout. First, a squad of men running, being over-taken by men on bicycles, followed by a limber at a gallop, and the whole being overtaken by a Panther tank crowded with men and doing well up to 30 mph, all with the main idea of getting away as fast as they could.[14]

Anyone dying on top of those rolling steel coffins was just pitched overboard, so that a living man could take his place. The never-ending detonations, soldiers waving at us, begging for help – the dead, their faces still screwed up in agony, huddle everywhere in trenches and shelters – the officers and men who had lost their nerve, burning vehicles from which piercing screams could be heard and men, driven crazy, crying, shouting, swearing, laughing hysterically – and horses, some still harnessed to the shafts, screaming terribly, trying to escape the slaughter on the stumps of their hind legs.[15]

A German ambulance column had been shot to pieces by enemy fighter-bombers. It was the most horrible sight of my entire wartime experience. The ambulances were burnt out. In the incinerated vehicles . . . humans, so shrunk by the heat that they were the size of children's dolls. Others lay as they fell, beside the wrecked vehicles and inside, one could easily see that that the victims had been helpless, already wounded men.[16]

(Map 8)

Harmel's general plan for what remained of his Division, now amounting to little more than a reinforced Panzer-Grenadier Regiment, was that it should form into three basic KGs. The first, comprising Brinkmann's 10th SS Reconnaissance Battalion and the few surviving SPWs of 1st/21st SS Panzer-Grenadier Battalion, was to move at 0300 hours on the 20th and secure crossings over the Dives at St Lambert and Chambois. The other KGs, which were to start moving at 0400, were based on the 21st and 22nd Regiments, with the Divisional staff and the 10th SS Pioneer Battalion survivors joining the 21st and the other Divisional units the 22nd. Needless to say, the intense artillery fire, 'fog of war' and the overall chaos of the Pocket soon disrupted the plan and the main KGs did not start their moves until after 0900 hours. Although Brinkmann's KG managed to get to the designated crossing points, his men received conflicting orders from the many senior officers passing through and there was no way the KG could hold them for use by a specific unit. To add to this confusion, many wounded individuals who had become separated from their units – SS men, Luftwaffe paratroopers, ordinary army personnel – littered and blocked the few routes available. Some tried to join the fragmented Frundsberg KGs but unless they had weapons, they were rejected.

The march-out, over the crossings at St Lambert, Moissy and Chambois continued all day. The route leading north-east from Moissy became known as 'The Corridor of Death'. The Divisional rearguard, under the command of SS Lieutenant Colonel Paetsch, the commander of the 10th SS Panzer Regiment, crossed the Dives and reached the comparative safety of the II SS Panzer Corps lines late in the evening. Nevertheless, for the men of the Frundsberg their ordeal was far from over – it was more than 100km to the Seine over which an American Division had already established a bridgehead at Mantes (Map 4).

The Tiger Battalion
(Map 7)

The last time we heard of Weiss's 102nd Tiger Battalion was on 9 August when it was being sent back to join Sepp Dietrich's I SS Panzer Corps, north of Falaise. We know that thirteen of its Tigers passed through Condé at midday on the 9th and that they were refuelled in or near Falaise that night. On the 10th and 11th seven Tigers of the 1st and 3rd Companies were with KG Wünsche of the Hitlerjugend, covering the Caen–Falaise road north of Potigny, and another six of Schroif's 2nd Company were with the 271st Infantry Division east of Thury-Harcourt. The latter claimed five British tanks knocked out on the 10th.

On 12 August an advance by Canadian troops[17] via Barbery, 8km south of Bretteville, ran into four 2nd Company Tigers at Cingal. Five Shermans were knocked out for the loss of one Tiger. On the eastern flank, north of Potigny, the few remaining tanks of the 1st and 3rd Companies, operating with the Hitlerjugend between the 12th and 15th, were heavily engaged against the Canadians trying to advance south towards Falaise on the east side of the Caen road.

On 16 August two Tigers fought with KG Krause of the Hitlerjugend in Falaise itself before withdrawing to Villy, just to the east of the city, whilst others fought against British troops[18] near Nécy, on the Falaise–Argentan road. Hausser's Command Post was located there on the 16th.

The last three operational Tigers west of the Dives 'met their ends' at Nécy on the 19th. By then, SS Lieutenant Colonel Weiss, the Battalion commander, had been severely wounded and taken prisoner near Trun. He had been on his way to Vimoutiers to take command of those Tigers which had managed to withdraw across the Dives and which had been made operational for use in the planned II SS Panzer Corps counter-attack.

The Counter-attack
(Map 8)

On 19 August II SS Panzer Corps was ordered to break into the Falaise Pocket from the north-east and link up with a coordinated escape attempt by the remaining formations of Hausser's Seventh Army[19], including the Leibstandarte and Hitlerjugend Divisions. Bittrich immediately gave orders for the Hohenstaufen to advance in two groups – a flanking group through St Gervais and Louviers and the main body down the Vimoutiers–Trun road. The remains of the 2nd SS Panzer Division Das Reich had been placed under his command on 13 August, and it was ordered to advance on St Lambert and Chambois through Champosoult and Ménil-Hubert respectively. The 102nd SS Werfer Battalion was to be in support.

The attack by Bock's Hohenstaufen was a failure – hardly surprising when one considers that, once again, its exhausted, depleted and ill-supported ranks were being asked to go into the attack without preparation, reconnaissance or even adequate rest. It began at 0400 hours on the 20th, with Gräbner's much weakened 9th SS Reconnaissance Battalion on the northern flank, protecting the main body. Wilhelm Tieke describes events as follows:

> The main body advanced through Champeaux [in fact Hostellerie Faroult on the Vimoutiers–Trun road] and attacked the 1st Polish Armoured Division, which denied it any further progress, on the heights of St Gervais–Champeaux. The few Panzers and StuGs of the Hohenstaufen were unable to push back the enemy tanks and the Panzer-Grenadier Companies that had just escaped from the Pocket were no longer in a condition to attack decisively.[20]

In fact, it was the Canadians[21] who halted the Hohenstaufen; the Poles, as we shall discover shortly, were farther to the east. Despite the failure of the attack, Bock was awarded Oakleaves to his Knight's Cross for his leadership of the Division over this period.

Das Reich's counter-attack was more successful. Its commander, SS Colonel Otto Baum, had taken over only three weeks earlier when the highly decorated Christian Tychsen had been wounded and captured by the Americans. He died a prisoner.[22] Already the commander of the 17th SS Panzer-Grenadier Division, Götz von Berlichingen and the holder of a Knight's Cross with Oakleaves, Baum was to be awarded Swords for his part in the coming battle.

Das Reich advanced on three routes. The Der Führer Regiment, under Otto Weidinger, with two SS Panzer-Grenadier Battalions of about 120 men each and probably six tanks, including at least one Panther, took the Fresnay–Champosoult–Coudehard–St Lambert road. The 2nd SS Reconnaissance Battalion, with some assault guns of the Divisional Sturmgeschütz Battalion, moved through Survie towards St Pierre-la-Rivière to provide flank protection, and the Deutschland Regiment, also with two weak SS Panzer-Grenadier Battalions took the Mardilly and Ménil-Herbert road with St Pierre-la-Rivière as its objective. The number of tanks and assault guns available to Das Reich in this counter-attack is unclear. Unit records mention only one Panther and two Mk IVs; though on the day *after* the attack the Division had fifteen tanks and assault guns on strength and it seems likely that more than six participated on 20 August.

Unknown to the Das Reich KGs, General Maczek's 1st Polish Armoured Division was barring their way. On Point 262 (North) – known to the Poles as 'Maczuga' (The Mace), but better known as Mont Ormel – there were over eighty tanks, some twenty anti-tank guns and 1,500 infantry-men, and at Coudehard Boisjos, 2km to the north of Coudehard, there was another infantry Battalion with an anti-tank company. The important feature, Point 262 (South) was, however, unoccupied. Also unknown to the Germans was the fact that the Poles were isolated and running short of fuel, food and ammunition.

SS Captain Werner's 3rd SPW Battalion led the Der Führer advance, with the tanks, Weidinger's command group and the 2nd Battalion fol-lowing. No opposition was met in the early stages and there was no interference from enemy aircraft. The KG ran into literally hundreds of Germans soldiers pouring out of the Pocket.[23] At about 0900 hours the first resistance was encountered. SS Captain Zwörner's 2nd SS Panzer-Grenadier Battalion was deployed into woods on the east of the road to protect the southern flank and, after artillery and mortar fire was brought in against Mont Ormel and the Boisjos position, the advance continued. Fortunately for Weidinger, the Polish tanks were basically facing towards the escape routes from the Pocket and could not deploy easily against his advance. In one well-recorded incident, a Panther with the KG picked off five Polish Shermans on Mont Ormel. They were all side-on to the German tank.

By early afternoon Weidinger's KG had secured the important road fork 1km north-east of Coudehard and this led to claims that it had 'opened' the Falaise Pocket. In fact, it had never been fully closed. Owing to confusion, lack of coordination, incompetence and worries about 'Blue on Blue' incidents, no Allied infantry were deployed on the 5km stretch of the Dives river between Magny and Moissy (a stretch which could be waded in certain parts by men on their feet) and the vehicle crossings at Magny, St Lambert and Moissy, although interdicted by indirect fire, therefore remained open.

According to Otto Weidinger[24], it was at this point, after he had cap-tured the road fork north of Coudehard, that he was ordered by Baum to continue his advance towards St Lambert and Chambois. He believed, however, that if he did this his KG would become isolated and caught in the Pocket, and he goes on to say that he ignored the order, remaining north of Coudehard and Mont Ormel until 1600 hours. At that time Weidinger judged that no more troops were escaping from the Pocket through his sector and he began a successful withdrawal to the north-east. In contradiction, a Polish report says that as late as 1700 hours, Grenadiers and Mk IVs penetrated into their perimeter on Mont Ormel and that it took until 1900 hours to expel them. The Germans are said to have lost three Mk IVs in this fighting.[25]

The Deutschland KG began its move at 0520 hours but it is said that the heavily wooded and difficult nature of the country west of Mardilly slowed the advance to only 500m in two hours. The Germans claimed that their 'battalions were fired at by Shermans from the 1st Polish Armoured Division, but these were attacked and destroyed at close range'. They go on to say that the KG reached St Pierre-la-Rivière by 1530 hours and 'opened' the Pocket. This author finds the report of the fighting with the Polish tanks difficult to accept. There was not one anywhere near St Pierre-la-Rivière (the farthest point of the KG Deutschland advance). The nearest Polish tanks were 4km away on Point 262 (North). Nevertheless, this is no reason to doubt the claim that the commander of the Regiment's 2nd SS Panzer-Grenadier Battalion, SS Lieutenant Macher, was wounded for a twelfth time on this day. A day later came the news that he had been awarded Oakleaves to his Knight's Cross.

Later on the 20th, the Deutschland KG also withdrew to the north-east, covered by SS Major Ernst Krag's 2nd SS Reconnaissance Battalion with its assault guns and an Army Panther unit which had attached itself to his group during the breakout.

By 2000 hours the following day, the gap between St Lambert and Chambois was finally sealed. The last battle of Normandy was over. Three weeks later, when the 15th Scottish Division passed through the Pocket, its soldiers were shocked by what they saw:

> Everywhere around there was the slaughter, destruction and stench of war. Upturned tanks, smashed armoured cars, burnt-out transport lined every road. Paths for single-line traffic had been bulldozed through the mess of stranded vehicles and corpses. Noteworthy, even in this museum of the macabre was 'Dead Horse Alley', where for seven miles, the carcasses of horses and mules were piled high in the ditches – and the stench was unbelievable. Such was the 'Killing Ground' of Falaise.[26]

The 21st Army Group's 2nd Operational Research Section carried out an intensive investigation of the area enclosed by the towns and villages of Pierrefitte–Argentan–Chambois–Vimoutiers–Trun–Pierrefitte (Map 7), the 'inner' Pocket or 'the Shambles' as it is called in its official report.[27] It found 3,043 German vehicles – 187 tanks and assault guns, 252 artillery pieces, 157 light armoured vehicles, 1,778 trucks and 669 'cars'; most of the tanks had been destroyed or abandoned by their crews. Many more vehicles and pieces of equipment had of course been lost or abandoned during the Fifth Panzer and Seventh Army's retreats across Normandy, including a further 300 tanks and assault guns.[28]

It is impossible to give accurate figures for German personnel losses. The best are probably those of Hermann Jung[29] and Chester Wilmot[30], who both calculated that 10,000 Germans lay dead and 50,000 were taken prisoner. Of the senior commanders, Paul Hausser, although wounded, escaped, as did four of the five Corps commanders, including Bittrich, and twelve of the fifteen Divisional commanders, including Wisch of the Leibstandarte, and Kurt Meyer of the Hitlerjugend. As we have already heard, the commanders of the 2nd, 9th and 10th SS Panzer Divisions also survived the Falaise Pocket fighting.

In the period 1 to 23 August, the First Canadian Army suffered 12,659 casualties – 7,415 Canadians, 3,870 British and 1,374 Poles.[31]

It is also difficult to determine total casualty figures for the Normandy fighting. The 21st Army Group War Diary for 29 August says there were 83,045 British, Canadian and Polish ground casualties, including 15,995 killed. According to Carlo D'Este, in his admirable book, *Decision in Normandy*, 125,847 American soldiers were listed as killed wounded or missing, including 20,838 killed. This comes to a total of 208,892 Allied casualties. In the case of the Germans, Chester Wilmot[32] has a figure of 183,663, but other historians come up with much higher figures, usually in the region of 200,000 killed, wounded or missing and another 200,000 taken prisoner.

NOTES

1. The author can find no reference to such an action in British or Canadian records.
2. Basically 4 Armd Div.
3. Allied Air Forces flew 2,029 attack sorties on 17 Aug – AEAF Ops Summary No. 211 dated 18 Aug 44.
4. Lt Col Koszutski's 2nd Armd Bn, with infantrymen of the 8th Bn mounted and an a/tk Coy.
5. Tieke, *In the Firestorm of the Last Years of the War*, p. 190.
6. Ibid., p. 191 & Harzer, MS # P-162.
7. This is the only detailed account of the Frundsberg's actions at this time known to the author.
8. 11 Armd Div War Diary, 16 Aug 44.
9. Rosse, *The Story of the Guards Armoured Division*, p. 79.
10. 5 Gds Armd Bde War Diary, 18 & 19 Aug 44.
11. Hitler suspected von Kluge of trying to negotiate with the Allies during a time he had been out of touch with his Headquarters on the 15th. He was ordered to report in person to the Führer but on the 18th, during a flight home, this holder of the Knight's Cross with Oakleaves and Swords committed suicide by taking cyanide.
12. On the afternoon of 9 Aug, Hitler sacked the commander of the XLVII Pz

Corps, Hans von Funck, and created Pz Gp Eberbach. It comprised the XLVII and LVIII Pz Corps.
13. AEAF Ops Summaries No. 212 dated 19 Aug 44 & No. 213 dated 20 Aug 44. Thereafter, the near impossibility of identifying specific ground targets caused the air effort to be switched farther east to the Seine and its approaches.
14. Bellfield & Essame, *The Battle for Normandy*, p. 209.
15. Senior Sgt Erich Braun of 2 Pz Div.
16. Tieke, op. cit., p. 190.
17. Of the 2 Inf Div & 2 Cdn Armd Bde.
18. 53 Inf Div.
19. Hausser himself had been reported missing, and so on the 20th the Seventh Army was placed under command of the Fifth Pz Army, then located near Rouen.
20. Tieke, op. cit., p. 197.
21. 4 Cdn Armd Bde, part of 4 Cdn Armd Div.
22. For details see Mark Bando's book, *Breakout at Normandy*.
23. The Adjutants of the 3rd Bn and Der Führer Regt estimated 8–10,000.
24. Weidinger, *Comrades to the End*, p. 330.
25. Stanislaw Grabowski (Polish veteran) to author 29 Aug 96.
26. Martin, *History of the 15th Scottish Division 1939–1945*, p. 110.
27. PRO WO 106/4348.
28. Ibid.
29. Jung, *Die Ardennen Offensive 1944–45*.
30. Wilmot, *The Struggle for Europe*, p. 424.
31. Stacey, *The Official History of the Canadian Army in the Second World War, Vol III, The Victory Campaign*, p. 271.
32. Wilmot, op. cit., pp. 386 & 424.

CHAPTER XI

Normandy to Holland: 21 August – 8 September

Dives to Seine

(Map 9)

As early as 17 August all the non-essential vehicles of II SS Panzer Corps had been ordered to withdraw across the Orne and the Dives and a significant number had therefore survived the carnage of the Falaise Pocket. As they withdrew north-east from Vimoutiers, the Divisions were thus able to link up with some of their transport and take into use numerous other vehicles that had been abandoned with minor break-downs. Combat vehicles were a different matter. Few reliable figures survive but it is recorded that the 9th SS Panzer Division had only nine tanks or StuGs, and the 10th seven, on 21 August.[1] In terms of manpower, both the Hohenstaufen and Frundsberg had increased their fighting potential by picking up the many armed soldiers coming out of the Pocket who were only too willing to join an organised formation. According to the Chief of Staff of the Hohenstaufen[2], his Division had strength of about 6,000 men when it began its withdrawal towards the Seine, and Wilhelm Tieke says the Frundsberg was more or less the same.[3]

Immediately following the disaster of the Falaise Pocket, the German commanders in northern France faced another crisis – how to prevent a further encirclement and the destruction of more than 150,000 troops between the Dives and Seine rivers. Field Marshal Walter Model had taken over as CinC West on 18 August and Sepp Dietrich had been made the temporary commander of the Fifth Panzer Army. Heinrich Eberbach had assumed command of the Seventh Army after Paul Hausser had been wounded during the breakout from the Pocket.

In order to achieve the Allied aim of destroying the German forces west of the Seine, the American 12th Army Group, which had already reached the line Dreux–Chartres–Orléans by 16 August, was ordered to attack north-east, whilst the British 21st Army Group on its left was to advance as rapidly as possible towards Rouen. On 18 August, in fulfilment of this directive, an American Division moved on Mantes, which had been left unguarded when the German troops guarding the Seine crossings in that sector had been sent, on Hitler's orders, to cover the direct approach to Paris. The following day the Americans ran into a scratch force made up from elements of the Leibstandarte and Hitlerjugend[4] SS Panzer Divisions and three other divisions, which were protecting the southern flank along a line from l'Aigle, through Verneuil and Dreux, to the Seine at Mantes. Although this force may have delayed the Americans' advance and misled them as to the real German strengths in the area, they still reached the river on the 19th. The following day they established a bridgehead on the north bank – at the very time the men of the Hohenstaufen and Das Reich were counter-attacking back towards the Falaise Pocket, 100km to the west. A second crossing was seized by the Americans 50km south-east of Paris on the 23rd. This meant that the only way out of this second 'Pocket' was across a 60km stretch of the Seine between Louviers and the sea – a stretch on which no bridges remained except one badly damaged railway bridge at Rouen.

On the 21st Army Group front things did not move so quickly. The British, Canadians and Poles were, to some extent, still tied up in the Falaise Pocket, but one has to wonder why, at this critical time, the British Guards Armoured Division was still 'resting'. As one young officer wrote:

Beyond Condé-sur-Noireau, still well behind the battlefront, we ... passed the time peacefully. There was even a Brigade boxing tournament . . . The world may have wondered why, in the midst of a war, soldiers on the same side should fight each other instead of the enemy.[5]

Fortunately, when Bradley suggested that his men should advance into the 21st Army Group sector to cut off the German retreat, Montgomery agreed. An American armoured Division was immediately ordered to strike north from Verneuil into the German flank. It advanced 60km in four days but on the 24th ran into heavy opposition in the Louviers area, where a determined German force, including a relatively strong Hitlerjugend KG, reinforced by parts of the Leibstandarte, was protecting the sixty or so ferries and pontoons being used to evacuate the remnants of the Seventh Army across the lower Seine.[6]

The same thing happened to the Canadians. They reached Orbec on the 22nd, but when they tried to move north-east the following day, they too ran into strong opposition. This time it was provided by units of the Hohenstaufen located north of the town, the 10th SS Reconnaissance Battalion at Bernay and other elements of the Frundsberg on both sides of Brionne. These small KGs held on until the night of the 24th, when they withdrew to the general area of Bourgtheroulde, near Rouen. On arrival, they found their comrades of the 2nd SS Panzer Division Das Reich already in position between there and Elbeuf. While these KGs of both I and II SS Panzer Corps, and another from the 116th Panzer Division under Lieutenant General von Schwerin, protected the southern flank of this new 'Pocket', the three German infantry Divisions which had been located in the coastal areas to the north of Falaise carried out the equally vital task of defending the Seine crossing points against the British and Canadians[7] advancing from the west. These German Divisions, and others which had been sent, far too late, from the Fifteenth Army in the Pas de Calais to reinforce the Seventh Army, had been forced to withdraw towards the Seine as their left flank was exposed by the Allied advance.

The German resistance in the Louviers–Elbeuf area on the 23rd and 24th enabled the majority of the 150,000 German soldiers east of the Dives to escape across the Seine, though most of their heavy equipment had to be abandoned. In that regard, Dietrich is quoted as saying, 'the Seine crossing was almost as great a disaster as the Falaise Pocket.' Nevertheless, the War Diary of the Fifth Panzer Army records that 25,000 vehicles of all types were transported across the Seine between 20 and 24 August, and many more would cross before the end of the month. Although some 300 barges were destroyed in air attacks between 16 and 23 August, bad weather after that made it difficult for the Allied Air Forces to maintain their attacks on the ferry and pontoon sites. Two recollections will suffice to give some idea of the difficulties involved in the crossing:

On the march to the Seine, little groups formed by chance. Ours was one of them. It contained elements of the Regimental staff and the Signals platoon, about ten SPWs .... and several personnel carriers and trucks. By bartering with other elements of the Army, we got fuel and supplies.... We reached the huge bottleneck at Elbeuf on the Seine. The bridges there were no longer useable.... A naval unit had built a ferry out of two barges ... but they could not be persuaded to take us across in the day. A second attempt, however, with bottles of cognac and other drinks was more successful. By noon we were loaded up and on the river ... We were in the middle of the Seine when a Lightning [US fighter-bomber] appeared. The plane flew over us though, and continued on its way. It must have had other orders.[8]

All approaches to Oissel [where the Frundsberg was ordered to cross] are hopelessly jammed, the columns in double and triple rows, radiator to radiator, wheel to wheel ... We estimate 5,000 to 7,000 vehicles. Rain rules the day and keeps away the enemy airplanes. Beside the roads, in woods and fields small fires flicker. Boxes, files, apparatus and rubbish are burning. What seemed valuable a few hours ago is now set on fire ... Officers of the Waffen-SS direct traffic with pistols in hand ... A clearing group of about eight men stationed on the bridge has the assignment of tipping any vehicle off that has broken down.[9]

On 25 August Paris was liberated and it was obvious to the German commanders that there was no chance of making even a temporary stand on the Seine. Model ordered an immediate withdrawal to the Somme.

The overall situation facing CinC West at this time was later described by his Chief of Staff, General Günther Blumentritt:

The Seine was expected to hold for at least seven days and then defensive positions to have been taken up through ... Amiens–Soissons–Châlons ... But there were no troops available to man either the Seine or the Somme, and the Allies cut through France with little opposition.[10]

As just mentioned, the crossing point for the Frundsberg was Oissel, 6km south of Rouen. With Brinkmann's 10th SS Reconnaissance Battalion securing the damaged railway bridge and an emergency crossing farther downstream, and the 10th SS Flak Battalion providing air defence, the heavy vehicles of the Division crossed during the night of the 25th and the main body completed its crossing on the evening of the 27th.

The emergency bridge that the 10th SS Reconnaissance Battalion had discovered and put back into service, was reserved by the Division and held against the attempts of other units to barge their way in.[11]

The Hohenstaufen's crossing point was nearby at Duclair, 17km north-west of Rouen. SS Lieutenant Colonel Otto Meyer, the commander of the Division's Panzer Regiment, was put in charge and maximum use made of a 100-ton steam ferry run by the Navy (already mentioned). 20mm flak guns provided air cover. Beside the naval ferry, the 9th SS Pioneers manned pontoon ferries, rubber rafts and assault boats for foot soldiers and light vehicles. On the 24th good flying weather enabled the Allies to destroy the Elbeuf bridge and damage those at Oissel and Rouen. In the late afternoon a formation of Thunderbolts attacked the Duclair ferry. Meyer was killed and his Adjutant, SS Captain Frölich, had his arm torn off. Lieutenant Suhrkämper of the 9th SS Pioneers was also killed. Despite these attacks the bulk of the Hohenstaufen crossed to the relative safety of the north bank by nightfall on the 29th with the Division's SS Panzer-Grenadiers, led by SS Lieutenant Colonel Zollhöfer, holding a bridgehead south of Duclair, strongly supported by batteries of the 102nd SS Werfer Battalion, also south of the river. The last Company[12] of SS Panzer-Grenadier Regiment Hohenstaufen, after being cut off and still with Zollhöfer present, constructed emergency ferries from fuel cans and timber and crossed the Seine that night. The two Werfer Batteries, under SS Captain Nickmann, crossed early on the 30th, blowing the ferry behind them.

And what of the Tigers of the 102nd SS Heavy Panzer Battalion? Few details are available. Several are said to have taken part in the II SS Panzer Corps counter-attack on 20 August in the Champosoult area but they seem to have achieved little; one still stands at Vimoutiers. Wilhelm Tieke says that all the remaining Tigers had to be blown up by their crews before they could get back across the Seine[13], but this is contradicted by Wolfgang Schneider[14], who says that five crossed the river on the 28th. Four of those were destroyed by their crews near the Somme and the last one abandoned by its crew in Belgium after they rendered the gun useless. Nevertheless, we shall hear more of this Battalion in the later stages of WWII.

Before we describe the final withdrawal from France, it is of interest to mention the incredible losses incurred by the Germans in the Normandy campaign. The respected German historian, Hermann Jung, gives the following figures, taken from the files of the Berlin Headquarters of the Army Surgeon's Department, for the period 6 June to 31 August – 23,019 killed, 198,616 missing or captured, 67,240 wounded. If anything, these figures can be said to be on the conservative side.

It is also worth recording that, despite all the criticisms of Montgomery, it had been a brilliant victory for the Allies – the Seine had been reached two weeks ahead of schedule and the whole campaign fought in accordance with *his* original strategy.

The Seine to the Dutch Border
(Map 10)

On 27 August, well before the Hohenstaufen had completed its crossing of the Seine, Bittrich ordered Bock to form a new KG and move it as soon as possible to the Amiens sector of the Somme. Bock himself was to continue on towards the Dutch border with the Divisional administrative units and all non-essential vehicles. By 29 August a KG of about 3,500 men, under the command of the Divisional Chief of Staff, SS Lieutenant Colonel Walther Harzer, had been formed in the area of Barenthin and was on the move, through Neufchâtel, to Amiens. Having been stationed in that part of France for nine months in 1943–44, the region was well known and the move went smoothly with the KG arriving in Amiens on the 30th. Harzer's KG comprised the remnants of the 19th and 20th SS Panzer-Grenadier Regiments, Gräbner's 9th SS Reconnaissance Battalion (at about 50% strength), the Divisional Escort Company, the 9th SS Flak Battalion, a company of the 9th SS Pioneer Battalion, a motorized artillery platoon, and a small administrative and supply group.[15] These men were unaware that only the day before the British had broken out of their bridgehead across the Seine at Vernon and that the leading units of the 11th Armoured Division were only 60km away.

Also on the 27th the Frundsberg, whilst re-organising in the woods east of Rouen, had been ordered to send all non-essential vehicles and administrative personnel as far to the east as possible, and move its combat-effective elements at once to the Beauvais area. It arrived there on the 29th, only to receive orders from LXXXI Corps to continue moving, via Montdidier, to the Bray–Peronne sector of the Somme. This continued movement was necessary because the VII Corps of the US First Army had already reached Soissons and Patton's Third Army columns had captured Châlons and were approaching Reims. The next day American troops broke through in the Laon area and threatened to encircle all German troops west of that city, including those of II SS Panzer Corps. Harzer's Hohenstaufen KG hurried out of Amiens that afternoon, under orders to take up a blocking position north-west of Laon, but it was too late for any effective action. Rather than risk being outflanked by the US armoured columns streaming north, Harzer withdrew during the night of 1 September through St Quentin to Cambrai.

Meanwhile on the 30th, Heinz Harmel, who had lost contact with LXXXI Corps, ran into Fritz Kraemer, the acting commander of I SS

Panzer Corps. After being briefed on the worsening situation, he agreed to take up defensive positions on the Somme at Bray and Peronne. At this time his comrades in I SS Panzer Corps were already in action 100km to the east around Marle and Rozoy.

Harmel organised his Division into two main KGs and a command group made up from part of Brinkmann's SS Reconnaissance Battalion and the Divisional Escort Company. KG Paetsch, under the 10th SS Panzer Regiment's commander, deployed at Peronne with the remnants of his own unit and sub-units of the Reconnaissance, Flak and Pioneer Battalions. KG Schultze set up at Bray with what was left of the two Frundsberg SS Panzer-Grenadier Regiments, plus a light artillery group and another part of the Reconnaissance Battalion. He also took the precaution of deploying part of his force on the Amiens–Albert road.

By the evening of 31 August, it was reported that the British had captured Amiens (and General Eberbach, the commander of Panzer Group West, in the process) and that with three of the four bridges in the town still intact, their tanks were advancing on Albert. Schultze decided he had no option but to pull back to defend Albert, while Paetsch held on at Peronne. When this situation was reported to I SS Panzer Corps, the order came back that Albert was to be held to the last man. KG Paetsch continued to defend its sector until the night of 1 September, when it fell back on Cambrai, where, as we shall hear, Harzer's Hohenstaufen KG was taking up positions to cover the main road into Belgium. That same night KG Schultze was surrounded in Albert; its commander was killed along with many of his men. The survivors fought their way out of the town on the 2nd.

It was then that Model, in order to avoid yet another encirclement, ordered a general retreat to a new line running from the mouth of the Scheldt, through Antwerp and then along the Albert canal to Maastricht and the West Wall (Siegfried Line) (Map11).

As part of the plan to facilitate this general German withdrawal into Belgium, Harzer's KG Hohenstaufen was ordered[16] to hold Cambrai throughout the hours of daylight on the 2nd. He still had a reasonably strong KG, including the eighteen 88mm guns of the 9th SS Flak Battalion which had managed to catch up with him after deployment with the Fifteenth Army. While SS Pioneers destroyed as many of the bridges over the three canals in the area as possible, Harzer deployed his flak guns to cover the main approach roads from Bapaume and Arras. Men of the Reconnaissance Battalion watched the northern and southern flanks and SS Panzer-Grenadiers provided close protection for the guns. The positions were prepared by 0900 hours. Harzer[17] himself later gave a vivid description of the daylong battle which followed between '200' American tanks and accompanying infantry and his KG.[18] He claimed that by 1500 hours forty enemy tanks had been put out of action and that only the

Escaut canal finally blocked the American advance. His account undoubtedly exaggerated the numbers of tanks involved; but it is clear that by the end of the day, after he had ordered his men to withdraw, KG Hohenstaufen had lost most of its 88mm guns, Harzer and his command group were cut off, and the enemy had captured Cambrai. It is also certain that by nightfall British troops moving on the axis Arras–Brussels had reached the Belgian border near Lille, and that American units, having bypassed Cambrai, were nearing Mons. One British and two American Corps were lining up on the Belgian frontier.[19]

The battle of France was at an end and for the surviving Germans it was now a race to reach the safety of the West Wall – or, as we shall see, the relative safety of the Dutch river and canal system.

A 'snapshot' of part of the Hohenstaufen's retreat down the Cambrai–Mons road that night is graphically portrayed by Wilhelm Tieke:

The highway was overcrowded with fleeing vehicles. At the end of the stream drove the last prime movers of the 4th SS Flak battery with its sixteen survivors, among them many severely wounded. Shortly before Valenciennes, one of the vehicles broke down. The badly wounded were no longer able to endure the torments of the hasty retreat. The courageous Battery medical orderly, Gottschalk, remained with those wounded who could no longer be transported and went into captivity with them.[20]

By the morning of the 3rd, the depleted Hohenstaufen KG was back in Mons where it found a new addition to the Division – SS Captain von Allwörden's 9th SS Panzerjäger Battalion. This recently organised and equipped unit had arrived from East Prussia only a few days previously, but had lost a number of its twenty-one Jagdpanzer IVs both in an Allied air attack as they were being unloaded from railway flat-cars and then later in a series of short rear-guard actions which had followed in the Mons area.

With the remnants of the Hohenstaufen withdrawing just ahead of them, the tank columns of the British Guards Armoured Division liberated Brussels on the 3rd. Bock's men had passed to the south of the city, helping themselves to food, ammunition, weapons and vehicles as they passed the numerous army supply depots in Belgium. By 5 September they reached a new II SS Panzer Corps assembly point at Hasselt where, to their surprise, they found Harzer with his small command group. Their escape from Cambrai had been remarkable and had involved flying British and American flags on their vehicles and looting the many unattended Allied trucks they found parked on the roadsides. On the 7th the retreat towards the Maas–Scheldt canal continued on two routes through Venlo and Eindhoven and eventually, on the 8th, the exhausted remnants of the 9th SS Panzer Division reached their final assembly area in the peaceful and rich countryside near Arnhem.

We left the Frundsberg KGs on the night of 1 September retreating towards Cambrai. On reaching the town, Harmel received orders to take his Division back to the II SS Panzer Corps assembly area at Hasselt. The subsequent move back was difficult and chaotic, with other units clogging the roads and a constant fear of Allied encirclement. Like their comrades in the Hohenstaufen, Harmel's men salvaged vehicles abandoned by other groups and weapons and equipment from deserted army depots – their biggest find being a train halted on an open stretch of track during a bombing raid. It was without guards and loaded with twelve brand new howitzers. Harmel's artillerymen helped themselves.[21]

On 4 September Harmel met his Corps commander, Bittrich, and received new orders. He was to occupy an 8km wide defensive bridgehead west of the Maas and Albert canal at Maastricht. Fortunately for the Frundsberg, Harmel received a change of orders twenty-four hours after arriving there and, during the night of the 5th, he was told to go back to the new Corps assembly and re-fitting area north and east of Arnhem. The Division arrived there on 7 September. With both Divisions of II SS Panzer Corps in the Arnhem area, the scene was set for another momentous chapter in the history of the Second World War.

NOTES

1. Tieke, *In the Firestorm of the Last Years of the War*, p. 200.
2. Harzer, MS # P-162.
3. Tieke, op. cit., p. 200.
4. Made up from sub-units left behind in Belgium in June and skeleton units which had been pulled out of Normandy early for re-manning and re-equipping.
5. Wilson, *The Ever Open Eye*, pp. 57–8.
6. More detailed accounts of these actions between the Dives and the Seine can be found in the author's book, *Men of Steel: I SS Panzer Corps The Ardennes and Eastern Front 1944–45*.
7. I British & II Cdn Corps.
8. Lehmann & Tiemann, *The Leibstandarte IV/1*, p. 230.
9. Tieke, op. cit., p. 203.
10. Interview Blumentritt – Milton Shulman, Feb 45.
11. Tieke, op. cit., p. 205.
12. Formed from the Recce Coys of 19 & 20 SS Pz-Gren Regts.
13. Tieke, op. cit., p. 203.
14. Schneider, *Tigers in Combat II*, p. 333.
15. Harzer, MS # P-162.
16. It is not clear who gave this order. Tieke implies that Harzer, unable to make contact with LXXXI Corps in Cambrai, decided on his own initiative to defend the town. In the circumstances, this seems unlikely.
17. Harzer, MS # P-162.

18. Tieke repeated it in his book, pp. 216–18.
19. The British XXX and American VII & XIX Corps.
20. Tieke, op. cit., p. 218.
21. Harmel in an interview with Robert Kershaw, 27 Oct 87. Dugdale, *Panzer Divisions, Panzer Grenadier Divisions, Panzer Brigades, Vol I, Part 1,* p. 93, says twenty guns were obtained.

CHAPTER XII

MARKET GARDEN

Introduction

There is a widespread belief that the main reason for the failure of Operation MARKET GARDEN was the unexpected intervention of two Waffen-SS Panzer Divisions. Comments such as, 'the presence of a Panzer Corps in the area of Arnhem' and 'the presence of such a strong German armoured force in the Arnhem area'[1] are in fact totally misleading. As is a map in a famous book on the Operation, which shows Bittrich's II SS Panzer Corps being moved over 200km, from west of Coblenz in Germany to the Arnhem area, during the period 5/6 September.

The impression is also often given that the Divisions of Bittrich's Corps, the 9th and 10th SS Panzer, were merely resting and refitting in the Arnhem area, with little or no mention being made of their basic weaknesses in manpower and equipment. Their soldiers are variously described as 'fanatical products of the Hitler Youth organisation' or 'superbly equipped, battle-hardened SS veterans' and, even as late as 1977, the commander of XXX Corps, Lieutenant General Brian Horrocks[2], was still describing their 'overwhelming superiority in firepower'.[3]

Fortunately, readers are already aware of the true state of the Hohenstaufen and Frundsberg Divisions at the time of MARKET GARDEN. This will perhaps help them to understand why Montgomery did not consider the presence of II SS Panzer Corps in the Arnhem area significant enough to cancel or alter the Operation.[4] After the war, he accepted full responsibility for this decision. In his *Memoirs* he wrote, 'The 2nd SS Panzer Corps was refitting in the Arnhem area, having *limped up there after its mauling in Normandy* [author's italics]. We knew it was there'.[5]

No attempt will be made in this history to present the full details of the fighting, with numerous personal reminiscences. This has already been done in an exemplary manner by one of the participants, Geoffrey Powell, in his *The Devil's Birthday,* and by Martin Middlebrook in *Arnhem 1944 The Airborne Battle;* also by Cornelius Ryan in *A Bridge Too Far.* The

German side of the story has been well set out in Robert Kershaw's *It Never Snows in September*.

This account, being the history of II SS Panzer Corps, will of necessity have to repeat the basic scenario of MARKET GARDEN, but as far as possible it will concentrate on the parts played by the integral Divisions of that Corps over the period 8 to 26 September 1944.

Owing to the confused fighting and the fact that few records were kept by those directly involved, it is difficult to be precise about the timings of certain events during MARKET GARDEN. The timings that follow, particularly for events north of the lower Rhine, should therefore be treated with caution. It is also of note that German/Dutch time[6] was one hour ahead of that used by the Allies.

The Germans
(Map 11)

In the early afternoon of 4 September, the day the port of Antwerp fell to the British[7], General Kurt Student, the head of the German Parachute Arm, was telephoned in his Berlin office by General Jodl, head of the OKW Operations Staff, and briefed on the situation in Belgium and Holland. He was told that General von Zangen's Fifteenth Army of over 80,000 men was now isolated in north-east Belgium and could escape only by sea across the Scheldt estuary. Even if this were achieved, heavy losses were likely and it would take at least three weeks. The remnants of the Seventh Army were being pushed rapidly towards the Ardennes and the only troops available to deploy into the resulting 120km gap along the Albert canal between Antwerp and Maastricht were those of a Division badly depleted in the Normandy fighting[8] and a 'Fortress' Division which had been guarding the Dutch coastline.[9] Another 'Kranken' Division[10], composed of convalescents and men who had been invalided out of the army and then brought back, was currently entraining at Aachen in Germany and would be available in about two or three days.

Student was then told that he was to command a new Army, which would be subordinated to Field Marshal Model's Army Group 'B'. It was to be known as the First Parachute Army and its mission was to build and hold a new defensive front on the line of the Albert canal. Jodl ended his call with the words, 'This front is to be held at all costs'.

The First Parachute Army was to comprise all garrison, training and administrative troops already in Holland[11], the Divisions just mentioned and a new force of some thirty thousand Luftwaffe personnel. The latter, to the amazement of the OKH, had been volunteered by Hermann Goering and consisted of six Parachute Regiments in various stages of training or re-equipping, and some ten thousand Luftwaffe air and ground crew whose operations or training had been curtailed because of fuel shortages.

By any standards, what followed was an incredible feat of improvisation and organisation. The precise details are complicated and, thankfully, need not concern us. Suffice to say that by 13 September an organised, albeit fragile, defensive line had been established from the mouth of the Scheldt to Maastricht. It was manned by a mere thirty-two ad hoc battalions, stemming from four basic Divisions[12] (three of the Parachute Regiments had been grouped together to form the 7th Parachute Division under the command of a General Erdmann), backed by twenty-five assault guns. Nevertheless, a basic screen had been formed behind which further KGs could be formed and deployed. As Horrocks put it after the war, the Germans had: 'made one of the most remarkable military recoveries in history'.[13]

It was whilst this basic defence structure was being established that, on 8 September, the last elements of Willi Bittrich's II SS Panzer Corps arrived in central Holland – only nine days before the biggest airborne operation in the history of warfare was to be launched into the same area by the Allies. This administrative area, north of the lower Rhine and Waal rivers, was the responsibility of General Friedrich Christiansen, Armed Forces Commander Netherlands.

At this time the 9th SS Panzer Hohenstaufen and 10th SS Panzer Frundsberg Divisions numbered little more than about 6,000 to 7,000 men each[14], only about half of whom were combat troops; the remainder were in the Divisional service and supply units.

Model had hoped to replenish both II SS Panzer Corps' Divisions in Holland in order to create an Army Group reserve; in view, however, of problems in providing personnel replacements and bringing new equipment from the Reich, OKW gave orders that one Division should remain in Holland and the other return to Germany for refitting. Bittrich, whose Headquarters was in Doetinchem, 30km east of Arnhem, decided to keep the Frundsberg forward and send his old Division home. Accordingly, the Hohenstaufen was ordered to send all technical and non-essential personnel home at once, hand over two battalions of SS Panzer-Grenadiers, three artillery batteries and all its remaining heavy equipment to the Frundsberg, and to form its remaining personnel into combat-ready 'alarm' units, available for action up to the very moment they were due to leave for Germany. Not surprisingly, the Hohenstaufen veterans were loath to hand over their trophies, vehicles or indeed any weaponry which might come in useful again and so, by removing the tracks from their few remaining tanks and SPWs and important parts from their weapons, they managed, with Harzer's connivance, to hold on to a reasonable amount of equipment.

By the time the Allied air armada appeared over Holland on 17 September, Harzer's Division comprised a Divisional Escort Company, eleven Alarm Companies, Gräbner's 9th SS Reconnaissance Battalion of some 400 men with thirty-one armoured cars and SPWs, and the 9th SS Panzer Regiment, a Regiment in name only, with a mere handful of armoured vehicles on strength.[15] Ten of the Alarm Companies had been formed from what was left of the Division's Panzer, Panzer-Grenadier and Artillery Regiments and Pioneer and Flak Battalions. The eleventh came from SS Captain von Allwörden's 9th SS Panzerjäger Battalion, some 120 men, still waiting for their replacement Jagdpanzer IVs.[16] All the Companies were positioned in the approximate triangle formed by the towns of Arnhem, Apeldoorn and Zutphen. Harzer's Headquarters, with its Staff, Signals and police units, and his Divisional Escort Company were in Beekbergen, near Apeldoorn, 20km north of Arnhem. On 17 September, as the Allied aircraft approached Arnhem, the 9th SS Reconnaissance Battalion was on parade at Hoenderloo to see the Divisional commander present its commander with a Knight's Cross for his part in the recent Normandy fighting.

What of the Frundsberg? Harmel set up his own Headquarters with the Divisional Escort Company in Ruurlo, 50km east of Arnhem. Brinkmann's 10th SS Reconnaissance Battalion, partly motorized with nine armoured cars and twenty-five SPWs and partly on bicycles, together with the sixteen Mk IVs and four StuGs of the 2nd/10th SS Panzer Battalion[17], were located nearby. Harmel was still missing his 1st/10th SS Panzer Battalion – it was in Grafenwöhr, Germany, awaiting the issue of its Panthers. Two Hohenstaufen Panzer-Grenadier Battalions and three batteries of the 9th SS Artillery Regiment, including one with 100mm cannons had, however, as we have heard, been transferred to his command. The Grenadier Battalions were SS Captain Dr Segler's 2nd/19th and Battalion Euling, formed from the Divisional Replacement unit, and known initially after its commander, SS Captain Karl-Heinz Euling, but later as the 1st/22nd. These extra Battalions brought the 21st and 22nd SS Panzer-Grenadier Regiments up to two Battalions each – Battalions being made up of a heavy (support) company and two rifle companies. Harmel also had two well equipped, but only partly motorized, artillery Battalions, plus SS Pioneer and Flak Battalions, both weak in numbers and equipment and not fully motorized – exact details are unknown. All the Frundsberg units were stationed north of the Rhine and between Arnhem and the German frontier.

Soon after his arrival in the Arnhem area on 6 September, Harmel was warned that he might have to provide KGs at short notice for use on any threatened part of the front, and four days later he was ordered to provide a strong KG as a reserve for the First Parachute Army. The KG was named KG Heinke, after its commander SS Major Heinke, and comprised two SS Panzer-Grenadier Battalions (SS Captain Dr Segler's and another from the 21st Regiment), companies from Brinkmann's Reconnaissance and Tröbinger's Pioneer Battalions, and an artillery Battalion. Arriving south of Eindhoven on the 10th, Heinke took under command SS Captain Roestel's 10th Frundsberg SS Panzerjäger Battalion, with twenty-one Jagdpanzer IVs and a company of twelve 40mm towed anti-tank guns, which was already in the area.

On the eve of the Allied airborne landings, as the Frundsberg continued its refitting programme, Harmel kept an appointment at the Waffen-SS Command Headquarters in Berlin – a sure sign that no enemy activity was expected in the Arnhem area. His intention was to discuss reinforcements and he succeeded in obtaining an undertaking that 1,500 Waffen-SS replacements would be forthcoming in the near future. In his absence, SS Lieutenant Colonel Paetsch, the commander of the almost tank-less 10th SS Panzer Regiment, took command of the Division.

Walther Model, the commander of Army Group 'B', had set up his own Headquarters on 15 September (just a day before the opening of MARKET GARDEN) in the Hartenstein Hotel in Oosterbeek, a mainly residential area of about 10,000 people, a few kilometres to the west of Arnhem. Some commentators have suggested that Model's selection of this location for his Headquarters was based on a foreknowledge of the impending Allied landings. They ignore that fact that his operational area (Army Group 'B') ran from the Scheldt to the Moselle river. Since it was highly unlikely that the Allies would attempt an advance through the Ardennes and the Eifel, Model needed to find a location between the Scheldt and a line drawn from Aachen to Cologne. Anywhere between the Maas and Rhine rivers or near the Ruhr was clearly unsuitable. Seen from this perspective, the Arnhem area makes complete sense. It was a sheer coincidence that he found himself less than 4km from one of the British landing zones (LZs) and that Bittrich, the remaining units of the Hohenstaufen and the whole of the Frundsberg Division were within 50km of all the LZs.

The Allies

(Map 4)

By the beginning of September 1944, the Allied advance towards Germany had been halted through a lack of supplies, particularly fuel. As George Patton is alleged to have said, 'My men can eat their belts, but my tanks have gotta have gas!'. No major port east of the Seine had been captured, the British supply lines stretched 500km, all the way back to Bayeux, and those of the Americans ran even farther, 600km, through Paris to the Cotentin peninsula. There were sufficient stocks of all commodities already ashore in Normandy but the problem remained of getting them to the forward units in the quantities needed. The first supply

SONS OF THE REICH

train reached Paris from the Normandy bridgehead on 30 August, but the bulk of the supplies still had to be transported by road. As Chester Wilmot put it in *The Struggle for Europe*:

> The destruction of the bridges over the lower Seine, the devastation of the marshalling yards and the general disruption of the railway system – all the result of the air attacks which had contributed so greatly to the German defeat in Normandy – now saved the Wehrmacht from pursuit by the full strength of Eisenhower's forces.[18]

It is, however, of interest that after the war Horrocks wrote:

> I believe that if we had taken the chance and carried straight on with our advance instead of halting in Brussels the whole course of the war in Europe might have been changed. On 3rd September we still had 100 miles of petrol per vehicle, and one further day's supply within reach ... When we were allowed to advance on 7th September, the situation had worsened drastically ... Within three days, instead of being on a fifty-mile front ... the Corps was concentrated on a five-mile front engaged in a tough battle. The Guards Armoured Division took four days to advance over the next ten miles up to the Meuse–Escaut Canal.[19]

He confirmed this view in the television series, *World At War*, when he said that after liberating Brussels on 3 September:

> We were ordered to halt. The reason was that we were outrunning our supplies. Now this was wrong ... They [he did not specify who, but he was presumably speaking of Dempsey and Montgomery] should have taken a chance ... We could have brushed straight through them [the Germans]. We could have bounced the crossings on the Rhine. Unquestionably. It was, to my mind, a very bad mistake.

It is also clear that shortages of fuel and ammunition did not prevent Patton, with Bradley's blessing, resuming his offensive on 5 September. There seems little doubt therefore, that had the British pushed on into Holland on 4 September, instead of waiting until the 7th, the consequences for the Germans might have been disastrous. The fact that they did not is even more surprising in view of the SHAEF Intelligence Summary for the week ending 4 September. It describes the German Army in front of Second British Army as, 'no longer a cohesive force but a number of fugitive battlegroups, disorganised and even demoralised, short of equipment and arms'.

In addition to the supply problem, there was at this point in the

104

campaign, a serious argument between the Allied leaders over whether to proceed on a 'broad front', with Montgomery's 21st Army Group advancing in the north towards the Ruhr and Bradley's 12th Army Group moving at the same time in the south towards the Saar, or in a 'single thrust' by just one of the Army Groups. The relative merits of each case need not concern us – they have been set out clearly in the many books describing the strategy of the European campaign. From our point of view only the results of the argument matter. On 4 September, the day Hitler re-appointed Field Marshal von Rundstedt as CinC West, Eisenhower issued a Directive, which ordered Montgomery's Army Group and two Corps of the First US Army to 'reach the sector of the Rhine covering the Ruhr and then seize the Ruhr'. At the same time, the Third US Army and one Corps of the First US Army were to 'occupy the sector of the Siegfried line [West Wall] covering the Saar and then seize Frankfurt' (Map 1).

(Map 11)

This Directive, whilst apparently giving Monty a 'green light', presented him with a problem. Surprising though it may seem, he had insufficient forces to exploit the German weaknesses on his front. Of the fourteen divisions and seven armoured brigades in his 21st Army Group, only two Armoured Divisions were ready to continue the advance – the Guards and the 11th of Horrocks' XXX Corps. The six Canadian Divisions had been given the essential task of clearing Le Havre (Map 4) and the Pas de Calais ports (Map 10). XII Corps was committed to pushing the German Fifteenth Army back to the Scheldt estuary and VIII Corps was still immobilised back at the Seine owing to a lack of transport.[20] Nevertheless, XXX Corps was told to push on and on 4 September Antwerp was captured by the 11th Armoured Division. Unfortunately, by the time it was ordered to cross the Albert canal and advance towards 'S-Hertogenbosch a day later, all the bridges had been blown. This failure to seize the Albert bridges on the 4th has been criticised[21], but the Divisional War Diary, whilst agreeing that it might have been possible, claims that there had been no indication in any previous orders of this proposed thrust to the north. It points out that its commander, Major General 'Pip' Roberts, thought his job was to secure the vital dock facilities rather than the bridges, and that the next move would be towards Germany rather than Holland. In either case, however, the Albert canal had to be crossed and Antwerp screened in order to prevent it coming under German artillery fire, so the criticism would seem to have been justified. Certainly, when a small bridgehead was eventually established two days later, it was so strongly counter-attacked by the Germans that neither a bridge nor ferry site could be constructed and Roberts was told to move his

Division to the east, towards Beeringen (sometimes spelled Beringen), where the Guards had already crossed the canal.

In the afternoon of 10 September armoured cars[22], operating in front of the Guards Armoured Division, by-passed German positions at Hechtel and 'bounced' an intact bridge over the Albert canal at Neerpelt. By last light an armoured group[23] had secured a bridgehead and the foothold required by Monty for his 'single thrust' towards the Ruhr was a reality. One can only wonder at what might have happened at this stage if the situations had been reversed and the Germans had established such a bridgehead against a British Army in headlong retreat? Or, if George Patton or one of his senior commanders had been in command at this moment? As one young British Guards officer wrote later, echoing the words, already quoted, of his Corps commander:

> We wondered why we were sitting still. Having captured a bridge against minimal opposition, it would be reasonable to suppose that the advance would continue at once, keeping up the momentum and not giving the Germans any time to organise defence ... From 11 to 16 September, the Guards Armoured Division sat immobile for six whole days, giving the Germans ample time to organise ... The delay apparently arose because the Chiefs of Staff, with the enthusiastic backing of pushy airborne generals, had decided on an airborne operation ... There have been claims that the six days delay [before the resumed advance of the Guards Armoured Division] was also necessary to allow supplies of food, fuel and ammunition to reach the ... units of 30 Corps ... But the supply situation was never desperate ... if necessary, air drops of supplies could have been organised. Instead of that, a priceless opportunity was thrown away.[24]

That same afternoon Montgomery and Eisenhower met at Brussels airfield. After an acrimonious opening discussion, during which Ike had to remind Monty that he was a subordinate, the Supreme Commander eventually approved the latter's latest plan. This envisaged the First Allied Airborne Army, Eisenhower's only strategic reserve, securing crossings over the Maas, Waal and lower Rhine, and then British armour advancing rapidly to outflank the West Wall and the Ruhr. The plan had the added advantage that, if successful, it would cut off all the Germans in western Holland, including those of the Fifteenth Army.

Both generals were aware of the need to launch the operation quickly – before the Germans could build up their defences in Holland and in order to eliminate the V2 rocket bases in the west of the country.[25] There was, however, at least in the minds of the senior British commanders, a major problem to be solved before the plan could be put into operation. With the Americans now turning east, the right flank of the proposed

British armoured thrust would be exposed and Dempsey considered it essential to bring up VIII Corps to protect it. Monty agreed and warned Eisenhower that unless he could be provided with more transport to move the Corps and build up the necessary stocks, he could not launch the combined airborne and armoured assault before the 23rd. The threat worked and on the 12th Montgomery was promised that 1,000 tons of supplies a day would be delivered to Brussels by road and air. He was also led to believe[26] that the American drive on the Saar would be halted and that the bulk of Bradley's Army Group resources would go to his First US Army, which would co-operate closely with Montgomery's 21st Army Group. On this basis, Monty gave the go-ahead for Operation MARKET GARDEN to be launched on 17 September. In fact, with Bradley's agreement, the attacks by both the First and Third US Armies continued, and it is interesting to note that as far as the senior American commander responsible for Operation MARKET (the airborne part of the Operation) was concerned, these attacks were seen as an essential part of the overall plan:

> Stonewall Jackson said: 'Mystify, mislead, and surprise.' That's what we tried to do in our advance build-up for Operation MARKET. In order to make the enemy believe that our supply situation would make it impossible for the Northern Group of Armies to advance, patrols of the 30th Corps were withdrawn as much as ten miles in some instances. At the time the US First and Third Armies made attacks into Germany and across the Moselle.[27]

The First Allied Airborne Army was under the command of US Air Force Lieutenant General Lewis H Brereton, formerly the commander of the US Ninth Air Force. His deputy was British Lieutenant General 'Boy' Browning and he had a mixed staff of Americans, British and Poles. Brereton's Army had two Corps, one American and one British. XVIII US Airborne Corps, under Lieutenant General Matthew Ridgway, comprised the 82nd and 101st Airborne Divisions, and the 17th Airborne which was still assembling and not yet operational. The 82nd and 101st were experienced Parachute Divisions, having dropped and fought in Sicily and, more recently, Normandy. I British Airborne Corps, under the command of the 'double-hatted' General Browning, consisted of the 1st British Airborne Division, the 6th British Airborne Division, which had just been pulled out of Normandy after three months' fighting, and the 1st Polish Independent Parachute Brigade Group. The 52nd (Lowland) Division was in reserve and available to be flown in as the situation demanded or permitted, but it was not officially part of Browning's Corps.

The soldiers of the First Airborne Army were 'like coins burning in

SHAEF's pocket'. Since early July most of them had been on stand-by for a whole series of operations, none of which had been launched, either because the ground troops had moved so quickly that the proposed operation became redundant or because the necessary aircraft were being misused for aerial re-supply.[28] It was therefore with relief and enthusiasm that Brereton and his staff began their planning to employ three and one-third airborne Divisions, to be dropped in three different areas and, hopefully, to be relieved within three days by the ground troops of Horrocks' XXX Corps.[29]

The aim of Operation MARKET was to capture and hold the five major crossings over the canals and rivers lying across the British Second Army's axis of advance between and including Eindhoven and Arnhem, as well as a number of other strategic objectives. Command was vested in the British deputy commander of First Airborne Army, 'Boy' Browning. The decision to give him command was surprising for three reasons: first, because 75% of the troops taking part in the operation were to be American; second, because the US Corps commander, Ridgway, was far more experienced; and third, because Browning's Headquarters was basically a planning, administrative and training organisation and certainly not a command Headquarters. Inevitably, it had no means of communicating with the two American Divisions and this meant that US manpower and equipment had to be added to it at the last minute. In addition, the imposition of this Headquarters on the ground meant that as soon as the ground troops linked up, there would be two Corps Headquarters controlling operations in the same area. In the event, Browning and his Headquarters, due to totally inadequate communications, played little part in the forthcoming battle and wasted thirty-eight gliders badly needed by the 1st British Airborne Division to increase its first lift.

The basic plan was for the US 101st Airborne Division to seize the several bridges and defiles between Eindhoven and Grave and the US 82nd Airborne to capture the Maas crossing at Grave, at least one of the four bridges over the Maas–Waal canal and then, after securing the high ground between Nijmegen and Groesbeek (described in the Operation Order as an 'imperative' task) to capture the vast Waal road bridge in Nijmegen.[30] At the same time, the 1st British Airborne Division, later aided by the 1st Polish Independent Brigade Group, was to capture 'the bridges over the lower Rhine at Arnhem with sufficient bridgeheads to facilitate the passage of XXX Corps.'[31] The XXX Corps Operation Instruction made it clear that its advance (Operation GARDEN), was to be carried out 'at maximum speed' and included the prophetic words: 'the success of this operation depends largely on speed of advance'.[32]

It will not have escaped the reader's notice that the extent of the missions given to the American Divisions was infinitely greater than that given to the British and Poles. The latter had to hold on for a longer period but at least their operational area was limited in size. In an attempt to deal with this problem, the Americans reinforced each of their Divisions with an extra Regiment, giving them four rather than the normal three.[33] Even so, the sheer magnitude of their operational areas virtually guaranteed that the Americans would have problems holding them until they were relieved. It should be noted that the 101st Airborne Division was to come under the command of XXX British Corps on landing.

The armoured advance of just over 100km was to be made on a very narrow front. There was only one main road, varying in width between six and nine metres, for most of the way.[34] VIII Corps would be responsible for right flank protection and XII Corps would advance on the west side of XXX Corps' axis with a similar task. Once north of Arnhem, three bridgeheads were to be established[35] across the IJssel, at Zwolle, Deventer and Zutphen, followed by an advance to the east into Germany.

The risks inherent in Operation MARKET are well known and need not be repeated in detail. Put simply, they were: first, the weather; second, insufficient aircraft and gliders to carry out all the landings in one lift; third, dropping the British Airborne Division a long way from its objectives; and fourth, carrying out the assault in daylight. The first two were connected. The Air Commander for the operation[36], with Brereton's support, decided that no more than one lift should be flown each day. This was due not only to the difficulties of navigating and keeping formation in the pre-dawn or post-dusk flights which would have been necessary if two separate lifts had been launched in a single autumn day, but to there being insufficient ground staff to turnaround and repair aircraft in the time available. The knock-on effect of this decision was that three consecutive days of good flying weather would be needed to land the whole force.

The decision to land the British so far from their primary objective, the road bridge[37] over the lower Rhine at Arnhem, has been the subject of much post-war discussion and not a little criticism – especially from those who took part. When the American commander of the 82nd Airborne Division, Jim Gavin, heard General Urquhart describe the plan, he exclaimed, 'My God, he can't mean it!'[38] In fact, it was the senior RAF officer involved who made the decision.[39] His reasons were that the extensive open area immediately south of the Rhine road and rail bridges was unsuitable for large-scale glider operations and that his aircraft would have to fly out over the flak batteries known to be north of Arnhem. Allied Intelligence believed there were 112 light and forty-four heavy flak guns in the Arnhem area, with a particularly heavy concentration around Deelen airfield, 10km north of the city. In fact, following an Allied bombing raid on 3 September, which rendered the airfield temporarily unusable, those defending the airfield had been withdrawn. This was confirmed by photographic reconnaissance on 6 September but this critical information was apparently unknown to those responsible for the aerial delivery of the troops.

Urquhart's request that at least part of his Division should be landed near the bridges as a coup-de-main force, which had the support of the Commander Glider Pilots,[40] was also rejected. This decision was made in spite of the fact that there was sufficient space for just such a force, including gliders, in three separate places: one, on the good meadow land south of the rail bridge; two, immediately south of the road bridge; and three, north of the river between the Heveadorp ferry and the railway bridge. Even more puzzling is the fact that this rejection was made in contradiction of the fact that the Polish Brigade were due to be dropped south of the river, less than 2km from the road bridge, on Day 3 of the Operation. This LZ had been Urquhart's first choice. It seems the lessons and the outstanding success of the Pegasus Bridge operation in Normandy had been forgotten or were ignored.

Montgomery later took full responsibility for allowing Urquhart's men to be dropped too far from the bridge:

> The airborne forces at Arnhem were dropped too far away from the vital objective – the bridge ... I take the blame for this mistake. I should have ordered Second Army and 1 Airborne Corps to arrange that at least one complete Parachute Brigade was dropped quite close to the bridge, so that it could have been captured in a matter of minutes and its defence soundly organised with time to spare. I did not do so.[41]

Dempsey, the Second British Army commander, appears to have been unaware of even the basic framework of the operation. After a post-battle, personal briefing by Roy Urquhart on 28 September, he wrote in his Diary:

> The Parachute Brigade had to march 8 miles to Arnhem to secure the bridge and the Air Landing Brigade had to remain 8 miles from Arnhem to guard the drop zone for the subsequent arrivals. *As was almost inevitable* [author's italics], the enemy came in between the two Brigades, each of which became isolated.[42]

The associated problems and dangers of sending a complete Corps of over 20,000 vehicles down a narrow corridor, across a series of six major canals and waterways, to link up with the airborne bridgehead 100km away, were obvious. In anticipation of this problem, 9,000 British and Canadian Royal Engineers and all the bridging resources of the 21st Army Group, involving some 5,000 vehicles, were brought together for the Operation.

Before describing the fighting in MARKET GARDEN, it is important to address the subject of close air support. This had been a major factor in the Allied victory in Normandy, but it was to be sadly lacking in Holland, particularly north of the lower Rhine. There were two reasons: first, the ground attack aircraft of the Second Allied Tactical Air Force based on the Continent were forbidden to operate over the battle area when troops or supplies were being landed or dropped; and second, the lack of reliable communications between the troops on the ground and their supporting aircraft. The first reason is understandable owing to the danger of 'blue on blue' engagements between fighter escorts and close support aircraft. Unfortunately, this restriction, when coupled with the poor weather conditions which pertained during much of MARKET GARDEN, meant that close air support was often restricted to just a few hours, usually late in the day. The second reason resulted from an over-complicated command and communications system, lack of operator training and poor equipment. In the event, neither of the two air-support signals units that landed with the 1st British Airborne Division ever established radio contact with any outside Army or Air Force formations. As the Divisional commander was to write later:

I was much annoyed at the disappointingly meagre offensive air support we were receiving. The resupply boys' gallantry had been magnificent, but the fighters were rare friends. We needed the Typhoons and Tempests to carry out rocket attacks on the Germans' gun and mortar positions.

It is surprising that he did not go on to complain about the almost total lack of planned interdiction attacks against German troop movements, particularly those of their armoured forces, towards the airborne bridgeheads and XXX Corps corridor. The German Intelligence Summary, covering MARKET GARDEN and issued by CinC West on 1 October, stresses this point, 'Our own troop movements in spite of good weather were practically undisturbed'.[43]

NOTES

1. Both taken from the script of an official 1994 British Army Battlefield Tour.
2. Knighted in 1945.
3. Horrocks, *Corps Commander*, p. 104.
4. He knew of this through ULTRA, aerial reconnaissance and Dutch Resistance reports.
5. Montgomery, *Memoirs*, p. 297.
6. When the Germans took over in May 1940, they introduced German time throughout Holland and Belgium. All clocks had to be put forward 100 minutes at midnight on 16 May.

7. The British advance was so swift that the German Garrison did not have time to sabotage the vital port facilities.
8. The 85th under Lt Gen Chill.
9. The 719th under Lt Gen Sievers.
10. The 176th under Col Landau.
11. These included a Hermann Goering Luftwaffe Regt, a Dutch SS Guard Bn, an SS NCO School, an SS Pz-Gren Depot & Reserve Bn, some ad hoc Luftwaffe bns formed from ground personnel fleeing from France and naval bns formed from non sea-going personnel and coastal arty units.
12. 85, 176 & 719 Inf Divs and 7 Para Div.
13. Horrocks, *A Full Life*, p. 232.
14. Tieke, *In the Firestorm of the Last Years of the War*, p. 222 & Dugdale, *Panzer Divisions, Panzer Grenadier Divisions, Panzer Brigades, Vol I, Part 1*, p. 79.
15. Estimates vary from five Panthers (Dugdale) to four Mk IVs, eight StuGs & three Command Mk IIIs.
16. The unit had only two JgPz IVs and a few towed 75mm guns left after the withdrawal from Belgium.
17. Dugdale, op. cit., p. 89.
18. Wilmot, *The Struggle for Europe*, p. 472.
19. Horrocks, *A Full Life*, pp. 205–6.
20. All its 2nd line transport & half its 1st line had been reallocated to XII & XXX Corps.
21. Wilmot, op. cit., p. 486.
22. A Sqn, 2 HCR.
23. 2 Armd IG & 3 IG; the bridge was christened 'Joe's Bridge' after the commanding officer of 2 Armd IG, Lt Col J O E 'Joe' Vandeleur.
24. Wilson, *The Ever Open Eye*, pp. 94–5.
25. The first V2 rocket had fallen on London two days previously.
26. By Lt Gen Bedell Smith, Eisenhower's Chief of Staff. The Confirmatory Notes of this meeting made it clear that the daily airlift of 500 tons would have to be suspended during the period of the airborne operation.
27. Brereton, *The Brereton Diaries*, p. 342.
28. Ibid., p. 343.
29. The original plan for seizing the river and canal crossings in Holland, Operation COMET, had foreseen the use of only the 1st British Airborne Div & the 1st Polish Airborne Bde.
30. The Waal is 250m wide, the bridge over it 600m long, with a centre span of 250m & four smaller spans supported by four massive stone buttresses.
31. Guards Armd Div, 43 & 50 Inf Divs, 8 Armd Bde & a Dutch Bde.
32. Appx B to XXX Corps Op Order No. 24 of 15 Sep 44.
33. American & British airborne divs normally comprised two para inf & one glider inf regts/bdes – each of three bns. The only major differences between them were in arty – US divs had thirty-six 75mm pack hows & twelve 105mm hows to the British twenty-four 75mm pack hows. On the other hand, 1 Airborne Div had sixteen 17-pdr a/tk guns, whereas the largest calibre available to the Americans was 57mm.
34. The width of a Sherman tank was 2.6m.
35. By the Gds Armd, 43 & 50 Inf Divs.
36. US Maj Gen Paul L Williams, commander IX Troop Carrier Command, USAAF.
37. This bridge had been blown by the Dutch on 10 May 40 and the rebuild was not completed until Aug 44, just before MARKET GARDEN.

38. Gavin, *On to Berlin*, p. 150.
39. Air Vice Marshall L N Hollinghurst, commander 38 Group.
40. Col Chatterton.
41. Montgomery, op. cit., p. 297.
42. Dempsey Diaries, PRO, WO 285/10.
43. ULTRA decrypt, PRO, HW 1/3249.

CHAPTER XIII

MARKET GARDEN:
Sunday 17 September

The Aerial Assault

(Maps 11 & 12)

Operation MARKET began during the night 16/17 September with 200 Lancaster heavy bombers and twenty-three Mosquitoes attacking four airfields in the general area of the proposed drop zones. Shortly after first light, fifty-four more Lancasters and five Mosquitoes attacked known flak positions and a further eighty-five Lancasters and fifteen Mosquitoes pulverised the German coastal batteries on Walcheren. Then, just before the troop-carrying aircraft flew in, 816 Flying Fortresses, escorted by a total of 373 Mustangs and P-47s, attacked an additional 117 known flak positions on the approaches to and near the LZs.

The airborne armada, protected by 919 Tempests, Spitfires, Mosquitoes, Thunderbolts, Mustangs and Lightnings, comprised 1,544 troop-carrying aircraft and 478 gliders. Beginning at 1025 hours, they took off over a period of one and a half hours from seventeen US and nine British bases in England.

In the early afternoon the sky became black with aircraft; wave after wave of Dakotas and gliders passed over, their escort fighters darting around them like destroyers round a convoy. It was an uplifting sight.[1]

At 1240 hours the first parachutes opened in the Arnhem area as the men tasked with marking the main LZs began their descent.[2] At 1300 hours the first gliders landed and fifty minutes later the main drop began.[3] Casualties were comparatively light – no British transports were lost, although thirty-eight gliders failed to arrive (mainly due to broken tow-ropes), and the Americans lost thirty-five transports and thirteen gliders, mainly due to flak. Seventy-three fighters and bombers failed to return.

Only thirty Luftwaffe fighters were seen and, not surprisingly, seven of these were shot down.[4]

A good impression of what it was like for the men of the First Allied Airborne Army was given in a broadcast by Ed Murrow, of Columbia Broadcasting, as he flew in one of the transport aircraft:

> I'm standing here, looking down the length of the ship now. The crew chief is on his knees back in the rear, talking into his inter-com ... They're looking out of the window rather curiously, almost as if they were passengers on a peacetime airline. You occasionally see a man rub the palm of his hand across his trouser leg.... Our fighters are down there, just almost nosing along the hedgerows, searching the little villages, and are up above us and on both sides. This is the real meaning of air power ... I look back at the door and the pilot gives me the clenched fist salute, like a boxer ... Tracers are going across us, in front of our nose ... In just about forty seconds now our ship will drop the men ... There they go! ... Fifteen ... sixteen. Now every man is out! ... The whole sky is filled with parachutes. They're all going down so slowly. It seems as though they should get to the ground much faster.

A less heroic, but perhaps more realistic, account of what it was like for those taking part was given by a doctor with a Battalion which landed on the second day:

> One of our gliders lay forlornly like a child's broken toy in an empty playground. There was nobody to be seen in the vicinity and I wondered what had happened to its occupants as we were still some way from the target ... As though in a dream I saw a black puff appear immediately below an adjacent Dakota ... Then another nearby aircraft started to bank slowly out of formation, dragging a wing with dirty yellow flames and black smoke trailing from the engine, and with horrible inevitability spiralled slowly earthwards. I could imagine all too clearly the scene inside; imprisoned paratroopers waiting like ourselves for the order to jump, while the pilot fought to keep height and on course. It was already too late, half way to the ground before men appeared, jettisoning themselves with hopelessly slow precision. The first dozen or so parachutes opened, the last few had no time, and as the Dakota hit the ground and burst into flames a man was still framed in the doorway. I noticed the red light flick on but could not have been more alerted and ready to jump than now, for it was requiring all my will-power to control an overwhelming desire to push past the two men in front of me and escape into the air.[5]

Both Field Marshal Model and General Kurt Student had expected a major British ground offensive towards Eindhoven, but Operation MARKET came as a complete surprise. When the SS commander in Holland had suggested to Model the possibility of an airborne landing, he had replied, 'Montgomery is a very cautious general, not inclined to plunge into mad adventures.'[6] In addition, the fact that the American First and Third Armies, much to Montgomery's irritation, were still attacking towards the West Wall and across the Moselle, did much to divert German attention – as intended by Eisenhower. It was therefore, quite literally, a 'bolt from the blue' when the Allied air armada began to appear over southern Holland, and it was to be some hours before the senior German commanders became aware of the size and scope of the whole operation. Fortunately for them, however, an American glider was shot down near Student's Headquarters during the early afternoon and 'a few hours later the orders for the complete airborne operation were on my desk'.[7]

As well as the heavy attacks against airfields and known flak positions, all the barracks in and around Arnhem were hit – except the one intended for use by the Headquarters of the 1st British Airborne Division.[8] Considerable damage was caused in the city and its surrounding area and 249 civilians were killed.[9]

Inevitably, reports of hundreds of Allied aircraft flying north-east began to arrive at the various German Headquarters but, surprisingly, few of the duty officers on this warm, sunny afternoon appreciated their significance. One senior officer who did was the commander of II SS Panzer Corps, Willi Bittrich. He received his first enemy situation report at 1330 hours (German time) and ten minutes later issued a warning order to both his Divisions. The Hohenstaufen was told to assemble its units for operations to secure Arnhem and its bridge and engage enemy air-landings to the west of the city. The Frundsberg was told to assemble for an immediate move to Nijmegen, where it was to occupy the bridges over the Waal and then advance to the southern edge of the city.

Bittrich's warning order was quickly passed on by the Hohenstaufen Headquarters to Harzer at Hoenderloo, 12km north of Arnhem, where, it will be recalled, he had been presenting Gräbner with his Knight's Cross. As a result of this quick reaction, all the Hohenstaufen Alarm Companies received orders within one hour, and sixty minutes later Gräbner's 9th SS Reconnaissance Battalion had some thirty armoured cars and SPWs ready for action. Bittrich then transferred the Battalion to the Frundsberg and ordered Gräbner to proceed at once towards Nijmegen to secure the route for that Division. This involved using, and if necessary securing, the Arnhem and Nijmegen road bridges.

Another officer to react quickly, but of necessity rather than instinct, was Field Marshal Model. His Sunday lunch in his quarters at the Hotel Tafelberg in Oosterbeek had been suddenly interrupted by a series of heavy explosions, followed by his Chief of Staff returning from a telephone call to announce that they had one to two enemy parachute divisions landing on top of them. Model drove immediately, via his own logistic Headquarters, to see Bittrich in Doetinchem. He arrived there at about 1500 hours and, after a short briefing, agreed Bittrich's immediate counter-measures. He then placed Bittrich and his Corps under his own direct command.

At 1600 hours Bittrich issued firm orders for the Hohenstaufen to assemble in the Velp area, just to the north-east of Arnhem, from where it was to be prepared to attack 'the enemy who has landed in Oosterbeek in approximately brigade strength'.

At 1730 hours Bittrich issued more detailed orders. In general terms, the Hohenstaufen was told to eliminate the landings west of Arnhem and the Frundsberg those around Nijmegen. It was stressed that the enemy in the Nijmegen area was to be prevented from linking up with those at Arnhem.

In the meantime, Model had returned to his own Headquarters and, as more information began to emerge of the Allied landings and of the British XXX Corps attack out of its Neerpelt bridgehead, he was able to come up with a positive plan for dealing with what was by then a crisis situation. He divided the relevant area into three sectors, roughly equating to those of the Allies. He allocated responsibility for dealing with the British ground attack at Neerpelt and the American 101st Airborne Division's landings in the Eindhoven area to the First Parachute Army. To help Student with this mission, he promised him additional forces. These will be described later.

The Nijmegen sector and the US 82nd Airborne Division's LZs became the task of Military District VI. This was an Administrative Command, totally unsuited for controlling combat operations. Nevertheless, as will become apparent, it was able to play a significant part in the forthcoming fighting. Again, Model promised its commander additional troops in the form of a complete Parachute Corps which would be brought from the Cologne area.

Responsibility for the British landings in the Arnhem sector remained with Bittrich's II SS Panzer Corps, particularly the Hohenstaufen, but General Christiansen, Armed Forces Commander Netherlands, was given the task of attacking Arnhem from the north and north-west with another ad hoc force, which again will be described later. Further reinforcements were also promised to Bittrich as they became available.

Model issued confirmatory orders to his outline plan at 2315 hours. That such a plan could be initiated at all, and that the necessary forces could not only be earmarked but actually warned in such a short time is, at least to this author, nothing short of incredible.

The Arnhem Sector
(Maps 12 & 13)

Slightly more than 8,900 men of the 1st British Parachute Division[10] had landed during the afternoon of 17 September, virtually without opposition, on three LZs to the north and west of the village of Wolfheze. Their primary objective, the road bridge over the lower Rhine in Arnhem, was nearly 11km away. The British plan was, nevertheless, relatively simple. First, a Reconnaissance Squadron in jeeps would drive along the Ede–Arnhem road to the bridge, remove any demolition charges and then hold on until relieved. Second, a reinforced Parachute Battalion[11] would advance on foot along the north bank of the lower Rhine, capture the railway bridge near Oosterbeek and a floating ship bridge (usually referred to as a 'pontoon' bridge)[12] 4km to its east, and then go on to secure the road bridge in Arnhem, establishing one company at the southern end. Third, another reinforced Parachute Battalion[13] would take the main road into Arnhem, again on foot, and if necessary assist in the capture of the road bridge and hold the northern end. And fourth, a similarly reinforced Parachute Battalion[14] would, on the order of the Brigade commander[15], follow the Reconnaissance Squadron's route on foot and secure the high ground north of Arnhem, with the intention of blocking any German counterattack from the direction of Apeldoorn. Meanwhile the glider-borne force[16] would secure the LZs for the arrival of a second Parachute Brigade[17] and more heavy equipment the following day.

The first thing to go wrong for the British was the failure of the Reconnaissance Squadron to reach the road bridge. After a delayed start, the leading jeep ran into German troops shortly after passing through Wolfheze and was shot up; the remainder of the Squadron, after suffering more casualties, was forced to pull back. The Germans were from SS Panzer-Grenadier Training and Replacement Battalion 16, under the command of SS Captain Sepp Krafft. His unit, soon to be known as KG Krafft, had been bivouacked in the woods north-west of Oosterbeek and as soon as he saw the British parachutes open, he correctly deduced the mission of the British troops. Without further direction, he deployed his 435 men[18] into a blocking position, which ran south-east from Wolfheze and covered the main road and railway line leading into Arnhem from the west. This position was completed by 1530 hours – within an hour and a half of the airborne landings. Perhaps not surprisingly, after the battle of Arnhem, Krafft received a congratulatory note signed personally by Heinrich Himmler.

KG Krafft continued to cause problems for the British trying to advance into Arnhem during the late afternoon. The leading elements of the Parachute Battalion Group[19] following the main road into Arnhem ran into one of its armoured cars at around 1700 hours and, as well as being delayed for an hour, suffered five wounded and lost one of its 6-pounder anti-tank guns. Just before this, in an amazing incident, soldiers of the same Battalion had shot dead the German City Commandant of Arnhem, General Friedrich Kussin. He had responsibility for the defence of the city itself, including its vital road bridge, and was just returning to his Headquarters after a visit to Krafft when his staff car encountered the British paratroopers.

KG Krafft caused further delays to the same Battalion during the evening but, at about 1800 hours, Krafft realised he was being outflanked and decided to withdraw as soon as darkness fell. This happened at approximately 2130 hours. At about the same time, in a decision that has been criticised many times since, the commander of the British Battalion following the main road into Arnhem, decided, with the concurrence of his Brigade commander, to halt his Battalion where it was, in the area of the Hartenstein hotel (now the main Operation MARKET museum) in Oosterbeek (Map 17). A single company, which he had previously detached to the north, was able to get into the western suburbs of Arnhem using the axis of the railway line without opposition and later, during the night, nearly half this company reached the area of the Arnhem road bridge.

By 1730 hours Walther Harzer of the Hohenstaufen knew that KG Krafft was in action against the British and that he had to extend Krafft's blocking line to the north and to the south down to the lower Rhine. He decided therefore to concentrate most of his Alarm Companies under the command of SS Lieutenant Colonel Ludwig Spindler, the commander of the 9th SS Artillery Regiment, and to order this new KG (Spindler) to advance along the main east–west roads through Arnhem. Harzer himself moved into General Kussin's Headquarters in Arnhem.

Spindler's command was made up of over 350 men in two companies from his own 9th Artillery Regiment, some 100 SS Pioneers in SPWs from SS Captain Hans Möller's 9th Pioneer Battalion, the four remaining SS Panzer-Grenadier companies of the 19th and 20th Regiments, and an eighty-five-man force with a single 88mm and one 20mm from the 9th SS Flak Battalion under the command of SS Lieutenant Gropp. The whole KG was to number over 1,000 men. Inevitably, it took time for these individual units to arrive in Arnhem and for them to be formed into a composite KG. By the time Spindler was ready to move west towards Oosterbeek, KG Krafft had already begun its withdrawal and Spindler was therefore forced to take up a blocking position on the western edge of Arnhem, covering the Ede–Arnhem road and Wolfheze–Arnhem railway line. This he did some time before midnight and KG Krafft reached the same line at about 2230 hours.

Two other KGs arrived in the Arnhem area during the afternoon and evening but did not initially form part of KG Spindler. They were KG Allwörden, with about 140 men of the 9th SS Panzerjäger Battalion, supplemented by some 100 naval personnel to make three companies, and KG Harder, under SS Lieutenant Harder, with about 350 dismounted crewmen and administrative personnel from the 9th SS Panzer Regiment and again, some 100 naval personnel to thicken up its three companies. The latter formed up behind and to the south of KG Spindler, but KG Allwörden, which arrived from the Apeldoorn direction with two Jagdpanzer IVs and a few towed 75mm guns, became engaged in a prolonged and fierce battle north-east of Oosterbeek with another of the Parachute Battalion Groups[20] trying to advance towards Arnhem. Finding the Ede–Arnhem road firmly blocked by KG Allwörden, this Battalion diverted through the woods to the south of the road, but by midnight it had suffered over 100 casualties and was less than half-way to its objective. In fact, the commander of this Battalion, tasked with securing the high ground north of Arnhem, had decided with good reason to advance towards the Arnhem road bridge instead.

The most successful British move was by the Parachute Battalion Group[21] that followed the old road into Arnhem, running along the edge of the lower Rhine through Oosterbeek. As already mentioned, it was tasked with capturing both the rail and road bridges, with priority given to the latter, and capturing the German Headquarters in the city. The first opposition it met was a small vehicle convoy, probably a reconnaissance element of KG Krafft, which it quickly eliminated. Then in the early evening, after moving through nearly 5km of woods and meeting only very light opposition, the leading company reached Oosterbeek. At about this time, the armoured cars and SPWs of Gräbner's 9th SS Reconnaissance Battalion were thundering across the main British objective, 5km to the east, on their way to Nijmegen.

The inhabitants of Oosterbeek showered the British paratroopers with gifts in a rapturous welcome, but despite their assurances that all the Germans had withdrawn into Arnhem, sporadic firing soon broke out. The warm welcome and shooting inevitably caused some delay but the advance eventually continued and some time between 1700 and 1800 hours, a platoon managed to get up onto the railway bridge:

> We reached the north end of the bridge and climbed up the embankment. We got there without any trouble. . . . We were running on the metal plates . . . We got about fifty yards and then needed a pause . . . The centre span of the bridge exploded . . . and the metal plates in front of me heaved up into the air.[22]

The demolition ended any real chance of crossing to the south bank of the river and capturing the southern end of the road bridge. Unfortunately, the Battalion had already passed the fully operational Heveadorp ferry and had not been briefed that it was capable of carrying eight jeep-loads of men across the river in a single lift.

The blowing of the railway bridge remains something of a mystery. Who ordered it? According to SS Captain Hans Möller, the commander of the Hohenstaufen's SS Pioneer Battalion, it came as a surprise to him. He claimed later that even 'Bittrich had no idea of any plans [to blow the bridge] . . . [and we were] quite concerned about what was going on in our rear'.[23] This statement clearly contradicts another, which claims that an SS Pioneer Company, 'blew the bridge and withdrew'.[24] It seems most likely therefore that the demolition, which was of a major nature and destroyed the bridge in three places, was carried out by the permanent bridge guard, acting on the orders of the City Commandant, General Kussin. If this was the case, his orders apparently allowed the guard commander to blow the bridge on his own initiative.

At about 1900 hours the British advance towards the road bridge was again held up, this time by heavy machine-gun fire from its left flank. Möller's 9th SS Pioneer Battalion had taken up positions there during the late afternoon and a complete Parachute Company had to be detached to deal with it. This action enabled the remainder of the Battalion[25] to reach and occupy the area at the north end of the Arnhem road bridge by 2000 hours without opposition. It is clear that the German need to use the bridge for the reinforcement of the Nijmegen sector had precluded any attempt to prepare it for demolition. Even if orders *had* been given for it to be prepared, Bittrich would certainly have countermanded them on his arrival at Kussin's Headquarters in the afternoon.

British attempts to move across the bridge failed in the face of fire from the area of one of two 2.8m high towers situated on the bridge, some 50m short of the main span. The Germans had built a wooden structure on top of the western tower to house a 20mm flak gun and a couple of huts to accommodate the twenty or so members of the bridge guard and their stores.[26] Although these guards fled when their ammunition and petrol store exploded after being hit by a round from a PIAT (hand-held anti-tank weapon), the paratroopers were unable to advance any farther across the bridge in the face of continuing German machine-gun fire from the southern end. An attempt by an unknown group of Germans in four lorries to cross from their side shortly after the explosion was halted by the British with numerous casualties. The blazing lorries only added to the general inferno caused by the burning ammunition and petrol store – even the paintwork on the bridge caught fire. By midnight, each side controlled one end of the vital structure but neither could prevail against the other.[27] The British force, which included the 1st Parachute Brigade Headquarters[28], now numbered just over 700 men.

The Nijmegen Sector
(Map 14)

On this same day, 20km to the south of Arnhem, 7,277 paratroopers and forty-eight gliders of the US 82nd Airborne Division, under the command of Brigadier General Jim Gavin, had landed successfully and achieved all their initial tasks. Whilst one Parachute Company captured the vital bridge over the Maas at Grave, other troopers of the same Regiment[29] secured another over the Maas–Waal canal. These actions were completed by 1930 hours. This meant that as soon as the British armour arrived, it would be able to advance straight towards Nijmegen. Meanwhile, the other two Regiments[30], together with the Divisional Engineer Battalion and an artillery Battalion with twelve 75mm howitzers, occupied the strategically vital ground around, and to the south-east of, Groesbeek.[31] In one particularly unfortunate incident, two American paratroopers[32] were captured and summarily executed by a local Gauleiter in the village of Kranenburg, just inside Germany. This caused the local population to flee in fear of reprisals.[33]

The original orders to the 82nd Airborne specified that no attempt was to be made to take the main Nijmegen road bridge until the bridge over the Maas, at least one of those over Maas–Waal canal, and the high ground covering the approaches from Germany at Groesbeek had been secured. Indeed, control of the Groesbeek feature was considered vital to the success of the whole Grave–Nijmegen operation.[34] Accordingly, Gavin had briefed the commander of one of the Regiments[35] responsible for Groesbeek area, that he should only send a Battalion against the Nijmegen bridge if the situation in the Groesbeek area was in hand and only then under the cover of darkness.[36] Since the situation seemed favourable for such an attempt by 1800 hours, the necessary orders were issued and at 2200 hours the move towards the bridge began. Three Companies from two separate Battalions were eventually committed but the leading Companies[37] ran into heavy opposition in the area of the main traffic island in the city and could make no further headway.

It will be remembered that on 17 September Heinz Harmel was in Berlin and control of the Frundsberg was in the hands of SS Lieutenant Colonel Paetsch, the commander of the 10th SS Panzer Regiment; also that Gräbner's 9th SS Reconnaissance Battalion, now under his command, had crossed the Arnhem bridge at 1800 hours with the mission of securing the route to Nijmegen for use by the Frundsberg. Gräbner's Battalion reached Elst (Map 19) at about 1900 hours and continued on to the main Nijmegen road bridge where it met German troops already in position. These troops were a scratch force of about 750 men from various training and reserve units in and around the city, cobbled together by a Colonel

Henke, the commander of a spare Parachute Training Regimental Head-quarters – another perfect example of German initiative and military competence. Henke also ensured that the twenty-nine 88mm flak guns and some additional 20mm weapons, sited to protect the bridges, were capable of firing in a ground role.

Gräbner's orders were to remain in Nijmegen, but it seems that by now he was aware that British troops had reached the area of the Arnhem road bridge. Seeing that the Nijmegen bridge was already secure, he decided therefore to leave some SPWs mounting 75mm guns in Elst and return to Arnhem, leaving KG Henke and others of Military District VI to deal with the 82nd Airborne.

The Eindhoven Sector
(Map 15)

The third component of Operation MARKET, Major General Maxwell Taylor's 101st US Airborne Division, had also been largely successful in fulfilling its missions. By the end of the 17th nearly 7,000 troopers of its three Parachute Regiments[38] had captured all but one of the bridges in the 25km-corridor between Eindhoven and Veghel. This corridor became known to the Americans as 'Hell's Highway'. The only important bridge not to be captured was the one at Son (sometimes spelled Zon) over the Wilhelmina canal. A KG from the Hermann Goering Training Regiment had managed to hold on long enough against part of the US 506th Parachute Infantry Regiment for it to be blown at about 1600 hours. Nonetheless, during the night the Americans crossed the canal on a makeshift bridge and soon after dawn they were approaching Eindhoven, where they were expecting to link up with the British armour coming up from the south. Indeed, one Armoured Group[39] was to come under its operational command as soon as it arrived to aid in the task of keeping open the XXX Corps axis.

(Map 11)

Recall that Field Marshal Model had given General Student's First Parachute Army the task of dealing with this airborne assault and that Student was in possession of the relevant part of the Allied plan. Fortunately for him, the leading elements of a very under-strength Division[40] of the Fifteenth Army, having escaped across the Scheldt, were just beginning to arrive in western Holland. Orders were given immediately for them to detrain at Tilburg, only 25km north-west of Eindhoven, and by early evening the first Regiment of this Division had been directed towards Son. An ULTRA decrypt dated 16 September reveals that this Division had a strength of only about 3,000 men.

In the same way, two scratch Battalions of paratroopers from a Training and Reinforcement unit in 'S-Hertogenbosch, a similar distance north of Eindhoven, were ordered to advance towards the American bridgeheads at St Oedenrode and Veghel (Map 15). Most important of all from the German point of view, Panzer Brigade 107, with a Battalion of Panthers, a Panzer-Grenadier unit in SPWs, and a company each of StuGs and SPW-mounted Pioneers, had been diverted from the Aachen area and was expected to be in action in just over twenty-four hours.

The Neerpelt Sector

(Map 16)

At 1415 hours on the 17th, the massed guns of XXX Corps[41] engaged known German positions north of the Neerpelt bridgehead and began a rolling barrage, 1.8km wide, along the Eindhoven road. Twenty minutes later, the leading armoured Battlegroup[42] of the Guards Armoured Division[43] rolled forward across 'Joe's bridge'.[44] Standing ready to support the Guards on their flanks were the infantrymen of another Division.[45] Overhead, ground attack aircraft kept up constant rocket and machine-gun attacks on suspected enemy positions.[46]

The basic plan was for the 5th Guards Armoured Brigade to lead the advance as far as Vaalkenswaard where, whilst it would continue on to Eindhoven, the 32nd Guards Brigade would turn off to the east through Leende and Helmond (Map 15). Both Brigades would then head for Grave on parallel routes.

Barring XXX Corps' way was part of KG Walther. This KG had been formed on Student's orders under the command of Luftwaffe Colonel Walther only four days previously. Walther had commanded a parachute Regiment for several years and was destined to become a divisional commander. His KG comprised Baron von der Heydte's 6th Parachute Regiment with three Battalions of about 150 to 200 men each, plus a 'Heavy' Battalion with mortar, anti-tank, reconnaissance, pioneer and flak companies; a similar but weaker Regiment under Colonel von Hoffmann, formed only three weeks before from a Parachute Training Depot; a 'Penal' Battalion and, most significantly from our point of view, KG Heinke. This was made up of the Hohenstaufen's 2nd/19th SS Panzer-Grenadier Battalion, under SS Captain Dr Segler, the Frundsberg's 2nd/21st Battalion under SS Captain Richter, and the 10th SS Panzerjäger Battalion with about fifteen Jagdpanzer IVs and some towed 75mm anti-tank guns under SS Captain Roestel. A number of his Jagdpanzer IVs had been lost in the fighting against the Neerpelt bridgehead during the previous few days. Readers will recall that KG Heinke had arrived in this sector on 10 September.

By the morning of 17 September, KG Walther was firmly in position. KG Hoffmann, with a Frundsberg SS Pioneer Company, was astride the Eindhoven road to the north of Neerpelt, von der Heydte's 6th Parachute Regiment was to the west and the two Frundsberg SS Panzer-Grenadier Battalions (Segler's on loan from the Hohenstaufen) to the east. To the east of KG Walther was Parachute Division 'Erdmann', hastily formed from three newly raised Parachute Regiments and named after its commander, and to its west the remains of the 85th Infantry Division, renamed KG Chill after its commander. Also present were a number of 88mm flak guns, unable to move because they had no tractors, but covering the intended British axis of advance.

Not surprisingly, the weight of the British attack succeeded in breaking through KG Hoffmann's defences and by 1730 hours the leading tanks had reached the bridge just south of Valkenswaard. 'The reshuffle of the group [companies] and the crossing of the bridge took a considerable time' but the town was eventually entered against very minor opposition just after dark.[47]

There had been much confusion on the German side, caused not least by a breakdown of communications within KG Walther. Again, this is hardly surprising in view of its disparate composition. All eight of Hoffmann's 75mm anti-tank guns had been destroyed by the initial artillery barrage and KG Roestel was down to only eight Jagdpanzer IVs at the end of the day. All the 88mm flak guns had been overrun or abandoned. Richter's SS Panzer-Grenadiers were forced to pull back to the east and von der Heydte's paratroopers had to conform to the general withdrawal in a similar way. There are no reports of what happened to Segler's Grenadiers but it seems likely they too were pushed back to the north beyond Valkenswaard. But the British did not have it all their own way. The ground in this area is very similar to the old British Army training areas at Sennelager and Soltau in Germany[48], with sandy soil and many cypress plantations. The latter provided good cover for ambush parties and allowed paratroopers and Grenadiers with Panzerfausts to engage the rear of the leading Irish Guards Squadron and the head of the second Squadron. A member of the Reconnaissance Regiment[49] with the Guards Armoured Division wrote in his diary:

The Micks [Irish Guards] have now run into an 88 gun and bazooka [Panzerfaust] trap and lost nine tanks ... two of our own Daimler armoured cars have gone up on mines. We stopped for the night five miles over the Dutch border.[50]

And so it was. After an advance of 12km during the afternoon and evening, and with a major breakthrough in the offing, orders were issued at 2200 hours for the advance to be halted and not to continue until

0700 hours the following morning. After recording that the leading tank Battalion, despite having nine tanks knocked out, had suffered only eight killed and 'several wounded', the unit War Diary continues, 'The Battalion then went to sleep'.[51] The infantry Battalion had lost seven killed and nineteen wounded during the seven-hour advance and it too, after preparing to move 'the following morning in the same order of march ... went to sleep'.[52] There is little doubt that properly directed infantry, and there was more than enough available, could have covered the 8km to Eindhoven on their feet and entered the city that night. An Irish Guards officer wrote later:

> It is a sad reflection that we should never have stayed the night in Valkenswaard but should have continued to advance all night to Eindhoven and beyond non-stop ... It made no sense to stop, bearing in mind the distance to be covered to Arnhem and the river crossings ahead. The main road to Eindhoven was easy to follow, apart from the skill of the Household Cavalry in discovering routes ahead of the main armour. If need be, another regimental group could have gone ahead.[53]

The order to halt was given by the commander of the 5th Guards Armoured Brigade, Brigadier Gwatkin, on the grounds that the Irish Guards Group 'had been fighting hard and tanks require maintenance'. Since Horrocks specifically mentions it in his own book, *Corps Commander*[54], the order was presumably given with his agreement. The idea of ordering the Grenadier Guards Group to take over the advance does not seem to have occurred to either commander. Furthermore, the statement that the tanks needed to stop overnight for maintenance, or even for fuel, has to be dismissed – after only 12km a Sherman tank needed neither. It is of interest that the Divisional War Diary records that sufficient petrol was being carried 'on wheels' at this time for another 300km.

Horrocks also claimed later that, 'As anticipated, the Germans soon counter-attacked [Valkenswaard] but we were well prepared and the 50th Division repulsed them without difficulty'.[55] An eye-witness with the leading battlegroup described this event rather differently:

> We were all parked on the main road at Valkenswaard and, some time in the night, some German troops tore through the town in transport tossing out grenades. There was some damage and casualties.[56]

Sadly for the British at Arnhem, the failure to continue the advance during the night was to give the Germans a much needed second chance.

NOTES

1. Martin, *History of the 15th Scottish Division* 1939–1945, p. 142.
2. Maj B A Wilson's 21 Indep Parachute (Para) Coy.
3. In the ten days beginning 17 Sep, 21,074 men were delivered into Holland by parachute and a further 18,546 by glider – most of them on the first day.
4. The above figures are taken from *The Brereton Diaries*.
5. Mawson, *Arnhem Doctor*, pp. 27–8.
6. Wilmot, *The Struggle for Europe*, p. 502, Note 2.
7. In fact, it covered only the 101 Airborne Div's part in the operation and the XXX Corps' order of battle.
8. Artillery Park Barracks.
9. Including eighty-seven in the Wolfheze Mental Asylum.
10. 1st Para Bde Group & 1st Air-Landing Bde Group under the command of Maj Gen Roy Urquhart.
11. Lt Col John Frost's 2 Para Bn with engrs & an a/tk Bty.
12. The Dutch and Germans had been using this pontoon bridge every day since 1940 when the road bridge had been destroyed to delay the German advance.
13. Lt Col John Fitch's 3 Para Bn with engrs & an a/tk Bty.
14. Lt Col David Dobie's 1 Para Bn with engrs & an a/tk Bty.
15. Brig Gerald Lathbury.
16. Brig 'Pip' Hicks's 1st Air-Landing Bde.
17. Brig John (Shan) Hackett's 4th Para Bde.
18. Nos 2 & 4 Coys were recruit Coys & No 9 (Hy) Coy comprised mortar, a/tk & flak pls.
19. 3 Para.
20. 1 Para. It is likely that another small KG (Weber) of fewer than 100 men from the 213 Sigs Bn also participated in the fighting against this Bn.
21. 2 Para.
22. Middlebrook, *Arnhem 1944 The Airborne Battle*, pp. 147–8, and confirmed to the author by Lt Mike (Peter) Barry, 15 Nov 2000.
23. Kershaw, *It Never Snows in September*, p. 93, quoting Hans Möller's own account, *Die Schlacht um Arnhem–Oosterbeek*.
24. Tieke, *In the Firestorm of the Last Years of the War*, p. 236.
25. A, HQ & Support Coys only.
26. The myth has grown up since the war that the Germans on the bridge were occupying a 'pill box' or 'bunker'. The tower described was, and is, mainly ornamental and designed to protect pedestrians climbing the steps leading up to the bridge.
27. The British claimed that their attempts that night to re-assemble the pontoon bridge, the centre section of which had been removed and anchored to the north bank, failed due to a lack of boats. There were in fact, as shown in aerial photographs, plenty of boats in the adjacent (now non-existent) harbour, although this area was under German fire from KG Harder.
28. The Bde commander, Brig Lathbury, had become separated from his HQ during the day and in the general confusion of the advance, had been unable to rejoin it. The same thing happened to the Div commander, Maj Gen Urquhart.
29. Col Reuben Tucker's 504 Para Inf Regt.
30. Col William Ekman's 505 & Col Roy Lindquist's 508 Para Inf Regts.
31. Owing to the enormity of the task, the majority of the defensive positions were little more than platoon-sized road blocks.

32. 1/508 Para Inf Regt.
33. Michels & Sliepenbeek, *Niederrheinisches Land im Krieg*. The officer, SS Lt Col Klüttgen, was hanged for this atrocity in Oct 48.
34. Even forty-eight hours later Browning was still of the opinion that control of the high ground at Groesbeek was more important than the capture of Nijmegen itself – see Fitzgerald, *The History of the Irish Guards in the Second World War*, p. 498.
35. Col Roy Lindquist of the 508 Para Inf Regt.
36. Gavin, *On to Berlin*, p. 151.
37. A & E/508 Para Inf Regt.
38. At Browning's insistance, the 101st had been given priority in the airlift to ensure that the southern bridges were captured quickly for use by XXX Corps.
39. 15/19 H with sqn Royals & bty 86 Fd Regt RA.
40. 59 Inf Div.
41. One hy, four med & ten fd arty Regts, totalling 350 guns – Horrocks, *Corps Commander*, p. 99.
42. Three, full strength sqns of 2 Armd IG & three coys of 3 IG (due to manpower shortages, one coy of 3 IG had been temporarily dispersed to the other three).
43. The Div had been re-organised into four Regtl Battlegroups on 2 Sep: Gren Gds & IG under 5 Gds Armd Bde, & Coldm Gds & WG under 32 Gds Bde, each with one tk and one inf bn.
44. The bridge was a composite, wooden & steel girder bridge.
45. 231 Inf Bde of 50 Inf Div.
46. There have been statements that eleven Typhoon sqns participated, flying some 230 sorties. Horrocks, op. cit., p. 99, in a summary of his orders for the Op, says, 'The Typhoons of the 83 Gp will give close support.' 83 Gp had ten Sqns. RAF records held in the PRO London (Air 27) reveal that only nos.174,175, 247 & 440 Sqns took part in Operation GARDEN on 17 Sep 44. Remarkably few positive claims were made. Others Sqns were relocating to forward airfields or did not fly due to bad weather.
47. Fitzgerald, op. cit., p. 494,
48. A Belgian army camp and tk trg area is currently located just to the south-west of Neerpelt, at Beverlo. In 1944 it was a Waffen-SS training area & barracks.
49. 2 HCR.
50. Cooper, *Dangerous Liaison*, p. 56.
51. 2 Armd IG War Diary, 17 Sep 44.
52. Fitzgerald, op. cit., p. 495.
53. Wilson, *The Ever Open Eye*, p. 112.
54. Horrocks, op. cit., p. 103.
55. Ibid.
56. Cantlay, *A Sapper's War*, p. 11.

CHAPTER XIV
MARKET GARDEN:
Monday 18 September

The Arnhem Sector
(Maps 11, 12 & 17)

The commander of II SS Panzer Corps knew only too well that if he was to stop the British armoured advance towards Arnhem he had to get his Frundsberg Division down to Nijmegen. The only way to do this quickly was to use the Arnhem bridge and therefore, during the night of the 17th/18th, he gave Harzer the Frundsberg's 10th SS Reconnaissance Battalion (KG Brinkmann) and told him to re-capture the bridge as a matter of urgency. In addition, he gave him a Battery of the Corps' 102nd SS Werfer Battalion.

Brinkmann launched his first attack against the British[1] at the northern end of the road bridge soon after dawn on the 18th. When this infantry assault failed, he followed up with a second incorporating armoured cars and SPWs. Two British 6-pounder anti-tank guns played a major role in defeating this armoured attack and it soon became clear that the Frundsberg would have to find an alternative route to Nijmegen – at least in the short term.

The next major action by the Germans in Arnhem on the 18th occurred at 0930 hours. In a move that surprised both sides, Gräbner's 9th SS Reconnaissance Battalion attempted to drive across the Arnhem bridge from the south. Recall that Gräbner had decided to return from Nijmegen on his own initiative. Before the British could react, the first few armoured cars managed to get across the bridge, but then there was carnage. The fighting went on for nearly two hours but at the end of it, at least eight SPWs and a similar number of other vehicles had been knocked out and Gräbner and some seventy of his men killed. The remainder of his Battalion took up positions at the southern end of the bridge, which itself remained a no-man's-land, with destroyed vehicles blocking the way. These men subsequently moved into a brick factory on the south side of the river, from where they could control the north bank, west of the bridge.

As soon as Heinz Harmel returned from Berlin, early on the 18th, he reported to his Corps commander. Bittrich made it clear to him that as far as he was concerned the key to winning the battle in Holland was the city of Nijmegen with its two bridges over the Waal. Harmel was therefore to concentrate his Division north of the city as quickly as possible. He was also to take over responsibility for the Arnhem bridge which was needed not only for his own Division, but also for use by additional forces which Bittrich had been promised, including a heavy Panzer Battalion. Harzer's Hohenstaufen would remain responsible for dealing with the British forces in and to the west of Arnhem.

Faced with the double problem of capturing the Arnhem bridge and moving his Division to Nijmegen quickly, Harmel came up with a new and innovative plan. He would use KG Brinkmann, which Bittrich had just returned to his command, and an additional unit that had been allocated to him, KG Knaust, to capture the bridge. At the same time, he would move another part of his force to a ferry site that was already under construction at Pannerden, 20km to the south-east of Arnhem on the lower Rhine (Map 11).[2] Battalion Euling, the second weak SS Panzer-Grenadier Battalion which had been detached from the Hohenstaufen to the Frundsberg, had already closed up to KG Brinkmann in readiness to cross the Arnhem bridge, but it was now placed under a KG Reinhold (formed from the 2nd/10th SS Panzer Battalion, in an infantry role, under SS Major Leo Reinhold) and ordered to divert to the ferry site. On arrival, KG Reinhold was to cross the river using rubber rafts and ferries manned by the Division's SS Pioneers and then advance to Nijmegen along the north side of the Waal. Harmel decided to remain north of the Rhine with the bulk of the Frundsberg and delegate responsibility for the forward elements to Reinhold. The degree of flexibility and speed of implementation of this new plan have to be admired.

The additional unit allocated to Harmel, KG Knaust, was a Panzer-Grenadier Training and Replacement Battalion from Germany, under the command of Major Hans-Peter Knaust. This unit contained a large number of highly experienced, but convalescent, soldiers – even Knaust had only one leg! Eight Mk III and IV tanks, which had been extracted from a Panzer Reinforcement unit where they were being used for driver training, were also on their way to join the KG.

As soon as it arrived in Arnhem, KG Knaust relieved Euling's Battalion at the north end of the road bridge and the thus reinforced KG Brinkmann renewed its attack. Hand-to-hand fighting ensued and after several of the houses occupied by the British were set on fire, they were forced to make limited withdrawals. This simple tactic of burning the British paratroopers out of their defensive positions ensured that, unless they were quickly reinforced, they would soon be overwhelmed. However, barring the way of those reinforcements were KGs Krafft, Spindler and Harder.

KG Krafft was holding the northern sector of the blocking line, covering the Ede–Arnhem road, and KG Spindler was in position along the line of the north-south road on the western edge of Arnhem, to as far south as the railway line. Additional positions had been occupied by the same KG along the railway embankment and the line of the main east-west road into Arnhem to a point where it meets the river (Map 17). Included in KG Spindler were Allwörden's 9th SS Panzerjägers, Möller's 9th SS Pioneers and the eighty-seven men of the 9th SS Flak. KG Harder formed a second line of defence nearer to the bridge. Two additional alarm units were formed during the morning from personnel arriving in trucks and on bicycles from elsewhere in Holland and from Germany, and these were immediately integrated into KGs Allwörden and Harder to bring them up to over 400 men each.

The British attempt to break through to the Arnhem bridge began before first light, when the Battalion Group[3] which had halted for the night in Oosterbeek (with the permission of its Divisional and Brigade commanders[4]), switched to the southern route running along the lower Rhine. All went well at first, with no opposition, but a little after dawn a major part of the Battalion, including all its heavy mortars and machine-guns and all but one of its anti-tank guns took a wrong turning and became separated. Some time after this, the leading element, including the commanding officer and the Divisional and Brigade commanders, came under heavy fire from the survivors of Gräbner's 9th SS Reconnaissance Battalion in the brick factory across the river and were pinned down for over six hours. Another attempt to advance, at about 1430 hours, along a route farther away from the river also resulted in failure. The remnants of the Battalion ended up in two groups sheltering for the night in houses to the west of the St Elizabeth hospital, still more than 2km west of the bridge. The Battalion suffered fifteen men killed and about forty to fifty wounded during the day.

Meanwhile, the Battalion Group[5] that had kept moving during the night had cut south onto the main east-west road into Arnhem. Soon after 0530 hours it too ran into heavy fire, this time from Möller's SS Pioneers on the railway embankment, and so cut south again in an attempt to follow the lower road already taken by its sister Battalion. In the process, it picked up part of the heavy weapons group of that Battalion. At about 0800 hours it encountered more heavy opposition from KG Spindler and, having no way of sidestepping it, a full attack was mounted. The fighting which ensued was mostly at close quarters and through houses and gardens. It took eight hours and twenty-three killed for the Battalion Group to reach the same area as its sister Battalion, near the St Elizabeth hospital. Both units were exhausted.

Major problems for the British at this time were caused by the failure of many of their radios and the fact that both the Divisional commander and the commander of the 1st Parachute Brigade had become separated from their respective Headquarters. Early on the morning of the 18th their whereabouts was still unknown. At Urquhart's Headquarters there was consternation, for his staff knew that if there was to be any chance of capturing the Arnhem bridge, more troops were needed in the forward area and needed quickly. The only troops immediately available were those of the 1st Air-Landing Brigade whose task, however, was to protect the LZs for the second assault wave.[6] The commander[7] of the Air-Landing Brigade was therefore persuaded to take over and, at 1030 hours, he ordered part of his force[8] to advance in support of the paratroopers already in Oosterbeek and Arnhem. At 1400 hours he gave further orders that, as soon as possible after landing, a Battalion[9] of the 4th Parachute Brigade, which was due to arrive later that day, was also to move into Arnhem.

Most accounts of the fighting in Oosterbeek and Arnhem mention the fact that many of the British radios failed or, at best, worked only intermittently. Whilst it is certainly true that most of the sets were unreliable and had limited range, particularly in built-up areas, it is not widely known that many of these failures were due to static interference, caused by the high level of iron in the soil of this area.

Thick fog had shrouded the UK airfields on the morning of the 18th, with the consequence that the first aircraft and gliders of the second assault wave did not arrive over the Arnhem area until 1509 hours – over four hours late. This delay might well have proved disastrous for, late on the 17th, a number of ad hoc SS, Naval and Luftwaffe units, under General Hans von Tettau, the 'Commander Training' in Holland, had been ordered by General Christiansen to move east and attack the LZs. Fortunately for the British, this substantial KG failed to arrive in time to disrupt the new landings and although there was some minor fighting between small German parties and the British troops[10] defending the LZs north and west of Wolfheze, there was no serious interference. Nevertheless, significant disruption was caused by aircraft losses and men landing away from the designated drop zones. Nearly 400 of the 2,000 or so British paratroopers who were dropped on the 18th were missing when the units formed up for their advance into Arnhem. Thirty-two men were killed in the actual drop and in immediate actions on the ground.

Needless to say, when the commander of the incoming Parachute Brigade[11] heard that, without consultation, one of his units was to be taken from his command and ordered into Arnhem by an officer of equal rank, he was highly displeased. Even so, the need to move troops in the forward area was obvious and by midnight the two additional units[12] had caught up with the two depleted Parachute Battalions near the St Elizabeth hospital. Thus, by the end of Day 2 of Operation MARKET, there were four British Battalions within 2km of the Arnhem bridge but, unlike the Germans who seem to have had no trouble in finding overall commanders in a crisis, no one took charge of this force. This was particularly ironic, since the Divisional commander and at least one Brigade commander, the latter albeit wounded, were hiding in nearby houses. Major General Urquhart and Brigadier Lathbury had attempted to reach safety at about 1600 hours that afternoon. Unfortunately, they and two other officers ran towards rather than away from the Germans. Lathbury was wounded and had to be left in one house, whilst Urquhart and the others ended up hiding in another, less than 50m from the St Elizabeth hospital, for the next twelve hours.

What of the other Parachute Battalions of the incoming Brigade? One[13] remained on, and in the vicinity of, the drop zone and the other[14], in accordance with the original plan, set off at 1700 hours to occupy the northern district of Arnhem. At this stage, their Brigade commander had no idea of the current situation in the city and was simply complying with his original orders. This Battalion ran into part of KG Spindler at about midnight and, believing the opposition too strong to attack on its own, halted for the night.

At about 2300 hours the commander of the 4th Parachute Brigade received new orders from the acting Divisional commander.[15] He was to capture a ridge of high ground just to the north-east of Oosterbeek and then approach Arnhem on the left flank of the depleted 1st Parachute Brigade in what was hoped would become a joint attack towards the Arnhem bridge.

Meanwhile, late on the 18th the Divisional Headquarters moved to the Hartenstein Hotel in Oosterbeek, one of the Air-Landing Brigade's Battalions[16] moved to its Phase II positions in the western part of the same town, and the other[17] moved off to secure a LZ just to the north-west for the planned arrival of the third-lift gliders the following day.

The end of the 18th saw the 1st British Airborne Division in a state of chaos. Its acting commander had no communications with his home base, the Allied aircraft in the skies above him, his Corps commander, the forward Brigade or the group holding the north end of the bridge. Only two of the four senior commanders in the Division were in touch with each other (and they did not see eye to eye) and, perhaps most serious of all, its three Brigades were uncoordinated and its leading units fragmented. The chances of the Arnhem bridgehead being secured for the further advance of the ground troops were fast diminishing. In contrast, all the senior German commanders were in close touch, including the Commander-in-Chief of Army Group 'B', and their forces were fully coordinated and growing in strength by the hour.

The Nijmegen Sector

(Map 14)

By early on 18 September the 10th SS Pioneers had the ferry service running across the Rhine at Pannerden. They used anything they could find – canal barges, rubber dinghies, rowing boats and so on, and later in the day they were assisted by Army engineers who provided a 40-ton capacity ferry which allowed armoured vehicles to cross the river. The whole process was inevitably very slow and, despite the limited protection provided by the Frundsberg's 10th SS Flak Battalion, Allied aircraft transiting the area caused further delays. Nonetheless, the first combat troops of the Division were across during the morning and later in the day Harmel moved his advanced Command Post to the crossing site.

The first troops to make contact with the force already protecting the Waal bridges in Nijmegen, KG Henke, were those of SS Major Reinhold and an advance party of Frundsberg Pioneers, led by SS Second Lieutenant Baumgärtel. The Pioneers immediately started preparing the massive road and railway bridges for emergency demolition, while Henke briefed Reinhold on his defensive layout. After being told that a scratch force was already defending a line running approximately a kilometre south of the Waal bridges and that two 20mm and one 88mm flak guns were covering the Waal railway bridge, Reinhold decided to deploy his men on the north bank of the river immediately adjacent to the bridges.

Next to arrive, at about midday, was SS Captain Karl-Heinz Euling's SS Panzer-Grenadier Battalion. Reinhold gave orders that it was to secure the immediate approaches to the road bridge and placed the various Army and Police detachments already manning strong-points in the area under Euling's command. The latter set up his Command Post near the Valkhof, the citadel of Nijmegen and the highest point in the city, not far from the southern ramp of the bridge while his men took up positions covering all the approaches to the large traffic island near the south end of the bridge. Four StuGs[18] that arrived later from Pannerden were also allocated to Euling. Meanwhile, on the north bank, Reinhold ensured that the 88mm flak guns, already protecting the bridges from air attack, were re-sited amongst the houses at the water's edge so that they could engage with direct fire any vehicles attempting to cross. As further Frundsberg units arrived, including a few Mk III and IV tanks, they were incorporated into the overall defensive system and used to strengthen KG Henke. Mines were laid, and various buildings, including factory chimneys and even church towers, demolished to create obstacles.

What of the Americans during this time? Brigadier General Jim Gavin, the commander of the 82nd Airborne Division, knew full well that until the arrival of his second lift, he did not have the strength to hold the vital Groesbeek area and at the same time mount a strong enough attack on the Nijmegen road bridge. To compound his problems, the abortive attempt to take the Nijmegen bridge the previous night had depleted his forces covering the LZs and the approaches from the Reichswald. There were, however, two factors in his favour. One, there were, and still are, no roads or even reasonable tracks leading from the Reichswald towards the thickly wooded high ground at Groesbeek; and two, the Maas–Escaut canal and waterways flowing into the Waal just to the east of Nijmegen channelled any German attack towards the Groesbeek ridge.

At 0630 hours on the morning of the 18th, the Germans launched their long awaited counter-attack. In another amazing feat of inventiveness, organisation and military competence, they had assembled an ad hoc force of four battalions armed with twenty-four mortars and 130 light and medium machine-guns, three artillery batteries and even a few armoured cars and SPWs mounting flak guns.[19] Totalling over 3,000 men, many of whom had never received even basic infantry training, this group[20] was ordered to attack and drive the Americans back across the Maas. Perhaps not surprisingly, in view of the very thin American defences, the German attacks made some progress and parts of the LZs were overrun. With the expected fly-in due at 1300 hours, Gavin was forced to withdraw his men from Nijmegen and throw in his last reserves.[21] Even so, fighting was still going on when the first of 450 Dakotas, towing 450 gliders, appeared overhead at 1400 hours – bad weather in England had delayed their take-off. Although some casualties were suffered, the fly-in was amazingly successful[22] and caused panic amongst the Germans who fled. Ninety-seven close air support sorties were flown during this action.

The Americans had suffered few casualties during the day, but the German counter-attack and the late arrival of his reinforcements had ended Gavin's chances of mounting a proper attack against the Nijmegen bridges. His best hope now was a combined attack with the British armour which he was told was due to arrive at the Grave bridge at 0830 hours the following morning.

The Eindhoven Sector
(Map 15)

At 0700 hours on 18 September, the 5th Guards Armoured Brigade resumed its advance towards Aalst, led by armoured cars of its attached armoured Reconnaissance unit.[23] By this time the German command structure in the area was in danger of breaking down and indeed, as early as 0415 hours that morning, the War Diary of the relevant Corps has the entry, 'There is no doubt about it, the enemy has broken through.'[24] Whilst this was certainly an exaggeration, the only immediate opposition in the way of the Guards was the remnants of KG Hoffmann[25] and one or maybe two Jagdpanzer IVs, almost certainly from Roestel's 10th SS Panzerjäger unit, operating on the eastern flank of the British advance at this time. Even so, with close air support unavailable during the first part of the day due to poor flying weather, it took until midday for the leading British Battlegroup[26] to cover the 5km to Aalst. Then, just to the north of the village, four 88mm guns were encountered covering another waterway and the approach road to Eindhoven. Armoured cars managed to bypass this opposition to the west and in an attempt to exploit this opportunity the reserve Battlegroup was told to follow up. However, the weakness of the bridges in the area frustrated the advance of the heavier tanks and it was a further six hours before the leading elements of the Division covered the last 2km to Eindhoven and made contact with a Regiment[27] of the US 101st Airborne Division already in the city. Afterwards, one young Irish Guards officer wrote ruefully, 'One wonders whether the guns would have been there if the advance had continued overnight instead of some twelve hours later'.[28]

Another officer with the Guards Armoured Division wrote in his diary:

Held up all day. The enemy holding a strong line here south of Eindhoven with tanks and 88s – we Typhoon them and eventually break through at about 5.30 in the evening ... We stop for the night by a canal crossing.[29]

Eindhoven itself was undefended:

On the outskirts of Eindhoven we passed our first American soldier standing at the side of the road and holding the hand of a small child. He waved and shouted, 'Great stuff, boys.' More and more Americans appeared, strolling round the town. It was surprising to see them in an almost peacetime atmosphere. There were no barricades at main roads, machine-guns posts, anti-tank guns, or other static defences.[30]

The canal mentioned was the Wilhelmina at Son. Recall that the Germans had managed to blow the bridge there just before the arrival of the American paratroopers. The British tanks reached it at 2100 hours and engineers arrived shortly afterwards to begin bridging the gap. Fortunately, a heavy German bombing attack on Eindhoven during the night did not interfere with this work.

With the way to the north through Veghel and Uden already secured by the Americans and civilian reports that Helmond was strongly held by the Germans, the planned advance by the 32nd Guards Brigade on the eastern axis was consequently cancelled.

By 0615 hours on 19 September, a 40-ton Bailey bridge was spanning the Wilhelmina and the tanks of the Guards Armoured Division were ready to continue their advance.

NOTES

1. A, most of B, HQ & Support Coys 2 Para (C Coy was forced to surrender on this day while still well west of the bridge); five guns of 1 Air-Landing A/Tk Bty RA; HQ 1 Para Bde, including the Defence Platoon; a large part of 1 Para Sqn RE; a platoon of 9 Fd Coy RE; part of C Coy 3 Para; a RASC platoon; and a miscellaneous group of about sixty men including glider pilots & artillerymen – total fewer than 750.
2. The existing ferry, capable of taking six cars across the 30m wide, fast-flowing river, had been destroyed by the ferryman.
3. 3 Para.
4. Both Maj Gen Urquhart & Brig Lathbury had become separated from their respective HQs on the 17th and had ended up with the 3 Para Group.
5. 1 Para.
6. 4 Para Bde under Brig Hackett and more heavy equipment.
7. Brig Hicks.
8. Just over half of Lt Col Derek McCardie's 2nd Bn, The South Staffords (2 S Staffs), which had arrived the previous day.
9. Lt Col George Lea's 11 Para.
10. Lt Col Tommy Haddon's 1st Bn, The Border Regt (1 Border) & Lt Col Robert Payton-Reid's 7th Bn, King's Own Scottish Borderers (7 KOSB).
11. Brig 'Shan' Hackett.
12. Both Bns ran into some minor opposition during their moves into Arnhem; 2 S Staffs suffered two killed and several wounded and 11 Para at least three men killed.
13. Lt Col Ken Smyth's 10 Para.
14. Lt Col Sir Richard des Voeux's 156 Para.
15. Brig Hicks.
16. 1 Border.
17. 7 KOSB.
18. These may well have been JgPz IVs.
19. Kershaw, *It Never Snows in September*, p. 122.
20. Designated 406 Div under Lt Gen Scherbening, all these units came from Military District (Mil Dist) VI and formed part of Corps 'Feldt', commanded by cavalry Gen Kurt Feldt.
21. Two coys of the 307 Engr Bn.
22. This was the 82nd's heavy lift. Another eighteen howitzers & eight 57mm a/tk guns were landed successfully.
23. 2 HCR.
24. LXXXVIII Corps War Diary, 18 Sep 44.
25. The remnants of the 1 & 3 Para Bns, plus up to eleven 75mm a/tk guns without towing vehicles. Hoffmann himself had been killed the previous day.
26. 2 Armd & 3 IG BG.
27. 506 Para Inf Regt.
28. Wilson, *The Ever Open Eye*, p. 114.
29. Cooper, *Dangerous Liaison*, p. 58.
30. Wilson, op. cit., p. 118.

CHAPTER XV

MARKET GARDEN:
Tuesday 19 September

The Arnhem Sector
(Map 12)

By the morning of 19 September the British holding the north end of the Arnhem bridge knew that the XXX Corps armoured column, due to link up with them within three days, was still south of Nijmegen. It also became obvious as the day progressed that the sounds of battle to their west were decreasing rather than increasing and that the planned drop of the Polish Parachute Brigade on the south side of the bridge had been delayed or cancelled. They were indeed in a parlous position. As we shall hear shortly, the attempt to reinforce them from the west was ending in failure and bad weather had prevented the Polish Brigade even taking off, let alone landing.

Recall that Heinz Harmel of the Frundsberg Division had two KGs, Brinkmann and Knaust, attacking the British from the north and east sides of the bridge. He also had other troops capable of firing directly across the river from the south bank, and artillery and Nebelwerfers[1] in action in an indirect fire role. By now Harmel had resolved to literally 'blast' the British out of the dozen or so houses they were still occupying. Flame-throwers, Panzerfausts and explosives were all brought into use, and the task was made that much easier when KG Knaust was reinforced during the morning by the promised eight Mk III and IV tanks from the Panzer Reinforcement unit. Before starting his attacks, however, Harmel sent a prisoner back to British lines with an offer of surrender. It was curtly rejected. Shortly after this, three Mk IIIs were deployed on the eastern flank and they, with the existing armoured vehicles of KG Brinkmann and the artillery, set about systematically destroying the houses occupied by the British. Panzer-Grenadiers then took over the ruins. One Mk III was knocked out by a PIAT (hand-held anti-tank weapon) and the others withdrew, but were later replaced by what have been described as two 'Tiger' tanks. Although, as we shall hear, Mk VI Tigers did appear later in the battle, it seems much more likely that these two tanks were the Mk IVs with KG Knaust. Whatever the truth, their high velocity 75mm shells had a devastating effect on the British positions and by the evening, having lost another nineteen killed, and with wounded now totalling some 150, it was obvious that the small British perimeter would soon be overrun.

The pre-dawn attempt by four British Battalions to break through to the bridge from the west ended in disaster. Their advance was made on two axes (Map 18). The remnants of the two Parachute Battalions[2] which had ended up just to the west of the St Elizabeth hospital moved on the road beside the Rhine, and the other two Battalions[3] advanced along the main road running just to the south of the railway line. Resisting them, in what Wilhelm Tieke describes as 'a steel wall'[4], were all the Hohenstaufen KGs and KG Krafft, reinforced by ten StuGs from Assault Gun Brigade 280. The outposts, which had held up the advance of the British the previous evening, had been withdrawn to a much stronger line and the StuGs were soon distributed between KGs Spindler and Harder. On the north flank, covering the Ede–Arnhem road and facing south, was KG Krafft. Gropp's 9th SS Flak gunners overlooked the main Utrecht road to the south of the railway line and Möller's 9th SS Pioneers were in the houses flanking the same road. The rest of KG Spindler and KG Harder completed the 'steel wall' to as far south as the river, facing due west towards the advancing British Battalions. Most importantly, what was left of the 9th SS Reconnaissance Battalion was still in the brickworks, south of the river, covering the riverside road. What happened next was inevitable. The Germans held all the vital ground, had all the heavy weapons, including some armour, were led by experienced commanders and were operating under a unified command. The British were unco-ordinated, mostly inexperienced, lightly armed, short of ammunition and without artillery or armoured support. Their advance has been equated to the Charge of the Light Brigade in the Crimean War and their defeat called a massacre. In the event, their advance lacked the impetus of the former and, since relatively few men were killed, the result hardly qualifies as 'indiscriminate and brutal slaughter'.

On the river road, the battle was all over by 0630 hours. The para-troopers were caught in the open by the machine-guns and cannons of KGs Spindler and Harder and the 9th SS Reconnaissance Battalion across the river. They were forced to take cover wherever they could find it, and then, having run out of anti-tank ammunition, to retreat.

On the main road, the fighting lasted longer – until mid-morning – but the result was the same. At 0900 hours Major General Urquhart, now back in command of his Division and distraught at the way his units were being committed piecemeal into a hopeless battle, gave orders that the follow-up Battalion[5] on the main road should not get involved and that the lead unit should pull back. Sadly, it took two hours for these orders to reach those concerned and by that time the leading Battalion[6], having already been shot up from three sides, was being decimated by German counter-attacks. Most of the British infantrymen were taken prisoner. But worse was to come. The follow-up Battalion[7] had subsequently been ordered to move across the railway and secure the high ground one kilometre north-west of the St Elizabeth hospital for use by the rest of Hackett's Parachute Brigade in its advance towards Arnhem from the LZs. At about 1430 hours this Battalion was caught in the open by Harzer's mortars and artillery. His armour and Panzer-Grenadiers finished the job and the Battalion was annihilated. Only about 150 men got back to British lines.

Following the landings, five British Battalions, totalling more than 3,000 men, had advanced into Arnhem. By nightfall on the 19th they totalled fewer than 1,000. About 120 had been killed and over 1,700, many of them wounded, were prisoners of the Germans. Four of the five Battalion commanders had been killed or wounded. The rout was complete – the survivors of the fighting in western Arnhem took up positions behind the Oosterbeek railway bridge.

What of the remainder of Hackett's 4th Parachute Brigade[8]? Recall that they had been ordered to move north of the railway line on the left flank of the troops already in the city. The leading Battalion[9] advanced soon after dawn but ran straight into the men of the Hohenstaufen. Some twin and quadruple 20mm flak guns of unknown origin, but quite possibly including some from the Hohenstaufen itself, formed part of this end of the 'steel wall'. By 1400 hours, despite repeated attempts to get forward, the British had suffered nearly 50% casualties. They were ordered to pull back. The other Battalion[10] set off at 0430 hours but, although it suffered only ten men killed, its attack too soon bogged down. By the time Roy Urquhart met up with the Brigade commander at about 1330 hours, it was obvious that the advance had 'run out of steam'. Another Battalion[11] had been attached to the Brigade, but it was still tasked with protecting the LZ for the next glider lift. In addition, there was more bad news – powerful German forces were reported to be closing in from the west and threatening the rear of the Brigade and the LZs. Not surprisingly, the decision was taken to withdraw the Brigade to the south of the railway line and concentrate in the Oosterbeek area. In the event, the report was in error and led to a further unnecessary disaster.

The German forces in question were those of KG Tettau. They comprised three Battalion groups from the SS NCO School 'Arnheim', under the command of SS Colonel Hans Lippert (KG Lippert), a Dutch SS Guard Battalion (KG Helle), an SS 'Depot' Battalion[12] (KG Eberwein) and a security Regiment of mixed origin but which including a Luftwaffe Flak Battalion (KG Knoche).[13]

KG Tettau had advanced with KG Knoche on the axis of the Ede–Arnhem road, KG Eberwein along the railway line and KG Lippert south of the railway towards Oosterbeek (Map 12); a shortage of radios, however, made coordination, both within the KG and with Harzer's Headquarters, extremely difficult and this resulted, fortunately for the British, in a sluggish approach. The only Battalion[14] to come under attack from the west on this day was the one dug in on the western edge of Ooster-beek, having withdrawn there the previous evening in accordance with the original plan. It reported:

> At 1900 hrs light probing attacks were made on all Company positions as von Tettau's units moved from the west towards Oosterbeek. These attacks were repulsed without difficulty.[15]

The ordered withdrawal of the 4th Parachute Brigade was complicated by the fact that, due to the high embankment, there were only two vehicle crossing points over the railway which separated the Brigade from both Oosterbeek and the remnants of the 1st Parachute Brigade. As one of these was already in German hands there was an urgent need to secure the other, near Wolfheze. The nearest Battalion[16], some 4km away to the east, was given the task, but its route, through the woods north of the railway line, took it to the open area where the next glider lift was due to land. This LZ was more than 3km to the east of the others, which were covered with gliders from the previous lifts. Inevitably, when the gliders containing the Polish heavy equipment came in at about 1600 hours, they came under fire not only from German flak but from KG Krafft which had just been reinforced by two Marine Regiments, a Police company[17] and some StuGs. They also landed amongst the withdrawing British paratroopers. Chaos ensued. Krafft's men fired on the slow moving gliders and at the same time German fighter aircraft appeared overhead. A Polish war correspondent with the force wrote later:

> Several gliders caught fire and, rolling over from wing to wing, dived in a mad flight to the ground. Several others landed helplessly with shattered undercarriages. Even from some distance, we could see the torn sides and hanging rudders. One of the gliders broke up in the air like a child's toy and a jeep, an anti-tank gun and men fell out of it. We never expected things to be so bad, so very bad.[18]

Despite the delayed take-off in England and the loss of fifteen aircraft in transit, twenty-eight gliders eventually reached the LZ. But the arrival of the Poles, in unfamiliar berets and speaking a different language, only added to the general confusion. The British took some of them for enemy and in turn, the Poles are said to have fired on friend and foe alike. Nine of them died – two on the fly-in and seven after landing – and to add to this chapter of mishaps, only three of their ten precious anti-tank guns were successfully unloaded. According to Wilhelm Tieke[19], thirteen gliders landed in German territory and a quarter of the Polish material ended up in German hands, including a jeep containing a suitcase of the commander of the Polish Parachute Brigade, Major General Sosabowski. This led the Germans to broadcast an announcement that he was dead – in fact, he was still in England![20]

Despite the pressure from KG Krafft, some three-quarters of the remnants of the second Parachute Battalion[21] and most of Hackett's Headquarters managed to get back to a rendezvous south of the railway line. A narrow tunnel beneath the railway, wide enough to take jeeps, was discovered during the afternoon but in the undisciplined scramble to use it, many vehicles were abandoned. Meanwhile, the Parachute Battalion[22] still north of the railway, after extricating itself from the chaos of the LZ, moved to the vehicle crossing near Wolfheze, which it held until the late afternoon. It then took up defensive positions in the village itself. At that time, it still numbered just over 400 men. The third Battalion[23] of the Brigade, after carrying out its primary task of defending the LZ, withdrew to Oosterbeek independently, losing two-thirds of its strength in the process – one company remained near the rail tunnel and another, after moving in the wrong direction, was forced to surrender. The Battalion commander, wrote later:

It is against textbook teaching to break off an engagement and withdraw from the battlefield in broad daylight . . . As a result, this fine Scottish Borderer battalion . . . was reduced, within the hour, to a third of its strength.[24]

By nightfall Hackett's Brigade had been reduced to about half strength. It had suffered an estimated fifty-four men killed during the day – again the rest, many of them wounded, were prisoners. Some sub-units were still north of the railway but fortunately for them, and for the group in Wolfheze, Krafft and the elements of KG Tettau moving in from the west did not, as we have heard, press forward in any strength.

Some time during the evening or early part of the night, Roy Urquhart ordered what was left of Hackett's Brigade back to Oosterbeek, where a defensive perimeter was already being set up by the exhausted survivors of the 1st Parachute Brigade. After talking to Headquarters 1st Parachute Division by radio, Hackett, fearing that his men might be fired on by those within the perimeter, decided not to withdraw until first light the following morning.

Before leaving the events in the Arnhem sector, it is important to note that at about midday on the 19th a complete Flak Brigade with ample ammunition arrived from Germany. Its four Battalions, which were immediately subordinated to Harzer's Division, were equipped with a total of thirty-three 88mm, six 37mm and twenty-nine 20mm flak guns. By mid-afternoon they were covering all the British LZs. At about the same time, a Luftwaffe liaison officer joined Harzer's Headquarters. This gave him the capability of calling on the 300 fighter aircraft of the 3rd

Luftwaffe Fighter Division based only ten minutes' flying time away in Germany. This accounts for the German aircraft over the LZ when the Polish gliders arrived. Luftwaffe personnel in Dunkirk (Map 10), where the beleaguered garrison was still holding out, had signalled their approach. On top of all this, Harzer's Intelligence officers had by now discovered from captured British documents the instructions for the laying out of identification panels for further supply drops. As Wilhelm Tieke puts it, 'from then on, the Germans smoked English cigarettes and ate English chocolate.'[25] Eighteen out of 190 aircraft trying to drop supplies to the 1st British Airborne Division were lost on this day[26], and some 390 tons of ammunition and food dropped by parachute fell into German hands.[27] This was mainly because the pre-arranged drop zone was outside the British perimeter and Urquhart's message suggesting a new DZ had failed to reach England.

There was another significant change on the 20th. Field Marshal Model, who was a constant visitor to Harzer's Headquarters during this period, authorised the Hohenstaufen to deal directly with his own Army Group 'B' Headquarters. This allowed the Division to request on a priority basis, urgent supplies, additional weapons and even specialist units, such as a Pioneer Battalion[28] specifically training and equipped for street fighting.

The Nijmegen Sector
(Map 14)

The bad weather in England affected the Americans even more than the British and Poles. The IX Troop Carrier Command launched a total of 445 aircraft and 385 gliders on the 19th, of which twenty-seven aircraft were lost and only 221 gliders reached their LZs.[29] The failure to launch 258 of their gliders[30], carrying the 82nd Airborne Division's 325th Glider Infantry Regiment, was to end any hope Brigadier Jim Gavin might have had of capturing one of the vital Nijmegen bridges on this day. Just as bad, only forty of the 265 tons of essential stores and ammunition destined for his Division was recovered. Similarly, only 1,341 out of 2,310 troops and 40% of the artillery pieces bound for the 101st Airborne Division defending 'Hell's Highway', got through.[31] Fortunately for Maxwell Taylor, however, two of his Glider Infantry Battalions had been landed successfully the previous afternoon.

On the ground, the British began their advance from Son at 0615 hours with armoured cars in the lead and a mixed Battlegroup of the Guards Armoured Division following.[32] The Grave bridge was reached at 1100 hours and the commander was met by 'Boy' Browning, the Airborne Corps commander, and Jim Gavin. Browning said he believed that a concerted 'rush' could succeed in capturing the Nijmegen road bridge and, after a short conference, it was agreed that Gavin would place a Parachute Battalion[33] under British command for this mission. As a quid pro quo, the British gave Gavin a mixed Battlegroup[34] to help him defend his vital 40km perimeter facing the Reichswald. He said later, 'So far, we had been spared a major German armored attack, but now, with the availability of British armor, we felt equal to anything that could happen'.[35]

The advance into Nijmegen, by three combined British/American columns, began at 1600 hours. The smallest group, made up of an infantry company and four tanks, was given the main Post Office as its objective in the belief that it contained the demolition control point for blowing the bridges. It was captured without difficulty but nothing was found. Stronger, simultaneous attacks were launched against the men of KG Euling defending the road bridge and KG Henke at the rail bridge. The road bridge attack was carried out by an American Parachute Battalion[36], less a company, but with twelve British tanks and a British infantry company attached, and that against the rail bridge by single British and American infantry companies and twelve British tanks.[37] Neither was successful. Wilhelm Tieke gives the German version of what happened:

Heavy fire burst from all the houses and parks around the two bridges over the Waal against the attackers. On the approaches to the railroad bridge, several Shermans were knocked out by an 88mm. At the highway bridge they did not get anywhere near as close. 20mm flak hammered the length of the streets and two StuGs attacked from well-concealed ambush positions and shot up several enemy tanks. With the fall of darkness, the infantry attack was repulsed. The American paratroopers and British tanks took positions for the night 400m from the bridges.[38]

British reports differ in detail. The History of the Grenadier Guards says one Sherman was knocked out and two damaged in the road bridge attack with:

practically no [personnel] loss to themselves . . . However, at no stage in the battle did the forces directed on the two bridges look like being able to rush them or even seriously disturb the German defences.[39]

Another account says five Shermans were lost.[40] The personnel casualties are confirmed as 'light' in the relevant War Diary.[41]

A British liaison officer with the Americans in forward positions overlooking the bridge from its east side, wrote later:

The plan had been to rush the bridge with the Grenadier Guards Motor Battalion but this failed as German SS troops and others were holding both ends of the bridge and the northern part of the town in strength ... The Grenadiers, together with the Americans, fought on all afternoon and after very bitter fighting reached a roundabout just short of the bridge where they were finally held up. These American troops are splendid types, brave and cheerful, and seemingly indifferent to the worst.[42]

Later in the day, the commander of XXX Corps, Lieutenant General Horrocks, came forward and met Gavin, Browning and Major General Adair, commander of the Guards Armoured Division. They were all acutely aware that the attempts to take the bridges had failed and that, with the Germans on both banks, their men had little chance of capturing either intact. It seemed obvious that, rather than risk losing a bridge, the Germans would demolish it. In fact, in the case of the road bridge, Field Marshal Model had expressly forbidden such an act. He was determined to use it in a counter-offensive.

The Allied commanders were now facing a crisis. The British force at Arnhem was in deep trouble, the 82nd Airborne Division's eastern perimeter was under heavy pressure[43] and the extremely narrow XXX Corps corridor was under ground attack from both flanks[44] and intermittent air attack.[45] In similar circumstances, most commanders would have given up trying to fight their way to the bridges through a built-up area and would have carried out a river crossing on one of the flanks, followed by a bridging operation. But these were far from normal circumstances and the time needed to mount and carry out such complicated operations would have spelled annihilation for the British at Arnhem. As Gavin put it: 'If I did nothing more than pour infantry and British armor into the battle at our end of the bridge, we could be fighting there for days and Urquhart would be lost.'[46] He came up therefore with a daring, but extremely risky, plan to attack both ends of the bridge at once.

NOTES

1. Kershaw, *It Never Snows in September*, p. 230, says there were twelve 320mm Nebelwerfers operating in the Arnhem area from 17 Sep.
2. 1 & 3 Para.
3. 2 S Staffs & 11 Para, the latter at more or less full strength.
4. Tieke, *In the Firestorm of the Last Years of the War*, p. 246.
5. 11 Para.
6. 2 S Staffs, now reinforced by its remaining companies which had arrived with the second lift.
7. 11 Para.
8. 10 & 156 Para.
9. 156 Para.
10. 10 Para.

11. 7 KOSB.
12. The precise makeup of this unit is unknown.
13. Kershaw, op. cit., pp. 109, 111–13, 163 & 235.
14. 1 Border.
15. Eastwood, *When Dragons Flew*, p. 125.
16. 10 Para.
17. Kershaw, op. cit., p. 202.
18. Swiecicki, *With the Red Devils at Arnhem*, p. 26.
19. Tieke, op. cit., p. 247.
20. Middlebrook, *Arnhem 1944 The Airborne Battle*, p. 272.
21. 156 Para.
22. 10 Para.
23. 7 KOSB.
24. Powell, *The Devil's Birthday*, p. 127.
25. Tieke, op. cit., p. 248.
26. Brereton, *The Brereton Diaries*, p. 350.
27. Wilmot, *The Struggle for Europe*, p. 511.
28. Pnr Trg Bn 9 arrived at Deelen airfield on the night 20/21 Sep.
29. Brereton, op. cit., p. 350. Ryan, *A Bridge Too Far*, p. 305, gives different figures: 655 aircraft and 431 gliders launched and some 112 gliders and forty transports lost.
30. Ryan, *A Bridge Too Far*, p. 305
31. Ibid.
32. 2 HCR followed by 2 Armd Gren Gds and 1 Gren Gds.
33. 2/505 Para Inf.
34. 1 Armd Coldm & 5 Coldm Gds.
35. Gavin, *On to Berlin*, p. 169.
36. 2/505 Para Inf.
37. All the British troops came from the Gren Gds Group.
38. Tieke, op. cit., p. 248.
39. Forbes, *The Grenadier Guards in the War of 1939–45*, p. 134.
40. Powell. op. cit., p. 132, says one in the attack on the rail bridge and four in the attack on the road bridge.
41. 1 (Mot) Gren Gds War Diary, 19 Sep 44.
42. Cooper, *Dangerous Liaison*, pp. 59–60.
43. From Corps Feldt.
44. By two Regts of 59 Div from the west and Pz Bde 107 from the east.
45. Rosse, *The Story of the Guards Armoured Division*, p. 147, mentions attacks by fifteen aircraft on 19 Sep & six FW 190s on the Grave bridge on the 20th. Four were shot down.
46. Gavin, op. cit., p. 170.

CHAPTER XVI
MARKET GARDEN:
Wednesday 20 September

The Arnhem Sector
(Map 12)

At dawn on 20 September, dark clouds and drizzle added to the already deeply depressing situation for the British at the northern end of the Arnhem bridge. The Germans subjected the small force on either side of the ramp to a virtually incessant artillery and mortar barrage and, as the day wore on, to combined infantry and tank attacks from the eastern flank, followed by infiltrations from the west.

Lieutenant Colonel John Frost, the British commander, was at last in radio contact with his Divisional commander, but the news he received could not have been more disturbing. There was no hope of reinforcements reaching him from the west, the planned Polish drop south of the river had had to be postponed and XXX Corps had not even crossed the Waal, let alone started its advance towards the Arnhem bridge. Then, to add 'injury to insult', at about 1330 hours Frost was wounded in both legs by mortar fire.

British resistance was clearly collapsing and Bittrich's urgent requirement to move reinforcements across the bridge to reinforce the advance elements of Harmel's Frundsberg Division in the Nijmegen sector looked as though it would soon be realised. A further Battalion of the Frundsberg's 21st SS Panzer-Grenadier Regiment had already arrived in Arnhem and been subordinated to KG Brinkmann and this enabled KG Knaust to re-group in readiness for the move south.

Some time in the evening, a two-hour truce was arranged at the request of the British to allow approximately 300 wounded, including about 100 Germans and Dutch civilians, to be evacuated. Frost later described their captors as 'kind, chivalrous and even comforting'[1], and most reached the St Elizabeth hospital safely where they found two British surgical teams working alongside the German medical staff and Dutch nurses. For the remainder, wounded or otherwise, the choice was stark – surrender or try to escape through the surrounding German lines.

Whilst the Frost group at the Arnhem bridge fought its last battle, the remainder of 1st British Airborne Division spent the 20th struggling to set up and hold a defensive perimeter in Oosterbeek. There, Urquhart, realising that it was only a matter of time before the foothold at the

146

bridge was lost, still hoped to maintain a bridgehead for the eventual use of XXX Corps. Bittrich and Harzer were under strict orders from Model to prevent this happening and, whilst keeping up the pressure on the eastern flank throughout the day, they prepared for an all-out assault in the Oosterbeek area on the 21st. To this end, KG Tettau was subordinated to II SS Panzer Corps, all Dutch civilians, except Police, medical staffs, air-raid rescue teams and the critically sick or injured, were evacuated and additional units brought under Harzer's command. These included two coastal Machine-Gun Battalions, an Artillery Regiment[2] and an Army Panzer-Grenadier Battalion (KG Bruhn). All existing non-SS artillery units were then placed under the command of the Artillery Regiment, which was itself then subordinated to the Hohenstaufen. KG Bruhn was deployed on the western flank of KG Krafft, where it would be used to attack the northern edge of the British perimeter.

Satisfied that Harzer had sufficient forces to deal with the British north of the lower Rhine, and still convinced that the key to the battle was the Waal front north of Nijmegen, Bittrich moved that night to Harmel's advanced Command Post, 3km west of Pannerden (Map 11).

Bittrich's opposite number on the Allied side was Lieutenant General 'Boy' Browning, of whom we have heard little. The first important decision he was required to take came on this day, when he received a signal from England offering to fly in an additional Brigade by glider and land it as close as possible to Urquhart's men. This Brigade was part of the Division[3] earmarked in the original plan to fly in to Deelen airfield on the 21st. Browning, displaying a total ignorance of the real situation in Arnhem and Oosterbeek, replied, 'offer not, repeat not, required as situation better than you think. We want lifts as already planned, including Poles.'

The Nijmegen Sector
(Map 14)

The commander of the 82nd Airborne Division, Brigadier General Jim Gavin, described 20 September 1944 as 'a day unprecedented in the Division's combat history. Each of the three Regiments fought a critical battle in its own area and won over heavy odds.'[4] This was indeed the case. To the south-east of Nijmegen, two of his Regiments[5] fought a desperate battle to hold off German forces[6] attacking from the direction of the Reichswald, and in the city itself the third Regiment, as we shall hear shortly, played a decisive part in the capture of the bridges over the Waal. General 'Boy' Browning witnessed this latter event, together with Horrocks of XXX Corps, and is said to have exclaimed, 'I have never seen a more gallant action'.[7]

The German attacks from the direction of the Reichswald, which even today looks like a great wave about to break into this part of Holland, were launched by three KGs[8] at around 0800 hours. By early evening they had made considerable progress against the badly over-stretched Americans, having captured the villages of Wyler, Beek and Mook and at one stage threatening the only bridge available to XXX Corps over the Maas–Waal canal.[9] This critical situation was eventually restored that night and the following morning by strong American counter-attacks, those at Mook and Beek being supported by elements of the attached British armoured group.[10]

Despite its obvious dangers, both Horrocks and Adair, the commander of the Guards Armoured Division, readily gave their approval to Gavin's plan[11] for the capture of the Nijmegen bridges. It involved joint Anglo-American attacks to secure the southern ends of the rail and road bridges and most of an American Parachute Regiment crossing the river in assault boats to the west of the railway bridge with the aim of securing the northern bank. In the case of the road bridge, British tanks were to make a dash across it in conjunction with the American attack. The dangers of the Germans blowing the bridge at this point were obvious.

It took five hours, until 1330 hours, to clear the jumping-off area for the final assault on the southern ends of the bridges, and the bank of the Waal from which the river crossing was to be made. Further delays were then experienced in bringing forward thirty-two British assault boats[12] from the XXX Corps column. A major cause of this delay was another extremely heavy Luftwaffe raid on Eindhoven the previous night[13] which had blocked roads and caused numerous civilian casualties.[14]

Just before 1500 hours, following an air strike by eight Typhoons[15] and a fifteen-minute artillery barrage, the boats, each with thirteen men[16], set off across the 400m wide river. The 3rd Battalion[17] of Colonel Reuben Tucker's 504th Parachute Infantry Regiment led the way, with the 1st Battalion[18] following, in a total of six waves. The 2nd Battalion[19] and thirty British tanks[20] provided direct fire support from the south bank near the power station, and some 100 American guns and mortars provided indirect fire support. Smoke rounds were included in the fire plan to give cover to the highly vulnerable paratroopers, but much of it blew away before it could be effective.

The story of the incredibly gallant Waal river crossing and the seizure of the north bank of the river by the men of the 504th Parachute Infantry Regiment has been told many times and portrayed vividly in the film, *A Bridge Too Far*. It is unnecessary to repeat it.

Meanwhile, the complementary assault against KG Euling at the southern end of the road bridge was reaching its climax. By early evening, despite a considerable number of casualties and the loss of a Sherman, the attack[21] finally overwhelmed the German defenders:

All serious German resistance seemed to crack . . . a patrol from No. 4

Company [Grenadier Guards] moved down to the bridge and, apart from a considerable number of shell-shocked Germans, found it clear ... It remained for the 2nd Battalion [the Grenadier Guards tank Battalion] to move over the bridge. At 1830, a troop [platoon of four tanks], which had been held in readiness by the round-about, edged forward along the embankment, but it was still too light; they were met by strong anti-tank fire and forced to withdraw.[22]

By this time the brave but depleted American paratroopers[23] had secured the north end of the railway bridge[24] and were continuing their advance to the north and to the east. At 1900 hours, as they approached the north end of the massive road bridge, the troop of four Grenadier Guards Shermans[25] was ordered to advance again. Despite the fading light they came under fire from two 88mm guns on the far side, a StuG firing straight down the bridge and from men with hand-held anti-tank weapons and machine-guns on the structure itself. The two rear tanks were hit but, against all expectations, the other two succeeded in crossing and after knocking out the StuG, linked up with Tucker's valiant paratroopers about a kilometre up the road.[26] The time was 1915 hours. Within an hour the Americans had eliminated the anti-tank threat and British engineers, more Shermans (including one of those hit on the bridge), four 17-pounder anti-tank guns and two companies of infantry had reinforced the slender bridgehead.[27]

With the remnants of the beleaguered 1st Airborne Division at Arnhem, less than 18km away to the north, the Americans naturally expected the British armour to move rapidly to their rescue – but nothing happened. Reuben Tucker was, understandably, furious. He is said to have told a Guards major, 'Your boys are hurting up there at Arnhem. You'd better go.'[28] There is even a report that one American company commander was so angry about the failure to advance that he actually threatened a British officer with his sub machine-gun, causing him to close the hatches on his Sherman. Certainly Tucker said to Jim Gavin the next morning, 'What in the hell are they doing? We've been in this position for over twelve hours and all they seem to be doing is brewing tea'.[29] In view of the casualties his Regiment had suffered securing the north bank of the Waal, his anger would seem to be justified.

A British Guards officer wrote later:

Patrols of Americans, wearing rubber-soled boots that made no sound, kept passing through us, alert and eager to engage the enemy. For our part, we just sat in our positions all night ... The situation in Arnhem remained desperate. Yet the Guards Armoured Division did nothing.[30]

Sadly, it was true. It would be eighteen hours before the advance was resumed and yet for five hours, from 1900 until midnight, there was virtually nothing to stop an advance up the Elst–Arnhem road (Map 19). Once again, however, British caution ruled the day. The plight of those at the Arnhem bridge and in Oosterbeek seems to have taken second place to worries about the XXX corridor south of Nijmegen.[31] Or was it perhaps lethargy, military incompetence, or an unwillingness to accept a few casualties for the good of the majority – not least the Dutch people north of the Waal? Whilst it is certainly true that it would have been difficult to assemble quickly the Battalion which had secured the southern bank of the river (it already suffered heavy casualties), this was certainly not true of the two infantry companies sent across the Waal 'as soon as the Grenadiers captured the bridge', or of their 'Battalion HQ and the other companies . . . comfortably and securely lodged in a large school south of the river.'[32] This Battalion had been in reserve for forty-eight hours.

Many excuses have been offered for the failure of the Guards Armoured Division to advance on the evening of 20 September, but none of them is totally satisfactory. Lack of infantry is the most common. Surprisingly, Chester Wilmot in *The Struggle for Europe* writes:

> In the Nijmegen bridgehead Horrocks had one parachute regiment [the US 504th] and two groups of Guards [the Grenadier and Irish Guards Battlegroups], but the latter could not resume the offensive until they were relieved by infantry of the 43rd Division which was only just crossing the Maas.[33]

Even so, he does not explain *why* the Guards had to be relieved and it is inconceivable that the Germans or Americans would have considered it necessary to do so at such a critical stage in the battle. Only nine tanks had been lost[34] and two infantry companies[35] of the immediate reserve were already north of the river. One junior Irish Guards officer wrote later:

> I led my platoon over the [Waal] bridge in the dark to take up a position astride the road ahead. Again, we sat there all night, with no German counter-attack . . . It was a moment when you would have expected the commanders to order the Grenadiers [in Shermans] to continue hell for leather to Arnhem, with the 3rd Battalion Irish Guards riding on the tanks. Neither battalion was otherwise seriously engaged all night.[36]

In the same way, it is strange that the third Battlegroup of the Division, the Welsh Guards, which had seen no action other than 'a small flank action near Valkenswaard'[37], was not transferred immediately from the reserve to the forward Brigade in order to continue the advance. Suggestions that it was fully committed protecting the Grave bridge are not credible. Two brigades of the 43rd Wessex Division were in the Grave area, which was not under attack anyway. Sadly, the Welsh Guards were left south of the river at this critical time.

The failure of Horrocks to order the advance to continue 'hell for leather' that evening, or of Adair to seize the initiative and give the necessary orders, was to result in tragic events on both sides of the lower Rhine.

It is also of note that Wilmot's statement that the 43rd Division was 'only just crossing the Maas' is wrong. Two of its Brigades spent the night south of the river, one of them stating in its War Diary that it 'decided to halt till daylight just south of Grave'[38] (see above). The same applied to its attached Armoured Brigade, which sat immobile for the first three days of the Operation and was not even ordered to move forward into Holland until 1600 hours on the 20th.[39] Whilst there is no doubt that the severe congestion on the only available road to Nijmegen, and the difficulties of getting convoys through bomb-damaged Eindhoven, made it inevitable that the vehicles of the 43rd Division would take a long time to reach the Maas, it is surprising that its infantry were allowed to sit in traffic jams instead of being made to march the 75km or so. In this context, it has to be pointed out that many of the Germans attacking the XXX Corps corridor had marched just that sort of distance[40], as had many of the Frundsberg Panzer-Grenadiers in their move to the Nijmegen front.

Not surprisingly, the situation in front of the Nijmegen bridgehead on the night of 20/21 September soon began to change and, shortly after midnight, a new German defensive line, some 4km north of the bridge, began to build. It was manned initially by KG Reinhold, and by dawn the following day it had been reinforced by sixteen Mk IVs and StuGs and a Battalion of the Frundsberg's 22nd SS Panzer-Grenadier Regiment, newly arrived from the Pannerden crossing.

There remains the question of why the Germans failed to blow the vital Nijmegen bridge on 20 September. We have already heard that Frundsberg Pioneers set to work to prepare it for demolition as soon as they arrived on the 18th. This work was confirmed by British engineers[41] who searched the bridge immediately after its capture. As well as cutting numerous wires and cables, they found Teller mines in one of the piers at the southern end and cutting charges under the deck girders at the northern end. Since Harmel had been personally responsible for the defence of the Waal in the Nijmegen sector since early on the 18th, he clearly had ample time in which to specify the conditions under which the bridge could be blown. We have heard too that he had been expressly forbidden to do so by Model. Twelve years after the event, in the safety of post-war Germany, Heinz Harmel gave his version of what happened when he arrived in the area north of the bridge as, or soon after, the first British tanks crossed:

I now gave the order, on my own responsibility, to blow the road bridge, over which further tanks continued to advance. It failed to go up – probably because the initiation cable had been cut by artillery fire.[42]

Whilst this may well be true, it seems highly unlikely that even in these circumstances he would risk disobeying the Field Marshal's order – particularly since Model was one of Hitler's favourites! The full facts will probably never be known.

In an episode almost as amazing as the American crossing of the Waal, SS Captain Karl-Heinz Euling led the sixty or so survivors of his KG to safety that night. They fought on until around 2225 hours in various locations near the bridge and then managed to slip away, quite literally under the noses of the British, to find rowing boats and join their Frundsberg comrades on the north side of the river. Euling was later awarded the Knight's Cross for his actions on this day.

NOTES

1. Powell, *The Devil's Birthday*, p. 149.
2. Arty Regt 191.
3. 52 (Lowland) Div.
4. Gavin, *On to Berlin*, p. 177.
5. 505 (less a Bn) & 508 Para Inf Regts.
6. Corps Feldt.
7. Gavin, op. cit., p. 179.
8. KGs Becker, Herman & Greschick with men from II Para Corps & Mil Dist VI.
9. According to Powell, op. cit., p. 133, the 82nd had by this time suffered 150 killed and 600 wounded. Casualties in the Mook battle alone were twenty killed, fifty-four wounded and seven missing.
10. Coldm Gds Group including four 17-pdrs of Q Bty, 21 A/Tk Regt.
11. In *Corps Commander*, p. 111, Horrocks claims that he and Browning suggested the idea of crossing the Waal in assault boats.
12. Fitzgerald, *The History of the Irish Guards in the Second World War*, p. 501, says six of these boats were lost when the lorry carrying them was destroyed by German fire as it approached the off-loading point.
13. According to its War Diary, the Gds Armd Div lost sixteen ammunition & seven fuel trucks in this raid.
14. 227 civilians died in air raids on the city during MARKET GARDEN.
15. 247 Sqn, 2 ATAF.
16. Manned by C Coy, 307 Airborne Engr Bn. Incredibly, one of the boats used in the Waal crossing was found intact in a farmer's barn near Nijmegen in Jun 2001.
17. Maj Julian Cook.
18. Lt Col William Harrison.
19. Maj Edward Wellems.
20. 2 Armd IG.

21. Lt Col Edward Goulburn's 1 Gren Gds & LTC Ben Vandervoort's 2/505 Para Inf Bn (less D Coy), both supported by Shermans of Lt Col Moore's 2 Armd Gren Gds.
22. Forbes, *The Grenadier Guards in the War of 1939–45*, p. 138.
23. The 504th suffered 134 casualties, killed, wounded or missing, in this action. Sixteen of the assault boats were sunk or swamped. D/504 Para Inf crossed the Waal at 1900 hrs but E & F Coys remained south of the river to guard PWs.
24. The southern end was not captured until 0900 hrs the following day. According to Rosse, *The Story of the Guards Armoured Division*, p. 142, 417 German dead were counted on and in the immediate vicinity of the bridge.
25. Commanded by Sgt Robinson of 2 Armd Gren Gds. Sgt C Pacey's tk was in the lead.
26. Details taken from Robinson's and Pacey's Citations for bravery.
27. 1 & 3 Tps 14 Fd Sqn RE, a Tp of Q Bty 21 A/tk Regt & Nos 2 & 4 Coys 3 IG.
28. Ryan, *A Bridge Too Far*, p. 355.
29. Gavin, op. cit., p. 181.
30. Wilson, *The Ever Open Eye*, p. 131.
31. It had in fact been cut for a short time on this day, at Son, by Panzer Brigade 107.
32. Fitzgerald, op. cit., p. 505. Horrocks' statement in *Corps Commander*, p. 118, that 3 IG was down to only 'five platoons' is incorrect.
33. Wilmot, *The Struggle for Europe*, p. 514.
34. Gds Armd Div War Diary, 20 Sep 44.
35. 2 & 4 Coys 3 IG.
36. Wilson, op. cit., p. 181.
37. Ellis, *The Welsh Guards at War*, p. 69.
38. 130 Inf Bde.
39. 8 Armd Bde War Diary for period 17–20 Sep 44.
40. Kershaw, *It Never Snows in September*, pp. 251–2, claims that teenage soldiers of the 6 Para Regt marched 63km in thirty-six hrs on 21/22 Sep, carrying weapons, ammunition and rations.
41. Lt A Jones, Lt A Vivian & Sgt V Zimmer of 14 Fd Sqn RE.
42. Waffen-SS veterans' magazine, *Der Freiwillige*, Sep 56.

CHAPTER XVII

MARKET GARDEN:
Thursday 21 September

The Arnhem Sector

(Map 12)

By 0500 hours on 21 September, organised resistance at the north end of the Arnhem bridge had ceased. The British had held their positions for three days and four nights and won the respect of their adversaries.

SONS OF THE REICH

Above all they had engaged important elements of the Frundsberg Division, particularly KG Brinkmann, and prevented them being used against the US 82nd Airborne Division and XXX Corps at Nijmegen. It is estimated that eighty-one British paratroopers died in the fighting around the bridge (of which thirty-one have no known grave)[1] – virtually all the others who fought there were wounded and/or captured. Most of the survivors agreed that the men of the Frundsberg fought 'correctly' and treated them with consideration after the fighting ceased. The relationship which gradually, but not always, developed between prisoners and captors is well described by a British doctor who experienced it later in the Oosterbeek area:

> The fundamental antipathy between both sides could not be disguised. The points of view, from which each side regarded the other, were such poles apart that no common ground could be found, except the impersonal and abstract one of interpreting the correct medical usages of war. Since both parties subscribed, unlike the Russians, to the Geneva Convention, an appeal to its code could be made without fundamental antagonism, and it was here that the areas of agreement were defined. The Germans agreed to remove their armed troops, apart from those guards necessary to prevent the possible escape of lesser-wounded back to their units and the fight. They agreed to provide food and medical supplies, and to arrange the evacuation of the seriously wounded as soon as possible.[2]

As far as Harmel and Bittrich were concerned the most important aspect of this victory was that KGs Knaust and Brinkmann, and the Hohenstaufen's 9th SS Reconnaissance Battalion in the brick factory south of the river, were now available for re-deployment. The first to move was KG Knaust which, with eight Mk III and IV tanks, set off towards the British bridgehead at Nijmegen at midday.

The Oosterbeek 'perimeter', as it became known, was initially about 5km in length and encompassed only about one third of the built-up part of the village. It was defended by some 3,500 men, under the overall command of Major General Roy Urquhart. Brigadier 'Shan' Hackett commanded the eastern side of the perimeter with about 500 men and Brigadier 'Pip' Hicks the much larger north-west and western side with the remainder. In terms of heavy weaponry, twenty-three of the twenty-four 75mm howitzers[3], eight of the sixteen 17-pounder and thirteen of the fifty-two 6-pounder anti-tank guns[4] which had left England were still in action. Six Polish 6-pounders were also operational. Trapped within the perimeter were more than 3,000 Dutch civilians.

Bittrich's plan for eliminating the Oosterbeek bridgehead was for concentric attacks by the Hohenstaufen from the north and east and by KG

Tettau from the west. Whilst apparently simple in theory, this plan proved difficult to implement in practice. The main problem was the overall shortage of radios and basic command facilities, particularly in KG Tettau, which made coordination between KGs extremely difficult. Added to this was an ignorance of the precise locations of the British. Nevertheless, at 0800 hours on 21 September KGs Lippert and Eberwein and a Battalion of the Hermann Goering Training and Reinforcement Regiment, supported by four converted Renault Char B tanks, attacked the reinforced British Battalion[5] holding the two and a half kilometre western side of the perimeter. Despite the numerical superiority of the Germans, their only significant success was the capture of the 30m high bluff, overlooking the lower Rhine, known as the Westerbouwing (Map 17). Its significance lay in the fact that it dominated the north bank of the river in the direction of the railway bridge and in particular, the Heveadorp ferry site. Although the Dutch ferryman had cut the cable and sunk the ferry the previous day, the site itself, with its approach roads, remained the best potential crossing place for XXX Corps. With the benefit of hindsight, it seems remarkable that the British made no attempt to use this ferry on the 18th and 19th in order to attack the southern end of the road bridge – Dutch civilians are said to have used it to cross to Oosterbeek to buy bread as late as the morning of the 20th. In much the same way, the Germans seem to have failed to appreciate the importance of the Westerbouwing or to exploit it as a jumping off point to attack the British bridgehead.

In the north and north-east the attacks by KGs Bruhn and Krafft made little progress in the wooded terrain, interspersed with houses. The defenders[6] held on tenaciously.

In the east, with KG Spindler[7] centred on the main east-west Utrecht road, and KGs Allwörden and Harder[8] on its left to as far south as the river, Harzer's SS men slammed their way forward into the battle-weary remnants of many of the units that had tried to reinforce Frost's men at the road bridge.[9] Each KG was reinforced with three StuGs from Assault Gun Brigade 280 and a few Mk III and IV tanks, and the guns and mortars of Artillery Regiment 191 were in indirect support. Some penetrations were achieved, but despite the German strength, the British perimeter remained intact.

In the midst of all this fighting on Thursday 21 September, some important new participants entered the scene – men of the 1st Independent Polish Parachute Brigade Group. Originally due to drop south of the Arnhem road bridge on the Tuesday, bad weather had caused delays until this unfortunate moment. Unfortunate for three reasons: first, because of the failure of the 1st Airborne Division to secure the Arnhem bridge and its other objectives, the LZ had to be changed to an area immediately south of the Heveadorp ferry site, near Driel (Map 12);

SONS OF THE REICH

second, because German flak and fighter aircraft were fully active by this time; and third, because by the time the Poles arrived the Heveadorp ferry had been sunk and the site had been in German hands for over two hours.[10]

We have already heard of the disastrous landing of the jeeps and anti-tank guns of the Polish Brigade on the north side of the river on the Tuesday. What happened two days later was another tragedy. 114 transport aircraft carrying 1,568 men took off in the early afternoon. Forty-one C-47s, carrying a complete parachute Battalion, turned back after receiving re-call messages sent out because of bad weather at the mounting airfields, and German fighters and flak shot down a further five aircraft over Holland. Despite these setbacks, 1,003 Poles landed near Driel and made their way to the southern bank of the lower Rhine, only to find the ferry sunk and Germans (KG Harder) on the north side. Without boats or rafts, there was simply no way the Poles could get across to reinforce the Oosterbeek perimeter. The Polish commander, 51-year-old Major General Sosabowski, who had no radio contact with Urquhart's Headquarters only 2km away, reluctantly ordered his men to remain under the cover of the steep riverbank. They had suffered only five killed and twenty-five wounded, but they had no artillery support and nothing bigger than PIATs to use against any tanks which might attack them.

The German reaction to the Polish drop was immediate and effective. The commander of Artillery Regiment 191 re-deployed some of his units to cover the new LZ, whilst one of the coastal Machine-Gun Battalions with forty heavy machine-guns, together with four Battalion sized units totalling some 3,275 men[11] were formed into 'Blocking Group Harzer'. This new group was then deployed to defend the line of the Arnhem–Nijmegen railway (Map 19) and link up with KG Harder on the north side of the lower Rhine near the railway bridge.

North of Nijmegen
(Map 19)

Early on 21 September Bittrich ordered the Frundsberg to attack the bridgehead north of the Waal from the east and throw the Allies back across the river. At the same time, his opposite number, Horrocks, at last ordered the Guards Armoured Division to strike north 'as early as possible and at maximum speed' and the 43rd Division to move into Nijmegen with a view to following up. Later in the day, Dempsey, the Second British Army commander, met Horrocks and Browning and made it clear to them that his first priority was 'to hold the Nijmegen bridgehead'.[12] It is also of note that Horrocks' order for the Guards Division to continue leading the advance contradicts Chester Wilmot's statement that XXX Corps 'could not resume the offensive until they [the Guards] were relieved by the infantry of the 43rd Division'.

At 0900 hours a British XXX Corps medium artillery Regiment (Battalion) established radio contact with Urquhart's Headquarters in Oosterbeek[13] and received the following message:

> Enemy attacking main bridge in strength. Situation critical for slender force. Enemy also attacking divisional position from Heelsum vicinity and west from Arnhem. Situation serious but am forming close perimeter around Hartenstein with remainder of division. Relief essential both areas earliest possible. Still retain control ferry-crossing Heveadorp.

Horrocks, not unreasonably, concluded from this that the airborne bridgehead was still large enough to be exploited. He therefore gave further orders that if the Guards found the direct route to Arnhem blocked, they should divert to the west and head for the Heveadorp ferry site. In this way they might avoid the main German defences, link up with the Polish Parachute Brigade due to drop that afternoon (Map 12) and establish a crossing site opposite Oosterbeek.

By the time Horrocks gave his second order, the Nijmegen bridge was under German air attack and the Frundsberg force opposing the Guards consisted of one and a half SS Panzer-Grenadier Battalions from Schultze's 22nd Regiment, Reinhold's 2nd SS Panzer Battalion with sixteen Mk IVs and StuGs, the 10th SS Pioneers and an Army unit known as KG Hartung. The 2nd Battalion of the 10th SS Artillery Regiment was in direct support and other units of the Regiment were capable of giving additional support from the right bank of the lower Rhine. The general line established by this force ran from Bemmel to Elst, where elements of the Hohenstaufen's 9th SS Reconnaissance Battalion, left there by Gräbner on the 18th, were still in position. As the day wore on, units of Deisenhofer's 21st SS Panzer-Grenadier Regiment crossed the river at Pannerden to thicken up the line and, as we have already heard, KG Knaust, with eight tanks began its move south from Arnhem to Elst at midday. The new boundary between the Frundsberg and the Hohenstaufen ran from the junction of the lower Rhine and the Ijssel to Elst.

The route the British were planning to take to Arnhem was the shortest but fraught with difficulties in that it ran across reclaimed land – in fact, the whole area between the Waal and lower Rhine was nicknamed 'The Island'. It is well described in the History of the Irish Guards:

> 90% water. Surrounded by water, based on water, criss-crossed by innumerable waterways, below water level and completely flat, so that

if the rivers burst their dykes it was also under water. The soil was rich with river mud, excellent for fruit trees, which the Dutch farmers planted industriously, lining the main road to Arnhem with orchards. This road [the only direct one from Nijmegen to Arnhem ran more or less due north through Elst] was embanked high [2m] above the surrounding fields and cut off from them by a deep drainage ditch on either side.[14]

The greatest drawback to using this route was the near impossibility of tanks moving off the embanked road if they ran into trouble. That said, it is worth noting that whilst the British claimed that their tanks could not move cross-country in this area, it seems that the Mk IIIs and IVs, StuGs and even some Tiger IIs with KGs Reinhold and Knaust were able to deploy off road to good effect.

The orders to advance up the Arnhem road reached the Irish Guards Battlegroup at 1100 hours but the first of its fifty-two tanks[15] did not move off until 1330, over eighteen hours after the Nijmegen bridge had been captured and hardly in accordance with Horrocks' later assertion that, 'no troops could have done more or advanced more rapidly than had 30 Corps'.[16] Ten minutes and 3km later the leading squadron ran into the German anti-tank screen in front of Elst and the first three Shermans went up in flames. Their accompanying infantry dismounted and took cover, only to come under intense mortar and artillery fire. Lacking artillery support for the next three hours – a new experience for the British – and unable to call in the Typhoons circling above them owing to radio problems, the advance came to an abrupt halt.[17] At 1730 hours an attempt by a supporting Battlegroup[18] to find a way round the left flank, towards Oosterhout, was halted after it ran into the leading elements of KG Knaust, newly arrived from Arnhem. Although three German tanks were allegedly knocked out, it was getting dark and:

the Higher Command ... decided that before any further advance could be made the bridgehead must be enlarged so that more troops could be brought [forward]. The Welsh Guards [a tank Battalion and an infantry Battalion] were ordered to withdraw to harbour [rest] near the bridge.[19]

During the night KG Knaust took up positions in Elst, thus ensuring that future British attempts to advance towards Arnhem would be even more difficult. When Elst was finally captured, several days later, eleven 75mm and two 88mm guns were found abandoned or destroyed in the area where the Guards had been halted.[20] Knaust himself was to receive a Knight's Cross from Model personally for his KG's actions in this fighting.

Meanwhile, between 0830 and 1130 hours on 21 September, two Brigades of the long awaited 43rd (Wessex) Division arrived in Nijmegen. In view of the situation in Oosterbeek, one would have expected them to continue to the north side of the Waal, but instead both remained in the city. One Brigade[21] was used to relieve the two Guards Battalions that had been involved in the capture of the Nijmegen bridge and spent the rest of the day guarding the bridges and searching for non-existent Germans. The Guards in turn moved to the south of Nijmegen and were told, 'no move for some time.'[22] The other Wessex Brigade remained, virtually inactive, for the rest of the day[23] – indeed, one Battalion, misdirected in traffic chaos, could not even find its way to the railway bridge.

NOTES

1. Middlebrook, *Arnhem 1944 The Airborne Battle*, p. 321.
2. Mawson, *Arnhem Doctor*, pp. 135–6.
3. 1 Air-Landing Lt Regt RA.
4. 1 & 2 Air-Landing A/Tk Btys RA.
5. 1 Border, reinforced with engrs & glider pilots.
6. 7 KOSB, 21 Indep Para Coy, 1 Airborne Recce Sqn, 4 Para Sqn, 9 (Airborne) Fd & 261 (Airborne) Fd Pk Coys RE, and E & F Sqns The Glider Pilot Regt.
7. Including KG Möller.
8. Reinforced by KG Weber.
9. Lonsdale Force (2 S Staffs, 1, 3 & 11 Para), D & G Sqns The Glider Pilot Regt, 10 & 156 Para, all supported by the 75mm howitzers of 1 Air-Landing Lt Regt RA.
10. Urquhart had sent a message at 0430 hrs confirming that the Heveadorp ferry was in British hands. This message still exists in the Sikorski Museum in London.
11. One each from the Army (Schörken), Navy (Köhnen), Luftwaffe (Kauer) & Dutch SS (3rd Landsturm Nederland).
12. Dempsey Diaries, PRO London, WO 285/10.
13. This contact enabled the Regt to provide badly needed heavy arty support for those within the Oosterbeek perimeter.
14. Fitzgerald, *The History of the Irish Guards in the Second World War*, p. 506.
15. Ibid., p. 508.
16. Horrocks, *A Full Life*, p. 223.
17. Details of this action are taken from the 2 Armd IG War Diary, 21 Sep 44.
18. 2 Armd WG & 1 WG.
19. Ellis, *The Welsh Guards at War*, p. 228.
20. 2 Armd IG War Diary, 24 Sep 44.
21. 130 Inf Bde with two tk sqns under command.
22. 1 (Mot) Gren Gds War Diary, 21 Sep 44.
23. 214 Inf Bde War Diary, 21 Sep 44.

CHAPTER XVIII

MARKET GARDEN: 'Black Friday'
22 September.[1]

North of the Lower Rhine

The siege of Urquhart's force in Oosterbeek was to last another four days. During this period the Germans maintained constant pressure but their attacks, whether by infantry or armoured vehicles or a combination of both, were limited in scope. Model, Bittrich, and Harzer all knew that as long as reinforcements and supplies could be prevented from reaching the encircled defenders, it was only a matter of time before they would have to surrender. Bittrich resolved therefore to 'batter the British into submission'. 110 guns and heavy mortars were to be brought into action and, with no shortage of ammunition, the Germans were able to maintain a virtually incessant bombardment, particularly at night. The only effective assistance Urquhart's exhausted men received during the siege was from the XXX Corps artillery. By the end of the week, fourteen batteries were firing in support and a total of 160 fire missions were carried out, some within 150m of the defenders' positions.

For those who wish to read detailed accounts of the close-quarter fighting which took place in these last days of the Oosterbeek perimeter, and the personal stories of many of those involved, Martin Middlebrook's *Arnhem 1944 The Airborne Battle*, and Robert Kershaw's *It Never Snows in September* are particularly recommended. For our purposes, Urquhart's own description, sent in a radio message at 2015 hours on the 23rd will suffice:

> Many attacks during day by small parties infantry, SP guns, tanks, including flame-thrower tanks[2]. Each attack accompanied by very heavy mortaring and shelling within Div perimeter. After many alarms and excursions the latter remains substantially unchanged, although very thinly held. Physical contact not yet made with those on south bank of river. Re-supply a flop, small quantities of ammo only gathered in. Still no food and all ranks very dirty owing to shortage of water. Morale still adequate, but continued heavy mortaring and shelling is having obvious effects.

Between the Waal and the Lower Rhine
(Map 19)

The lost opportunity of the previous night was to cost the British – and the Poles – dear. Faced now with substantial German forces blocking the main road to Arnhem and the ground on either side unsuitable for armour, Horrocks knew he would have to deploy infantry in strength and find an alternative route. The previous evening Urquhart had reported, 'balance of division in very tight perimeter . . . Relief within twenty-four hours vital'. Early on the 22nd Horrocks replied, '43 Div ordered to take all risks to effect relief today and are directed on ferry [Heveadorp]'. He still believed that 'with a fresh infantry Division available . . . I would be able to join up with them [the Poles] and force a crossing'.[3] Despite the assurance he had given Urquhart that the 43rd Division would 'take all risks', Horrocks in fact told Thomas 'to advance with all speed but, and this is most important, . . . artillery ammunition must be used with the utmost economy'.[4]

Good news came early on the 22nd, when armoured cars[5] reported that, after taking advantage of the early morning mist, they had managed to slip through Oosterhout and Valburg, 4km west of Elst, and make contact with the Poles at Driel. Unfortunately, by the time this news was received, Major General Thomas's 43rd Wessex Division had taken over responsibility for the advance and the potential of the reserve Battlegroup[6] of Adair's Guards Armoured Division, which had harboured north of the road bridge the previous evening, was wasted. Just as serious for those in the Oosterbeek perimeter was the fact that Thomas's Division, which had arrived in Nijmegen the previous day, was still incomplete on the north side of the Waal. By the time it was ready to advance, at 0830 hours, the mist had cleared.

The leading infantry Brigade[7] (in effect, the leading platoon of the leading company of the leading Battalion[8]) eventually advanced through the Irish Guards on the Arnhem road towards Elst whilst another Brigade with tank support[9], in the same configuration, pushed forward farther west towards the village of Oosterhout. The third Brigade remained in Nijmegen guarding the bridges.

Within an hour, both advances had ground to a halt in front of KGs Knaust and Reinhold. This was hardly surprising, given the restriction Horrocks had placed on artillery support. KG Reinhold defended Oosterhout successfully all day and it took three attacks[10], the last finally supported by 100 guns and two tank platoons, to overcome the men of the Frundsberg at 1730 hours. The British took 139 prisoners and found a Mk III tank, one 88mm and five 20mm guns in the village. They claimed three other Mk IIIs knocked out.[11] General Thomas seems to have failed to pass on Horrocks' order 'to take all risks' and as a result the British suffered only nineteen wounded and wasted yet another day. This limited success, however, enabled a squadron of tanks carrying two companies of infantry[12] to make a dash for Driel. The fact that visibility was generally restricted to some 100m by the profusion of fruit trees in the area undoubtedly helped their advance and by 2015 hours they had covered the difficult 16km and linked up with the Poles. Their arrival after dark was fortunate since the Polish defensive perimeter in the village had been subjected throughout the day to spasmodic infantry attacks by Blocking Group Harzer and constant mortar and artillery fire from north of the river. The Polish defenders had waited in vain for the rest of their Brigade to join them, but bad weather had again prevented the troop carrying aircraft leaving England. With the LZ under German observation and fire, the airborne operation would almost certainly have ended in disaster anyway.

Included in the British column reaching Driel were two large amphibious vehicles carrying much needed supplies for the airborne men north of the lower Rhine. They were also intended for use in getting the Poles across the river, but the banks were found to be too steep for them to be launched. Consequently, only fifty-two Poles, using small dinghies and improvised rafts, and minimal amounts of food and ammunition, reached Oosterbeek that night. With the minor road through Valburg under fire from KG Knaust in Elst, and a reinforced Blocking Group Harzer just east of Driel on the line of the Arnhem–Elst railway, the prospects for reinforcing and re-supplying Urquhart's men looked bleak. This latter Group, now commanded by a Colonel Gerhard but still under Harzer's overall command, comprised a hotchpotch of thirteen Alarm companies from all three Services and the Machine-Gun Battalion[13] mentioned in the last Chapter. Later that evening KG Brinkmann joined the Group and, despite the unsuitable ground, was ordered to advance against the Poles. After being engaged from the flank by the rear elements of the British Battalion[14] that had joined up with the Poles, Brinkmann decided to withdraw back to the Arnhem railway line and rejoin the rest of the Blocking Group. The British claimed three 'Tiger' tanks knocked out and two 'ditched' in this action.[15] In fact, there were no Tigers with KG Brinkmann. The Tiger IIs of the 506th Heavy Panzer Battalion did not arrive from Germany until two days later and the vehicles mentioned were most probably armoured cars or personnel carriers, or perhaps Mk III or IV tanks or StuGs. Tank recognition was notoriously bad amongst Allied infantrymen.

Hell's Highway
(Map 15)

Readers will recall that the American 101st Airborne Division had already nicknamed the 45km-corridor between Eindhoven and Grave, 'Hell's

Highway'. Maxwell Taylor's paratroopers had successfully defended it against the relatively weak forces of General Student's First Parachute Army until the 21st but their difficult task had been prolonged by the slow progress of the British Corps on either flank. By the morning of the 22nd, when the major attack ordered by Field Marshal Model against the Veghel area was launched, VIII Corps was still south-east of Eindhoven and XII Corps around Best, 8km west of Son. The Germans had managed to blow the bridge at Best too, but the threat from that flank[16] had drawn in a substantial proportion of the 101st Airborne Division. In fact by now the 101st was so stretched that in places the 'front' was quite literally the edges of the main Eindhoven–Nijmegen road and defended only by the XXX Corps troops moving along it.

The failure of the flanking British Corps to keep pace with XXX Corps and thus relieve the pressure on the Americans defending Hell's Highway has been the subject of much post-war discussion. The bare facts are that XII Corps was not ready to advance on 17 September and three days later had covered only 15km to reach the Turnhout–Eindhoven road, while VIII Corps, which did not begin its advance until the 20th[17], took six days to reach the Maas river, 25km south-east of Nijmegen (Map 11). Although no one would question the bravery of the junior officers and soldiers (VIII and XII Corps suffered 3,874 casualties during the period of Operation GARDEN), or the severity of the fighting, one has to question the motivation of some of their superiors and compare it with that of their opponents. It is significant that, long after the war, O'Connor, the commander of VIII Corps, admitted that he had been instructed 'not to press too hard' on his flank![18]

The attack ordered by Model was launched at 0900 hours on the 22nd from both sides of Hell's Highway. KG Huber[19] attacked from the west, with a Parachute Regiment[20] following up, but not reaching the battle area until the following day. The heaviest assault came from the east and was mounted by a reconstituted KG Walther[21] – it will be remembered that the original KG Walther had been badly mauled in the Neerpelt sector on the first day of Operation GARDEN. Included in this KG was Major Freiherr von Maltzahn's Panzer Brigade 107 and the Frundsberg's KG Heinke.[22] But the latter was missing Segler's SS 2nd/19th Panzer-Grenadier and Roestel's 10th SS Panzerjäger Battalion which were still tied up in another sector and would not arrive in time for the fighting on the 22nd. The same was true of a Parachute Battalion which had also been allocated to Walther's KG. Panzer Brigade 107 was a very powerful formation made up of a Panzer Battalion with thirty-six Panthers and eleven Jagdpanzer IVs, a full strength Panzer-Grenadier Battalion with 116 SPWs and eight 120mm mortars, and an SPW mounted Pioneer Company. Readers may recall that it had been in action two days previously when it had cut the XXX Corps corridor at Son for a short time. In doing so, however, it had lost 10% of its armour.

Maxwell Taylor's 101st Airborne Division had been defending Hell's Highway, virtually without support, for five days and its Regiments were inevitably too thinly spread to resist a strong attack at a single point. Only one Battalion[23] was positioned in Veghel and the two other Parachute Battalions of Colonel Johnson's 501st Regiment were already involved 5km to the east of Uden which was undefended. Fortunately for the Divisional commander, members of the Dutch resistance had warned Taylor of a German build-up during the night on both sides of the corridor and he was able to start deploying some of his slender reserves[24] as the battle started.

The German attacks were violent and although not fully coordinated, succeeded in cutting the road between Uden and Veghel by 1330 hours. Panthers of the Panzer Brigade then turned south towards Veghel and shortly afterwards KG Huber, advancing from the west, was able to bring fire to bear on the vital bridge over the Willems canal. The Americans, however, were able to pull back their Battalions from west of Uden to support their comrades in Veghel and these Battalions were able to engage and virtually annihilate KG Huber from the rear. Meanwhile, the arrival of a small reserve force heading for Uden, supported by a squadron of British tanks[25] and a Battalion of Glider infantrymen from the main Divisional LZ, halted the move of Maltzahn's tanks from the north and stabilised the situation. According to the US Official History[26], the Americans 'requested air support, but unfavorable weather denied any substantial assistance from that quarter'. This statement is contradicted by Lieutenant General Brereton, the commander of the First Allied Airborne Army, who claimed that 119 Typhoon sorties were flown in support of the ground troops on this day.[27] RAF records show a total of seventy-four Typhoon sorties being flown; sixty-six in the 101st Airborne sector where the alleged target was up to '100 tanks', and eight in the Reichswald area. One Squadron reported firing 119 rockets but few significant claims were made.[28]

By last light the 101st Airborne Division was holding the Veghel area in some strength[29], but it was not strong enough to reopen the corridor through Uden and then continue to hold it open for the movement of the XXX Corps units and supplies urgently needed north of Nijmegen. Reluctantly, but knowing that the Germans would intensify their attacks during the night and the next day, Horrocks gave orders that part of the Guards Armoured Division in Nijmegen was to be sent back down the corridor to help the Americans. Readers will no doubt be surprised to learn that the units chosen were the tank and infantry Battalions which had done all the fighting in Nijmegen on the 19th and 20th.[30] Unfortunately for them, they were now in reserve and the only ones readily available. They received the order to move at 1230 hours and, after making contact with elements of KG Walther south of Uden, went firm in the town as darkness fell.

In the meantime Dempsey, in an indication of how seriously he viewed the situation, placed the US 101st Airborne Division under VIII Corps and told the VIII Corps commander to move one of his Divisions[31] to Veghel.[32]

NOTES

1. For reasons which will become obvious, the XXX Corps commander called 22 Sep 'Black Friday'.
2. It is most unlikely that any flame-throwing tanks took part in this battle; however, an ex-French Renault Char B1 (bis) flame tank was found at Deventer in Holland at the end of the war. It is quite possible that the weapon system in question was a flame -throwing SPW; there was certainly one SPW 251/16 with Recke's Recce Bn – see Dugdale, *Panzer Divisions, Panzer Grenadier Divisions, Panzer Brigades of the Army and the Waffen SS in the West, Volume I [Part 1]*, p. 83.
3. Horrocks, *Corps Commander*, p. 119.
4. Horrocks, *A Full Life*, p. 224.
5. C Sqn, 2 HCR.
6. 2 Armd WG & 1 WG.
7. 129 Inf Bde.
8. 4 Wilts.
9. 214 Inf Bde, with a Bn of tks (4/7 DG) from 8 Armd Bde under command.
10. By 7 SLI.
11. 4/7 DG War Diary 22 Sep 44.
12. Tks of B Sqn 4/7 DG & inf of 5 DCLI.
13. MS # P-162.
14. 5 DCLI.
15. Powell, *The Devil's Birthday*, p. 195.
16. From the 59 Inf Div.
17. Due to lack of transport it did not even cross the Seine until 16 Sep.
18. Powell, op. cit., p. 139.
19. With three inf bns, an arty bn, flak bty & seven a/tk guns from 59 Inf Div and four Jagdpanthers from the 559 PzJg Bn.
20. Von der Heydte's 6 Para Regt.
21. A Pz-Gren Bn, arty Bn & flak Bty from 180 Inf Div & 1/21 Para Regt.
22. Segler's 2/19 & Richter's 2/21 SS Pz-Gren Bns & Roestel's 10 SS JgPz Bn.
23. LTC Robert Ballard's 2/501 Para Regt.
24. LTC Ray Allen's Bn of 327 Glider Inf Regt, 150 men of Col Sink's 506 Para Inf Regt & 44 RTR (a British tk Bn).
25. 44 RTR.
26. MacDonald, *US Army in World War II, ETO, The Siegfried Line Campaign*, p. 190.
27. Brereton, *The Brereton Diaries*, p. 354.
28. PRO London, Air 27.
29. Eight Bns of Para & Glider inf & two sqns of British tanks – MacDonald, op. cit., p. 191.
30. 2 Armd Gren & 1 (Mot) Gren Gds.
31. 50 Inf Div.
32. Dempsey Diaries.

CHAPTER XIX
MARKET GARDEN:
Saturday – Tuesday, 23 – 26 September

North of the Waal – Saturday 23 September
(Map 19)

While Urquhart's valiant men continued to suffer at Oosterbeek, the 43rd (Wessex) Infantry Division struggled to reach the lower Rhine. The Brigade[1] trying to advance north towards Elst was told to keep the Oosterhout crossroads, which were under German artillery fire, clear until 1300 hours so that its sister Brigade[2], relieved from its guard duties in Nijmegen, could come through and move via Valburg to join up with the Poles at Driel. The third Brigade[3] was to be used to shield this move and at the same time attack Elst from the west, whilst a Battlegroup[4] of the Guards Armoured Division was to attack in the direction of Bemmel. In the event, the Wessex units attacking Elst from the south and west found themselves up against the significant defences of KG Knaust[5] and the Guards ran into the Frundsbergers holding the Bemmel part of the line. No significant progress was made.[6] It remains unclear why another Guards Battlegroup[7], sitting 4km south of Elst, was not used to support these attacks. It 'had a quiet day, save for a few mortar bombs, suffering mostly from the steady pouring rain'.[8]

Nevertheless, in spite of the confusion and congestion in the Oosterhout area, the bulk of the Brigade[9] moving on the western flank reached the lower Rhine, west of Driel, soon after dark. Unfortunately, it arrived too late to join the Poles in a coordinated attempt to cross the river that night but it did bring with it twelve assault boats.

In the meantime, Harzer had ordered the 1st Company of the Frundsberg's 10th SS Reconnaissance Battalion to move from the brick factory, west along the south bank of the river until it was directly south of the Oosterbeek perimeter (Map 17).

The Nijmegen Sector
(Map 14)

By last light on 23 September, the 82nd Airborne Division had expanded its Nijmegen defensive perimeter to an average depth of 7km in the east and 12km in the south-east. Although Corps Feldt had been reinforced[10], the American paratroopers had fought it to a standstill and this expanded American bridgehead between the Maas and the Waal provided a much needed firm base for the further advance of the British VIII Corps. It also provided greater protection for the vital Nijmegen bridges. With the safe, if belated, arrival of the 325th Glider Infantry Regiment (3,385 men) on this day, Gavin could be justly proud of his Division's achievements. His own performance had been remarkable – he had been in constant pain from a suspected broken back following his parachute landing on the 17th.

Hell's Highway
(Map 15)

Farther south, in the 101st Airborne Division's sector, the situation was less stable. The balance of the Frundsberg's KG Heinke – Segler's 2nd/ 19th SS Panzer-Grenadiers and Roestel's 10th SS Panzerjägers – had closed up to KG Walther, as had the missing Battalion of paratroopers. Thus reinforced, Walther resumed his attack on the Veghel sector of Hell's Highway. In conjunction with this attack from the east, a Parachute Regiment[11], already exhausted after a forty-eight hour approach march, was ordered to attack from the west – on basically the same axis as that taken by the ill-fated KG Huber the previous day. Neither attack was successful. By midday the paratroopers from the west had been halted by their American counterparts and, at about the same time, Walther, no longer able to ignore the steady advance of the British VIII Corps to his left rear, decided to pull back. An hour later the overall American commander in Veghel, Brigadier General Anthony McAuliffe[12], sent two Battalions, with British tank support[13], north to clear the road and by 1520 hours his men had linked up with the British units[14] moving south from Uden. After twenty-four hours, Hell's Highway was open again. The War Diary of one of the British units describes its men finding three knocked out tanks and 'lots of half-tracks' in the area between Uden and Veghel.[15] German reports confirm that Panzer Brigade 107 lost sixteen Panthers, twenty-four SPWs and over 300 men in its struggle to cut the Highway.[16]

A further Allied success on this day was the safe delivery by glider of the remaining artillery and 3,000 men of the 101st Airborne Division.

The Germans

The arrival of another airborne armada bringing reinforcements to the two American airborne Divisions had been a nasty surprise for Field Marshal Model and, after conferring with Bittrich, he decided to change his command structure. With effect from the 24th, General von Zangen's Fifteenth Army would be responsible for all forces west of the XXX Corps corridor, and General Student's First Parachute Army was to take over Bittrich's II SS Panzer Corps (including KG Tettau), General Meindl's II Parachute Corps, Corps Feldt and two other Corps which need not concern us.

Model had come to the conclusion that if he was to contain XXX Corps and the reinforced American Airborne Divisions, he needed every tank and Panzer-Grenadier he could lay his hands on. He did not believe the Frundsberg and KG Knaust on the Elst–Bemmel line were strong enough to resist an attack from the west by the 43rd Infantry Division, part of the Guards Division and the Poles and, as far as he was concerned, Harzer's Hohenstaufen and KG Tettau were being wasted around the Oosterbeek perimeter. He therefore gave Bittrich twenty-four hours to eliminate the British north of the river. Bittrich in turn told Harzer to 'intensify all attacks against the airborne tomorrow. I want the whole affair ended.'

In an interview given shortly after the war to American interrogators[17], Harzer listed the forces available to him for this task: KG Spindler (over 1,000 men) with four SS Panzer-Grenadier Companies, two each from the Hohenstaufen's 19th and 20th Regiments, an artillery Battalion of two batteries acting in an infantry role, plus four 20mm flak guns; KG Allwörden (410 men) with anti-tank, Pioneer and supply companies, all acting in an infantry role and supplemented by naval personnel; KG Harder (460 men) with the personnel of two Panzer companies and an administrative company, again all operating as infantrymen and reinforced with naval ratings; KG Bruhn with nearly 1,000 men in eight companies; KG Krafft (nearly 500 men) with a four company Battalion, now including a military police company acting as infantry; Pioneer Training Battalion 9 (560 men) with three companies; Artillery Regiment 191 with twenty-four 105mm towed howitzers; Flak Brigade Swoboda with thirty-three 88mm, eight 37mm and twenty-nine 20mm flak guns; II SS Panzer Corps' 102nd SS Werfer Battalion with sixteen heavy Neb- elwerfers and two 100mm Kanons; fifteen Tiger IIs of Heavy Panzer Battalion 506 (we shall hear more of these shortly), three Panthers of his own 9th SS Panzer Regiment and ten StuGs of Assault Brigade 280. He also listed KG Brinkmann, with three companies totalling three armoured cars and thirty-six SPWs but, as we have heard, this was operating south of the river with the Blocking Group.

North of the Waal – Sunday 24 September

Major General Sosabowski's Poles made their second attempt to cross the lower Rhine on the Saturday/Sunday night, using the twelve assault boats brought forward by Thomas's 43rd Division – two and a half hours later than expected and capable of holding only twelve men rather than the planned sixteen. Worse still, there were no crews to man them and the Poles, untrained in watermanship, had to take over. Inevitably, the crossing, which began at 0300 hours and took place under fire, was far less successful than had been hoped for, with only 153 Poles reaching the north bank and not all those making it into the airborne perimeter. Sosabowski and the rest of his men returned to Driel.

One of the most critical happenings on the Allied side on the Sunday was a conference held in Valburg by Horrocks, with Browning and Thomas and Sosabowski in attendance. To the dismay and anger of the Polish commander, he was placed under Thomas's command and one of his Battalions attached to a British Brigade[18] . Furthermore, this Battalion, together with a British Battalion[19], was to take part in a river crossing that night at the Heveadorp ferry site, whilst the rest of his men were to cross farther to the east. Sosabowski's well made points that it was asking for trouble to cross directly below the German-held Westerbouwing and that the crossing should be made either directly opposite the Oosterbeek perimeter or farther downstream were ignored. So was his contention that if there could be no major reinforcement of the Oosterbeek perimeter that night, Urquhart's men should be withdrawn. H-Hour for the crossings was confirmed as 2200 hours.

The Oosterbeek Perimeter

North of the river in Oosterbeek, Sunday saw the appearance of the first Tiger II. Forty-five of these 69-ton monsters[20], totally unsuited for action in towns, had been sent to Holland on the personal order of Adolf Hitler. Armoured vehicles operating in built-up areas, even with close infantry protection, are always highly vulnerable and the fighting in Oosterbeek had already proved this point. By the time the first Tiger appeared, all eight tanks operating with KG Lippert, two Panthers with the Hermann Goering Battalion and three or four StuGs from Assault Gun Brigade 280 had been lost to British and Polish PIATs, 6 and 17-pounder anti-tank guns and even 75mm howitzers firing over open sights.

The first of Lieutenant Hummel's fifteen Tigers attached to the Hohenstaufen suffered the same fate. Harzer had deployed them with KG Spindler on the east side of the perimeter[21], and a random mortar round hitting the air vent on the fuel tank of one of them caused a major explosion, totally disabling the Tiger.

By now the plight of some 1,400 wounded men within the perimeter had become intolerable. The very limited British medical services within the siege area were clearly being overwhelmed. The wounded were lying within the sound and even the range of the fighting; they were cold, hungry and thirsty, and fully aware of dead comrades being quietly removed. A vivid description of their plight was later given by one of the doctors struggling to cope:

> Macabre scenes developed as already wounded men received fresh injuries as they lay helpless; jagged pieces of metal whirred indiscriminately through broken windows whenever a missile was exploded at high level by a tree . . .

> a piece of metal flashing through the window practically severed his right hand from his wrist. . . . a man lying face downward because of a wound in his buttock, having his shoulder sliced open as though he had been struck with a razor sharp whip; and the medical orderly, standing over a stretcher, who suddenly collapsed onto the wounded man beneath him, and lay there dead with a hole in the back of his head, until others pulled him off.[22]

The most senior of the wounded was the commander of the eastern side of the perimeter, Brigadier 'Shan' Hackett, who was hit in the stomach and thigh by mortar splinters. Shortly afterwards the senior British medical officer, Colonel Graeme Warrack, suggested to Urquhart that an attempt should be made to persuade the Germans to evacuate the most seriously wounded to hospitals in the surrounding area. Warrack arranged to be driven through German lines by a German doctor and negotiated an agreement with the commander of II SS Panzer Corps, Wilhelm Bittrich. Over 500 of the worst cases were removed later that day in what Urquhart described as 'a strange afternoon of not quite total war'.

Hell's Highway
(Map 15)

The commander of XXX Corps, Brian Horrocks, came forward early on the Sunday to see Sosabowski at Driel. He could not have been optimistic about what he saw from the village church tower and admitted later to not feeling well and being depressed with the way MARKET GARDEN was going. He was still suffering from wounds received earlier in the war but in addition, he had begun:

> To find it difficult to sleep. In fact I had to be very firm with myself in order to banish from my mind, during those midnight hours when everything seems to be at its worst, the picture of the airborne troops fighting their desperate battle on the other side of the river in front. I had had sufficient experience of war to know that any commander who finds it difficult to sleep will soon be unfit to be responsible

for other men's lives. And here I was going that way myself – an unpleasant thought.[23]

Horrocks' depression must have deepened even further when he received news during the morning that the Germans had again cut Hell's Highway.

Now under the command of the Fifteenth Army, and supported by an ad hoc KG[24] hastily put together by the 59th Infantry Division, the German Parachute Regiment[25] which had already tried and failed at Veghel attacked again at 1000 hours. Tenacious fighting followed between the German and American paratroopers and, whilst this was going on, men of the attached KG found an undefended section of the highway, 6km south-west of Veghel. Within twenty-four hours of Hell's Highway being reopened, it was cut again. Despite heavy interdiction from American and British guns, German paratroopers successfully reinforced the KG during the night and it soon became clear that much stronger Allied forces would be needed to reopen the vital road to Nijmegen.

North of the Waal – Monday 25 September
(Map 19)

The Allied assault crossing of the lower Rhine ordered for the Sunday/ Monday night did not go according to plan. Owing to the problems on Hell's Highway, the assault boats were again late arriving and when they did there were fewer than expected. After a barrage by three Regiments of artillery and heavy mortars, and under the cover of medium machine-guns firing on fixed lines, the first boats entered the water at 0100 hours. By 0215 hours, when the operation was called off due to increasing German fire, only just over 300 men of the British Battalion[26] had been ferried across. Opposition from the north bank led inevitably to dispersed landings and over 200 of those who made it to the north bank were quickly rounded up and made prisoners. The Polish crossing farther downstream had to be cancelled because of the shortage of boats.

The failure of the river crossing and the severing of the XXX Corps corridor on the Sunday had dramatic repercussions for the men in the Oosterbeek perimeter. Just after 0600 hours in the morning, Roy Urquhart received a letter from the commander of the 43rd Division, telling him that Second Army had abandoned the attempt to reinforce and maintain his bridgehead and that the remnants of his Division could withdraw across the river whenever he wished.[27] Shortly after 0800 hours, Urquhart told Thomas he wanted the evacuation plan implemented that night, and, at 1030 he and his senior commanders started planning the withdrawal.

South of the lower Rhine, the British attacks against the Elst–Bemmel line were renewed with the aim of expanding the narrow wedge between Oosterhout and Driel and, in the process, of preventing the Germans from attacking it. By early evening the British infantrymen had fought their way into the first houses of Elst but elsewhere there was no progress. Farther east, another British Brigade[28] was brought forward during the day for use against the Bemmel end of the German line.

Hell's Highway
(Map 15)

At 0830 hours on the Monday morning, a combined attack by American and British forces was launched to clear the Germans off Hell's Highway. The men of one US Parachute Infantry Regiment[29] advanced from the direction of Veghel, whilst a reinforced Battalion of another[30], together with British infantry[31], moved up from St Oedenrode. British tanks supported both groups.[32] Although they were surrounded on three sides, the Germans held on and sensibly used their time to heavily mine the whole area. Although they eventually withdrew after dark that evening, it took Allied engineers until 1400 hours the following day to clear the mines and finally declare Hell's Highway safe for use. From now on, the Germans would have to resort to artillery fire and aircraft to interdict the constant flow of traffic. In this respect, a major attack by forty German aircraft took place against the Nijmegen road bridge on the 25th. One bomb hit, but the bridge remained passable.[33]

The Oosterbeek Perimeter

By the time Urquhart and his officers started planning their withdrawal, the Oosterbeek perimeter had shrunk to a mere one kilometre by a kilometre and a half. Model had authorised the use of more heavy weapons and these naturally attracted retaliatory strikes from British medium and heavy guns sited south of the river and ground attack aircraft. The whole area was becoming an inferno and bad weather and rain added to the general misery.

Bittrich's order to Harzer that he wanted the 'whole affair ended' caused the latter to change his approach to the problem. Many of the 'alarm' companies included in the Hohenstaufen KGs on the eastern side of the perimeter consisted of poorly trained or novice personnel. Their combat capability was inevitably low. He decided therefore to withdraw these companies and rely instead on his own veterans. Accordingly, early on the 25th his KGs were reorganised so that they included only men of the Hohenstaufen. At the same time he allocated Tiger II tanks to the KGs operating between the main Utrecht road and the river – KGs Allwörden

1. Paul Hausser, commander of the first Waffen-SS Division (SS-Verfügungstruppe-Division, first SS Panzer Corps, first commander II SS Panzer Corps, commander Seventh Army in Normandy from 29th June 1944 and Army Group G on the Eastern Front in 1945. He was wounded in Russia in October 1941, losing an eye.

2. Willi Bittrich, first commander of the 9th SS Panzer Division Hohenstaufen and commander II SS Panzer Corps from 29th June 1944 until the end of the war.

3. Sylvester Stadler, commander of the 9th SS Panzer Division Hohenstaufen in Normandy from early July 1944 until wounded on the 29th of that month and then from October 1944 until the end of the war.

4. Heinz Harmel (left) with his driver in November 1944. He commanded the Frundsberg Division from April 1944 until the end of the war. (Ryan Collection, Ohio University)

5. Tiger I of the 2nd Company, 102nd SS Heavy Panzer Battalion in Normandy, July 1944.

6. Hohenstaufen Panther in Normandy with SS Panzer-Grenadiers mounted.

7. Das Reich Mk IV tank halted beside the command StuG of Ernst Krag, commander 2nd SS Reconnaissance Battalion, during the move to Normandy.

8. Otto Meyer, commander 9th SS Panzer Regiment Hohenstaufen during July and August 1944.

9. Otto Paetsch, commander of the 1st SS Panzer Battalion Frundsberg in Normandy and the 10th SS Panzer Regiment Frundsberg on the Eastern Front until killed in March 1945.

10. Hans Weiss, commander 102nd SS Heavy Panzer Battalion in Normandy.

11. Alois Kalls, commander 1st Company, 102nd/502nd SS Heavy Panzer Battalion – killed on 2nd May 1945.

12. Allied commanders in Normandy, August 1944. From the left: Courtney H. Hodges, commander First US Army, Henry Crerar, commander First Canadian Army, Monty, commander 21st British/Canadian Army Group, Omar N. Bradley, commander 12th US Army Group and Miles Dempsey, commander Second British Army. (Imperial War Museum)

13. Tiger I of the 2nd Company, 102nd SS Heavy Panzer Battalion abandoned near Falaise, August 1944.

14. The railway bridge over the Seine at Oissel in late August 1944.

15. The road bridge over the lower Rhine at Arnhem on the afternoon of Monday, 18th September 1944. The knocked out vehicles of Gräbner's 9th SS Reconnaissance Battalion lie scattered at the north end. (Airborne Museum Hartenstein)

16. The railway bridge over the lower Rhine at Arnhem, demolished by the Germans during the afternoon of 17th September 1944. (Airborne Museum Hartenstein)

17. Montgomery, 'Shan' Hackett, commander 4th Parachute Brigade, and Roy Urquhart, commander 1st Airborne Division, six months before MARKET GARDEN. The airborne troops on this parade were apparently not impressed by Monty's gesture of wearing a 'Red Beret'. (Imperial War Museum)

18. Jim Gavin, commander 82nd Airborne Division during MARKET GARDEN and in the Ardennes. (US Army)

19. Maxwell Taylor, commander 101st Airborne Division during MARKET GARDEN. (US Army)

20. Left to right: Walther Model, commander Army Group B during MARKET GARDEN and AUTUMN MIST, Willi Bittrich, commander II SS Panzer Corps, Hans-Peter Knaust, commander SS Panzer-Grenadier Training and Replacement Battalion 'Bocholt' and KG Knaust during MARKET GARDEN and Heinz Harmel, commander 10th SS Panzer Division Frundsberg. Knaust had just been awarded the Knight's Cross – 28th September 1944. (Ryan Collection, Ohio University)

21. Sepp Krafft, commander SS Panzer-Grenadier Training and Replacement Battalion 16 and KG Krafft during MARKET GARDEN.

22. Ludwig Spindler, commander 9th SS Artillery Panzer Regiment Hohenstaufen and KG Spindler during MARKET GARDEN.

23. Panoramic view of Nijmegen and its road bridge over the Waal after the fighting. (US Army, Ryan Collection, Ohio University)

24. Nijmegen road bridge over the Waal, taken shortly after its capture. (US Army, Ryan Collection, Ohio University)

25. Reuben Tucker, commander 504th Parachute Infantry Regiment, 82nd Airborne Division, during MARKET GARDEN and in the Ardennes.

26. Vehicles of XXX Corps halted by German counter-attacks on Hell's Highway between Eindhoven and Nijmegen during MARKET GARDEN. (Ryan Collection, Ohio University)

27. Brian Horrocks, commander XXX Corps, with Monty and Prince Bernhard of the Netherlands shortly before MARKET GARDEN. (Ryan Collection, Ohio University)

28. 'Boy' Browning, commander Allied Airborne Corps, with Jim Gavin, commander 82nd Airborne Division shortly before MARKET GARDEN. (Ryan Collection, Ohio University)

29. Maj Gen S. F. Sosabowski (centre), commander 1st Polish Independent Airborne Brigade Group, with Maj Gen G. I. Thomas, commander 43rd Infantry Division, near Valburg on 24th September 1944. Lt Col R. Stevens, British liaison officer with the Brigade, on the left. (Polish Institute and Sikorski Museum. London)

30. Walther Harzer, commander 9th SS Panzer Division Hohenstaufen during the retreat from France and during MARKET GARDEN. (Ryan Collection, Ohio University)

31. Hans von Tettau, commander Training Netherlands and KG Tettau during MARKET GARDEN.

32. Kurt Student, commander First Parachute Army during MARKET GARDEN.

33. Karl-Heinz Euling, commander KG Euling of the Frundsberg Division during MARKET GARDEN and the 1st SS Panzer-Grenadier Battalion of the Division's 22nd Regiment in Alsace and on the Eastern Front.

34. Frundsberg Panzer-Grenadier killed on the Nijmegen bridge. A flare pistol lies by his left hand. (US Army, Ryan Collection, Ohio University)

35. A trooper of the 82nd Airborne Division with a 45 calibre sub-machine-gun. (US Army, Ryan Collection, Ohio University)

36. Tiger II knocked out during the last attack on the east side of the Oosterbeek perimeter – 25th September 1944. The building in the rear was a school, since demolished. (Airborne Museum Hartenstein)

37. Sherman of the Guards Armoured Division knocked out in Nijmegen on the 19th or 20th September 1944. (US Army, Ryan Collection, Ohio University)

38. Heinz Lammerding, commander 2nd SS Panzer Division Das Reich from 7th March until 26th July 1944 when he was wounded by artillery fire and from 23rd October 1944 until 20th January 1945 when he joined Himmler's staff.

39. Otto Weidinger, commander 4th SS Panzer-Grenadier Regiment Der Führer in Normandy, the Ardennes and on the Eastern Front in 1945.

40. Günther Wisliceny, commander 3rd SS Panzer-Grenadier Regiment Deutschland in Normandy, the Ardennes and on the Eastern Front 1945.

41. Ernst-August Krag, commander 2nd SS Reconnaissance Battalion Das Reich in Normandy, the Ardennes and on the Eastern Front 1945.

42. Rudolf Enseling, commander 2nd SS Panzer Regiment Das Reich in Normandy, the Ardennes and on the Eastern Front 1945. (left)

43. Eberhard Telkamp, commander 9th SS Panzer Regiment Hohenstaufen in the Ardennes and on the Eastern Front 1945. (above)

44. Ernst Barkmann, Panther commander in the Ardennes and platoon commander in the 1st SS Panzer Battalion Das Reich on the Eastern Front in 1945. (left)

45. Josef Stalin II heavy tank.

46. Das Reich Mk IV near the Floridsdorf bridge in Vienna, 13th April 1945. Otto Weidinger, commander Der Führer Regiment of Das Reich, walking towards the camera wearing a long coat.

47. Soviet Sherman, sent to Russia under the 'Lease/Lend Agreement' between the US and the Soviet Union, in the streets of Vienna, 14th April 1945.

48. Hermann Balck, commander XLVIII Panzer Corps in the Ukraine in early 1944 and the Sixth Army in Hungary in 1945.

49. Rudolf von Bünau (right), City Commandant of Vienna in April 1945, with Otto Weidinger, commander Der Führer Regiment of Das Reich. Taken near the Floridsorf bridge in Vienna on 13th April 1945.

50. Rudolf Lehmann, Chief of Staff I SS Panzer Corps in Hungary in 1945 until 12th March when he took over command of the 2nd SS Panzer Division Das Reich. He was wounded on 8th April in Vienna.

51. Karl Kreutz, commander 2nd SS Panzer Artillery Regiment Das Reich in Normandy, the Ardennes and on the Eastern Front in 1945. He took over command of Das Reich from 9th April 1945 until the end of the war.

52. Armoured personnel carriers of the Waffen-SS carry wounded personnel into captivity in Austria, May 1945. (US Army)

53. German POWs marching into captivity past a Sherman of Patton's Third Army in May 1945. (US Army)

and Harder. The new tactics began to pay off but still did not achieve the required result. The most significant success occurred during the afternoon on the eastern side of the perimeter. KG Allwörden broke through the defences, a battery of 75mm guns was overrun, and the attack only brought to a halt when it was 600m from the western edge of the perimeter and within 500m of Urquhart's Headquarters in the Hotel Hartenstein. It was to be the last major attack against the Oosterbeek perimeter.

Monday/Tuesday Night – 25/26 September

The withdrawal of the British and Polish survivors of Operation MARKET took place between 2140 hours on the 25th and 0530 hours on the 26th in heavy rain. The area chosen for the evacuation across the lower Rhine was the only one possible – between the Heveadorp ferry site and the railway bridge (Map 12). Fortunately, the river water was not cold[34] and a well prepared artillery fire plan, unselfishness and good discipline on the part of the evacuees, and courageous and dedicated work by the British and Canadian engineers[35], ensured its success. Some men got lost, some were dispersed by German fire, some had to swim the river, an estimated ninety-five men died (bringing the total killed in the last twenty-four hours of the fighting north of the river to 258), and between 150 and 300 men were left behind on the north bank. On the credit side, nearly 2,300 men reached safety, including 160 Poles. Surprisingly, many of the survivors had then to march all the way back to Nijmegen which they reached as dawn was breaking.

Conclusion

Operation MARKET GARDEN was over. It had cost the Allies over 16,000 soldiers and 248 airmen.[36] Just under 12,000 men of the 1st British Airborne Division and Polish Independent Brigade Group had taken part of which 1,446 British (including 229 glider pilots) and ninety-seven Poles were killed and 6,414 British and 111 Poles became prisoners, many of whom had been wounded.[37] XXX Corps suffered 1,480 casualties and VIII and XII Corps lost 3,874 men between them.

During Operation MARKET 29,628 American troops were delivered into Holland by parachute or glider.[38] The 82nd Airborne Division lost 215 killed, 790 wounded and 427 missing; the 101st suffered 315 killed, 1,248 wounded and 547 missing; and 122 glider pilots were lost of whom twelve were killed.[39]

Precise details of German casualties do not exist but they totalled about 6,400. Robert Kershaw[40]estimates that, in addition to some 2,565 lost north of the lower Rhine, including 1,240 men of the Hohenstaufen, the

Germans may have lost another 3,750 men in the fighting around the XXX Corps corridor, including 750 men from the Frundsberg.

With the war still in progress, it was inevitable that MARKET GARDEN would be presented to the British and American people as a victory. Churchill described it as 'a decided victory' and Montgomery claimed it was 90% successful since 90% of the ground specified in the Operation Order had been taken. To this latter claim, Prince Bernhard of the Netherlands is said to have replied: 'My country can never again afford the luxury of a Montgomery success.'

In reality, it was a strategic failure. The West Wall had not been out-flanked, Second Army was not positioned for an attack on the north flank of the Ruhr, the German Fifteenth Army had not been cut off[41] and there had been no collapse of German arms. The salient achieved led nowhere and was to prove extremely costly in the coming months.

The vast majority of those involved in MARKET GARDEN, of whatever nationality, displayed great bravery and earned the respect of their adversaries. In the case of two of the major participants, the Americans and Germans, their senior ground commanders – Gavin, Taylor, Model, Bittrich, Harmel and Harzer – demonstrated outstanding military competence. The same cannot be said of the British. The seven most directly involved – Montgomery, Dempsey, Browning, Horrocks, Adair, Urquhart and Thomas – must bear responsibility for the failure of the Operation.

It is also clear that, whilst the German commanders were prepared to take all necessary measures and risks to win the battle, even to the point of using men untrained in ground warfare, their British adversaries were cautious in their use of manpower and reluctant to take risks. Why this difference? There are four basic reasons. One: the British were war-weary and facing a manpower crisis. Two: most British considered the war would be 'over by Christmas' and that it would be wrong to undertake offensive actions which might incur heavy casualties. Three: for the first time, the Germans were defending the borders of the Reich itself. And, four: many Germans still believed that if they could just buy enough time for their Führer, he would produce a series of war-winning weapons in the same vein as the V1 flying bomb, V2 rocket and ME 262 jet.

The aftermath for those who returned from MARKET GARDEN differed markedly, depended on their nationality. The British survivors of Oosterbeek were flown back to England on 30 September and welcomed as heroes. In a surprisingly generous move by Eisenhower and the American authorities, the two US Airborne Divisions were left under Montgomery's command and stayed in the line in Holland for a further six weeks. They suffered another 3,594 casualties, including 685 killed.[42] Sadly, Brereton's prediction that, 'In the years to come everyone will remember Arnhem, but no one will remember that two American divisions fought their hearts out in the Dutch canal country' became all too accurate. Few today are aware of the contribution and sacrifice made by the Americans in MARKET GARDEN. Horrocks, however, was in no doubt when he wrote after the war:

> As this difficult battle progressed I became more and more impressed with the fighting qualities of the 82nd and 101st US Airborne Divisions . . . What impressed me so much about them was their quickness into action [was he remembering the failure of his own Corps on the evening of 20 September after the Waal crossing?] . . .
>
> They were commanded by two outstanding men . . . Both were as unlike the popular cartoon conception of the loud-voiced, boastful, cigar-chewing American as it would be possible to imagine. They were quiet, sensitive-looking men of great charm, with an almost British passion for understatement . . . Under their deceptively gentle exterior both Maxwell Taylor and Gavin were very tough characters indeed. They had to be, because the men they commanded were some of the toughest troops I have ever come across in my life.[43]

The Poles, after marching back to Nijmegen under occasional mortar fire, spent the next ten days on guard and patrol duties there before being returned to England. Their commander, Major General Sosabowski, was sacked on 9 December – undoubtedly at British (Montgomery and Browning) insistence. Not surprisingly, two of his Battalions went on what turned out to be an unsuccessful hunger strike.

For the Dutch people the aftermath of the fighting was to be the most bitter and painful of all. Some 100,000 people had been forced out of the Arnhem and Oosterbeek area. Their homes had been destroyed and systematically looted by the Germans, who then cut their rations to less than 500 calories a day in what became known as the 'Hunger Winter'. In retaliation for their assistance to the Allies during MARKET GARDEN and a countrywide railway strike begun by Dutch workers on 17 September, the Germans stopped all inland shipping. Without trains or barges it was impossible to move sufficient food from the agricultural east to the towns and cities of the west – it has been estimated that some 25,000 Dutch people died of starvation that winter. As they died, they wondered why the Allies did not continue their advance to free them. The answer was simple – the Germans were too strong and the ground too difficult. Any major advance would almost certainly have led to a level of destruction which would have resulted in the flooding of most of the Netherlands. The Allies turned instead towards the Rhine.

For the men of II SS Panzer Corps there was to be no respite:

175

The main body of the 9th SS Panzer Division Hohenstaufen transferred to the area of Oosterbeek and to the northern part of Arnhem, cleared up the battlefield for the next few days and collected the booty.[44]

On 30 September the Division was relieved by elements of two other Divisions and a day later withdrawn to Germany for refitting and re-equipping. Hitler already had a new task in mind for it.

The 10th SS Panzer Division Frundsberg was to continue in action in the area between the Waal and lower Rhine for a further seven weeks.

NOTES

1. 129 Inf Bde, with a tk sqn of the 13th/18th Hussars (13/18 H), part of 8 Armd Bde, under command.
2. 130 Inf Bde, with two 13/18 H tk sqns under command.
3. 214 Inf Bde, with two 4th/7th Royal Dragoon Guards (4/7 DG) tk sqns under command.
4. 2 Armd WG & 1 WG.
5. The 8 Armd Bde War Diary claims the 4/7 DG encountered 'at least one Tiger and four Panthers' on this day. Readers will recall that KG Knaust had no Tigers with it.
6. According to 1 WG War Diary, 23 Sep 44, the Bn suffered nineteen casualties. Ellis's *The Welsh Guards at War*, p. 229, says 2 Armd WG lost one tk.
7. 2 Armd & 3 IG.
8. Fitzgerald, *The History of the Irish Guards in the Second World War*, p. 514.
9. 130 Inf Bde.
10. By seven bns of II Para Corps.
11. Von der Heydte's 6 Para Regt.
12. The 101 Airborne Div Arty commander. He was to gain even greater fame in the siege of Bastogne in Dec 44.
13. 44 RTR which lost two tks on this day.
14. The Gren & Coldm Gds Groups.
15. 1 (Mot) Gren Gds War Diary, 23 Sep 44.
16. Dugdale, *Panzer Divisions, Panzer Grenadier Divisions, Panzer Brigades, Vol I, Part 1*, p. 143.
17. MS # P-162. Confirmation of these details is also provided by Dugdale, op. cit., p. 84.
18. 130 Inf Bde.
19. 4 Dorset.
20. Hy Pz Bn 506 under the command of Maj Lange.
21. The other two Tiger II Companies were allocated to Harmel's Frundsberg Division and deployed in support of the Elst–Bemmel line, which both Model and Bittrich still considered vital to their whole defensive posture. Although providing substantial additional firepower in defence, the Tigers were useless in offensive actions, proving too heavy for the canal bridges and soft terrain.
22. Mawson, *Arnhem Doctor*, pp. 99 & 101.
23. Horrocks, *A Full Life*, p. 228.
24. KG Jungwirth with at least one JgPz.

25. Von der Heydte's 6 Para Regt of four weak Bns, supported by a few aslt guns and/or JgPzs.
26. 4 Dorset.
27. According to his Diary (PRO, WO 285/10), Dempsey met Montgomery at 1100 hrs and obtained his agreement and he confirmed this to Horrocks 'on the air' at 1215 hrs. In his *Memoirs*, p. 295, Monty claimed: 'I gave orders that the remnants of the division were to be withdrawn . . .'
28. 69 Inf Bde of 50 Inf Div.
29. 506 Para Inf.
30. 502 Para Inf.
31. From 50 Inf Div.
32. From 44 RTR which lost another six tks on this day.
33. Brereton, *The Brereton Diaries*, p. 356.
34. The current in the river is much slower today than in 1944 due to the construction of new weirs.
35. 260 (Wessex) Fd Coy RE & 23 Fd Coy RCE.
36. Hey, *Roll of Honour Battle of Arnhem September 1944*.
37. Hey, op. cit. The author has been unable to determine the number of wounded. The Germans gave a figure of 1,700 (26%), but the Dutch authorities, in whose hospitals most of the wounded prisoners were treated initially, put the figure at about 38%.
38. Brereton, op. cit., p. 357.
39. MacDonald, *US Official History, ETO, The Siegfried Line Campaign*, p. 199.
40. Kershaw, *It Never Snows in September*, pp. 339–40.
41. The bulk of this Army escaped to play an important part in defending the West Wall and in the Ardennes Offensive of Dec 44.
42. MacDonald, op. cit., p. 206.
43. Horrocks, op. cit., p. 228–9.
44. Tieke, *In the Firestorm of the Last Years of the War*, p. 269.

CHAPTER XX

II SS Panzer Corps: 26 September – 18 November

(Maps 11 & 19)

The 100km Allied salient into central Holland can be likened to an arrow with a broken head. The failure of XXX Corps to cross the lower Rhine meant it posed no direct threat to the territory of the Third Reich in general or to the Ruhr in particular. In fact an attack on the Ruhr, by Montgomery's 21st Army Group from the north in concert with a US First Army attack from the south, had just been authorised by Eisenhower at a major planning conference held at Versailles on 22 September. The failure of MARKET GARDEN four days later put an end to any such grandiose plans. On 7 October, Montgomery told Ike that for logistical reasons he could not launch an offensive into the Rhineland. First, he needed to drive the Germans from the Sheldt estuary and from the area south of the Maas, thereby opening up the vital port of Antwerp. Two days later the Supreme commander gave orders that the opening of Antwerp was to take priority over all other operations.

Just as the Allied commanders tended to overestimate German strengths, so Hitler, without the benefit of an ULTRA-type intelligence service, underestimated the Allied supply problems and shortages of trained manpower. As far as he was concerned, the XXX Corps salient posed a severe threat in that further airborne, and/or even seaborne, landings in western and northern Holland could support and extend it. He gave orders therefore for an offensive to be mounted to clear all Allied troops from north of the Maas river and, to this end, directed that the 9th and 116th Panzer Divisions be moved from the Aachen sector to join Bittrich's II SS Panzer Corps.

On 26 September Model told his senior commanders how he intended to carry out the Führer's order. The Fifteenth Army was to attack eastwards towards Grave, General Meindl's II Parachute Corps was to attack again, west from the Reichswald towards Groesbeek and Nijmegen, and Bittrich, with the Frundsberg, 9th and 116th Panzer Divisions was to strike westwards between the lower Rhine and the Waal. A new XII SS Army Corps, under SS General von Gottberg, with a new Volks-Grenadier Division (see Appendix VII), the 363rd, was to take over the front in the Arnhem–Oosterbeek area from the Hohenstaufen and support Bittrich's attack from north of the river.

The main drawback to this plan was that, due to fuel shortages and Allied air interdiction, neither the 9th nor 116th Panzer Division could arrive in time to be ready to join in the II Parachute Corps and Fifteenth Army attacks planned for the 28th.

By 1 October, when the Hohenstaufen was withdrawn to Germany, both Elst[1] and Bemmel had been lost to the British. The Frundsberg, still with its various Alarm units under command, was holding a 5km deep bridgehead west of the lower Rhine running roughly from Elden in the north to Haalderen, a kilometre north of the Waal, in the south. It was into this bridgehead that the 9th and 116th Panzer Divisions moved in readiness for the II SS Panzer Corps attack. The 116th, on the northern flank, took under command Blocking Gerhard (Harzer) in the Elden area, left behind by the Hohenstaufen, whilst the 9th, in the Huissen area in the centre, received KGs Knaust and Bruhn and the Tiger IIs of Heavy Panzer Battalion 506 from the Frundsberg, Their initial objectives were Driel and Elst respectively.

The Frundsberg, on the southern flank of the newly constituted II SS Panzer Corps, was tasked with re-taking the Bemmel sector. By now

Harmel had restructured his Division into two KGs, based on the 21st and 22nd SS Panzer-Grenadier Regiments. Included in these KGs was an incredible hotchpotch of units including personnel from three air bases, a Battalion of men with stomach ailments, a bicycle Battalion which had received no weapon training, a Fortress machine-gun Battalion with old maxim guns and some left over Alarm units from Nijmegen.[2]

In an attempt to prevent the Allies reinforcing their bridgehead north of the Waal, German aircraft attacked the Nijmegen bridge on the 27th and 28th. Included in the attacks on the second day was a glider, filled with explosives, which caused some damage to the railway bridge; otherwise the attacks were unsuccessful. Then on 29 September, German divers, under the cover of darkness, managed to place sub-surface explosive charges against the buttresses of both bridges. The resulting explosions caused the centre section of the railway bridge to collapse and seriously damaged the road bridge, but by 1 October the latter was back in use.

The attack by II Parachute Corps against the 82nd Airborne Division positions facing the Reichswald was launched on 28 September. It failed with heavy loss, as did the Fifteenth Army attack towards Grave.

Bittrich's II SS Panzer Corps launched its attack on 1 October. Foggy weather and difficult ground conditions complicated the whole operation and the assault soon broke down in the face of intense Allied defensive fire. 'What had begun as a unified attack broke up into many local operations.'[3] One of the attacks was supported by four Tiger IIs, but 'one of the Tigers got bogged and the others gave up the attack to drag it out of the mud'.[4] When the skies cleared later in the day, ground attack aircraft of the Second Allied Tactical Air Force struck the German artillery positions and the ferry sites at Pannerden and Huissen. Further attacks during the night of the 1st/2nd, which included the use of several Panthers, were no more successful – 'we were surprised that they could approach us over the sodden ground'[5].

II Parachute Corps renewed its attack against the 82nd Airborne in the Groesbeek sector on the 1st, but by the evening of the 2nd it had reported to Model's Headquarters: 'The attempted attack was unsuccessful. Massive enemy air superiority during the day. Troop training too poor for night attacks.'

By 5 October the British VIII and XII Corps had advanced sufficiently far north to relieve the US 101st Airborne Division of its responsibility for Hell's Highway and the Division was moved north of the Waal to join XXX Corps. The commander of the First Allied Airborne Army, General Brereton, was infuriated. He wrote, 'Keeping airborne soldiers in the front lines as infantry is a violation of the cardinal rules of airborne warfare.'

By this time the British 43rd Division and 8th Armoured Brigade were holding the arc to the west of Elst and the 50th Infantry Division, with support from the infantry of the Guards Armoured Division, held the arc to the east. On the German side, the Frundsberg, renamed KG Harmel in view of its much-reduced strength, had been forced on to the defensive on the line of the Kanal de Linge and it was clear that the 9th and 116th Panzer Divisions' attacks against Elst and Driel had also failed.

On 7 October, with the Aachen sector now under heavy pressure from the Americans, Model ordered Bittrich to go on to the defensive and pull the 116th Panzer Division out of the line for use at Aachen. On the same day the bridge over the lower Rhine at Arnhem was destroyed in an Allied air attack. That evening the 9th Panzer Division and Blocking Group Gerhard (Harzer) took over the 116th Division's sector and, together with KG Harmel, set up bridgeheads south and west of the lower Rhine around the Arnhem road bridge site and at Elden, Huissen, Angeren, and opposite Pannerden. During the night of 13/14 October, the 9th Panzer Division withdrew successfully behind the lower Rhine and left Bittrich's command. KG Harmel and Blocking Group Gerhard (Harzer) continued to man the bridgeheads west of the river. The follow-ing day XII SS Corps was also withdrawn to the Aachen area and its 363rd Volks-Grenadier Division, which was responsible for the Arnhem/ Oosterbeek sector, transferred to II SS Panzer Corps. Bittrich thus became responsible for the whole lower Rhine front from Oosterbeek to the junc-tion with the Waal.

After the failure of his offensive to clear the Allies from the salient north of the Waal, Model considered plans to flood the whole area and withdraw his forces behind the lower Rhine. SS Major Brandt, now in com-mand of the Frundsberg's 10th SS Pioneer Battalion, carried out the neces-sary reconnaissances but in the end Model decided against the plan. Instead, the forward defences were thinned out and only strongpoints left west of the river. Brinkmann's 10th SS Reconnaissance Battalion manned those at Huissen and Angeren, Brandt's SS Pioneers held the one opposite their ferry site at Pannerden, and Blocking Group Gerhard (Harzer) remained at Elden. Harmel kept his artillery batteries well back from the river and the few remaining Mk IV tanks and StuGs of the 5th and 8th Companies of Reinhold's 2nd/10th SS Panzer Battalion were sited some 30km east of the lower Rhine where they could carry out long-overdue maintenance in safety and await the issue of new equipment. On the 15th Roestal's 10th SS Panzerjäger Battalion, which readers will recall had been operating with KG Walther south of the Maas, rejoined the Division. Three days previously 1,600 reinforcements, including 500 Luftwaffe personnel, had joined Harmel's command but they were kept with the Divisional Replacement Battalion at Doetinchem for further training.

The following days 'passed peacefully' as the Frundsberg, 'refitted its units and added to their weapons and equipment'. The 21st and 22nd SS Panzer-Grenadier Regiments 'pulled one battalion at a time (in rotation) out of the front for rest and reorganisation'.[6] For the British and

Americans the misery continued. As October drew to a close, even part of Gavin's 82nd Airborne Division was moved north of the Waal where, 'the men huddled in shallow foxholes dug no more than three feet deep lest they fill with water seepage'. It was to be 13 November before they were finally pulled out of the line and the 27th of that month, seventy-one days after their parachutes had opened over Holland, before the last of Maxwell Taylor's men left 'The Island'. By then, their combined casualties for the period 17 September to 27 November totalled a staggering 7,136, including 1,215 killed. This was 24% of their total strength and exceeded the combined losses of the British VIII, XII and XXX Corps.

On 18 November the 10th SS Panzer Division Frundsberg left II SS Panzer Corps for emergency action against the US Ninth Army which had broken into the West Wall 100km away to the south. Hitler's plan for it to remain with Bittrich's Corps for use in his last great offensive in the West was to be thwarted. So, as the Frundsberg leaves II SS Panzer Corps, it leaves our main picture too. Its subsequent actions, and those of the II SS Panzer Corps' 102nd SS Heavy Panzer Battalion, are described in Appendix I.

NOTES

1. The Germans evacuated Elst on the evening of 25 Sep.
2. Tieke, *In the Firestorm of the Last Years of the War*, p. 269.
3. Ibid., p. 272.
4. Fitzgerald, *The History of the Irish Guards in the Second World War*, pp. 522–3.
5. Fitzgerald, op. cit., p. 526.
6. Tieke, op. cit., p. 275.

CHAPTER XXI

A Reconstituted II SS Panzer Corps

Hohenstaufen

(Map 20)

The remnants of the 9th SS Panzer Division Hohenstaufen arrived in the Siegen area of Germany, 100km east of Cologne, in early October. Being hilly and forested, it was a totally unsuitable area for a Panzer Division, but at least it was safe from Allied air attention; and waiting for Harzer's men were the first of the reinforcements designed to bring it back up to strength. Some 30% of them were former Luftwaffe and Naval personnel, the vast majority of whom had no combat experience and only the most rudimentary military training. Many of the remainder were ethnic Germans from Hungary and Yugoslavia. The absorption of such a disparate group into an elite Waffen-SS formation was obviously fraught with difficulties and the fact that it was achieved so effectively is sound evidence of the leadership qualities of the Platoon, Company and Battalion commanders of the Division. It was also achieved in an amazingly short period. It had to be – Hitler needed the Hohenstaufen for his new offensive in the West planned to begin in late November.

Wilhelm Tieke, in his *In the Firestorm of the Last Years of the War*, quotes two examples of how easily and effectively the new men were absorbed. A battery commander in the 9th SS Panzer Regiment, SS Lieutenant Steinbach, wrote:

> The transfer into the Waffen-SS at first made them shudder, but our warm-hearted and comradely welcome and our 'nose' for recognising valuable men, soon made them part of us.

And SS Lieutenant Franke, a Company commander in the Divisional Signals Battalion, wrote later:

> There was understandable scepticism on both sides. Not only was there an essentially greater age of the [new] men, ... but there was also a certain arrogance among our men, who had proved themselves in action. ... The comrades, most of whom had not volunteered to transfer from the Luftwaffe to the Waffen-SS, proved that they could fulfil the missions assigned to them just as reliably as the others.[1]

On 10 October SS Senior Colonel Sylvester Stadler returned to take command of the Hohenstaufen. Readers will recall he had been wounded in Normandy. Walther Harzer, who had commanded the Division during the retreat across France and throughout MARKET GARDEN, was made Commandant of the Divisional Commanders' Course in Hirschberg.

On 18 October the Hohenstaufen was placed once again under the command of Willi Bittrich's II SS Panzer Corps and between that date and the 27th, it moved to a more suitable area (one well known to all British soldiers who have served in Germany) between Paderborn and Münster. Many former members of the Division rejoined from hospital and convalescence at this time and by 1 November the strength of the Hohenstaufen had risen to 14,861. A strength return dated 3 November shows thirty-two Mk IV tanks, two Panthers, twenty-two Jagdpanzer IVs and 118 SPWs with the Division, and fifty-eight Panthers, twenty-eight StuGs and sixty-three SPWs due for delivery.

On 9 December the Hohenstaufen, using sixty-two trains, moved to the west bank of the Rhine and three days later, as part of Sepp Dietrich's Sixth Panzer Army, it formed up in the Bad Münstereifel area opposite the Ardennes region of Belgium. It now numbered 19,605 officers and men (17% below its official establishment) and its armoured strength totalled 142 vehicles (30% below establishment), made up of fifty-eight Panthers (including twenty-five in transit to the Division), thirty-two Mk IVs, twenty-one Jagdpanzer IVs and twenty-eight StuGs. In addition, it had 191 SPWs and armoured cars (50% below strength), eight Flakpanzer IVs, twelve 150mm SP and six 105mm SP guns and twenty-eight towed heavy artillery pieces (more or less correct in total). Its reconstitution as a Panzer Division, albeit weaker than planned, in such a short time and in the face of the Allied heavy bombing campaign, must be considered as nothing short of remarkable.

Das Reich

The Hohenstaufen's new partner in II SS Panzer Corps for the forth-coming offensive was the 2nd SS Panzer Division Das Reich. Recall that a KG Weidinger of this Division had fought with the Corps during Operation EPSOM in Normandy and what was left of Das Reich had taken part in the II SS Panzer Corps counter-attack into the Falaise Pocket in August.

Das Reich was the second most senior Waffen-SS Division and it had been in action constantly since the invasion of Poland in September 1939. Bittrich, Harmel and Stadler were all former Das Reich officers. Following the retreat from Normandy, the badly depleted Division spent a month defending German territory against American attempts to break through the West Wall. Then, in the second week in October, it was pulled out of the line for refitting and re-equipping in Germany. It spent two months in roughly the same area as the Hohenstaufen before being moved, between 11 and 24 November, to the Jülich area west of Cologne. Like the Hohenstaufen, it was part of the Sixth Panzer Army and had been positioned in this sector to mislead the Allies into thinking that it was part of a major counter-attack force protecting the Ruhr. As we shall hear, this ruse was highly successful and Hitler's real plans, for an offensive through the Ardennes, took the Allies completely by surprise.

On 13 December the 2nd SS Panzer Division Das Reich, under the command of SS Brigadier General Heinz Lammerding, began its move south to a new assembly area near Euskirchen for Operation AUTUMN MIST. Its strength was over 17,000 officers and men and it numbered just under 400 armoured vehicles, including fifty-eight Panthers, twenty-eight Mk IVs, twenty Jagdpanzer IVs, twenty-eight StuGs tanks, eight Flakpanzer IVs and 246 SPWs and armoured cars. On the other hand, winter clothing and boots were in short supply and there was a serious shortage of motor transport. For example, the 1st Battalion of the 3rd Deutschland

SS Panzer-Grenadier Regiment had no trucks to lift its Grenadiers, most of whom were issued with bicycles.

Heinz Lammerding had been a professional civil engineer with a degree from Munich University before joining the SS-VT. He had commanded a Pioneer Battalion in the Totenkopf in the Western campaigns of 1940 and later earned a Knight's Cross in Russia as commander of KG Das Reich. He led the 2nd SS Panzer Division Das Reich in Normandy until 26 July 1944 when he was wounded, but by November he had reassumed command. Following the Battle of the Bulge, he was to see out the war as Himmler's military Chief of Staff.

NOTES

1. Tieke, *In the Firestorm of the Last Years of the War*, p. 279.

CHAPTER XXII

WACHT AM RHEIN

By the autumn of 1944 it was obvious to the German High Command, and even to Adolf Hitler, that in the long term it would be impossible to conduct a successful defence of the Greater German Reich on three fronts. The Führer resolved therefore to deliver a massive blow on one of the two most important fronts, designed to render that particular enemy incapable of serious offensive action for a considerable period. This, he reasoned, would give him strategic freedom and provide the forces necessary to deliver other decisive blows and, most importantly, buy time for the perfection of his new war-winning weapons.

The sheer scale of the Eastern Front militated against an attack in that direction. As General Jodl, Chief of the OKW Operations Staff, put it after the war:

> The Russians had so many troops that even if we had succeeded in destroying thirty divisions it would have made no difference. On the other hand, if we destroyed thirty divisions in the West, it would amount to more than a third of the whole invasion army [in fact, half the Allied Expeditionary Force].[1]

This factor, coupled with the threat to the Ruhr and Hitler's low opinion of the fighting capabilities of both the American and British Armies, turned his eyes again to the Western Front. Once that front was stabilised, he believed he would have sufficient forces to resist the inevitable Soviet winter offensive. The fact that he was committing Germany's last reserves in men and resources gave the operation an air of finality – even Hitler predicted that the outcome of this offensive would bring life or death for the German nation. Nevertheless, in his eyes this desperate gamble, which invited disaster in the East, was the only course of action that might bring about his own survival and that of his Nazi regime.

(Map 21)

On 16 September Hitler revealed his basic plan and strategic goals to a small inner circle including Keitel, the Chief of OKW, and Jodl, Chief of the OKW Operations Staff. Despite objections, particularly from the two senior field commanders involved, von Rundstedt and Model, the final plan was basically unchanged when it was issued in late November. Essentially it called for three Armies under Model's Army Group 'B'[2] to break through the weak American front in the Ardennes and Luxembourg and then, with the main weight on the right flank, cross the Meuse south of Liège and exploit to the great port of Antwerp. This would cut off the British and Canadian 21st Army Group and American 9th Army, hope-fully causing mass surrenders and depriving the Allies of their most important port. Indeed, Hitler saw it as the basis of another 'Dunkirk', with a loss to the Allies of some twenty to thirty divisions. He even believed it might destroy the British and Canadian Armies once and for all.

Hitler's plan called for a huge force of seven Panzer and thirteen infantry divisions to be used in the initial assault, with a further two Panzer and seven infantry divisions to be thrown in later. In all, some 1,460 tanks, assault guns and self propelled anti-tank guns and 2,600 artillery pieces and rocket launchers were to be made available.

Sepp Dietrich's Sixth Panzer Army was destined by Hitler to gain the most honours in the forthcoming campaign and it was given the primary objective of Antwerp. The Fifth Panzer Army, under von Manteuffel, was to support this thrust on its left flank, crossing the Meuse astride Namur, with Brussels as its primary objective. General Erich Brandenberger's much weaker Seventh Army was to protect the southern flank of the whole offensive.

Hitler decreed the utmost secrecy in relation to his plan and the various Army staffs did not receive details of it until 29 November. Model, Diet-rich, von Manteuffel and many of the senior commanders responsible for the first wave of the offensive were briefed by the Führer himself at the Adlerhof, near Bad Nauheim, on 11 December. The ADC to Model later described the meeting:

Hitler went far back into history before getting to the Ardennes offensive itself. He spoke without notes, without moving his hands and was easy to understand. He was able to describe the objective of the operation – splitting the American and English forces through a lightning advance . . . the destruction of the English armies in an encirclement battle west of Aachen, in a vivid and convincing manner . . . He said in closing: 'Gentlemen, if our breakthrough via Liège to Antwerp is not successful, we will be approaching an end to the war which will be extremely bloody. Time is not working for us, but against us. This is really the last opportunity to turn the fate of this war in our favour.'[3]

Brandenberger, Bittrich and the senior commanders responsible for the second wave of the offensive received a similar briefing the following day.

(Map 22)

Dietrich was given three Corps: Hermann Priess's I SS Panzer Corps, with the 1st and 12th SS Panzer Divisions plus one Parachute and two Volks-Grenadier Divisions; Bittrich's II SS Panzer Corps, with the 2nd Das Reich and 9th Hohenstaufen SS Panzer Divisions; and Otto Hitzfeld's LXVII Corps with two Volks-Grenadier Divisions.

Hitler's plan called for the Parachute and Volks-Grenadier Divisions of I SS Panzer Corps to make a break in the crust of the American defences, and then form a hard shoulder on the right flank of the proposed advance. The 1st SS Leibstandarte and 12th SS Hitlerjugend Panzer Divisions would then surge to, and across, the Meuse south of Liège in one all-powerful wave; to be followed by Bittrich's II SS Panzer Corps, which 'regardless of flanks being threatened by the enemy' would carry out the exploitation phase to the north-west and seize Antwerp. In the meantime, von Manteuffel's Fifth Panzer Army would advance on the left flank and seize Brussels, whilst Branderberger's Seventh Army would advance to protect the left flank of the whole offensive. The codename for the planning of this operation was WACHT AM RHEIN (WATCH ON THE RHINE). The obvious defensive nature of this codename was chosen deliberately to mislead the enemy. The offensive itself was codenamed AUTUMN MIST.

The details of the plan called for the Divisions of I SS Panzer Corps, the Leibstandarte and Hitlerjugend, to form two powerful armoured KGs containing all the Corps' tanks. These were to advance side by side on parallel routes, with secondary, but strong KGs providing flank protection.

Following the devastation caused by Allied fighter-bombers in Normandy and during the retreat across France, Hitler had resolved to do everything possible to avoid this happening again. He decided therefore to protect his Panzer forces by launching his attack in bad weather and, despite the apparent contradiction, by ordering two associated air offensives at the same time. The first was designed to provide local air superiority for the Fifth and Sixth Panzer Armies at critical times and the second, codenamed BODENPLATTE, sought to destroy Allied aircraft on the ground by launching some 900 aircraft against eighteen airfields in Belgium and Holland in conjunction with the ground attack. After the war von Manteuffel recalled Hitler telling him:

> Goering has reported that he has 3,000 fighters available for the operation. You know Goering's reports. Discount 1,000, and that still leaves 1,000 to work with you and 1,000 for Sepp Dietrich.[4]

The real strength of the Luftwaffe in December 1944 was some 1,900 fighters and ground attack aircraft and 100 bombers.

In a further attempt to aid his Panzer divisions in their dash to the Meuse and beyond, Hitler ordered one special operation and reluctantly agreed to another. Operation GREIF was the Führer's own brainchild. It was to be led by one of his favourites and a former member of the Leibstandarte – Otto Skorzeny. He was told to form two English-speaking groups who would wear American uniforms and use American equipment. The task of the first group, comprising about fifty men in teams of four or five, was to penetrate US lines and then sabotage important installations and generally cause confusion. The second, much larger, group of some 3,000 men divided into three KGs, was to move at night on parallel lines to the advancing Panzer spearheads and seize bridges over the Meuse.

The second special operation, STÖSSER, involved a night parachute drop of some 800 men, to be carried out before H-Hour, with the aim of disrupting the movement of American units towards the right flank of the advance. Hitler, who again was to be proved right, did not believe the Luftwaffe was capable of carrying out the drop successfully but, under pressure from Field Marshal Model, he reluctantly gave approval.

(Maps 20 & 21)

What American forces were lying in the path of Hitler's offensive? Following the victorious advance across eastern France, Belgium and Holland, Eisenhower's Armies had ground to a halt through lack of supplies. Late September and October were spent building up thousands of tons of ammunition, fuel and other essentials, improving the road systems, rebuilding bridges and replacing the many casualties in men and vehicles. Once this had been achieved, Ike ordered the 21st and 12th Army Groups to close up to the Rhine. It proved a costly business. The British did not clear the Meuse until 4 December, the US Ninth Army could not close to the Roer river by that date, let alone the Rhine, and the US First Army became involved in a World War I type slogging match south of Aachen. Patton's Third Army took two weeks and many casualties to take Metz in the south. The unpalatable truth was that the Allies had run up against the West Wall, with all its inherent difficulties for the attacker and advantages for the defender.

In the Hürtgen Forest south of Aachen, Hodges' First Army had seen three of its Divisions cut to pieces. Two of them, the 4th and 28th Infantry, were so badly mauled that they had to be withdrawn and sent to quiet sectors in the southern Ardennes and Luxembourg. The untried 99th and 106th Infantry Divisions (see Appendix VIII) replaced them. All four would find themselves in the path of the German attack. The only immediate reserve available to Hodges was the unblooded 9th Armored Division, thinly spread across most of the front.

The SHAEF strategic reserve at this time was the XVIII Airborne Corps near Reims in France. It consisted of our old friends, the 82nd and 101st Airborne Divisions, resting and preparing for a further airborne operation after MARKET GARDEN.

Why were the Americans so ill prepared for an attack in the Ardennes? First, because no senior commander believed that the Germans were capable of launching an offensive in the West at this stage of the war; second, because the Allies thought the thick forests, deep valleys and fast flowing rivers of the Ardennes precluded any serious offensive action there during the winter; and third, because although the Allies knew of the existence of the Sixth Panzer Army they did not realise that by 15 December it had moved south from the Cologne area. They still thought, as Hitler intended, that it was a counter-penetration force designed to defeat any thrust towards the Rhine and the Ruhr. Moreover, because Hitler banned the use of radio and insisted that all communications before the offensive should be carried out on the telephone, ULTRA, the British decrypting organisation, failed to detect the build-up of German troops opposite the Ardennes front. In actual fact, there were a number of intelligence indicators, including the interception of messages between various Luftwaffe headquarters and bases which had ignored the radio ban, which should have alerted the Allies. Unfortunately, due to preconceived ideas, these intelligence indicators were ignored by the senior Allied staffs and their commanders.

NOTES

1. Jodl, ETHINT 50.
2. Harmel's 10th SS Pz Div Frundsberg was part of Model's Army Gp reserve

but was not committed as a Div. Only those units which participated directly will be mentioned.

3. Meyer, *The History of the 12th SS Panzer Division Hitlerjugend*, p. 238.
4. Price, *The Last Year of the Luftwaffe, May 1944 to May 1945*, pp. 112–13.

CHAPTER XXIII
AUTUMN MIST: 16 – 18 December

16 December
(Map 21)

Before describing the actions of II SS Panzer Corps in this offensive we need to know what happened to the supporting operations and the actions of the other Corps in the Sixth Panzer Army – Hermann Priess's I SS Panzer Corps. This was the formation tasked with advancing to, and crossing, the Meuse river in preparation for the exploitation phase by Bittrich's Divisions – Das Reich and Hohenstaufen.

Even before H-Hour on 16 December, Hitler's plan ran into trouble. Operation BODENPLATTE, the air offensive against Allied airfields, had to be postponed due to poor visibility and when the paratroopers of Operation STÖSSER tried to move to their mounting airfields they found there was insufficient transport. That operation too had to be postponed. It was eventually launched, twenty-four hours late, just before midnight on 16 December. Sixty-eight Junker 52 aircraft took off from two airfields with Luftwaffe Colonel Freiherr von der Heydte's 870 real and 300 dummy paratroopers; however, high winds, inexperienced pilots and both friendly and enemy AA fire led to a very dispersed drop, so that by last light on the 17th only some 300 of the 800 men, without heavy weapons or radios, had manage to form up in the Baraque Michel area to the north of Malmédy. In any case von der Heydte had arrived too late, with too little. A Regiment of the US 1st Infantry Division, which he might have delayed or disrupted, was already taking up positions to counter part of the thrust by Hermann Priess's I SS Panzer Corps.

In some respects though, STÖSSER was a success. Owing to the dispersed drop, the Americans gained the impression that there had been a very large parachute operation, with the result that hundreds of men were wasted looking for mythical paratroopers. Nevertheless, it is a fact that many veterans, and indeed many Belgians, together with most After Action Reports (AARs), talk about incidents with German airborne troops. Clearly, the few that did land behind American lines had an effect out of all proportion to their numbers.

Meanwhile, on the Sixth Panzer Army front, at precisely 0535 hours on 16 December, an intense German artillery barrage had broken the silence of the dark winter's morning. In the event, it achieved little other than to disrupt American communications, which at the time relied heavily on telephone lines. Most of their men were well dug in with good overhead cover, or sheltering from the bitterly cold weather in Belgian houses and farms. Few casualties were caused. Moreover, there was more bad news for the Germans. It soon became clear that in the critical northern sector, the Parachute and Volks-Grenadier Divisions[1] were failing in their attempts to break the crust of the American defences.

The decision to use infantry Divisions to make the initial breakthrough had been a surprising change of tactics. Maybe Hitler had learned from the lessons of Kursk, reinforced by those of the Mortain counter-offensive? Whatever the reason, in the case of I SS Panzer Corps in the Ardennes, it turned out to be a mistake – had its assault been led by tanks, it is most likely that the inexperienced American troops in its path would have fled. Similarly, as events would prove later, if the Corps' request for its attack frontage to be moved farther south had been agreed, and the whole Corps assault then led by tanks, it is more than likely that the Meuse would have been reached in accordance with the planned timetable. Hitler's refusal to listen to his generals when they pointed out that the road network and general topography in the Fifth Panzer Army's planned area of operations was far superior to that in the Sixth's, was to have disastrous results. The members of the Waffen-SS, who were expected to reach the Meuse in three days, would soon find their roads and tracks disintegrating and, unlike in Normandy, they would rarely be able to see as far as the effective range of their weapons.

(Map 23)

The senior commanders of I SS Panzer Corps were fully aware that the attack area assigned to them, and the refusal to allow them to lead with tanks, was asking for trouble. They knew that the state of training of their infantry divisions almost certainly precluded any chance of a rapid breakthrough and it came as no surprise to them therefore to discover that, by midnight on 16 December, the 1st SS Panzer Division's advance was over twelve hours behind schedule and that its two leading armoured Battlegroups were still in Germany – KG Peiper at Lanzerath and KG Hansen at Ormont. The situation on the 12th SS Panzer Division's front was even worse. The Americans, although by then reduced to half strength, were still holding most of their positions and the Volks-Grenadiers had failed to achieve any sort of breakthrough. The Hitlerjugend's armoured KGs – Kuhlmann and Müller – were also stalled in Germany.

The failure of the break-in battle inevitably affected Otto Skorzeny's Operation GREIF. But, whilst the conventional part of his force, the so-called '150 Panzer Brigade' was unable to advance, several of his commando teams did manage to penetrate American lines. By last light on the 16th, one group had even reached Huy on the Meuse (Map 21). After the war, Skorzeny said that forty-four of his men got through. Whatever the correct number there is no doubt that they achieved some success in that they made the Americans very jittery and security conscious, although as von Manteuffel said later: 'The importance of Operation GREIF has been grossly exaggerated.' The exploits of these commandos have been recounted many times before and need not be repeated. Twenty-three of them were captured and eighteen executed for contravening the Rules of War by wearing enemy uniforms.

How did the higher American echelons of command react to the events of 16 December? Apart from the Supreme Allied Commander himself, nobody seemed to appreciate the seriousness of the German attack. It was fortuitous that General Bradley, the commander of the 12th US Army Group, happened to be in Paris conferring with Eisenhower on that critical day. He was there to discuss the general problem of replacements. When, in the afternoon, they received a message from Bradley's Head-quarters in Luxembourg City giving word of the German attack, Ike suggested that he should perhaps, as a precaution, move the 7th Armored Division (see Appendix IX) down from the north and the 10th Armored up from the south. Bradley agreed.

Another important event occurred early on the 16th when Hodges, commanding the US First Army, telephoned Lieutenant General William Simpson of the US Ninth Army to discuss the overall situation. The result was a massive reinforcement from north to south starting the same day; this included the 1st and 30th Infantry Divisions and was to have a profound effect on the forthcoming battle.

17 December

17 December saw a dramatic breakthrough on the Leibstandarte front but little progress on that of the Hitlerjugend. The main Leibstandarte advance was led by the notorious SS Lieutenant Colonel Jochen Peiper – one time Adjutant to Heinrich Himmler and sometimes described as the 'Siegfried' of the Waffen-SS. Leaving Lanzerath in the early hours of the 17th, his powerful KG sliced its way through Honsfeld and Büllingen and then took a minor route to the west. At 1245 hours Peiper's advance guard burst onto the main Malmédy–St Vith road at a place that was to see one of the worst massacres of American troops in WWII – the Baugnez

crossroads. Full details of this tragic event can be found in the author's book *The Devil's Adjutant – Jochen Peiper, Panzer Leader*. It is sufficient to note here that eighty-four Americans died as a direct result of this meeting with Peiper's men and twenty-five were wounded. Fifty-six Americans survived the whole affair – there were no German casualties.

Continuing its advance westward, KG Peiper was eventually halted on the narrow road above the ancient town of Stavelot at about 1915 hours by a road block made up of just thirteen US engineers.[2] Although the engineers soon withdrew, Stavelot gave every appearance of being well defended and Peiper decided, with disastrous consequences, to delay his attack until the following morning. Little did he realise that his way through the town was clear and that its vital bridge, which he had to cross, was intact and had not been prepared for demolition. There is little doubt that at 2300 hours on 17 December KG Peiper could have driven straight through Stavelot and that had it done so, it would almost certainly have reached the Meuse the following day – with potentially catastrophic results for the Americans in particular and the Allies in general.

The second Leibstandarte Battlegroup, KG Hansen, also made significant progress on the 17th, reaching Recht by last light.

On the Hitlerjugend front progress was limited to a mere 5km. By last light, the 'Twin Villages' of Krinkelt and Rocherath and the Wirtzfeld area were still held by the Americans. In darkness and with snow falling the Hitlerjugend's Jagdpanzers and SS Grenadiers renewed their assault, but by 2315 hours they had been halted with heavy casualties. An American officer described the silence that descended on the battlefield as 'almost frightening'.

The failure to achieve any sort of breakthrough towards Malmédy in the northern part of the I SS Panzer Corps' front caused consternation at Headquarters Sixth Panzer Army. In an effort to break the deadlock, it was decided to reinforce success rather than failure and bring Bittrich's II SS Panzer Corps forward on the southern flank of the Leibstandarte. Accordingly, during the night of the 17th/18th, the Hohenstaufen began a move south-west towards Manderfeld. This would bring it into position behind KG Hansen at Recht. At the same time Das Reich started a move towards the vacated Hohenstaufen concentration area south-west of Blankenheim (Map 21). It was anticipated that one of Hasso von Manteuffel's Corps[3] would soon capture St Vith, thus clearing the way for Das Reich to come up on the Hohenstaufen's left flank. This would place three SS Panzer Divisions on a frontage of less than 20km and provide an armoured 'wave' which could then surge towards the Meuse.

The night of 17 December saw important happenings on 'the other side of the hill'. News of the massacre at the Baugnez crossroads, soon to be known as the 'Malmédy Massacre', reached Headquarters First US Army at Spa at 1640 hours. This was the first time anyone in the senior echelons of command knew just how far the Germans had advanced in the northern sector. And it did not take a military genius to work out that the enemy column (KG Peiper) would almost certainly turn west at Ligneuville, threatening both the strategic town of Malmédy and Hodges' own Headquarters at Spa. Not surprisingly, this new intelligence electrified the Americans. General Courtney Hodges was now faced with a breakthrough by enemy armour and he became so concerned that he asked his Army Group commander, General Omar Bradley, to press Eisenhower to release the Strategic Reserve to him. Under this combined pressure Ike agreed, and at 1900 hours the XVIII Airborne Corps near Reims in France received a warning order for a move to the Bastogne area (Map 20). The acting Corps commander, Major General Jim Gavin of Nijmegen fame, immediately drove to Spa, where he arrived to find a chaotic situation with the staff pulling out in any vehicle they could find. On learning that a German armoured column was probably only about 15km away, Gavin agreed to redirect his 82nd Airborne Division to the Werbomont area. The 101st Airborne Division would continue its move to Bastogne.

18 December

After a successful attack at Stavelot early on 18 December, the Leibstandarte's leading battlegroup, KG Peiper, continued its advance westwards and, despite a major diversion caused by blown bridges at Trois Ponts[4] and an air attack, it reached the Lienne river, 5km short of Werbomont, just before dark. After having the bridge there blown in his face as well[5], Peiper decided to reorganise and try again at first light on the following day, through Stoumont on his northern flank.

Also on the 18th the Hitlerjugend Division had renewed its attack on the Twin Villages with the aim of breaking through to Elsenborn. The fighting was as vicious as ever but at the end of the day the field of battle belonged to the Americans. Nevertheless, the US V Corps decided to abandon the Twin Villages and Wirtzfeld salient that night and take up stronger positions on the Elsenborn ridge, or 'North Shoulder' of the 'Bulge', as it became known. It was to prove impregnable and the 12th SS Panzer Division Hitlerjugend would have to seek glory elsewhere.

On the southern flank of I SS Panzer Corps on this day, KG Hansen of the Leibstandarte, after virtually annihilating a small Task Force of the 14th US Cavalry Group earlier in the day near Poteau, was preparing to advance to seize the Salm river bridge at Vielsalm when its commander received orders to withdraw to Recht and secure it for the advance of the 9th SS Panzer Division Hohenstaufen. At this moment the road to the Salm was wide open, with only an ad hoc force of stray tanks, infantry, cavalry and engineers in the way. The order to halt wasted an opportunity that would not be repeated. If Hansen had been allowed to strike for Vielsalm that afternoon there is little doubt he would have been successful – with potentially calamitous results for the Americans in the St Vith sector. The whole of the 7th Armored and 106th Infantry Divisions and CCB of the 9th Armored would have been put at risk. Instead, having broken contact, Hansen was told to be prepared to advance, by way of Logbiermé and Wanne, to Trois Ponts in support of KG Peiper. He said later:

> I became very angry with this Divisional order because I had been able to advance rapidly along my assigned route up to then and I was facing no strong enemy resistance.[6]

Maybe Sixth Panzer Army's idea of bringing up Bittrich's II SS Panzer Corps on the Leibstandarte's southern flank was sound in theory but, as we shall see, the move was to be plagued by fuel shortages, congested routes and, not least, American resistance; it was to be another five days before the Hohenstaufen would be able to advance beyond the Salm river. Similarly, the Fifth Panzer Army's failure to take St Vith until late on the 21st delayed the planned advance of Das Reich.

Hansen halted as ordered at Poteau and Recht and during the afternoon engaged an American armoured infantry Battalion and part of a tank Battalion from the 7th Armored Division, trying to advance towards Poteau. By last light there was stalemate – the Germans had no orders to attack and the Americans were not strong enough to do so.

Details of all I SS Panzer Corps' actions in this period, and subsequently in AUTUMN MIST, can be can be found in the author's book *Men of Steel, I SS Panzer Corps The Ardennes and Eastern Front 1944–45*.

It was during the night of the 18th that Sixth Panzer Army, very sensibly, changed the command structure of its attacking forces. Priess's I SS Panzer Corps could no longer be expected to control the Leibstandarte, the main part of which was now west of Ligneuville, and at the same time fight a breakthrough battle in the Elsenborn area. Hermann Priess's I SS Panzer Corps was therefore given the Hohenstaufen in place of the Hitlerjugend which was still entangled in the Büllingen area. At the same time Das Reich, moving towards St Vith, was also removed from Bittrich's command and became part of the Sixth Panzer Army reserve.

II SS Panzer Corps: 16 – 18 December

We have heard very little of II SS Panzer Corps during the first twenty-four hours of AUTUMN MIST. This is because the only unit to participate directly in the opening phase of the offensive was the Hohenstaufen's

9th SS Artillery Regiment. It was temporarily subordinated to one of the infantry Divisions[7] charged with opening the way for I SS Panzer Corps' KGs and joining in the opening bombardment. The rest of II SS Panzer Corps remained immobile in its assembly areas. Whilst ammunition had been provided on a plentiful scale, fuel shortages remained a major concern for Bittrich and his Divisional commanders. Allied air interdiction and the short preparation time for the offensive meant that stocks were well below the required levels – vehicles had sufficient for 100km only.

At midnight on 16 December, the Hohenstaufen at last began its move forward to a new concentration area just to the south-west of Blankenheim (Map 21). This was followed during the night of the 17th and on the 18th with a further move through Manderfeld towards Schönberg. As this placed the Division in the operational area of Hermann Preiss's I SS Panzer Corps, it was transferred, as we have heard, to his command the following day.

Meanwhile, Das Reich, due to a critical fuel shortage, struggled to follow on. By 18 December it had reached the concentration area vacated by the Hohenstaufen on the 17th, south-west of Blankenheim. The disruption to the railway system in the Third Reich meant that fuel had to be wasted bringing further supplies forward from depots in the Cologne area (Map 20) – a 120km round trip.

Fifth Panzer Army: 16 – 18 December
(Map 21)

Having described the happenings in the Sixth Panzer Army's sector up to 18 December, we should now take a look at events farther south – in the Fifth Panzer Army's area.

Von Manteuffel's tactics differed from those of Sepp Dietrich. He dispensed with a preliminary artillery barrage and used elements of his Panzer Divisions in the initial attack. He had three Corps and his plan was to envelop the Americans in the Schnee Eifel and then capture St Vith with one Corps, whilst the other two, comprising three Panzer and two Volks-Grenadier Divisions, were to secure Houffalize and Bastogne and then drive for the Meuse between Namur and Dinant.

By last light on 18 December, von Manteuffel had been only partially successful. One Corps[8] was across the Our river and ready to strike west to Houffalize, whilst another[9] had one Division[10] on the eastern outskirts of Bastogne, where the American 101st Airborne Division was just arriving, and another[11] beginning to bypass the town to its north. His third Corps[12], however, had failed to take the important road centre of St Vith and this meant that the route intended for Das Reich was blocked. With the approval of Army Group 'B', Dietrich and his Chief of Staff, Fritz

Kraemer, reluctantly ordered Lammerding's Division to divert even farther south through the Fifth Panzer Army sector. They knew it was bound to use up much of the Division's precious fuel.

NOTES

1. 12 & 277 VGD & 3 Para Div.
2. From C/291 Engr Bn.
3. LXVI with 18 & 62 VGDs.
4. By C/51 Engr Bn.
5. By A/291 Engr Bn.
6. Hansen to Lt Col Hans-Dieter Bechtold (Bundeswehr) 25 Nov 83 – Tiemann, *The Leibstandarte IV/2*, p. 423.
7. 277 VGD.
8. LVIII with 116 Pz & 560 VG Divs.
9. XXXXVII.
10. Pz Lehr Div.
11. 2 Pz Div.
12. LXVI with 18 & 62 VGDs.

CHAPTER XXIV
AUTUMN MIST: 19 – 23 December

Hohenstaufen

(Map 23)

The move of the Hohenstaufen, first to relieve KG Hansen at Recht and then to take over the advance on the left flank of I SS Panzer Corps, was plagued with problems. The few roads were jammed with the follow-up units and echelons of I SS Panzer Corps and had degenerated into rivers of mud. The weather remained atrocious and cross-country movement was still impossible for vehicles and impracticably slow for men on their feet. Shortages of transport (the Division had a deficiency of over 500 trucks) and fuel meant that most of the Panzer-Grenadiers of Stadler's Division had to march. Despite these problems, by 1400 hours on the 19th the leading elements of SS Captain Recke's 9th SS Reconnaissance Battalion reached Recht, where they started to relieve KG Hansen of the Leibstandarte. At about this time Zollhöfer's 19th SS Panzer-Regiment was approaching Born and the rest of the Hohenstaufen was spread out all the way back to Manderfeld and beyond. As its new Corps commander, Hermann Priess, put it in his post-war interrogation:

As no fuel supplies were at hand, only certain sections of the Reconnaissance Battalion could be sent forward. The Panzer-Grenadiers
began to move forward on foot; the artillery and tanks waited for the
arrival of fuel supplies.[1]

The following day, while part of Recke's 9th SS Reconnaissance Battalion
screened the important road junction at Poteau, Zollhöfer's men pushed
on due west through the forests towards Wanne.

By 2130 hours on 21 December, St Vith had fallen to the Germans,
releasing substantial elements of von Maunteuffel's forces[2] to push west
towards the Salm. But where was the Hohenstaufen? Wilhelm Tieke[3],
Herbert Fürbringer and the American historian Peter Elstob[4] all claim
that during the evening hours of the 21st part of the Division attacked
unsuccessfully into the woods east of Poteau. This sector was held by
part of CCA of the US 7th Armored Division on the northern edge of
the St Vith salient. The German authors both specify Recke's 9th SS
Reconnaissance Battalion and Mk IVs and StuGs of the 2nd/9th SS Panzer
Regiment, supported by guns of the 2nd/9th SS Artillery Regiment, as
the attacking force. They say that as the advancing armour tried to
advance along the axis of the Recht–Poteau road, it was taken in the flank
by US TDs and 'suffered losses'. This author can find no confirmation of
this attack in any US records and believes that it may have been confused
with a similar one that took place two days later. The fact that photographic evidence shows three Panthers, rather than Mk IVs and StuGs,
left on the battlefield again indicates that the attack took place on the
23rd rather than the 21st. The possibility that this attack did not take
place on the 21st raises the whole question of why we hear so little of
the 9th SS Panzer Division from the time it was ordered to move forward
on the night of the 17th/18th until late on the 22nd and more particularly
on the 23rd – a period of five days. Shortages of fuel and transport and
the fact that St Vith was still held by the Americans are usually offered
as reasons for the Division's slow progress and lack of offensive action.
These arguments ignore the fact that the Division's route through Manderfeld and Recht took it well north of St Vith and that, during the same
period and under the same weather and road conditions, Das Reich
completed a 100km move round the left flank into the northern part of
the Duchy of Luxembourg. It seems reasonable therefore to seek other,
or at least additional, explanations – the more so when one takes into
consideration that the two Volks-Grenadier Divisions of Lucht's
LXVI Corps, with virtually no troop-carrying transport, not only fought
major battles and captured St Vith, but also reached the Salm at roughly
the same time as the Hohenstaufen. So how can one account for the
sluggish moves of the 9th SS Panzer Division and the fact that it was
uninvolved in the fighting for so long? This author believes it may well

have been due to confusion and incompetence within the overall German command organisation. Stadler's Division had been removed from Bittrich's command and placed under Priess's I SS Panzer Corps but, whilst still part of Dietrich's Sixth Panzer Army, it was in fact moving astride the boundary with von Manteuffel's Fifth Panzer Army. Hermann Priess was certainly more interested in events in the Hitlerjugend and Leibstandarte sectors than in the progress of the Hohenstaufen. Furthermore, he knew that the latter had little hope of crossing the Salm in the Trois Ponts sector; and even if it crossed farther south at Grand Halleux, it would still be south of the Amblève and in no position to reinforce the focal point of his attack. In the case of Model and von Manteuffel, their attention was focused on the major road centres of St Vith and Bastogne (Map 21) and the more important and potentially critical happenings between the Salm and the Ourthe. It seems more than possible therefore that Stadler was without firm and close direction, certainly until late on the 21st when St Vith was taken, or even until the 22nd when we hear of the first positive moves in the Grand Halleux–Vielsalm sector.

Whatever the truth about the slow progress of the Hohenstaufen, SS Captain Altrogge's 2nd SS Panzer-Grenadier Battalion of Zollhöfer's 19th Regiment, after a march of some 80km under atrocious conditions, reached the Wanne area on the 22nd. At 1200 hours, however, Priess had been told that the Hohenstaufen was to be returned to II SS Panzer Corps[5] and, as darkness fell, Altrogge's orders were changed. His exhausted Grenadiers were told to swing south through the dense forests to attack Grand Halleux. A member of the 6th Company describes what happened:

While the 5th Company, led by SS Sergeant-Major Jensen penetrated the south part of Grand Halleux ... and then turned north to the bridge over the Salm, the 6th Company, led by SS Senior Sergeant Mumberg, attacked the little town directly from the east and pushed forward as far as the bridge. The Americans were surprised but put up increasing opposition. We reached the bridge which was blown into the air right in front of us. In the meantime, daylight had arrived and it was impossible to cross the Salm since the Americans[6] kept us pinned down with heavy fire from armoured vehicles, artillery and a great numbers of mortars on the west bank.[7]

Jensen was severely wounded during this attack and later died. Nevertheless, by midday on the 23rd both the east bank of the Salm in the Grand Halleux sector and the southern flank of the Leibstandarte were secure and conditions were right for the Hohenstaufen to advance vigorously towards Vielsalm. The town and its bridge were vital to both sides – it was the only place where the Hohenstaufen could cross the Salm to the west, while for the Americans in the northern part of the St Vith salient it was their only viable escape route.[8]

The American withdrawal from the St Vith salient began at 0610 hours on 23 December and by midday Panther tanks of the 9th SS Panzer Regiment, led by the Regimental commander himself, were advancing on either side of the Recht–Poteau road. But, when they reached the area just to the north-east of Poteau, where KG Hansen had destroyed an American Task Force five days before, SS Major Eberhard Telkamp's own tank and four other Panthers were disabled by ten US Shermans and supporting TDs positioned in a semi-circle 'fronting from north-west to east'.[9] Telkamp survived unharmed but the advance inevitably came to an abrupt halt. At 1345 hours, however, as part of their planned withdrawal, the Americans in the Poteau area were ordered to pull back and shortly afterwards elements of Recke's 9th SS Reconnaissance Battalion with Panzer-Grenadiers of the 20th SS Regiment, now under the command of SS Lieutenant Colonel Geiger, occupied the crossroads. Then, just as the Germans were preparing to follow the Americans down the open valley to Petit Thier and Vielsalm, a squadron of US Lightnings struck the KG causing further delay and disruption. Units of the 18th Volks-Grenadier Division trying to move up from Rodt and use the Poteau crossroads at about this time were allegedly taken under fire by the men of the Hohenstaufen in the belief that they were retreating Americans. This only added to the general confusion and gave the American units even more time to reach the Vielsalm bridge.

During the same morning, units of Zollhöfer's 19th SS Panzer-Grenadier Regiment, advancing south from Grand Halleux, clashed with Americans at Petit Thier but they could not cut off or seriously interfere with the American withdrawal. The last US vehicles came under fire as they rushed to get away across the Vielsalm bridge, but by 1900 hours most of the Americans were safely across the river. Initial attempts to blow the bridge failed but shortly after midnight, despite the presence of Germans in the far bank, engineers of the 82nd Airborne Division were able to achieve a partial demolition.[10] In spite of heavy casualties, the American withdrawal has to be considered a success.[11]

Das Reich

We left the 2nd SS Panzer Division moving due south through the LXVI Corps area to the east of St Vith. The move via Prüm was carried out during the night of the 19th and on the 20th, and brought the Division into a new assembly area some 15km east of Houffalize by midday on the 21st. Not surprisingly, this detour of over 100km left Das Reich immobilised through lack of fuel. Some of its vehicles ran out of petrol before reaching the new area and had to be towed the last few kilometres.

By this time the advance of the right flank of the Sixth Panzer Army had already stalled in front of the Elsenborn ridge and just to the west of Stoumont. KG Peiper of the Leibstandarte had made the greatest progress, but it had been forced on to the defensive owing to lack of fuel and was now cut off by the Americans.[12] Attempts on this day (and subsequently) by KG Hansen to break through to Peiper from the Wanne area failed. This lack of progress in the Sixth Panzer Army sector led the Führer to modify his plan and move the focal point of the offensive farther south. On 20 September he directed that, whilst the first priority remained the seizure of the Meuse crossings between Huy and Dinant, crossings were acceptable anywhere – even as far south as Givet (Map 21). In accordance with this Directive, on 21 December Das Reich was ordered to advance north-west with all speed to secure the vital crossroads at the Baraque de Fraiture. This feature (known to the Americans, for reasons which will be explained, as 'Parker's Crossroads') stands 652 metres high and is the intersection of the Houffalize–Werbomont (N-15) and St Vith–La Roche highways. It is one of the bleakest and coldest areas in the whole Ardennes. This move was designed to bring Das Reich into position on the left shoulder of its partner, the Hohenstaufen, which as we have heard, was to cross the Salm in the Vielsalm sector. It would also threaten the withdrawal of the US forces in the southern part of the St Vith salient.[13]

The first re-supply of fuel reached Das Reich on the evening of the 21st and Lammerding immediately ordered a strong KG under the command of SS Major Ernst-August Krag to move north, through Joubiéval, with the aim of blocking one of the two main American escape routes from the St Vith salient – the road running west from Salmchâteau through the Baraque de Fraiture to La Roche. The KG was based on Krag's own 2nd SS Reconnaissance Battalion and was reinforced with the 2nd SS StuG and 1st SS Pioneer Companies and 1st (self-propelled) SS Artillery Battalion.

KG Krag set off soon after first light on the 22nd and after suffering 'continuous harassing fire', the Spitze (advance guard) reached Ottre at about 1415 hours[14] . According to Otto Weidinger's *Division Das Reich, Volume V*, Krag's 2nd SS Reconnaissance Company and StuGs were unable to advance through, or even attack, Joubiéval, due to intense artillery fire on Ottre which lasted until dusk and 'completely destroyed' the village. The commander of the 82nd Airborne Division, Jim Gavin, has a slightly different version of events: 'tanks entered Joubiéval. They were permitted to close up, then brought under devastating artillery fire'. Weidinger's claim that Joubiéval was occupied and defended at this time is unsupported by the available American AARs, although the US Official History mentions 'American outposts in villages south of the road [Salmchâteau–La Roche]'.[15]

According to Weidinger, the Spitze was forced on to the defensive at Ottre and was 'defending itself against tank attacks'. He goes on to say that the Americans managed to blow the bridge 2km south of the village during the night and that Krag's Pioneers had to repair it to allow the rest of the KG to close up. The author could find no American reports mentioning the tank attacks or bridge demolition.

During the night of the 22nd/23rd, Krag received new orders. He was told to seize Salmchâteau and complete the encirclement of the Americans trying to escape from the St Vith salient. Surprisingly, he made no move until just before last light and Weidinger's explanation for the delay raises as many questions as it answers. He claims that the Advance Party of Das Reich began the attack at 1600 hours, 'having previously been on standby'.[16] He then mentions a short but fierce battle in Provedroux, with StuGs knocking out enemy tanks and an enemy battery, after which the Krag's artillery Battalion opened fire on Salmchâteau.

As darkness fell the 3rd SS Reconnaissance Company reached the southern entrance of Salmchâteau [but] gained ground only slowly amidst very fierce street and house-to-house fighting in which enemy tanks and motorised vehicles attacked repeatedly. At about 2100 hours, the Salm bridge in the middle of the town was in our [German] hands. At 2200 hours the place was completely cleared of enemy . . . Throughout the night [the KG] had to fight off a series of enemy groups trying to break out of the encirclement . . . At about midnight the Führer Begleit Brigade . . . made contact with KG Krag.[17]

Thus, the noose was pulled tight. The American units involved in these actions were those withdrawing from the southern part of the St Vith salient. CCB of the 9th Armored Division, with infantrymen of the 424th Regiment, managed to clear Beho and Salmchâteau earlier in the day before Krag could cut them off, but a mixed group, known as TF Jones[18], and two companies of 28th Division's 112th Infantry Regiment were less fortunate. They found themselves trapped between the 62nd Volks-Grenadier Division on the east side of the river, the advance guard of Colonel Otto Remer's Führer Begleit Brigade (FBB)[19] coming up fast from the south-east, and KG Krag. The Stuart tanks leading the column were knocked out by Krag's men and 'most of the mechanised force at the tail was destroyed' by the FBB. The Official US History ends its description of this disaster as follows:

A trail had been discovered leading west out of the valley and most of the middle of the column, led by a light tank company, escaped over it . . . By midnight on the 23rd over two hundred men from the column had reached the 508th Parachute Infantry and many others straggled in before daylight. How many vehicles and men were captured by the enemy is impossible to say.[20]

Meanwhile, by the late afternoon of the previous day, the 22nd, sufficient fuel had arrived in the Das Reich assembly area for Otto Weidinger's 4th SS Panzer-Grenadier Regiment, with an artillery Battalion under command, to move off towards the Baraque de Fraiture. SS Lieutenant Colonel Günther Wisliceny's 3rd SS Panzer-Grenadier Regiment remained grounded through lack of petrol.

(Map 24)

According to Weidinger, his 2nd and 3rd Grenadier Battalions arrived in their new assembly area near Tailles (also called Les Tailles), 3km to the south-east of Baraque de Fraiture, during the late afternoon and night of the 22nd. He claims that his 1st Battalion was 'not operational' and that it did not catch up until the following afternoon – too late for the attack he was planning. Some of its men had to march, some moved on bicycles and many vehicles had to be towed.[21]

Weidinger found the forward elements of the 560th Volks-Grenadier Division stalled in front of a substantial, but very mixed, force of Americans in the crossroads area. This force had been gradually built up from late on 19 December when three 105mm howitzers and fewer than 100 men of the 589th Field Artillery Battalion under a Major Arthur Parker had been ordered to secure the Baraque de Fraiture.[22] Three probes by the 560th Volks-Grenadiers had been beaten off on the 21st and 22nd and more reinforcements in the form of a glider infantry Company from the 82nd Airborne and a platoon of TDs from the 3rd Armored Division had arrived on the fourth day.[23]

Weidinger's men relieved the Volks-Grenadiers and, following a pre-dawn artillery and mortar bombardment, the Grenadiers of his 2nd Battalion succeeded in overrunning the TD platoon which had been sited in front of the US main defence line without infantry support. The Americans lost eighteen men killed, wounded and missing and two guns. A counter-attack, however, by a Company of the 509th Parachute Infantry Battalion, sent in as a last-minute reinforcement from a 3rd Armored Division TF[24], soon retook the lost ground and Weidinger realised that nothing short of a full-scale attack would secure the crossroads.

During the morning the 7th SS (Mk IV) and 8th SS (StuG) Panzer Companies of the 2nd SS Panzer Battalion arrived to support his Regiment and Weidinger allocated them to his 2nd and 3rd Grenadier Battalions respectively.

The main attack was launched at around 1500 hours along the axes of the main roads leading into the crossroads from the west and south-east. By 1800 hours, after 'bitter fighting' in which four Mk IVs were lost, the Baraque de Fraiture was in the hands of the Waffen-SS. Weidinger claimed seventeen tanks, including eight Shermans, four armoured cars and thirty-three half-tracks and other vehicles destroyed or captured. This claim may be slightly exaggerated, but the Americans certainly suffered heavy casualties – only two of the Shermans and forty-four of the 116 glider infantrymen defending the crossroads survived this action.

In an attempt to exploit this success, Weidinger ordered his Grenadiers to move on down the slope and through the thick woods lying to the north-west of the Baraque de Fraiture. He was hoping they would reach the edge of the forest overlooking Odeigne and Malempré before last light. The 3rd Armored Division's TF Brewster[25] was blocking the way, however, at Belle-Haie, 3km north-west of the Baraque de Fraiture and in front of the crossroads leading to Odeigne and Malempré. In an abortive attempt to overcome this opposition, SS Captain Heinz Werner's 3rd Battalion suffered 'heavy casualties', including the loss of the commander of the 11th Company, SS Lieutenant Rosenstock.

Meanwhile, the first elements of the Deutschland Regiment – three Grenadier Companies and the Regimental Pioneer Company – had obtained enough fuel to move forward to a position 3km south of the Baraque de Fraiture.

II SS Panzer Corps

(Map 25)

It was on this same day, 23 December, that the commander of II SS Panzer Corps, Willi Bittrich, was called forward to reassume command of the Das Reich and Hohenstaufen Divisions. This was easier said than done. His own Headquarters had still to fight its way through the traffic jams and appalling weather conditions in order to catch up with him in St Vith and his Divisions were widely separated and uncoordinated. Recall that the Hohenstaufen was still on the east side of the Salm, and Das Reich 25km away on the west side, carrying out orders issued directly by Sixth Panzer Army and fighting in LVIII Panzer Corps' operational area. The only good news was that the 18th and 62nd Volks-Grenadier Divisions of General Walter Lucht's LXVI Corps had just been transferred from the Fifth to the Sixth Panzer Army with the aim of releasing Bittrich's Corps for use between the Salm and the Ourthe.

In his briefing on the overall situation by the Sixth Panzer Army Chief of Staff, Bittrich was told that the advanced elements of the 2nd Panzer Division were within 10km of the Meuse in the Dinant sector (Map 21), the 116th Panzer Division the same distance from Marche-en-Famenne and the 560th Volks-Grenadier Division north of La Roche. Furthermore, it was clear that if the offensive was to have any chance of reaching, let alone crossing, the Meuse, a fully coordinated II SS Panzer Corps had to be brought into play without delay on the right flank of Divisions just mentioned. Bittrich was ordered therefore to reassume command of Das Reich and Hohenstaufen, move the latter across the Salm as a matter of urgency and advance north-west, through Erezée and Durbuy to the Meuse between Namur and Huy (Map 21). Suggestions made in many books, that it was only *after* the capture of the Manhay crossroads that Model, Dietrich or Bittrich gave the order for Das Reich to turn west through Grandmenil and Erezée, rather than continuing north towards Liège, are incorrect. The intention was always for Das Reich to advance through Erezée to Durbuy and for the Hohenstaufen to move on the axis Lierneux–Manhay–Bomal.

NOTES

1. MS # A-877.
2. 18 & 62 VGDs & the Führer Begleit Bde (FBB). 3/10 SS Arty Regt and the Frundsberg's long-range Kanon Bty, from the Army Group 'B' reserve, fired from positions near Schönberg in support of this final attack.
3. Tieke, *In the Firestorm of the Last Years of the War*, p. 315.
4. Elstob, *Hitler's Last Offensive*, p. 294.
5. MS # A-877.
6. 505 Para Inf Regt, 82 Airborne Div.
7. Tieke, op. cit., p. 317.
8. 7 Armd Div.
9. Cole, *The Ardennes: The Battle of the Bulge*, p. 418.
10. Lt George Lamm was awarded a DSC for leading a series of charges to hold back the Germans and then detonating the explosives himself.
11. Cole, op. cit., p. 422: 'It is difficult to determine with surety how much of 7 Armd, CCB/9 Armd, 424 and 112 Inf Regts [were lost] during the fight for St. Vith. . .Casualty figures subsequently compiled for 7 Armd & 14 Cav Gp list 3,397 . . . killed, wounded or missing. . . . 7 Armd Div . . . lost fifty-nine med tks, twenty-nine lt tks & twenty-five armd cars.'
12. Units of 3 Armd, 30 Inf & 82 Airborne Divs.
13. 7 Armd Div, CCB/9 Armd Div, 112 & 424 Inf Regts.
14. 7 Armd Div G-4 Report, 22 Dec 44.
15. Cole, op. cit., p. 420.
16. Weidinger, *Division Das Reich, Vol V*, p. 386.
17. Weidinger, op. cit., pp. 386–7.
18. Some sub-units of the 7 Armd Div, remnants of the 14 Cav Gp, at least four TDs, a coy (+) of lt tks & C/965 FA Bn, all under the command of LTC Robert B Jones (CO 814 TD Bn).
19. Comprising twenty-three Mk IVs, forty-eight StuGs, three inf bns & an AA Regt.
20. Cole, op. cit., p. 421.
21. Weidinger, *Comrades to the End*, p. 362.
22. Four quad .50 cal half-tracks 203 AAA Bn, D/87 Recce Sqn & eleven Shermans & a recce pl from TF Kane 3 Armd Div. At least three of these Shermans

were later withdrawn to Lamormenil and the exact number at the crossroads on 23 Dec is uncertain.

23. F/325 Glider Inf Regt & 3/A/643rd TD Bn with four towed a/tk guns.
24. TF Richardson – 3 Armd Div AAR for Dec 44.
25. Part of TF Richardson/3 Armd Div, it comprised six tks of H/32 Armd Regt, A/509 Para Inf Bn & C/290 Inf Bn (both temporarily attached 3 Armd Div) & some survivors from the Baraque de Fraiture.

CHAPTER XXV
AUTUMN MIST: 24 – 27 December

Das Reich

(Map 25)

The most serious problem facing Major General Matthew Ridgway's XVIII Airborne Corps on 24 December was in the sector on its right flank around Manhay. This problem was exacerbated because the N-15 (now the N-30), running directly through the village to Liège 50km away to the north, was the boundary between Ridgway's Corps and Major General J Lawton Collins's VII Corps. To the east, Major General Jim Gavin's four Regiments were holding firm in a quadrant running from Trois Ponts, south along the Salm to Salmchâteau, and then west to Regné; but its frontage was far too long for a single Division. Major General Maurice Rose's 3rd Armored Division, less CCB which was detached to the 30th Infantry Division north of the Amblève, was located to the west of the N-15; but, despite the addition of two parachute Battalions[1], its operational area was also far too large and the Division badly needed reinforcing. Gavin had visited Rose on the 22nd and been told that the 3rd Armored was 'incapable of committing sufficient strength to the [Manhay] crossroads to guarantee its retention by our troops'.[2]

(Map 24)

Early on the 24th, in an attempt to rectify this situation, Ridgway ordered the 7th Armored Division to fill the gap and directed that particular attention be paid to the N-15. Despite a somewhat chaotic situation following the withdrawal from the St Vith salient, three TFs of the 7th Armored's CCA had been deployed by 0900 hours to cover the N-15 in the Manhay sector: one defended Malempré, one was located 2km south of Manhay on the east side of the N-15, looking out on Malempré and covering the main road immediately to its south, and the third was 2km farther down the N-15, behind TF Brewster and astride the crossroads leading to Malempré and Odeigne. Following the fighting in the St Vith salient, the 40th Tank, 48th Armored Infantry and 814th TD Battalions of CCA were well below strength and this allowed only a limited number of infantrymen, tanks and TDs to be allocated to each TF. In addition to a weak infantry company, the one at Malempré had ten Shermans, five Stuart tanks, four TDs and a detachment of armoured engineers, the one 2km south of Manhay nine Shermans, and the most southerly TF had seven Shermans and two TDs. The remaining two TDs were kept back in the village of Manhay. Also located in the Malempré area at this time was an Armored Infantry Battalion of CCB of the 9th Armored Division, but it was withdrawn during the afternoon into XVIII Corps Reserve near Hamoir (Map 25) on the Meuse.[3] TF Kane of the 3rd Armored Division, of which we shall hear more shortly, was covering the sector south of Grandmenil.

The continued fuel shortage still plagued Das Reich. One might have expected a Panzer Division, particularly of the Waffen-SS, to be given some priority, but because the Divisions of von Manteuffel's Fifth Panzer Army had been more successful in their advance westwards, they took priority over those of II SS Panzer Corps. It is interesting to note that the Americans were well aware of this problem. On 24 December the 7th Armored Division issued the following instruction: 'Do not abandon or surrender any supplies, especially gasoline. Defend them to the utmost and if necessary destroy'.[4]

By the early hours of the 24th, Lammerding, the Divisional commander, knew that the Americans were blocking the N-15 and holding the Manhay area in some strength. Nevertheless, he still hoped to avoid these forces by outflanking them to the west. He therefore ordered SS Lieutenant Colonel Günther Wisliceny's 3rd Deutschland SS Panzer-Grenadier Regiment to secure Odeigne on the left flank and the Divisional Pioneers to improve the track running through the forest from just west of the Baraque de Fraiture to that village. At the same time Weidinger's 4th Der Führer SS Panzer-Grenadier Regiment was ordered to clear and secure the woods south of Malempré, thus protecting the right flank of the planned advance. Lammerding's intention was to advance on two routes to his next major objective – Erezée. The first ran through Freyneux (spelt Freineux in 1944), Lamormenil and Amonines and the second through Oster and Grandmenil.

Odeigne was secured without serious trouble[5] although American artillery fire was still proving effective and interfering with the German preparations. SS Lieutenant Horst Gresiak, the commander of the 7th SS Panzer Company, was severely wounded during the morning but survived to be awarded the Knight's Cross for his part in the action the previous day at the Baraque de Fraiture.

Weidinger claims that the Grenadiers of his 1st and 2nd Battalions became involved in extremely fierce fighting in the woods and marshy ground south of Malempré, with one Company in particular suffering 'extraordinarily high' casualties. There are no American reports of this fighting. Weidinger then goes on to describe a sudden onset of frost causing numerous cases of men freezing to death during the night. He claims that 3 to 5% of fatalities his Regiment suffered at this time were due to exposure.[6]

SS Lieutenant Colonel Rudolf Enseling was given the task of co-ordinating the next part of the advance. A Pioneer officer with nine years' experience, Enseling was a surprising choice when he was appointed to command the 2nd SS Panzer Regiment in July 1944. Nevertheless, he had a sharp brain and was already the holder of a German Cross in Gold and a Knight's Cross. His plan, devised without the benefit of a proper reconnais-sance, saw two main thrusts. The first, from Dochamps to Lamormenil, was to be made by a Battalion of the 560th Volks-Grenadier Division, supported by SS Lieutenant Karl Mühleck's 1st SS Panzer Company. The main Das Reich attack, however, was to be made towards Freyneux and Oster by the 2nd and 3rd Panther Companies of SS Captain Wilhelm Matzke's 1st SS Panzer Battalion, supported by SS Lieutenant Grohmann's 1st Com-pany of the Deutschland's 1st SS Panzer-Grenadier Battalion. SS Lieuten-ant Alfred Hargesheimer's 2nd Panther Company, led by Knight's Cross holder SS Second Lieutenant Fritz Langanke, was targeted on Freyneux and SS Lieutenant Johann Veith's 3rd Company on Oster.

The ground over which the armoured assault was to be made could not have been more unsuitable. From Odeigne, a narrow twisting road, flanked by thick woods, led down to a road junction 2km from the village. There, the 2nd Panzer Company had to turn west and cross the small Aisne river towards Freyneux and Lamormenil, whilst the 3rd would carry on to Oster, a small hamlet completely dominated from the La Fosse ridge to its west.

Recall that TF Kane of the US 3rd Armored Division was positioned in the sector through which Lammerding's tanks were now about to advance. It was a mixed TF, with its Headquarters located in Grandmenil. Five Shermans were positioned in the dominating hamlet of La Fosse, four Shermans together with most of a Reconnaissance Company and four Stuarts were in Freyneux, a further three Shermans, two TDs and a Company of paratroopers in Lamormenil[7], and another infantry Com-pany, recently arrived and unblooded, in Oster.[8]

Not surprisingly, the German attacks were quickly halted. The three Panzer Companies each lost two Panthers, two more of Hargesheimer's 2nd Company were damaged and the Volks-Grenadiers suffered over

100 casualties. Karl Mühleck, the commander of the 1st SS Panzer Company and a Knight's Cross holder, received wounds from which he later died. With the advance stalled and US fighter-bombers soon appearing overhead, the Germans knew it was time to withdraw back into the protection of the woods around Odeigne. Confirmed American losses in this fighting were: one Sherman, one Stuart and a TD in the village of Freyneux, two Shermans, two assault guns, an armoured car and three half-tracks in the Lamormenil area, and four of the five Shermans which had tried to move south from La Fosse during the afternoon. With regard to these latter casualties, the History of the 9th Armored Division complains that they were deployed by the 3rd Armored Division without CCB's knowledge or that of the 82nd Airborne Division under whose command it was operating at the time.[9] It is estimated that a total of about 137 Americans, or 20% of those involved, became casualties[10] and that a considerable number of their 'soft-skinned' vehicles were put out of action or abandoned.

Readers interested in a more detailed account of this fighting are recommended to read George Winter's brilliantly researched account in *Freineux and Lamormenil – The Ardennes.*

It will be remembered that the original intention had been for the Hohenstaufen to advance concurrently on Lammerding's right flank through the Manhay area. Unfortunately, the non-appearance of the 9th SS Panzer Division on 24 December, for reasons which will be explained in the next Chapter, meant that Das Reich had now to protect its own flank in any future move to the north-west. The only course of action remaining to Lammerding was therefore to advance astride the N-15, with the aim of securing Manhay, Malempré and Vaux-Chavanne, before turning west through Grandmenil. These villages were of course the intermediate objectives of the Hohenstaufen and their capture would be of major benefit to that Division when it finally caught up.

SS Captain Ortwin Pohl's 4th SS Panzer Company, which had been held in reserve during the morning attack on Freyneux and Oster, was chosen to spearhead the advance from Odeigne to the N-15 and then to secure the vital crossroads at Manhay. The 2nd and 3rd Companies were to follow up while SS Captain Heinz Werner's 3rd Battalion of the 4th SS Panzer-Grenadier Regiment in SPWs was to provide close infantry support. Also in support on and to the west of the N-15 would be two Grenadier Battalions of the 3rd SS Panzer-Grenadier Regiment. The remaining two SS Panzer-Grenadier Battalions of Otto Weidinger's 4th Der Führer Regiment, with support from the 7th and 8th SS Panzer Companies, were to move on the right of the N-15 to secure Malempré and Vaux-Chavanne. Weidinger claimed later that his 1st Battalion was so ineffective that essentially he could only count on the 2nd Battalion and the Regimental units[11] (the SS Infantry Gun, Flak, Reconnaissance and Pioneer Companies). H-Hour for the attack was set for 2200 hours (2100 Allied time). It is interesting to note that, according to Ortwin Pohl, General Walter Krüger, the commander of LVIII Panzer Corps, a General in the Waffen-SS and a former commander of Das Reich, visited his Division during the day in an attempt to have the time of the attack brought forward. Since it was to take place in his operational area, he clearly felt he was entitled to interfere. Nevertheless, the time of H-Hour was not altered. This is hardly surprising in view of the time needed to organise such an attack and the dangers of launching it under the threat of more Allied air attacks.

According to Wilhelm Tieke[12], the Hohenstaufen's 9th SS Reconnaissance Battalion was temporarily subordinated to Das Reich at this time to provide left flank protection during the attack. Its Headquarters was located initially in Odeigne.

Having successfully deployed his units, Colonel Dwight Rosebaum, the commander of CCA 7th Armored Division, was surprised to be told at 1800 hours that his force was to withdraw to the north of Manhay at 2230 hours. TF Brewster, in front of him and due to withdraw through him that night in order to rejoin the 3rd Armored Division, was now to stay in position until his withdrawal was well under way.

(Map 25)

This new order stemmed from an overall directive issued earlier in the day by Field Marshal Montgomery, the recently appointed commander of all troops north of a line drawn from Givet to Houffalize (Map 21).[13] He had been authorised by Eisenhower 'to give up such ground as was necessary in order to assemble sufficient strength for a decisive counter-attack'.[14] He had concluded, not surprisingly, that the XVIII Corps line to the south and west of Trois Ponts was over-stretched and needed shortening and that Major General Lawton Collins should similarly draw back the left wing of his VII Corps (3rd Armored Division) to conform with the new XVIII Corps line. There has been a lot of post-war controversy about this decision but at the time it was clearly necessary and had the concurrence of most of the senior American commanders concerned, including Eisenhower, Ridgway and Gavin. In the case of Ridgway's Corps, the order involved Gavin's Regiments pulling back to a diagonal line running south-west from Trois Ponts to Bra and Vaux-Chavanne, and CCA of the 7th Armoured pulling back to the low hills just to the north of Manhay. A Regiment of the 75th Infantry Division was due to arrive later that day to the west of CCA's new position in order to support the 3rd Armored Division and block the roads running west and north-west from Grandmenil towards Erezée and Mormont respectively.

(Map 24)

There are two versions of how Rosebaum tried to disseminate the orders for this withdrawal to his three TF commanders. The Official US History[15] claims that just as the German advance began, he called them in to his Headquarters in Manhay to brief them personally. Another well researched account[16] says that, mindful of the need for secrecy, Rosebaum imposed a radio silence throughout his Command and ordered his Intelligence officer to go round personally and brief the TF commanders. It goes on to state that he was unable to make contact with the most southerly TF before the German attack started. In fact, it makes little difference which version is correct – the scene was already set for an American disaster.

At 2200 hours (2100 Allied time) on Christmas Eve, on a clear moonlit night, with Weidinger's Grenadiers already moving towards Malempré, the main German advance began. Many accounts speak of deep, frozen snow covering the ground. This is incorrect. There were a few centimetres of snow at the Baraque de Fraiture and on other nearby high points but little or none in the area of the German objectives.

What happened next has been told many times before by both German and American participants. For readers particularly interested in the details, George Winter's *Manhay The Ardennes Christmas 1944* is recommended. From the point of view of this history all we need to know is that within a few hours CCA of the 7th Armored Division had been routed, Manhay was in German hands and Weidinger's 1st and 2nd Grenadier Battalions had cleared Malempré. The American 'bug out' became, as the Official History puts it, a case of *'sauve qui peut'* and CCA quickly ceased to exist as a coherent fighting force. A combination of surprise and aggressive tactics, military competence and sheer bravery enabled the German tank crews and Panzer-Grenadiers to outflank, intermingle with and cut through the Americans in a way which has to be admired. The exploits of SS Senior Sergeant Ernst Barkmann, already a Knight's Cross holder, in this action have become legendary. Unexpectedly finding himself in the lead of the column of Panthers, Barkmann drove within a few hundred metres of the nine Shermans dug in 2km south of Manhay and then managed to penetrate right through the village, mixing with American vehicles and spreading panic and destruction as he did so. As well as being able to shoot into the crammed columns of CCA and TF Kane's echelons 'bugging out' from Grandmenil, he was personally credited with the destruction of seven tanks, two TDs, a half-track and two jeeps. The commander of the leading platoon of the 4th SS Panzer Company, SS Sergeant-Major Franz Frauscher, knocked out five of the Shermans by-passed by Barkmann and four more later in the battle. Not surprisingly, he was awarded the Knight's Cross. His Company commander, Ortwin Pohl, was credited with four tanks.

CCA lost twenty-one of its thirty-two tanks – the majority of them without firing a shot – and an untold number of half-tracks and other vehicles. The survivors took refuge with an Armored Infantry Battalion[17] holding the heavily wooded ridge a kilometre to the north of Manhay. The 40th Tank and 48th Armored Infantry Battalions lost a total of six men killed and nineteen wounded on this day – 436 were listed as 'Missing in Action', including eighteen officers.[18] The 3rd Armored Division losses are unspecified but certainly included two Shermans. TF Brewster lost two tanks in an attempt to withdraw via Malempré and, after finding his force cut off by the rapid German advance, the commander ordered his men to destroy their vehicles and withdraw on foot. It was after dawn the following day before some members of the TF[19] reached the safety of the 82nd Airborne Division's lines 8km away near Bra (Map 25).

Leaving Wisliceny's 3rd SS Panzer-Grenadier Battalion and a few tanks to secure Manhay, the bulk of the Panthers and Grenadiers turned west towards their next objective – Grandmenil. SS Sergeant-Major Frauscher's tank reached the crossroads in the centre of the village at about 0300 hours on Christmas morning. Two Shermans of the 3rd Armored Division positioned nearby accounted for the only other Panther left in his platoon, but Frauscher soon dealt with them and the advance, led now by Hargesheimer's 2nd Company, continued westwards towards the final objective – Erezée.

It will be remembered that a Regiment of the 75th Infantry Division had been due to arrive on Christmas Eve with the mission of blocking the roads running west and north-west from Grandmenil. The lead Battalion[20] of this Regiment, after encountering some tanks of the 3rd Armored Division fleeing to the west, received orders to dig in on the Erezée road and it was this Battalion group which the Germans encountered about a kilometre to the west of Grandmenil. The lead Panther was disabled and in the darkness, with a forested embankment on one side of the road and a steep drop on the other, the others found it impossible to deploy off the road. Dawn was about to break, bringing with it the threat of US air strikes[21] and the German commanders realised they had little chance of breaking through to Erezée. Not surprisingly, the decision was taken to withdraw back to the relative safety of Grandmenil.

The German attack had been a spectacular success but it had failed to achieve its ultimate goal and had been costly. The commanders of the 2nd and 4th SS Panzer Companies, Hargesheimer and Pohl, had been wounded[22] – the former by a pistol shot as he tried to disarm a GI – as had Heinz Werner, the commander of the 3rd SPW Panzer-Grenadier Battalion of Weidinger's Regiment and his immediate successor, SS Lieutenant Heinrich Manz. Panzer aces Ernst Barkmann and Fritz Frauscher were also amongst the many wounded. A minimum of eight Panthers had been lost in the 4th Company alone – four allegedly to mines laid between Manhay and Grandmenil.

Whilst the Germans completed their withdrawal back to Grandmenil, the Americans were beginning their moves to counter this serious penetration between their VII and XVIII Corps. At 0825 hours Ridgway ordered the depleted 7th Armored Division to 'attack and retake Manhay'. Its commander, Brigadier General Robert Hasbrouck, was told that a new TF from the 3rd Armored Division would be attacking at the same time from the west. After promising powerful artillery and air support, Ridgway closed his instructions with the words, 'I expect your entire effort behind this action to restore this part of the Corps' position with the minimum of delay'. This order was repeated at 1330 hours with the additional instruction that the operation was to be completed 'by dark tonight'.

In an attempt to comply with this order, Hasbrouck launched an attack with two under-strength tank companies and a company of armoured infantry, reinforced with an infantry Battalion from the 106th Division.[23] It was mounted from the ridge just to the north of Manhay, held by the Armored Infantry Battalion of the 9th Armored Division[24], 'plus tanks and stragglers that had worked their way past Manhay'.[25] Although it more or less coincided with the complementary assault by the 3rd Armored Division TF on Grandmenil, the attack never had any real chance of success against Wisliceny's SS Panzer-Grenadiers and some Panthers which had by now been carefully sited in the northern part of the village. Trees felled by the Americans during their retreat made it too difficult for the tanks to advance down the N-15 and when a company of six Shermans tried to move in from the east, they lost half their number – probably to Otto Weidinger's Der Führer Regimental group on that flank. Despite the artillery firing 6,409 rounds in support[26], the infantrymen attacking from the north were decimated, suffering 35% casualties. Towards the end of the day, Ridgway and Hasbrouck decided to resort to air power and the thirteen battalions of artillery within range to soften up the opposition before trying again. 8,600 more shells were to fall on Manhay and Grandmenil in the next thirty-six hours, devastating the villages and making them a hell on earth for the Germans and the few remaining local residents.

Meanwhile at 1130 hours, a TF McGeorge of the 3rd Armored Division had arrived in the area to the east of Erezée already held by the 289th Infantry Regiment. It had been rushed down from the La Gleize area (Map 25), where it had been heavily involved in the battle against KG Peiper, with orders to 'seize, occupy and defend at all costs Grandmenil [and the] high ground at La Fosse'. Unfortunately, at about 1430 hours, just as the TF's Sherman and Armoured Infantry Companies and a platoon of Stuarts[27] prepared to advance, they were bombed and strafed by eleven P-38s. Forty-one of McGeorge's men and four of the 289th infantrymen were killed and many others wounded. Even so, McGeorge still managed to launch his attack against Grandmenil at 1500 hours. Not surprisingly, with no time for reconnaissance and an advance restricted by the ground to a one-tank front, TF McGeorge was savagely repulsed by Wisliceny's 2nd SS Panzer-Grenadier Battalion and Panthers of Matzke's 1st Battalion. Das Reich was not going to give up its hard-won ground easily.

Soon after dark on Christmas Day, the remainder of McGeorge's tank Battalion and another armoured infantry Company[28] arrived, enabling him to launch a second attack at 2000 hours, supported by an infantry Company of the 289th Regiment.[29] Despite coming under fire and suffering casualties from their own artillery falling short and losing four of the five tanks in the leading platoon, McGeorge's men secured the western part of the village by 2200 hours. Inevitably, the Germans launched a violent counter-attack with tanks and Grenadiers causing the main part of the TF and its supporting infantry Company to withdraw. Unaware of this order, a single tank and a small detachment of armoured infantrymen remained in the western part of Grandmenil, saved only by the tank commander calling down friendly artillery fire on their own positions.[30]

Das Reich, whilst admittedly maintaining a firm grip on Manhay and Grandmenil, had still to achieve its primary mission of securing the Erezée to Mormont road. The problems facing Lammerding in this task were overwhelming. First, his Division was exhausted and had suffered heavy losses in both men and material; second, the fuel shortage was affecting not just his armour but also the supply of artillery ammunition; third, the clear skies meant that any vehicles moving by day were likely to come under immediate air attack; and fourth, due to the failure of the Hohenstaufen to come into line on his right shoulder, any move in the required direction would present an open flank to the enemy. In addition, the crammed and heavily interdicted lines of communication meant that only two battalions of the II SS Panzer Corps artillery had managed to cross the Salm and this, coupled with the general shortage of ammunition, meant the counter-battery fire against the massed American guns was severely restricted.

Before dawn on the 26th, in an attempt to protect his right flank and draw his enemy's attention, Lammerding ordered the 4th DF SS Panzer-Grenadier Regiment to mount a preliminary attack on the east side of Manhay towards Vaux-Chavanne. This was a difficult task because the hamlet of Vaux-Chavanne lies on the reverse slope of a high, forested ridge and on this ridge, covering the approach from Malempré, the Americans had positioned a glider infantry Battalion.[31] According to Weidinger his 2nd SS Panzer-Grenadier Battalion advanced through the densely wooded terrain and took the village of Vaux-Chavanne. A vigorous counter-attack, however, could not be held. The American version of this action reads, 'at 0630 hours one battalion of the 2nd SS Panzer Division attacked and succeeded in over-running a portion of the sector. Companies B and C promptly counter-attacked and restored all positions, inflicting heavy casualties on the enemy'.[32]

The main Das Reich effort was made by part of Matzke's now depleted 1st SS Panzer Battalion, supported by SS Captain Heinrich Bastian's 1st SS Panzer-Grenadier Battalion of the Deutschland Regiment. KG Krag, which had caught up the previous evening after its successful action at Salmchâteau, was positioned in the woods between Odeigne and Malempré, ready to exploit towards Mormont and Bomal.[33]

The Panther attack group advanced north-west from Grandmenil soon after first light; at the same time a secondary thrust was launched along the Erezée road by Wiscileny's 2nd SS Panzer-Grenadier Battalion which ran into a new American attack on Grandmenil. TF McGeorge and the 3rd Battalion of the 289th Infantry Regiment had advanced again at 0610 hours:

> [The American] leading elements ran into strong final protective fire [from German artillery and machine-guns] as well as fire from enemy tanks. Our tank losses were very heavy and at 1200 only two F Company tanks were left and both of their large caliber guns were jammed. At 1300, eight replacement tanks were brought forward and H Company of the 32nd Armored Regiment with eight tanks was attached to TF McGeorge for another attack which began at 1425.[34]

We will return to the action in Grandmenil shortly, but what of the main German advance towards Mormont? The commander of the American tank[35] that had survived the night in Grandmenil reported a column of at least twelve Panthers moving out of the village on the Mormont road soon after first light, and the strength of the column is confirmed by one of the armoured infantrymen who had also remained there:

> Someone up in the hayloft called down that there was a German tank approaching down a roadway which ran east of the barn. Soon a second tank was mentioned, then a third . . . This counting continued until he had numbered thirteen tanks, each one carrying a complement of infantry.[36]

The German column continued up the road which runs through 4km of thick forest and has a stream running along its left side. Deployment off the road was impossible. Hidden by the trees from a spotter aircraft sent up to find it, the lead tank soon ran into an abatis of felled trees behind which American infantry and TDs[37] had taken up positions. The Panther was quickly despatched, blocking the road, and American artillery fire prevented any further forward movement by the accompanying Grenadiers. Das Reich's attempt to advance west from Grandmenil was over.

We left TF McGeorge preparing to attack Grandmenil again at 1425 hours. Following a heavy concentration by three artillery battalions, the third assault was successful and by last light, after the tanks and armoured infantry had broken through the German defences, the 3rd Battalion of the 289th Infantry had occupied the main part of the village and the road to Manhay. More than fifty badly wounded Germans were taken prisoner. An American armoured infantryman later described the attack:

> The whole valley was now shrouded in smoke, giving us some degree of protection. No sooner did we reach the edge of the village, when again we were greeted with heavy machine-gun fire. The tanks, along with a few bazooka rounds eventually silenced some of them and we moved through quite rapidly ... When we entered one of the first partially intact houses on the left of the street, we were met by a Belgian woman who had somehow survived that ordeal of fire. [She was] standing in a large room with the floor literally covered from wall to wall in blood ...
>
> After we eliminated some of the machine-guns that held up our initial entry into the village, the fire subsided a little ... Later in the day we caught a particularly heavy barrage from what must have been that column of tanks that had withdrawn behind the village ... In the closing moments of the retaking of the village ... we approached a side street and literally bumped into an American coming up that side street, and who was it, but Major McGeorge, armed with nothing but his map case and a .45. What a remarkable man![38]

The 7th Armored Division's advance, designed to coincide with McGeorge's, was too weak to have any real chance of success. The few tanks that were scraped together for the attack began their move towards the Manhay–Grandmenil road during the afternoon but they had to cross open, sloping ground and were easy targets for the few Panthers still in the northern part of Manhay. They were halted several hundred metres north of their objective and fighter-bombers called in to help were ineffective. The American commanders then decided to change their tactics and launch a night attack with a fresh Battalion of Parachute Infantry.[39] And so, at 0220 hours, following a twenty-minute concentration of some 5,000 rounds fired by eight artillery battalions, the paratroopers advanced on the village. By 0400 hours on 27 December the battle of Manhay was over. Earlier in the night, while the Hohenstaufen's 9th Reconnaissance

Battalion held firm on the left flank in Oster and Freyneux[40] and Der Führer launched a holding attack on the right flank, Wisliceny's 3rd Deutschland Regiment and the remaining Panthers had begun pulling out of their exposed positions in Manhay towards Odeigne. This enabled the Americans to re-capture the village with surprisingly few casualties – ten killed and fourteen wounded. For the Germans it was a different story. Fifty of their dead remained in the village, together with twenty-five badly wounded, and Weidinger's holding attack proved extremely costly. A total of ten knocked out Panthers were found in and around the Grandmenil–Manhay area. It may well have been at this time that the commander of the 3rd SS Panzer Company, Johann Veith, was killed.

Das Reich's withdrawal was not solely due to the increasingly high casualty rate and American pressure. The reality was that by this time Hitler's great plan was in deep trouble. All four Waffen-SS Divisions had failed to achieve their primary missions. The Leibstandarte's thrust in the north had ended with the destruction of KG Peiper, the Hitlerjugend had failed at Elsenborn and Bütgenbach (Map 23), the Hohenstaufen had failed to come into line on Das Reich's right flank in time and the latter had failed to break through to Erezée.

Almost immediately after the loss of Manhay on 27 December, a dismayed Lammerding was told that Das Reich was to participate in a new attack being planned for that night.

NOTES

1. 509 & 1/517 Para Inf Bns.
2. Gavin's personal report to the US War Department.
3. AAR 27 Armd Inf Bn, dated 3 Jan 45.
4. 7 Armd Div G-4 Report, 24 Dec 44.
5. The five lt tks of A/32 Armd Regt & pl of D/83 Recce Bn withdrew with minimal casualties.
6. Weidinger, *Division Das Reich, Vol V*, p. 370.
7. Five Shermans from C/14 Tk Bn (CCB/9 Armd Div), seven from D/32 Armd Regt, C/517 Para Inf Regt (less a pl), two 3" guns A/643 TD Bn & parts of two Coys 83 Recce Bn including four Stuarts.
8. A/290 Inf Regt of 75 Div.
9. 9 Armd Div History, Dec 1944 (Excerpts), 609 – Ø.1, p. 53.
10. Winter, *Freineux and Lamorneil – The Ardennes*, p. 41.
11. Weidinger, *Comrades to the End*, p. 372.
12. Tieke, *In the Firestorm of the Last Years of the War*, p. 323.
13. This included most of the First US Army and the whole of the Ninth.
14. Cole, *The Ardennes: Battle of the Bulge*, p. 411.
15. Cole, op. cit., p. 588.
16. Winter, *Manhay The Ardennes Christmas 1944*, pp. 16–17.
17. 23 Armd Inf Bn of CCB/9 Armd Div.
18. 7 Armd Div G-4 Report, 25 Dec 44.
19. C/290 Inf Regt.

20. 3/289 Inf Regt.
21. At 1345 hours on 25 Dec, First Army told IX Tac Air Force that the Manhay/ Grandmenil sector had top priority for all missions – Cole, op. cit., p. 592.
22. Hargesheimer lost a leg from gangrene after being wounded again when the ambulance carrying him was strafed in a US air strike.
23. 2/424 Inf Regt.
24. 23 Armd Inf Bn.
25. Cole, op. cit., p. 590.
26. 7 Armd Div G-3 (Arty) Report, 25 Dec 44.
27. F/33 Armd, F/36 Armd Inf Regts & A/33 Recce Bn.
28. 2/33 Armd Regt & D/36 Armd Inf Regt.
29. L/289 Inf Regt.
30. Robert F Kauffman, D/36 Armd Inf Regt & a member of this group to the author 25 Nov 2000.
31. 2/325 Glider Inf Regt.
32. 82 Airborne Div AAR, 26 Dec 44.
33. Weidinger, *Division Das Reich, Vol V*, p. 389.
34. CCB/3 Armd Div AAR, 26 Dec 44.
35. Capt John Jordan.
36. *Personal Reminiscences and the Retaking of Grandmenil* by Robert F Kauffman, a member of D/36 Armd Inf Regt, sent to the author 25 Nov 2000.
37. L/289 Inf Regt & 629 TD Bn. A Sgt & Pte of the latter were both awarded posthumous DSCs for stopping an attack by 'fourteen tks' on this day – Cole, op. cit., p. 596.
38. Kauffman, op. cit.
39. 3/517 Para Inf Regt.
40. TF Kane had pulled out by 2100 hours on 26 Dec.

CHAPTER XXVI

AUTUMN MIST: 24 – 27 December

Hohenstaufen

(Map 25)

It will be remembered that soon after dark on 23 December the 2nd Battalion of Zollhöfer's 19th SS Panzer-Grenadier Regiment had secured the eastern part of Vielsalm but had been unable to prevent the Americans partially demolishing the Salm bridge. During the 24th, after leaving one Battalion in Grand Halleux, the rest of the 19th Regiment closed up and the first sub-units of Geiger's 20th SS Panzer-Grenadier Regiment and Recke's 9th SS Reconnaissance Battalion began to arrive in the town from the direction of Poteau. The Americans claimed that the Germans even managed to get a few patrols across the Salm by midday.[1] Fuel, however, remained a major problem for the Germans, resulting in most of the

Grenadiers having to march, and only a single artillery Battery, the 4th, reaching Petit Thier before dark.

Most of the Hohenstaufen's administrative units had reached the Recht area by midday on the 24th. Despite the protection offered by the 9th SS Flak Battalion, it was fortunate that a thirty-minute warning of an Allied air raid was received at 1400 hours allowing many of the units to evacuate the area before the first of several groups of medium bombers appeared overhead.

During the day Bittrich issued firm orders for the Division to cross the Salm that night and move with all speed to Manhay where it was to form up on the right flank of Das Reich for a further advance to Mormont and Bomal. Stadler instructed Zollhöfer's 19th Regiment to make the crossing against the paratroopers of the 82nd Airborne known to be holding the west bank.

Fortunately for the Germans their crossing and planned advance was destined to coincide with the phased withdrawal of Gavin's Division to a new, shortened line running, it will be recalled, from the Salm just south of Trois Ponts, through Erria and Bra, to Vaux-Chavanne. This withdrawal was due to begin at 2100 hours, but 'shells' (light screening forces) were expected to stay in position until 0400 hours on Christmas Day.

The American withdrawal went as planned except for two significant incidents. In the north, a Company of the 505th Parachute Infantry Regiment, pulling back from the Salm south of Trois Ponts, clashed with an 800-man German column trying to rejoin the Leibstandarte on the east bank of the river after escaping from the La Gleize pocket. It was being led by Jochen Peiper himself and was all that remained of his once powerful KG. Full details of this clash can be read in the author's book, *The Devil's Adjutant: Jochen Peiper, Panzer Leader*. It is sufficient for us to know that both sides went on to reach their planned destinations before daylight with only minor casualties.

The second incident is more pertinent to our history. The main body of the 508th Parachute Infantry carried out its 12km withdrawal without difficulty to a new line running from Basse Bodeux to Erria, leaving two platoons of its 1st Battalion as a covering force near the river at Vielsalm. These men came under heavy mortar and artillery fire around midnight and shortly afterwards found themselves under attack by Grenadiers of Zollhöfer's 19th Regiment who had used infantry pontoon bridges to cross the Salm or simply waded the river. The platoon nearest to the river was nearly overwhelmed but both sub-units finally managed to escape to rejoin their comrades in the new position. Wilhelm Tieke claims[2] that the grounds of the pre-war Belgian barracks (the ruins of which still exist) saw particularly intensive fighting. He goes on to claim that the Germans captured 300 Americans and found 'massive booty in the way of vehicles, guns, ammunition and fuel' in the barracks. This is almost certainly an exaggeration and his further statement that 'attacking Sherman tanks were knocked out with Panzerfäusten' has to be questioned. Any US tanks in Vielsalm that night could only have been stray vehicles trying to escape from the St Vith salient. Similarly, Tieke's assertion that 'sleep drunk Americans were routed out of scattered farmsteads' during the German advance is almost certainly fanciful.

By first light on Christmas day, Zollhöfer's Grenadiers had reached Abrefontaine and Geiger's 20th Regiment, led by elements of Rieke's 9th SS Reconnaissance Battalion, was nearing Lierneux. At least part of the Division's armour (Fürbringer says the 1st SS Panzer Battalion, but this author believes it was the 2nd), after crossing the river at Salmchâteau during the day, followed on through Joubiéval towards Lierneux.

During the early hours of Christmas day 'long columns of marching men and supply vehicles crammed all the roads and tracks between Recht and Lierneux'[3] as the Hohenstaufen struggled to catch up with Das Reich at Manhay. At 1140 hours the Intelligence log of the 504th Parachute Infantry Regiment has the entry, 'enemy vehicles including several half-tracks moving W into Lierneux'.

Meanwhile, by first light on the 25th, the 82nd Airborne had reformed their line. The 505th Regiment was covering from Trois Ponts to Basse Bodeux, the 504th Regiment had taken up positions on the right of the 508th between exclusive Erria to inclusive Bra, and the 325th Glider Infantry Regiment was on the right flank from exclusive Bra to inclusive Vaux-Chavanne. The line adopted was ideally suited for defence, incorporating all the vital ground in the sector between the Salm and Manhay and completely dominating the approaches from the south-east. The 504th and 505th each kept a Battalion in reserve, near Bra and north of Basse Bodeux respectively, and all units put out concertina wire and laid mines.

Readers will recall that Colonel Reuben Tucker's 504th Parachute Infantry Regiment had made the famous Waal river crossing in Nijmegen. In AUTUMN MIST it had already been heavily involved against KG Peiper near La Gleize and its 1st Battalion had suffered very heavy casualties. Details of this action can also be found in the author's book, *The Devil's Adjutant: Jochen Peiper, Panzer Leader*.

St Vith was virtually obliterated by American bombers on 25 December. Fortunately for most of those in the town, warning of the first raid was received in time for them to get out and casualties were minimal. Bittrich and his staff had already moved Headquarters II SS Panzer Corps to Vielsalm before the attack.

As already mentioned, Rieke's 9th SS Reconnaissance Battalion was detached to Das Reich during the 25th and took up a position on that Division's left flank at Odeigne. In the meantime, the SS Panzer-

Grenadiers of both the 19th and 20th Regiments prepared for their assault against the 82nd Airborne Division. In the event, no attacks could be launched during daylight on Christmas Day since none of the Grenadier Battalions were strong enough to do so and none of the Divisional artillery was within effective range. All were under air attack throughout the day, but in one particularly unfortunate incident for the Americans, a P-47 dropped a 500-lb bomb in the middle of D Company of the 505th Airborne, killing five men and seriously wounding four others.[4]

When the Hohenstaufen attacks were eventually launched, the 19th SS Panzer-Grenadier Regiment was tasked with breaking the American line between Erria and Bra and the 20th astride Vaux-Chavanne.

Zollhöfer's 19th Regiment, having crossed the Salm first, attacked on the night of the 25th. The Americans say that an attack 'supported by four half-tracks', against the left flank of the 508th Airborne was beaten back after a three-hour fight.[5]

The main Hohenstaufen attacks were launched during the day and night of the 26th. Reports differ. Tieke[6] claims that Zollhöfer's 19th Regiment captured the dominant village of Les Villettes after a short, intense fight and goes on to say that during the day Altrogge's 2nd SS Panzer-Grenadier Battalion, with support from the Hohenstaufen's 2nd SS Artillery Battalion, managed to get into the first houses of Bra. It had already suffered casualties from an air strike and 'furious defensive fire' and when an American counter-attack came in just before last light, it was forced back to its 'jump-off positions at the edge of the woods east of Bra'. The AAR of the 82nd Airborne merely states that the 2nd Battalion of the 504th Regiment 'broke up two enemy attacks launched by the 9th SS Panzer Division from the vicinity of Floret' (a kilometre south-west of Les Villettes). Tieke makes no mention of any attack on Erria. The 82nd AAR, however, states, 'F and G Companies [508th Regiment] attacked by an estimated two battalions of infantry of the 9th SS Panzer Division at 0120 hours [27 December]. G Company partially over-run. Enemy infiltrated into Erria. I Company (minus) committed to aid G company in destroying and ejecting the enemy. E Company (less one platoon) mopped up the town of Erria and the entire sector was cleared by 0430. Enemy casualties were heavy'. Another American version claims:

> Company G was driven out of the twin villages of Erria and Villettes ... but this penetration came to an abrupt halt when two artillery battalions went to work ... The following morning the commander of the 3rd Battalion (LTC Louis G Mendez) organised a counter-attack which swept through Erria ... and restored the line ... The American gunners had done much to take the sting out of the enemy force – over 100 German dead were counted around the village crossroad.[7]

What of Geiger's 20th SS Panzer-Grenadier Regiment? The Intelligence Journal of the 504th Parachute Infantry Regiment has a very relevant entry timed at 1400 hours on 27 December. It states that a Hohenstaufen prisoner had revealed that the 5th and 6th Panzer Companies of the 2nd Battalion of the 9th SS Panzer Regiment, with twenty-six Mk IVs, were in Verleumont (2km south-east of Lierneux) and the 7th and 8th Companies with twenty-eight Mk IIIs (StuGs) were in Lierneux itself. These figures are within the known equipment holdings of the Division at the time and it is a fact that on both the 26th and the 27th there were strong armoured attacks in the Vaux-Chavanne sector. These were carried out by Mk IVs and StuGs of the 2nd SS Panzer Regiment, supported by SPW mounted Grenadiers of the 3rd Battalion of the 20th Regiment and the self-propelled guns of the 1st SS Artillery Battalion. As already described in the last Chapter, the approach to Vaux-Chavanne was along a narrow, twisting, forested road and, not surprisingly, both attacks were halted by the 325th Glider Infantry Regiment, strongly supported by artillery and ground attack aircraft. As Tieke describes it:

> Hard attack and defensive battles went on the whole day long. The Companies melted away to strengths of forty to fifty men. The commander of the 2nd SS Panzer Battalion, SS Major Hilgenstock, was killed in an air attack.[8]

SS Major Rudolf Rettberg took over.

The other great loss on this day was that of SS Lieutenant Colonel Ludwig Spindler, the commander of the Hohenstaufen artillery Regiment. Readers will no doubt recall the actions of his KG in the battle of Arnhem, for which he was awarded the Knight's Cross. He was killed in an air attack in the Lierneux area when driving to visit one of his artillery Battalions. His place was taken by SS Lieutenant Colonel Jakob.

During the 27th Stadler, like his counterpart Lammerding, received news of another attack being planned for that night. The Hohenstaufen was not to be directly involved but, whilst continuing to defend its own sector, it was required to take over the whole of Das Reich's in order to release that Division for participation in the attack. Both Stadler and Lammerding knew that this would be extremely difficult, if not impossible, in the time available.

NOTES

1. Cole, *The Ardennes: Battle of the Bulge*, p. 599.
2. Tieke, *In the Firestorm of the Last Years of the War*, pp. 322–3.
3. Tieke, op. cit., p. 323.
4. Langdon, *Ready – A History of the 505th Parachute Infantry Regiment*, p. 247.

5. Cole, op. cit., p. 600 and 82 Airborne Div AAR dated 26 Dec 44.
6. Tieke, op. cit., pp. 324–5.
7. Cole, op. cit., p. 600.
8. Tieke, op. cit., p. 325.

CHAPTER XXVII

AUTUMN MIST: 27 – 30 December

Author's Note

Events during this period are difficult to describe with precision. Most of the American AARs are inadequate and sketchy and many of the German reports confusing. The following account differs in some important aspects from that to be found in other books, but is the result of the author's careful study of all available reports and undisputed facts.

Background
(Maps 21 & 25)

By last light on 27 December, the situation in the Ardennes had changed radically – in favour of the Americans. The Germans were being forced on to the defensive everywhere. The 'extended index finger', as it was called, of the 2nd Panzer Division had been cut off and destroyed within 10km of the Meuse near Dinant. This was to be the western limit of the German advance. As Chester Wilmot put it in his brilliant book, *The Struggle for Europe,* 'the spearhead of Manteuffel's Fifth Panzer Army lay broken in the snow. The Germans had looked upon the Meuse for the last time.'[1]

Hitler had directed that the Marche-en-Famenne plateau should be secured as a base for a concerted drive to the Meuse in support of von Manteuffel's leading elements; the resulting attack over Christmas by the rest of the 2nd Panzer Division, supported by Panzer Lehr and the 9th and 116th Panzer Divisions on the right flank had, however, come to nothing.

Taking the German front on the evening of 27 December from west to east we find: the severely weakened 2nd Panzer Division back at Rochefort with 9th Panzer on its right flank, the crippled 116th Panzer south-east of a line drawn from Marche-en-Famenne to Hotton and the 560th Volks-Grenadier Division holding a line drawn from Hotton to Amonines. The Hitlerjugend Division, after its mauling in the Elsenborn area had just been allocated to Bittrich's II SS Panzer Corps and was coming into line between the 560th at Amonines and Das Reich at Odeigne. On the right flank, the Hohenstaufen was defending an extended frontage to as far east as Basse Bodeux. Panzer Lehr had been pulled back and made responsible for the southern flank of the Fifth Panzer Army from Rochefort to Bastogne.

Despite the rapidly worsening situation, Hitler would still not give up his offensive. He had already refused a joint request by von Rundstedt and Model, made on 24 December, for the offensive to be curtailed. He firmly rejected their recommendation that a firm western flank should be established on the Meuse, followed by a drive north-east to eliminate the Allied salient at Aachen. Nevertheless, three days later the Führer and his senior commanders were at least agreed on one subject – Bastogne. The capture of this major road centre in the first few days of the offensive would have given von Manteuffel's armour a clear run to the Meuse, but it was still in American hands and quickly becoming the centre of gravity of the 'Battle of the Bulge'. When Patton's Third Army tanks raised the siege of Bastogne on the 26th, they created a salient in the side of the Fifth Panzer Army which posed a major threat to any further advance to the north-west – the advance which Hitler was still demanding.

Most of the senior German commanders, including Bittrich, Lammerding and Stadler, knew that a renewed attack by II SS Panzer Corps towards Durbuy, ordered by the Sixth Panzer Army in accordance with Hitler's Directive, had little chance of success. Even if it reached the Meuse, the forests, cliffs and built-up areas made it impossible to cross the river anywhere other than at existing bridge sites and these were now strongly held by the Americans and British. To make matters worse, Allied aircraft were crowding the skies, making the daylight movement of vehicles almost impossible.[2] Finally, substantial Allied reserves were beginning to arrive in theatre which would soon enable the Americans to go over to the offensive. A situation similar to that pertaining at Falaise and between the Dives and Somme rivers was returning to haunt the German commanders.

II SS Panzer Corps
(Maps 24 & 25)

The War Diary of Army Group 'B' has the following entry for the evening of 27 December: '2 and 12 SS Panzer Divisions are at present in the process of re-grouping for the attack on Sadzot and Erezée, planned for 1900 hours.' This was wishful thinking. The overall aim of the operation was the seizure of a major part of the ridge running from Hotton to Grandmenil. Das Reich was to attack through the 560th Volks-Grenadiers towards Soy and Erezée, whilst the Hitlerjugend was tasked with capturing the section of the Erezée to Grandmenil road between Sadzot and Briscol. A firm base would thus be provided from which the three SS Panzer Divisions – Das Reich, Hitlerjugend and Hohenstaufen – could launch their major thrust through Durbuy to the Meuse. It was hoped that the Hitlerjugend's armour, which had still to catch up, would rejoin in time for this advance and that even the Leibstandarte, now recovering and re-forming in the Vielsalm–St Vith area after the fighting on the northern flank, would be able to participate. In this event, the Hitlerjugend would leave Bittrich's command and rejoin Hermann Priess's I SS Panzer Corps.

(Map 24)

The move of the 12th SS Panzer Division Hitlerjugend to join II SS Panzer Corps took much longer than expected. The slow-moving columns of the Hohenstaufen jammed the roads, there were the usual fuel shortages and Allied air attacks restricted most of its movement to the hours of darkness. Nevertheless, by early on 27 December a significant part of the Division[3] had managed to concentrate in the Samrée–Dochamps sector. The Hitlerjugend's Panzer, Panzerjäger and attached Heavy Panzerjäger Battalions were still recovering from their costly and unsuccessful operations in the north but, as the ground over which the Division was due to move in the first phase of the forthcoming operation was unsuitable for armour, this was not considered critical. Two of the Division's SS Panzer-Grenadier Battalions[4] had been forced to march the final 38km to Samrée, with the result that they were unavailable for the operation which Bittrich, at Sixth Panzer Army insistence, had ordered for 1930 hours that evening.

The region through which the Hitlerjugend was to attack, between Dochamps and Briscol, was hilly and densely wooded. The Divisional commander was forced therefore to use SS Panzer-Grenadiers on their feet. The Chief of Staff of the Hitlerjugend claimed later that Kraas complained to II SS Panzer Corps about the whole operation:

> Because of the aerial situation, the attack would have to be carried out through broken, forested terrain at night. . . . Panzers, SPWs and wheeled vehicles could not be taken along or brought up later. On leaving the forest [in the area of the objectives], at the best, only medium mortars and Panzerfausts would be available to fight off tanks. Effective artillery support would be close to impossible due to uncertain communications in the hilly terrain.[5]

Despite these accepted difficulties, Bittrich insisted that the Hitlerjugend attack go ahead as ordered.

The next problem facing Bittrich was that the Hohenstaufen's planned relief of Das Reich did not go as planned. Stadler's frontage was already too large and not enough of his Division had arrived in the Malempré–Odeigne area to take over from Lammerding's men. By the evening of the 27th, none of Das Reich's forward units had been relieved and the only KG which could be made available for the planned attack was Ernst Krag's uncommitted 2nd SS Reconnaissance Battalion. Lammerding was ordered to reinforce the Battalion and hand it over to the 12th SS Panzer Division Hitlerjugend. He provided the 9th SPW Company of Weidinger's 4th SS Panzer-Grenadier Regiment, the Divisional Escort Company and his 3rd Artillery Battalion and the resulting KG was placed under the command of the only complete Hitlerjugend SS Panzer-Grenadier Regiment[6] to arrive in time for the attack. Krag was given the mission of advancing on the left flank of that Regiment to secure Amonines and the important villages of Erpigny and Hazeille to its north. Since no other Das Reich elements could be made available, the attack towards Soy was cancelled.

At this time the Erezée–Amonines–La Fosse–Grandmenil front was being held by elements of the 3rd Armored Division, reinforced by a few additional units. TF Orr, with six tanks and two infantry companies[7], was located at Amonines, a parachute infantry Battalion[8] and a small armoured group, known as TF Richardson[9], were to be found just to the west of Erezée, a reinforced tank Battalion had arrived in Soy at 1000 hours[10] on the 27th, and a Combat Team (CT), based on the 289th Infantry Regiment, was defending the line of the Aisne river from inclusive Erezée to inclusive Grandmenil. This latter position was potentially very strong but much too large for a single infantry Regiment with only three infantry Battalions, a field artillery Battalion and tank, TD, engineer and chemical Companies.[11]

Readers will recall that it was the 3rd Battalion of the 289th Infantry Regiment that had supported the successful assault on Grandmenil by TF McGeorge on the 26th. After McGeorge withdrew at 1115 hours on the 27th, the 3rd Battalion remained in position with all the CT's tanks and most of its TD Company. The weight of the CT was therefore on the eastern flank of its front at Grandmenil, opposite Das Reich. Meanwhile, the 1st and 2nd Battalions of the 289th had moved forward to secure the line of the Aisne river between Amonines and La Fosse. On the western flank the 1st Battalion did so without difficulty, but the 2nd Battalion became disorganised in the forest to the west of La Fosse and it was 1400 hours on the 26th before it reached the Aisne river line to the south-west of that hamlet. Even then, it had no contact with the 1st Battalion on its right flank and the resulting kilometre gap between the two Battalions was the one which the Hitlerjugend was about to exploit in a night infiltration operation.

The details of the Hitlerjugend Regimental attack need not concern us. For those particularly interested, a full account appears in the author's book, *Men of Steel*. All we need to know for this history is that it began at 1930 hours and by 0815 hours the next morning the Grenadiers[12] had captured Sadzot and reached the Erezée–Grandmenil road near Briscol.

Unfortunately for the Germans, the associated advance by KG Krag through a kilometre of thick forest towards the villages of Erpigny and Hazeille came to nothing. The Americans in Amonines were not even engaged. In a combat interview, given on 1 January 1945, Lieutenant Colonel Orr, stated, 'On 27 December, guided by officers from TF Orr, the relieving elements of the 75th Division moved into positions on either side of Amonines and the TF withdrew.'

The reasons for Krag's failure are fairly clear: the KG did not arrive in its assembly area for the attack until 2330 hours, no reconnaissance was possible and the artillery Battalion had to occupy its unsurveyed gun positions in the dark. Worse was to follow. In the confines of the narrow Aisne valley and the thick, hilly forest through which the KG was required to advance, radio communications failed. Contact within and between the various elements of the KG soon broke down and men and sub-units became separated. At first it was thought that many of the Grenadiers had become casualties in the confused fighting in the forest and certainly the commander of the attached 9th Der Führer SS Panzer-Grenadier Company, SS Second Lieutenant Cronjäger, had been wounded. However, most of the missing men reappeared soon after first light when the KG was withdrawn. At midday on the 28th it moved back to Dochamps, where it joined the SPW mounted SS Panzer-Grenadier Battalion of the Hitlerjugend[13] in preparation for another attack being planned for that night.

In the meantime, the American parachute infantry Battalion located near Erezée had launched a counter-attack towards Sadzot. It was joined, shortly after daylight, by TF Richardson's light tanks and this combined force, supported by effective artillery fire, soon forced the Hitlerjugend Grenadiers to pull back from the road near Briscol, take cover in the nearby woods and adopt a defensive posture. An anti-tank gun, one of only three that had been manhandled through the forest, fought off the pursuing light tanks. At 1115 hours the Headquarters of the 289th CT reported: '509 Parachute Battalion captured Sadzot, took 32 prisoners and 64 wounded. 3TDs and one platoon light tanks with them. Mediums [Shermans] coming up'.

The situation was in fact one of stalemate. The Germans, although outnumbering the Americans, could not advance against tanks and intensive artillery fire, and the American tanks dared not advance into woods full of infantrymen with anti-tank weapons.

As far as the Americans were concerned, the main task, now that the

German advance had been halted, was to close the gap on the Aisne river and prevent the Germans in the woods south of Sadzot escaping or being reinforced. Accordingly, at 1255 hours on the 28th an additional infantry Battalion was attached to the 289th CT and given the task of filling the gap.

From the German point of view, there could be no question of pulling out or 'escaping to the south'. The Army Group 'B' War Diary of 28 December has the following entry:

> 560 Volks-Grenadier Division has been attached to Sixth Panzer Army (II SS Panzer Corps) . . . [and] is on the attack against Wy . . . 9 SS Panzer Division has taken over the sector of 2 SS Panzer Division. The 2 SS Panzer Division has assembled for the attack along a line Frennex [Freyneux]–south of Amonines. 12 SS Panzer Division is regrouping for a further attack to the north.

Again, much of this was wishful thinking. Although it was certainly Bittrich's intention and hope that another attack would see significant elements of Das Reich and the Hitlerjugend Divisions holding the Hotton–Grandmenil road by first light on the 29th, he must have known it was unlikely.

The new plan saw two Battalions of Weidinger's Der Führer Regiment[14] advancing north from Devantave to secure Amonines, supported by KG Krag which, having reverted to Lammerding's command, was to clear the Dochamps–Amonines road and then continue on to secure the important road junction one kilometre west of Erezée. At the same time Wisliceny's Deutschland Regiment was to attack through the battle-weary and badly depleted 560th Volks-Grenadiers[15] to secure the Soy sector; whilst on the right flank, Grenadiers of the Hitlerjugend's SPW Battalion were to capture the villages of Hazeille and Erpigny.

The first thing to go wrong was that the two Battalions of Weidinger's Regiment could not be relieved from the Malempré sector in time for the attack. Only the 3rd SPW Battalion was able to pull out and reach its designated assembly area south-west of Dochamps. There it was held in reserve.

The second problem was fog, which although it helped the move of Wisliceny's Deutschland Regiment, via the Baraque de Fraiture, to an assembly area near Beffe on the left flank, made reconnaissance impossible and arrangements for the attack through the Volks-Grenadiers extremely difficult. Eventually, at midnight, the attack was cancelled. The US tank Battalion in Soy reported, 'There was some artillery fire on the town during the night but no casualties were suffered'.[16]

The KG Krag and Hitlerjugend part of the operation began slightly earlier, at 2230 hours. Krag's advance 'along the Amonines–Erezée road did not break through'[17] . Exactly what went wrong is unclear. Certainly, the Americans in Amonines were not subjected to any pressure. Charles L Miller, a platoon commander in the infantry Company[18] which had relieved TF Orr, reported, '[On 27 December] we moved into defensive positions in Amonines ... Our time in Amonines was mostly uneventful'.[19]

SS Sergeant Günther Burdack described what happened to the Hitlerjugend Grenadiers:

> The SPWs were left behind in a ravine south of Samrée. The crews ... marched via Dochamps ... The road was totally clogged by abandoned and destroyed enemy vehicles, mostly artillery, and was under constant heavy enemy shelling. After approximately 6km, the Battalion was directed by a liaison officer of the Der Führer Regiment to leave the road and advance in a northerly direction along a track toward the twin villages of Hazeille–Erpigny. After some 1.5km we reached the designated position at the edge of the forest. The villages could not be observed from the edge of the forest as they were at a higher location than our own position ... The deeply frozen ground did not allow us to dig in. The Battalion did not have any heavy weapons with it, only rifles and light machine-guns. Harassing fire covered the whole area.[20]

Soon after dawn the exposed Grenadiers were withdrawn in the face of increasing American artillery and mortar fire.

The Army Group 'B' War Diary for 29 December records:

> Attacks by 2 and 12 SS Panzer Divisions on Mormont are stalled ... [they] did not break through the enemy who fought tenaciously and was strongly supported by artillery ... advances from the Sadzot area as well as enemy armour attacks against the 560 Volks-Grenadier Division were repulsed.

US artillery fire was by now proving a battle-winning factor along the whole front.

Otto Weidinger claims that his 1st and 2nd SS Panzer-Grenadier Battalions eventually reached the assembly area for their attack on Amonines during the afternoon of the 29th.[21] They were a day late and that was too late. Their exhausted Waffen-SS and Volks-Grenadier comrades had already been pulled back and the whole II SS Panzer Corps attack abandoned. By dawn on the 30th the Americans had restored their original line and it was obvious to the German High Command that the piecemeal attempt to seize the Hotton–Grandmenil ridge had failed and that Sepp Dietrich's Sixth Panzer Army had made its last major effort in AUTUMN MIST. Field Marshal Model ordered it onto the defensive. It was to be stripped of its assets and, as its Chief of Staff put it after the war, left as 'a Panzer Army in little more than name'. Its remaining Panzer Corps, Bittrich's II SS, was to comprise three Volks-Grenadier Divisions and just one Panzer Division – Das Reich. The Hitlerjugend and Hohenstaufen were to be withdrawn for use by von Manteuffel's Fifth Panzer Army under Priess's I SS Panzer Corps.

By midday on 30 December, the 560th Volks-Grenadier Division was relieving the Hitlerjugend in the Samrée sector, the 12th Volks-Grenadier Division was beginning to take over the Hohenstaufen's front and Lammerding's Das Reich, with Deutschland on the left and Der Führer on the right, had been reformed and was located between the Ourthe and the Aisne, just to the south of Amonines. Its strength was now 15,286, indicating a loss of nearly 2,000 men since 16 December. The Division still had forty-seven Panthers, thirty-three Mk IVs, twenty Jagdpanzer IVs, twenty-three StuGs and 209 SPWs and armoured cars. This is an increase of five Mk IVs but a reduction of eleven Panthers, five StuGs and thirty-seven SPWs and armoured cars from its 16 December figures.

As postscript to this part of our history, it is worth noting an extraordinary event that took place on 28 December. After relief by the Hohenstaufen, the 3rd SPW Battalion of Weidinger's Der Führer Regiment, now under the command of SS Lieutenant von Eberstein, withdrew initially to an area around the Château St Jean, 4km south-west of the Baraque de Fraiture. Despite the gravity of the situation, the commanders of the Deutschland and Der Führer Regiments were called back to Lammerding's Headquarters in the Château. On arrival, they found their Army commander, Sepp Dietrich, waiting for them. He had come to award Oakleaves to their Knight's Crosses for 'the outstanding performances of their Regiments on the invasion front'.

NOTES

1. Wilmot, *The Struggle for Europe*, p. 602.
2. 15,000 sorties were flown in the period 25–28 Dec (ibid., p. 602).
3. 25 SS Pz-Gren Regt, 3/26 SPW SS Pz-Gren Bn, most of the HJ arty, 12 SS Werfer & 12 SS Flak Bns, Div Escort Coy.
4. Of 26 SS Pz-Gren Regt.
5. Meyer, *The History of the 12th SS Panzer Division Hitlerjugend*, p. 266.
6. 25 SS Pz-Gren Regt.
7. Three Shermans of H/33 Armd Regt, three Stuarts of B/83 Armd Recce Bn, A & C/36 Armd Inf Regt.
8. 509 Para Inf Bn.
9. Five Shermans, eighteen Stuarts & two inf pls.
10. 1/33 Armd Regt – AAR CCB/3 Armd Div, 27 Dec 44.
11. 730 Fd Arty, A/750 Tk, A/629 TD, A/275 Engr & B/87 Chemical. The latter

was a 4.2 inch mortar unit equipped to fire high explosive, white phosphorus and smoke rounds.

12. Of 25 SS Pz-Gren Regt.
13. 3/26 SS Pz-Gren Bn.
14. The 3rd (SPW) Bn was to be held in reserve south-west of Dochamps.
15. The acting Div commander later estimated that none of its three Regts had a combat strength of more than 300 men.
16. War Diary CCB/3 Armd Div 28 Dec 44.
17. Meyer, op. cit., p. 268.
18. A/290 Inf Regt.
19. Combat Interview, West Germany, Spring 45.
20. Meyer, op. cit., p. 266.
21. Weidinger, *Comrades to the End*, p. 367. He goes on to claim that his 16 SS Pnr Coy made a raid on Amonines that night which was halted by concentrated enemy fire. The Coy commander, SS Lt Wolf, was killed. The Americans make no mention of such an attack.

CHAPTER XXVIII
The Wider Picture

NORDWIND: 1 – 25 January 1945
(Map 20)

Operation NORDWIND, an attack into Alsace, had been planned at the same time as the Ardennes offensive. It was designed to take advantage of any weakening of the southern part of the American front brought about by the latter. The fact that the Americans had already been forced 'to withdraw something like 50% of their forces from the other fronts'[1] had convinced the Führer that his overall plan was working. On 28 December, therefore, he gave orders that NORDWIND was to go ahead and set H-Hour for one hour before midnight on New Year's Eve. In order for this attack to succeed, however, it was essential to tie down Patton's Third Army, so Hitler gave orders that a major attack against the Bastogne salient was to be made at the same time. This clearly suited Model, who that evening wrote his recommendations for the next phase in the offensive. It included the phrase, 'clench into a fist the hand which has till now been spread open.' He went on:

The final target of Antwerp must be abandoned for the time being. The task which now presents itself is to strike at the enemy with annihilating force to the east of the Meuse and in the Aachen area. . . The attacking arrowhead should be . . . pushed forwards in a northerly direction . . . in order to capture Liège and Maastricht and thus cut off the enemy units in the Aachen area. . . . After the successful conclusion of this partial attack . . . it should be possible to develop the operation against Antwerp.

This recommendation was in fact little more than a repetition of the 'Small Solution' which he had proposed the previous November as an alternative to Hitler's master plan. This time, however, Hitler went along with it since he believed NORDWIND would succeed and Model's clever inclusion of Antwerp as a final objective inevitably struck a responsive chord.

NORDWIND is of interest only in that it involved the Hohenstaufen's original partner in II SS Panzer Corps, the 10th SS Panzer Division Frundsberg. Harmel's Division was taken from Army Group 'B' reserve and allocated to Army Group 'G' to reinforce the attack. It began its move from the Euskirchen area at the beginning of January but did not cross the Rhine until 15 January and did not see action until the 17th. Despite some initial German successes, the Allies had retained all the militarily important ground and on 25 January the offensive was called off. The Frundsberg does not appear to have suffered any significant casualties in this fighting.

BODENPLATTE: 1 January 1945

Another operation ordered by the Führer at this time was BODENPLATTE. Readers may recall that this Luftwaffe operation, designed to cripple the Allied Air Forces on the ground, should have coincided with the opening of AUTUMN MIST but had had to be postponed due to bad weather. Hitler ordered its launch, to coincide with NORDWIND and events in the Bastogne sector, for the morning of New Year's Day.

The operation achieved considerable success in that at least 260 Allied aircraft were either destroyed or damaged. Even so, it cost the Luftwaffe some 227 aircraft and, more importantly, 214 irreplaceable pilots – 151 killed or missing. The Allies were able to make good their losses in less than two weeks and, as far as the ground troops were concerned, neither side noticed any difference in the skies above their heads. Indeed, the improved flying weather, which had begun on the 23rd, was proving a nightmare for the Germans. As Wilhelm Tieke described it:

The supply situation of the German troops had . . . grown to cata-strophic proportions. The enemy air force brought the railroad and highway traffic to a complete halt. Many transport trains had to be hidden in tunnels and created obstacles which could never be untangled. Only a few supplies reached the intended recipients.[2]

AUTUMN MIST: 29 December 1944 – 3 January 1945
(Map 21)

In fulfilment of Hitler's Directive that a major attack was to be launched against Bastogne, von Manteuffel held a conference with his senior commanders on 29 December and outlined his plan. In principle it was simple: first, close the ring around the town and then capture it. Phase I was to start on 30 December with the Leibstandarte and 167th Volks-Grenadier Divisions attacking the American corridor south of Bastogne from the east, and the 3rd Panzer-Grenadier Division and Führer Begleit Brigade attacking at the same time from the west.

The American corridor into Bastogne had been established on 26 December when Patton's 4th Armored Division had broken through to relieve the siege. A detailed description of events in the Bastogne area before this date is unnecessary for our understanding of what happened subsequently, but readers who are particularly interested in this part of the campaign are recommended to read S L A Marshall's *Bastogne – The First Eight Days*. The fighting which was about to take place was some of the most bitter and costly of the entire campaign and it will probably come as a surprise to many readers to learn that American casualties in the second half of the 'Battle of the Bulge' (30 December to 12 January), were nearly one third higher than in the first half.

The German counter-attack of 30 December failed to achieve its ultimate aim but did succeed in driving a wedge, 3km wide and 3km deep, into the eastern flank of the US corridor. CinC West's War Diary of 31 December has the following entry:

A report from Army Group 'B' at 1215 hours again described the ferocity of the fighting around Bastogne. The western attack group [3rd Panzer-Grenadier Division and the Führer Begleit Brigade] cannot advance any further without the support of the eastern group [Leibstandarte and 167th Volks-Grenadier Divisions]. The eastern group has indeed resumed the attack, but can only gain a little ground. The deployment of artillery will bring some relief. In spite of this, the forces committed so far appear to be insufficient to achieve the assigned objective.

By early on the 31st, Field Marshal Model had come to the conclusion that there was little or no chance of cutting the Bastogne corridor with the forces available and that a direct attack against the town was more likely to succeed.

As far as the Americans were concerned, and George Patton in particular, the German counter-attacks against the flanks of the Bastogne corridor were still presenting serious problems, but they did not see them as a reason to delay the planned attack by III US Corps towards St Vith scheduled for the 31st. This thrust was designed to link up in the region of Houffalize with another by Hodges' First US Army in the north and to cut off at least those German forces still west of a line drawn from Bastogne to Manhay. Montgomery, who remained concerned about the situation in the First US Army sector, finally gave his agreement on the 31st that the northern thrust could begin on 3 January.

In accordance with Patton's plan, his newly arrived 6th Armored Division was ordered to strike east and north-east out of the Bastogne salient on the 31st. Unfortunately, the delayed arrival of one of the Combat Commands, due to poor planning and road congestion, meant it went off 'at half cock'. It was finally launched at noon by a single Combat Command but by nightfall had advanced only a couple of kilometres.

Shortly after first light on New Year's Day the 6th Armored Division's attack was resumed, this time with two full Combat Commands, and although not fully successful, it caused a crisis in the German command. Von Manteuffel considered the threat to be so serious that at 1800 hours he told Priess that his existing orders for an attack on the western side of Bastogne corridor were cancelled and that I SS Panzer Corps was to take over the threatened sector to the north-east of the town at noon on 2 January. The Hitlerjugend, 340th Volks-Grenadier Division and parts of the Hohenstaufen were to be directed into this sector to strengthen his command.

Model visited Priess's Headquarters on the afternoon of the 2nd and insisted that a Corps counter-attack be launched towards Bastogne as soon as possible and at the latest on the following day. Although it was perfectly clear to Priess and his senior commanders that the Divisions could not possibly be assembled properly in time for such an attack, a request put to von Manteuffel for a postponement until the 4th was refused. The latter knew Model would never agree.

The commanders of the Hitlerjugend and Hohenstaufen SS Panzer Divisions and the 340th Volks-Grenadier Division spent the morning of 3 January desperately trying to assemble their units for the counter-attack demanded by Field Marshal Model. The Hohenstaufen was due to advance through the Compogne (called Rastadt in 1944) area on the west side of the main Houffalize–Bastogne road, the Volks-Grenadiers between that road and the Bourcy–Bastogne railway line, and the Hitlerjugend on the east side of the railway. The attack by the Hohenstaufen was scheduled for 0800 hours, but since there was no hope of the other Divisions being ready that early, their H-Hours were delayed until 1300 hours. In the event, the Hohenstaufen's attack had to be delayed as well.

NOTES

1. Hitler's words – Wilmot, *The Struggle for Europe*, p. 606.
2. Tieke, *In the Firestorm of the Last Years of the War*, p. 328.

CHAPTER XXIX
AUTUMN MIST: 3 – 5 January

Hohenstaufen
(Map 26)

Readers will be not be surprised to hear that the I SS Panzer Corps counter-attack of 3 January failed in its mission of pushing the Americans back inside their Bastogne perimeter. The 340th Volks-Grenadiers and Hitlerjugend, starting from the road running between Noville and Bourcy, ran into the 501st Parachute Infantry Regiment of the 101st Airborne and CCB of the 6th Armored Division respectively. The Hitlerjugend managed to achieve a penetration of 3km on the eastern flank and reach Arloncourt, but the Volks-Grenadiers clashed with an American attempted advance through the Bois Jacques and in the confused fighting which followed neither side could prevail. By dusk the German line ran west from Arloncourt, through the Azette wood and Bois Jacques, to Foy. This part of the counter-attack may have disappointed Model, von Manteuffel and Priess, but it still caused George Patton to exclaim, 'They are colder, hungrier and weaker than we, to be sure. But they are still doing a great piece of fighting.'

The associated advance on the western flank by the Hohenstaufen was less successful. Only part of the Division, Zollhöfer's 19th SS Panzer-Grenadier Regiment and 'about thirty Panzers and StuGs'[1] of the 2nd SS Panzer Battalion reached the Compogne (Rastadt) assembly area before the attack was launched on 3 January. The initial objectives were Longchamps and Monaville, held by units of TF Higgins.[2] Despite support from the Pioneer Company of Geiger's 20th SS Panzer-Grenadier Regiment, which caught up during the fighting, the attack stalled in the face of intense artillery and air attacks. The Commander of the 16th SS Pioneer Company, SS Captain Siegfried Klauck, was killed in front of Hill 497.

Hermann Priess, the Corps commander, said later:

In the first hours of the attack, they [the Hohenstaufen Grenadiers] succeeded in taking the heights to the south of the wood's edge, about one kilometre north of Monaville. This enabled the tanks to go in towards midday. They pressed forward under fire to both villages, but were driven back as they could find no cover on the open plain and they retired with some losses.[3]

According to Wilhelm Tieke, Field Marshal Model then personally intervened:

> and demanded that the attack be resumed. SS Lieutenant Steinbach[4] witnessed a confrontation between Model and the commander of the 9th SS Panzer Division, who refused to attack again in order to spare his men, weapons and armoured vehicles from being senselessly shot to pieces. It was eventually agreed to try to take Longchamps/Monaville in a night attack.[5]

This met with some success, but as Hermann Priess put it later: 'A surprise raid carried out in the night by the 9th SS Panzer Division brought it into Longchamps, but they met here with strong enemy resistance and had to retire.[6]

The AAR of the 101st Airborne Division has this to say about the Hohenstaufen attack:

> Although the force of the expected enemy attack was considerably lessened by our heavy artillery concentration on the enemy assembly areas, the attack was the heaviest to date [since the 101st arrived in Bastogne on 18 December]. A strong tank and infantry attack was repulsed by TF Higgins in the vicinity of Monaville between 1330 and 2200 on the 3rd. In the meantime 2nd Battalion, 327th Glider Infantry was attached to 502nd Parachute Infantry for the purpose of restoring the main line of resistance which had been breached by this attack.

Some idea of the difficulties experienced by Stadler's men at this time appears in a letter written on 5 January by one of his commanding officers, SS Captain Appel:

> For the last three days I have been the commander of the 1st Battalion of the 20th SS Panzer-Grenadier Regiment, for the moment under unpleasant conditions. We lie before Bastogne . . . Through unfavourable circumstances (inadequate training of the men and very serious shortages of supplies, in particular clothing and boots), I have very heavy casualties. They are mostly due to artillery and, whenever the weather clears, from Jabos [ground attack aircraft]. Yesterday I received 200 replacements but unfortunately, almost all are old men from the Ukraine, some of whom neither speak nor understand

SONS OF THE REICH

German. Everything is lacking. Here a man really has to prove himself. I have already experienced what it means to have to attack without any heavy weapons, since the anti-tank, infantry guns and artillery could not be brought forward due to a lack of prime movers, or because they had to be left, stuck fast in the frozen ground, as target practice for the enemy and the Jabos. The Companies have only a fraction of their fighting strength . . . on average, about forty to fifty men.[7]

In the meantime, on the night of the 4th, the 340th Volks-Grenadiers had resumed their advance through the Bois Jacques with the aim of reaching the Foy–Bizory track and, at 0400 hours, the Hitlerjugend followed suit with Bizory and Mageret as its objectives. On the right flank, the Hitlerjugend advance went well and by 0700 hours it had reached the line of the Foy–Mageret track against little opposition. Beyond that line American resistance stiffened with every metre being contested throughout the day. By 1100 hours the 340th had also reached the Foy–Mageret line but then, rather than attempt to advance farther, it spent the rest of the day clearing up the opposition it had bypassed in the Bois Jacques.

By dusk on 4 January the Hitlerjugend had gained another 2km and was only 3km from Bastogne. It was, however, exhausted and this was to be the high tide of the German counter-attack. Hitler's offensive through the Ardennes was over.

According to Priess:

In the morning [of the 5th], the [Fifth Panzer] Army ordered the [Hohenstaufen] Division to break off the engagement and proceed as quickly as possible to join the Sixth Panzer Army . . . As a result of enemy air activity, the 9th SS Panzer Division began the march with not many troops. The main body of the Division could only start after darkness had fallen.[8]

The reason for the Hohenstaufen's withdrawal was an American offensive from the north, begun on the 3rd, and designed to link up at Houffalize with Patton's Third Army drive from the south. Hodges' First Army attack had struck Dietrich's Sixth Panzer Army in its flank from Marche-en-Famenne to Basse Bodeux (Map 25) – and it was Bittrich's II SS Panzer Corps, in the centre, with just two infantry Divisions and Lammerding's Das Reich, that was bearing the brunt of the assault.

NOTES

1. Tieke, *In the Firestorm of the Last Years of the War*, p. 329.
2. Brig Gen G Higgins was the Assistant Div commander. His TF consisted of

502 Para Inf Regt, Team Cherry of CCB/10 Armd Div, B & C/705 TD Bn, and from 1530 hrs on 3 Jan, 375 Glider Inf Regt.
3. MS # A-877.
4. Commander 4/9 SS Arty Regt.
5. Tieke, op. cit., p. 328.
6. MS # A-877.
7. Tieke, op. cit., p. 330.
8. MS # A-877.

CHAPTER XXX

Defence and Withdrawal: 3 – 25 January

The Bigger Picture

(Map 25)

Major General 'Lightning Joe' Collins' VII Corps was given the key role in the new US First Army offensive. British troops had relieved the 2nd US Armored and 84th Infantry Divisions west of the Ourthe and this gave Collins four Divisions[1] east of the river for his attack. Launched on 3 January, from a line drawn roughly from Hotton, through Manhay, to Vaux-Chavanne, the 2nd Armored and 84th Infantry Divisions advanced west of the Manhay–Houffalize road (N-15) and the 3rd Armored and 83rd Infantry Divisions on the east side. The latter were responsible for the road itself and the capture of the crossroads at the Baraque de Fraiture. Jim Gavin's 82nd Airborne Division, part of Ridgway's XVIII Airborne Corps, was tasked with protecting the VII Corps flank and advancing to its old positions running south from Trois Ponts to Salmchâteau. To the dismay of many of the American generals, rather than attempting to cut off the German salient or 'Bulge' at the waist, they found they were advancing towards its shoulders. As Gavin put it later, 'the Army's attack plan was based on a huge turning action, pivoted on Stavelot. It was as though a huge stable door was being closed'.[2]

The First Army offensive was launched under the worst possible conditions. The snow was waist deep, the few roads were covered in ice and the temperatures often fell below zero.[3] Both sides suffered numerous casualties from frostbite but the Americans were far better off in terms of clothing, footwear and food; and, unlike the Germans, they had more than enough fuel and ammunition. Above all, Allied air superiority was proving a battle winning factor and negating the general German superiority in weaponry.

Despite the adverse conditions and stiff German resistance, the American advance proceeded steadily and relentlessly south-east towards Houffallize. By 9 January, when George Patton's Third Army, with eight Divisions, began its push towards Houffalize from the south, Dochamps in the west and the Baraque de Fraiture in the east had both been captured and Collins' 83rd Infantry Division was beginning its turn east towards St Vith – only 20km away. Hitler's order for the tip of the 'Bulge' to be pulled back on the same day and for the four Waffen-SS Panzer Divisions, Leibstandarte, Das Reich, Hohenstaufen and Hitlerjugend, and certain other formations to be withdrawn in order to create a reserve, was already being overtaken by events.

On 12 January the worst possible news reached the Führer – the Soviets had unleashed their winter offensive. Two days later he ordered Sepp Dietrich's Sixth Panzer Army to the Eastern Front. The danger from the Western Allies was serious but that from the 'sub-humans' in the East was intolerable. Nevertheless, it was to be another ten days before the last elements of II SS Panzer Corps could be extracted and brought back across the Rhine.

On 13 January V Corps joined the northern attack and thrust into the German flank north of St Vith and on the 16th the American pincers closed at Houffalize. It was exactly one month since the opening of AUTUMN MIST. Seven days later, on the 23rd, CCB of the 7th Armored Division broke through the German crust in front of St Vith and entered the town from which it had been driven just a month before. By early February the Germans were back behind the West Wall.

Das Reich: 3 – 9 January

(Map 24)

When the US VII Corps attack began on 3 January, Das Reich was still deployed with its 2nd SS Panzer and two SS Panzer-Grenadier Regiments to the west of Amonines, between the Ourthe and the Aisne. 3rd Deutschland was on the left, holding Trinal and the high ground just to the west, and Der Führer, less its 3rd SPW Battalion detached to KG Krag, was on the right, from Magoster to Hill 405 and thence to the Aisne. The 2nd SS Pioneer Battalion, less its 3rd SPW Company, was attached to the Deutschland and had been given the task of building a barrier line covering the roads running south through Trinal and Magoster to Devantave. The 560th Volks-Grenadier Division, on its right flank, was still responsible for the area to the north of Dochamps, including Odeigne, but there was no physical link between the two Divisions. A patrol sent out by Der Führer on the 3rd to make contact, ran into enemy on the Amonines–Dochamps road and was badly shot up.

As far as the Americans were concerned, the roads leading through

Devantave to Dochamps and from Amonines to Dochamps were vital. Until they were cleared, they had little hope of outflanking the German defences south of the Baraque de Fraiture or of reaching Houffalize from the north-west (Map 25).

The remaining element of Das Reich, KG Krag, had been inserted between the 560th Volks-Grenadiers at Odeigne and 12th Volks-Grenadiers holding Malempré, to cover the vital route south towards the Baraque de Fraiture. Operating under the latter's command, Krag had been given the 1st SS Panzer Company (Panthers) to add to his own 2nd SS Reconnaissance Battalion, Weidinger's 3rd SPW SS Panzer-Grenadier Battalion, an artillery Battalion and the 3rd SS Pioneer Company.

We will deal first with the attack between the Ourthe and Aisne by the tanks and infantry of the American 2nd Armored and 84th Infantry Divisions. This began on 3 January and met with some initial success. Trinal was captured by 1200 hours, but the troops who fought their way into Beffe were soon forced to withdraw. Contrary to Otto Weidinger's account of the fighting[4], the Americans say they cleared Magoster 'versus stiffening resistance . . . [and] the night was spent east of Magoster'. They say also that they knocked out four Mk IVs, two StuGs and three SPWs in the first day's fighting.

Both sides agree that Beffe, Magoster and Hill 405 fell to the Americans[5] on the 4th. There was still no link to the 560th Volks-Grenadiers on the eastern flank and during the day Lammerding's Headquarters lost contact with the 2nd Panzer Division to the west of the Ourthe. As if all this was not bad enough, that evening Lammerding was told that his Division was to be broken up even further. He was to leave Weidinger's Der Führer Regiment, the 2nd SS Pioneer Battalion less a Company, and an artillery Battalion in the Aisne–Ourthe position, while he, his Divisional Headquarters, Wisliceny's Deutschland Regiment, an artillery Battalion and the 2nd SS Flak Battalion were to be withdrawn into Sixth Panzer Army reserve just to the east of Houffalize. In that location they would be ideally placed to resist American thrusts from either Manhay or Bastogne. Rather surprisingly, Lammerding left his chief artillery officer, Knight's Cross holder SS Colonel Karl Kreutz, rather than Otto Weidinger, in charge of the Aisne–Ourthe group. It became known as KG Kreutz. This new configuration was to take effect at midnight.

What of Das Reich's armour at this time? According to Otto Weidinger[6], Enseling's 2nd SS Panzer Regiment stayed with the Aisne–Ourthe group except for the 1st SS Panzer Company, which had been allocated to KG Krag. There are only two reports, one German and one American, of German armour being used by KG Kreutz. The first, by Weidinger, mentions an attack by a StuG company on 5 January, and the second, by the US 2nd Armored Division, records ten Panthers resisting its attack towards Samrée on the 9th. It seems, at least to this author, most unlikely that Bittrich would have allowed the whole of Das Reich's 2nd SS Panzer Regiment to remain forward, under the overall command of an artillery officer, on the extreme left of his Corps and indeed of the Sixth Panzer Army. It seems much more likely that the majority of Enseling's Panthers and Mk IVs would have moved with Lammerding to the central reserve position. Whatever the truth, it took the Lammerding group until the late afternoon of the 5th to relocate near Houffalize.

The American AARs and Otto Weidinger differ widely in their accounts of exactly what happened between the 5th and the 9th. Weidinger claims that a counter-attack by the Divisional Escort Company and an unspecified StuG Company recaptured Magoster on 5 January, and that for the rest of that day and on the 6th, KG Kreutz continued to hold its sector against repeated attacks by the 335th Regiment of the 84th Infantry Division, supported by tanks. He admits that by last light on 7 January SS Captain Hannes Schulzer's 2nd SS Panzer-Grenadier Battalion had been pushed back to the woods south-east of Magoster and to a stream just to the north of Devantave. But he contends that his men continued to block the roads leading south from Marcouray and from Devantave to Dochamps throughout the 8th. On 9 January, however, Weidinger says the US 84th Infantry Division subjected KG Kreutz to a devastating attack and that, following a two-hour artillery barrage, 'eighty Panzers' burst through Devantave. The KG could not withstand such an attack and between noon and 1700 hours, it was forced back to a line about a kilometre west of the Dochamps–Samrée road.

The American reports have a very different version of events. Making no mention of the counter-attack on the 5th, the 84th Division claims that by midday on the 6th (three days earlier than Weidinger's account) its 335th Regiment and tanks had cleared Devantave and that following this success, two infantry Battalions[7] moved on into the woods between the village and the Ourthe river. The 2nd Armored Division, on the other hand, says that its CCA took until midnight on the 6th to clear all but the south-west end of Devantave. During the 7th and 8th, the Americans say they continued to drive south and, on the 9th, while the 2nd Armored tanks assaulted towards Samrée, the infantry of the 335th Regiment moved to take the hills north-east and north-west of Dochamps. The latter reached the edge of the woods, 500 yards from Samrée by dusk. They go on to say that, by 0930 hours on the 10th, the 1st and 3rd Battalions of the 335th Regiment had cleared Samrée.

In fact, it makes little difference which account is correct. Both versions confirm that KG Kreutz managed to prevent the Americans reaching the Samrée area until 9 January. Not for the first time, a successful delaying action by Das Reich had allowed numerous other Germans to escape a trap. Despite this, by the evening of the 9th KG Kreutz itself was being threatened with encirclement and orders were given, by whom is unclear, for it to pull back through the 560th Volks-Grenadiers during the night and join the main body of the Division near Houffalize.

(Map 25)

Meanwhile, what of KG Krag and the rest of the Division? The former had also come under heavy air and ground attack between Odeinge and Malempré on 3 January but had held its positions. The 12th Volks-Grenadier Division, on the other hand, lost Malempré to TF Lovelady of CCB of the 3rd Armored Division and was pushed back along the whole length of its 6km front. By the evening of the 5th, tanks of the 2nd Armored Division and the 333rd Infantry Regiment had fought their way into Odeigne, and by dusk the following day the 3rd Armored had captured the village of Fraiture, forcing KG Krag to pull back towards the Baraque de Fraiture or risk being cut off. Artillery support, which might have stemmed these US attacks, was largely ineffective. A lack of radio equipment apparently forced the artillery to fire by prediction only, resulting in entire salvoes falling amongst the Das Reich companies, causing a number of casualties and inevitably affecting morale.[8]

Ernst Krag was to receive Oakleaves to his Knight's Cross for his actions at this time. The relevant part of his citation, signed by Lammerding and Dietrich, reads:

> Because Krag, despite the threat of encirclement, held his positions in front of the crossroads Baraque de Fraiture with only a small number of men and weapons, he made it possible for our other units on the right and left to withdraw, allowed the higher command to make changes of position which had become urgently necessary, forced the enemy to regroup, and frustrated the enemy breakthrough to the south-east.

On this same day, 6 January, units of the 3rd Armored Division cut the La Roche–Salmchâteau road just north of Bihain and the first major 'changes of position' mentioned in Krag's citation took place. Lammerding deployed Wisliceny's 3rd SS Panzer-Grenadier Regiment Deutschland astride the N-15 between Tailles and Bihain. This allowed KG Krag, now reinforced by the II SS Panzer Corps Escort Company, to give up the crossroads and pull back to a new defensive line on the left of Wisliceny's men, running west from Tailles to Chabrenez. By 0930 hours on the 7th, TF Hogan and a Battalion of the 333rd Infantry Regiment had occupied the crossroads. The new line, strengthened on the 7th by the arrival of the 1st Battalion of the Hohenstaufen's 19th SS Panzer-Grenadier Regiment from the Bastogne sector, was more easily defended. Between Bihain and the N-15 there is 3km-stretch of marsh land, a kilometre wide, and similarly between the road and Tailles there are a number of marshy areas making cross-country difficult, if not impossible. Until Tailles, the N-15 and Bihain could be captured the American advance was therefore blocked.

During 7 January Lammerding re-assumed command of all Das Reich units in the N-15 sector, took under command the 12th Volks-Grenadiers in Bihain and inserted the Hohenstaufen Battalion between Wisliceny's Regiment and the 12th Volks-Grenadiers. KG Krag, now under Wisliceny's command, continued to defend the left flank.

The German defence held throughout the 7th and 8th, but by 1830 hours on 9 January Bihain had fallen to two Battalions of the 83rd Infantry Division.[9] They reported encountering eleven German tanks in the fighting. If this statement is accurate, they would undoubtedly have been from Enseling's 2nd SS Panzer Regiment.

Hohenstaufen: 5 – 9 January
(Map 25)

It will be remembered that the main body of the Hohenstaufen had begun its withdrawal from the Bastogne sector soon after dark on 5 January and that the 1st Battalion of Zollhöfer's 19th Panzer-Grenadier Regiment had joined Das Reich south-east of the Baraque de Fraiture on the 7th. Most of the Division's echelons were sent back to the Weiswampach area at this time, where they set up a new administrative area under the protection of the 9th SS Flak Battalion. A counter-order on the 6th for the Flak Battalion to rejoin the fighting elements could not be effected as the unit had run out of fuel.

In addition to the 1st Battalion of the 19th SS Panzer-Grenadier Regiment, the Hohenstaufen's 9th SS Reconnaissance Battalion and some of its Panthers were placed under Lammerding's command on the 8th. He deployed them on the right flank on the high ground to the west of Ottre. This happened at about the same time that the 82nd Airborne Division resumed its attack in the Abrefontaine area. According to Gavin: 'The Division swept on toward Vielsalm and the Salm river, where it was relieved by the 75th Infantry Division on January 9'[10] (from the VII Corps reserve). This new threat down the Salm valley was countered by the deployment of the Hohenstaufen's 20th SS Panzer-Grenadier Regiment and 2nd SS Panzer Battalion on both sides of Provedroux. Simultaneously, Zollhöfer's 19th SS Panzer-Grenadier Regiment, less its 1st Battalion with Das Reich, began to take up positions around Sterpigny, and Stadler's Headquarters moved into the village of Beho.

Side by Side: 10 – 25 January
(Map 25)

The American attack in the Salm valley began in earnest on the 10th but was held by the Grenadiers of the Hohenstaufen's 20th Regiment astride Provedroux, supported by Mk IVs and StuGs of the 2nd SS Panzer Battalion. On the same day, however, the Hohenstaufen's 9th Reconnaissance Battalion group at Ottre came under heavy pressure and was forced to pull back to the Petit Langlir area where it reverted to Stadler's command. During the night it linked up with the two Battalions of Zollhöfer's 19th SS Panzer-Grenadier Regiment already in position at Sterpigny and formed a new front facing west. Bittrich gave orders that if and when Das Reich was forced to withdraw, it was to take up new positions on the Hohenstaufen's left flank at Sommerain and Cherain.

On 11 January the American 83rd Infantry Division continued its attack towards Petit Langlir and reported 'heavy resistance'. This pressure led, during the night of the 11th, to the insertion of Weidinger's 4th Der Führer SS Panzer-Grenadier Regiment, less its 3rd SPW Battalion still with KG Krag, into the line on the east side of the N-15, between the Deutschland Regiment and the 12th Volks-Grenadiers. At this stage Das Reich and its attachments was defending a line running from the wood line south of Chabrenez and Tailles, to the N-15 just west of Pisserote and then east to link up with the Hohenstaufen at Petit Langlir and Provedroux.

American and German accounts of the final actions in this sector differ and it is difficult to make complete sense of the various movements and deployments described by Otto Weidinger[11] and Wilhelm Tieke.[12] According to the Americans, TF Hogan of the 3rd Armored cleared the high ground 2km south of Bihain on 12 January and, after encountering stiff resistance and suffering heavy tank losses in front of Sterpigny on the 15th, units of the 3rd Armored Division finally captured it along with Cherain and Sommerain on the 16th.

According to Otto Weidinger, KG Krag and Wisliceny's 3rd Deutschland Regiment were pulled back during the night of the 12th towards Sommerain and Cherain. His own Grenadiers continued to hold the north-south road running through Lomré throughout the 13th and 14th but their frontage was too wide and, after nearly being surrounded on the 15th, his Regiment withdrew to positions along the Cherain–Sommerain road. He goes on to claim that on the 16th Der Führer, in position at Sommerain, with the '12th Volks-Grenadier Division on the right and 560th Volks-Grenadier Division on the left', fought off attacks from the west. During these actions, the commander of his 2nd Battalion, Hannes Schulzer, was wounded and Weidinger himself had to take command of the unit. Strangely, he makes no mention at all of the Hohenstaufen units at Sterpigny, although it seems most likely that his Regiment withdrew through them, arriving in the Weiswampach area late on the 17th. According to Weidinger, the Deutschland Regiment was already on its way back to the West Wall at this time and Das Reich as a whole, after moving through Winterspelt on the 18th, reached the Prüm area (Map 23) on the 21st.

Wilhelm Tieke has Zollhöfer's 19th SS Panzer-Grenadier Regiment and 'the last battle-worthy Panzers of the 9th SS Panzer Regiment' in action at Sterpigny[13] until as late as the 17th, with Geiger's 20th Regiment on its right on both sides of Courtil. The final withdrawal began on the night of the 20th; first, to the line of the Salmchâteau–Weiswampach road and then on 25 January, when the Army's 9th Panzer Division relieved its Waffen-SS namesake, to the refitting area around Prüm.

Conclusion

For the men of Das Reich and Hohenstaufen the 'Battle of the Bulge' was over. Having taken part in their Führer's last offensive in the West, they and their comrades in the Leibstandarte and Hitlerjugend were about to be reinforced and re-equipped in order to lead his last great offensive on the Eastern Front.

How can we assess their performance in the Ardennes? Taking into consideration the overall state of the Waffen-SS after five years of war, the devastating number of casualties already suffered, the inadequate training of many of those taking part, the very limited amount of fuel available for an offensive operation, the almost total lack of air support, and the appalling weather conditions, it is doubtful if any other soldiers could have done as well or better – except possibly those of the American 82nd and 101st Airborne Divisions! Having said that, it is clear that both Divisions suffered from a lack of experienced and fully competent commanders at certain levels and that, due to the high number of casualties, there were far too many junior officers commanding at Battalion and Company level. Compounding this problem was the chaotic and fragmented way in which both Divisions were initially committed and then constantly re-deployed. One can only marvel at the way they performed, particularly Das Reich, often without adequate time or opportunity for reconnaissance or preparation, in every type of operation – advance to contact, attack, delay and withdrawal. And even when it was clear that the offensive had failed, and that a retreat to the West Wall was the only feasible option, they were still able to delay the advance of the US First Army from Erezée and Manhay to Houffalize, a distance of only 24km, for thirteen days and to the Salm valley south of Salmchâteau for a further five. Despite their overall defeat, the men of the 2nd and 9th SS Panzer Divisions had nothing of which to be ashamed.

NOTES

1. 2 & 3 Armd and 83 & 84 Inf Divs.
2. Gavin, *The Winter War*, p. 249.
3. Weidinger, *Comrades to the End*, p. 374, claims it was 20° below zero on 3 Jan.
4. Weidinger, *Division Das Reich, Vol V*, p. 399.
5. 335 Inf Regt.
6. Weidinger, *Division Das Reich, Vol V*, p. 406.
7. 2/334 of the 84 Inf Div & 1/290 Inf on loan from 75 Inf Div which went into VII Corps reserve on 3 Jan.
8. Weidinger, *Comrades to the End*, p. 375.
9. 1/329 & 1/330 Inf.
10. Gavin, op. cit., p. 254.
11. Weidinger, *Division Das Reich, Vol V*.
12. Tieke, *In the Firestorm of the Last Years of the War*.
13. There is photographic evidence of a Hohenstaufen Panther knocked out in Sterpigny.

CHAPTER XXXI
The Situation in early 1945
(Map 27)

Hitler's intention of delivering a devastating blow on the Western Front in order to buy the time and resources needed to deal with the deepening crisis in the East had come to nothing. Although the Ardennes offensive seemed to have bought him a short respite, it had in fact frittered away many of the men and much of the equipment needed to throw back and destroy the Soviet armies now threatening the Third Reich. As von Manteuffel said later:

The rapid advance by the Red Army [in January 1945] nullified the possible effects of the Ardennes offensive. It made a speedy end to the war inevitable. Time gained on the Western Front was thereby rendered illusory.[1]

Hungary

By the end of 1944 the Second and Third Ukrainian Fronts of the Red Army had surrounded Budapest and established strong defensive positions running from Esztergom on the Danube to Lake Balaton (known to the Germans as Plattensee). On the last day of the year the provisional government set up by the Soviets in those parts of Hungary occupied by the Red Army threw in its lot with the Allies and declared war on Germany. The last of Hitler's partners in his European Axis had deserted him – but not the Hungarian Army. In order to protect the country from the Bolsheviks, whom they feared and hated, what was left of the Hungarian Army continued to fight alongside the Germans.[2]

On New Year's Day 1945, the only sizeable German reserves on the Eastern Front launched an offensive code-named KONRAD, to relieve Budapest and secure the southern Hungarian oil reserves. By 6 January the 3rd Totenkopf and 5th Wiking SS Panzer Divisions of General Gille's IV SS Panzer Corps had come to within 25km of the Hungarian capital but then, in the face of rapidly re-deployed Soviet units, the attack stalled. On the same day the Russians launched an attack across the Gran river, north of the Danube, with the equivalent of two tank divisions and four infantry divisions[3] designed to disrupt the German offensive; it was successful and by the 8th they had advanced some 50km. German counter-measures succeeded in halting the attack and by the 14th the Russians had lost half their gains and some 200 tanks; nevertheless, they still held a sizeable bridgehead west of the Gran river.

In the meantime Gille's IV SS Panzer Corps had renewed its attack on 10 January and after three days, taking the Soviets completely by surprise, had advanced to within 21km of Budapest. Then, despite Herbert Gille's assurance that he was on the point of a breakthrough, Headquarters Army Group South inexplicably called a halt. SS Lieutenant Colonel Fritz Darges, commanding the Wiking's SS Panzer Regiment, said later:

> The head of our assault unit could see the panorama of the city in their binoculars. We were disappointed and we could not believe the attack was stopped. Our morale was excellent and we knew we could free our comrades the next day.

Be that as it may, Hitler and the OKW, as we have heard, had other plans. On 16 January von Rundstedt, more than 1000km away on the Western Front, received the following order:

> CinC West is to withdraw the following formations from operations immediately and refit them:

I SS Panzer Corps with 1st SS Panzer Division LAH and 12th SS Panzer Division HJ;
II SS Panzer Corps with 2nd SS Panzer Division DR and 9th SS Panzer Division H.
Last day of refitting is 30th January. Reinforcements will be provided under the authority of the SS Supreme Operations Office.[4]

Both SS Panzer Corps had been returned to Dietrich's command two days earlier and were already concentrating to the south of Cologne. But, as readers are already aware, both were in a wretched state and in urgent need of rest, reinforcements and new equipment. Nevertheless, at this time Hitler sent his personal adjutant, SS Major Otto Günsche, to Sepp Dietrich to warn him that he was sending the Sixth Panzer Army to the Eastern Front in order to launch a new offensive, code-named SPRING AWAKENING (FRÜHLINGSERWACHEN), designed to secure the vital oil deposits in southern Hungary and perhaps even regain the oil of Rumania. The refitting and move of Dietrich's Army was to be completed in less than a month. Both Dietrich and General Heinz Guderian, the Chief of Staff of the OKH, had wanted the Sixth Panzer Army deployed behind the Oder in order to protect Berlin and northern Germany, but Hitler would have none of it. The only natural oil deposits in German-controlled territory were those around Nagykanizsa in southern Hungary and, with Allied air attacks disrupting and often neutralising the synthetic gasoline production sites for long periods, it was essential to protect them. Without this crude oil the battle could not be continued – Dietrich and the trusted Divisions of the Waffen-SS were to be given responsibility for SPRING AWAKENING.

The decision to send the Sixth Panzer Army to Hungary meant that six of the seven SS Panzer Divisions were to be located in the Danube valley in the southern part of the Eastern Front and well away from Berlin.[5] When American intelligence became aware of this, it added to the suspicion that Hitler and his Nazi regime were planning to withdraw into some sort of mountain stronghold around Berchtesgaden:

The main trend of German defence policy does seem directed primarily to the safeguarding of the Alpine Zone. This area is, by the very nature of the terrain, practically impenetrable ... The evidence indicates that considerable numbers of SS and specially chosen units are being systematically withdrawn to Austria ... and that some of the most important ministries ... are already established in the Redoubt area.[6]

Although the idea of a National Redoubt turned out in the end to be mythical, it was realistic enough at the time to lead Eisenhower to conclude that the southern part of the European theatre was of greater significance than Berlin; this led in turn to acrimony between the Allies and to thirty-one American divisions being directed south-east towards the Danube valley and the so-called National Redoubt, leaving only eight on the direct route to Berlin. But we are getting ahead of ourselves and away from our main theme.

In view of the time needed to refit and move the Sixth Panzer Army to the Eastern Front and in order to secure the ground west of the Danube for the new offensive, Hitler ordered a third attack in Hungary on 18 January using much larger forces.[7] This attack was designed primarily to cut off and destroy all Soviet troops north of a line drawn from Lake Balaton, through Székesfehérvar (known to the Germans as Stuhlweissen-burg) to Budapest, and secondly to liberate that city – the Pest garrison had in fact withdrawn across the Danube to the hills of Buda the night before. Since the Russians had depleted their defences in this area to meet the previous German attacks in the north, the new offensive was initially very successful. Within three days, a large section of the west bank of the Danube had been secured 35km south of Budapest and the Germans then turned north and north-west, threatening to link up with other forces attacking in the north and to cut off an entire Soviet Front. By the 26th, however, with their forces in the south only 20km from Buda and in the north half that distance, the Germans were exhausted; and this was the moment when Marshal Malinovsky went over to the attack. Although Székesfehérvar and the ground between it and Lake Balaton was held, by 3 February the Germans were more or less back to their original positions – KONRAD had failed. Buda fell finally on the 14th – the siege had lasted fifty-one days and had cost the Axis over 70,000 men.

Meanwhile, Zhukov's and Konev's offensives in the north had advanced over 150km; Warsaw, Lodz and Cracow had fallen and a Soviet Army had entered East Prussia. The Red Army was now a mere 200km from Prague and, worst of all for the German people, it had crossed the Oder river and was only 70km from Berlin.

This then was the crisis into which the Sixth Panzer Army was about to be launched.

The Move to the East

Extraordinary measures were taken to conceal the fact that the Sixth Panzer Army was being moved to the Eastern Front – all ranks were ordered to remove their sleeve bands and special codenames were given to all components. Thus, II SS Panzer Corps became 'SS Training Staff South', Das Reich 'Training Group North' and the Hohenstaufen 'Training Group South'. Even Regiments were re-designated as 'Construction Teams'; for example, Der Führer became 'Otto North', after its commander, Otto Weidinger. Other deception measures included unloading part of the Sixth Panzer Army Staff near Berlin and making it known that their final destination was in the Frankfurt-am-Oder area and, despite the air threat, actually sending the Tiger IIs of I SS Panzer Corps' 501st SS Heavy Panzer Battalion via the Berlin area before routing them through Vienna to Hungary.[8]

The move of II SS Panzer Corps by rail began on 8 February. No one below Divisional commander and Chief of Staff level knew the final destination and, as the trains moved eastwards most junior ranks assumed they were heading for the Oder front to the east of Berlin. Even the railway staffs and crews were allowed to know only the destinations covered by their particular shift and, because of the air threat, trains moved only at night and took cover in tunnels by day. Once beyond the range of Allied fighter-bombers, however, movement was allowed by day and as they passed through Augsberg, Munich and Salzburg, the men realised they were heading for Hungary. In the case of some units the journey took nearly two weeks but, by the end of the third week of February, both Divisions had arrived in their new assembly areas south and south-west of Györ (known to the Germans as Raab). In this hilly and wooded part of Hungary, 100km south-east of Vienna and the same distance west of Budapest, there was no sign of war. It is a tourist region today.

Refitting

Needless to say it had proved impossible to fully refit any of the Sixth Panzer Army Divisions by 30 January and both personnel and material replacements continued to arrive during loading, during the move and even after arrival at Györ. Indeed, in view of the massive, and by now almost continuous, Allied air onslaught, the general state of the German war economy and not least, the appalling casualty rate sustained in five and a half years of war, it is astounding that Dietrich's Army was made ready for action in less than a month. More men were drafted in from the Luftwaffe and Navy, lightly wounded and sick returned to their parent formations and vehicles and tanks delivered direct from factories. Otto Weidinger wrote later that many convalescing officers, NCOs and men managed to return to his Division at this time. He described them being 'at home again at last'. Details of the rebuilding of the Waffen-SS Divisions will be provided only for those of II SS Panzer Corps. Readers interested in I SS Panzer Corps, and its actions between February and the capitulation in May 1945, should read the author's book, *Men of Steel – I SS Panzer Corps The Ardennes and Eastern Front 1944–45*.

By the time Bittrich's Divisions were committed to battle in early March, Das Reich was some 1,000 men over and the Hohenstaufen only 1,200 men under the authorised strength of a Waffen-SS Panzer Division

– approximately 18,500 all ranks.[9] Nevertheless, these figures do not reveal a severe shortfall in both officers and NCOs – roughly 30% and 50% respectively. Another important weakness was the fact that many of the reinforcements had received little or very limited military training and had no field experience with their units. As an extreme example, Wilhelm Tieke says SS Major Möller's 9th SS Pioneer Battalion received its last replacements 'shortly before the beginning of the attack. There was no time left to instruct the replacements, from the Luftwaffe, in any special pioneer skills'.[10]

The equipment state of both Divisions was surprisingly high. But with only 185 tanks, Jagdpanzers and StuGs between them, Das Reich and Hohenstaufen were still 50% below their total authorised holdings. The Hohenstaufen had nineteen Mk IVs, twenty-four Panthers, ten Jagdpanzer Vs, sixteen StuGs, 167 SPWs and fifteen heavy anti-tank guns on strength. Das Reich was even better off with twenty-four Mk IVs, thirty-four Panthers, nineteen Jagdpanzer IVs, ten Jagdpanzer Vs, twenty-nine StuGs, 258 SPWs and ten heavy anti-tank guns. Needless to say, the crews and the Divisional repair and maintenance teams had to work flat out to make these armoured vehicles combat-ready for the offensive; for example, on 25 February twenty-eight of Das Reich's Panthers and all its Mk IVs were still 'in repair'.

With regard to artillery pieces, it seems that while Das Reich was more or less up to strength, the Hohenstaufen had only five of ten authorised batteries. According to Tieke, 'units [batteries] of the 9th SS Artillery Regiment remained in Györ and waited for their guns and prime movers. They did not make it to the Division and, in retreat, joined up with the 2nd SS Panzer Division'.[11]

In an attempt to conceal the presence of the newly arrived Waffen-SS Divisions, camouflage was strictly enforced. Vehicle columns, groups of marching men and even the movement of single vehicles by day were strictly forbidden. Continuation training for the new recruits, which included the use of live ammunition, and familiarisation with the terrain for all ranks, was carried out only at night. The continuing shortage of fuel meant that even driver training had to be severely curtailed, as well as restricted to the hours of darkness.

Changes of Command

On 20 January, whilst still in the Ardennes, Heinz Lammerding had relinquished command of Das Reich to his chief artillery officer, SS Colonel Karl Kreutz and moved to Berlin to join Himmler's staff. Kreutz oversaw the move to Hungary, but on 10 February SS Major General Werner Ostendorff took over the Division. The latter held a Knight's Cross, dating from September 1941, and a German Cross in Gold. He had been wounded twice whilst commanding the 17th SS Panzer-Grenadier Division Götz von Berlichingen in 1944, once accidentally (according to Otto Weidinger) by his own men when leading an attack from the front. He was the fifth commander of Das Reich in less than seven months. Sylvester Stadler remained in command of the Hohenstaufen where the main changes involved the 19th SS Panzer-Grenadiers. SS Lieutenant Colonel Seela, the Corps Chief Pioneer officer, had taken over from Zollhöfer as the Regimental commander and SS Majors Lederer and Bartholomäi the 1st and 3rd Battalions and SS Captain Hey the 2nd.

Willi Bittrich remained in command of the Corps.

Morale

The remarkable esprit de corps of the premier Divisions of the Waffen-SS has already been described and it was inevitable that as the war progressed their soldiers felt an ever-stronger sense of comradeship. What is perhaps more remarkable is the fact that the non-volunteers and replacements from the Navy and Air Force who were drafted in after the Ardennes offensive were soon imbued with this same great sense of 'family' – all the more remarkable when one considers the parlous state of the Third Reich at this late stage of the war.

By February 1945 the soldiers of II SS Panzer Corps knew their country had no chance of winning WWII, but they were determined not to surrender 'unconditionally', as the Allies had demanded. Above all, they were determined to try to safeguard their Homeland from the Red Army whose members, they had been taught – and believed – were little more than sub-human. Moreover, since many of the members of Das Reich and Hohenstaufen came from the eastern territories of the Third Reich, they feared greatly for their families and homelands lying directly in the path of the Red Army. They, like their Führer, still harboured forlorn hopes that if Germany could just hold out long enough, the Western Allies would recognise the Bolsheviks as their real enemy and join Germany in a common crusade. This motivation, however flawed, explains, at least to some degree, the astonishing performance of these men in the final weeks of the war.

Another factor determining the performance of II SS Panzer Corps in these last months was that most of their leaders had fought together for over five years; they therefore knew each other's strong and weak points and, above all, they trusted each other. The vast majority of the officers we have mentioned – men like Bittrich, Stadler, Recke, Telkamp, Kreutz, Wisliceny, Weidinger, Enseling, Krag and so on – had fought together in the harshest conditions for year after year. They were not about to give up at this stage when the most feared and hated enemy of all was at the very gates of their beloved Heimat.

NOTES

1. Von Manteuffel, *The Fatal Decisions, The Ardennes*, p. 253.
2. The Third Hungarian Army was to play an important part in the forthcoming fighting.
3. IX Gds Mech Corps & V Gds Tk Corps of the Sixth Gds Tk Army & four Rifle Divs of the XXV Gds Rifle Corps; however, neither of these Mech & Tk Corps equated to more than a Waffen-SS Pz Div. The whole subject of Soviet organisations and strengths will be discussed in the next Chapter.
4. Meyer, *The History of the 12th SS Panzer Division Hitlerjugend*, p. 283.
5. The seventh, 10 SS Pz Div Frundsberg, was deployed 150km north-east of Berlin, in eastern Pomerania.
6. SHAEF Int Summary dated 11 Mar 45.
7. IV SS Pz Corps, III Pz Corps, I Cavalry Corps & VIII Hungarian Army Corps.
8. Schneider, *Tigers in Combat II*, p. 265.
9. Tieke, *In the Firestorm of the Last Years of the War*, p. 365.
10. Ibid., p. 364.
11. Ibid.

CHAPTER XXXII
The Soviet Side of the Hill

Although this history began with a description of II SS Panzer Corps' actions in western Ukraine in early 1944, it may help the reader to know a little more about the Eastern Front and the organisation, equipment and condition of the Red Army in early 1945. In the first place, the contrast between the Eastern and Western Fronts cannot be over-emphasised. The scale of the fighting, the topography, the weather, and in particular the enemy and his tactics, all differed greatly from those found in Normandy and the Ardennes. Moreover, because the majority of the officers and senior NCOs of II SS Panzer Corps had considerable experience of operations against the Red Army, none relished a return to that Front. As already mentioned, there was a terrible fear of being captured by an enemy whom they had been taught, and in some cases believed through experience, was uncivilized; and for those who had yet to serve in the East and who knew the vulnerability of the Third Reich at this stage of the war, the prospect was little short of terrifying – particularly for soldiers who wore SS runes on their collars.

The way the Germans viewed their Soviet enemies and the Eastern Front was described after the war by Lieutenant General Günther Blumentritt; in January 1945 he was the commander of the German Twenty-Fifth Army:

Eastern man is very different from his Western counterpart. He has a much greater capacity for enduring hardship, and this passivity induces a high degree of equanimity towards life and death. . . . Eastern man does not possess much initiative; he is accustomed to taking orders, to being led. . . . [The Russians] attach little importance to what they eat or wear. It is surprising how long they can survive on what to a Western man would be a starvation diet. . . . Close contact with nature enables these people to move freely by night or in fog, through woods and across swamps. They are not afraid of the dark, nor of their endless forests, nor of the cold . . .

The Siberian, who is partially or completely an Asiatic, is even tougher and has greater powers of resistance than his European compatriot . . . .

Distances in the East seem endless. . . . which inevitably affects the European with a sensation akin to awe. This is reinforced by the melancholy and monotonous nature of the . . . landscape, which is particularly oppressive during the gloomy days of autumn and the interminable winter darkness. The Russian is much influenced by the country in which he lives, and it is my belief that the landscape is largely responsible for his passivity and monotony.

The psychological effect of the country on the ordinary German soldier was considerable. He felt small and lost in that endless space. . . . A man who has survived the Russian enemy and the Russian climate has little more to learn about war.[1]

Organisation

A Soviet *Front*, the equivalent of an American or British Army Group usually comprised three or more *Combined Arms Armies* and sometimes one or two *Tank Armies* or mechanized groups. The former were made up basically of infantry, with formidable artillery support, and were used for defensive and breakthrough operations; independent *tank brigades and regiments* were assigned to provide extra punch during assault operations but training in the infantry support role meant that such units rarely performed well in tank versus tank engagements. Tank armies were normally employed in counter-penetration tasks, to complete a breakthrough and in the pursuit.

A *Combined Arms* army consisted of two to five *rifle corps*, usually three, and sometimes had *tank or mechanized corps* placed in support for operations requiring tactical mobility. Tank *armies* on the other hand had two or three *tank or mechanized corps* under command but, as already mentioned in Chapter I, *a tank and mechanized corps* (see Appendix III) even at full strength, was in practice the equivalent of no more than a Waffen-SS Panzer *division*.

A *Rifle corps* comprised two or three, and occasionally four, *rifle divisions* (see Appendix IV). Soviet formations and units that had distinguished themselves in action were usually given the title 'Guards'.

The terminology used in describing Red Army formations and units differed greatly from Western practice and has led to many misunderstandings about the size of the Soviet forces involved in various battles. Just as a Soviet *tank or mechanized corps* was only the equivalent of a Waffen-SS Panzer *division*, so Soviet tank *brigades* amounted to no more than Allied armoured *battalions* and Soviet tank *battalions* were only slightly larger than Allied or German tank *companies*. Soviet artillery *regiments*, like their British counterparts, were the size of American or German artillery *battalions*.

In order to avoid confusion and to assist the reader, the equivalent German organisation will be shown in brackets after the Soviet title in certain instances in this and subsequent Chapters.

Finally, on the subject of Soviet organisations, it is important to remember that the Red Army had been advancing since August 1944 and had suffered appalling casualties by this stage of the war – many of its formations, particularly the rifle divisions, were as much as 50% below strength. The scale of Soviet military casualties in WWII is difficult to comprehend: over five million deaths in action on land, sea and in the air, over one million died of wounds and nearly four and a half million missing.[2]

Equipment

The most famous item of Soviet equipment was of course the T-34. It became the most widely used tank of all time. When it first appeared on the battlefield in July 1941 it came as a complete surprise and instantly outclassed all German tanks then in service in fire-power, armour and performance.

By the Spring of 1944 the splendid T-34/85 had been introduced. It had an 85mm gun, adequate armoured protection and a three-man turret with all round vision; this was to be the main adversary of II SS Panzer Corps in 1945.

Other effective weapon systems in the Soviet armoury were the SU self-propelled gun series. These came in calibres of 76, 122 and 152mm and provided close fire support for tank and mechanized corps. The SU-100 was a self-propelled 100mm tank destroyer.

Soviet tanks and self-propelled guns, unlike their Allied and German counterparts, used diesel fuel rather than gasoline.

Women in the Red Army

There is a widely held belief that women regularly served alongside men in the Soviet ground forces in WWII and that there were even some all female combat units. Whilst it is true that about one million women were employed in the Red Army, three quarters of these were in fact conscripts and most served in air defence, medical, communications and logistic units. Female political workers accompanied some infantry units and there were a few volunteer female tank crews amongst the predominantly male units. Eighty-six women were made 'Heroes of the Soviet Union'. According to Charles Dick, an expert on the Red Army, the Soviet war-time propaganda machine exaggerated the ubiquity and contribution of its female combatants in order to boost morale. The conversion of the Soviet Army to sex equality in the front line, however, did not survive WWII. A few thousand women served in the armed forces during the Cold War but most were restricted to non-commissioned status and all to medical and support work.[3]

NOTES

1. Blumentritt, *The Fatal Decisions*, pp. 37–8.
2. According to figures published in Moscow in 1993.
3. These facts were provided by Charles Dick of the Conflict Studies Research Centre, Camberley, England.

CHAPTER XXXIII
The German Offensives

Author's Note
(Map 27)

For the benefit of readers who may visit the 1945 Slovakian, Hungarian and Slovenian battlefields, current place names are shown on Maps 27 to 33 and in the text, rather than those used in 1945. The only exception to this is the Gran river which is now called the Hron.

SOUTH WIND

Readers will recall that by mid-February 1945 the Red Army had succeeded, except in the Székesfehérvar area, in pushing the Germans back to their 1 January positions, and in retaining a considerable bridgehead across the Gran river north of Esztergom. This bridgehead was seen by the Germans as a potential assembly area for a major thrust towards Vienna and as such it had to be eliminated before they could launch their own Operation SPRING AWAKENING – the offensive to clear all Soviet forces from the area west of the Danube and north of the Drava rivers and to secure the Nagykanizsa oil deposits. This preliminary operation was given the code-name SOUTH WIND (SÜDWIND) and on 13 February Headquarters Army Group South ordered the commander of the German Eighth Army:

> To attack, concentrating all available infantry and armoured forces, and accepting the consequent weakening of other front sectors, with the newly arrived I SS Panzer Corps.... After a short artillery preparation, to thrust from the north, to destroy the enemy in the Gran bridgehead.

Eleven days later the Gran bridgehead had been eliminated. II SS Panzer Corps had not been involved in this operation, other than the Deutschland Regiment of Das Reich being moved across the Danube north of Györ as an emergency reserve force.

The Germans claimed seventy-one tanks, 179 guns, howitzers and anti-tank guns, 537 prisoners and 2,069 Russian dead in the fighting up to 22 February.[1] According to a return signed by Fritz Kraemer, the Chief of Staff of the Sixth Panzer Army, I SS Panzer Corps suffered 2,989 casualties, including 413 killed in the same period.

Operation SOUTH WIND was, without doubt, a brilliant success. In eight days I SS Panzer Corps, admittedly with valuable assistance from Panzer Corps Feldherrnhalle,[2] had recaptured over 400 square kilometres of territory, inflicted 8,800 casualties on the Red Army[3] and cleared seven infantry divisions and a Guards Mechanized Corps (Panzer Division) from west of the Gran. It is remarkable that such an effective fighting machine could have been produced within a month of the Ardennes disaster – the more so when one takes into account that many of the men involved had received only minimal training.

That said, the question arises as to whether this elite SS Panzer Corps should have been used in this operation at all. Despite all the measures taken to disguise the arrival of the Sixth Panzer Army on the Hungarian front, units of I SS Panzer Corps were soon detected in the Gran bridgehead operation. Its commitment there, rather than in the northern part of the Eastern Front, and the knowledge that yet another SS Panzer Corps had arrived in Hungary, immediately alerted the Soviets to the possibility of a German offensive. It is also obvious that the premature use of the Corps interrupted the proper refitting of its two SS Panzer Divisions and indeed, actually ensured that their effectiveness in SPRING AWAKENING would be reduced. Taken together, these facts indicate that the use of I SS Panzer Corps in Operation SOUTH WIND was a serious mistake. The Chief Operations Officer of the Sixth Panzer Army, SS Lieutenant Colonel Georg Maier, expressed similar thoughts in his book, *Drama zwischen Budapest und Vienna*, published in 1985.

SPRING AWAKENING
(Map 28)
The Setting

Hitler's aims for Operation SPRING AWAKENING were as wildly ambitious as those for AUTUMN MIST in the Ardennes three months previously. They were: to destroy the Soviet forces in the region bounded by Lake Balaton and the Danube and Drava rivers, secure the Hungarian oil deposits, and establish bridgeheads over the Danube with a view to further offensive operations.

The attack was to be carried out in the north by Sepp Dietrich's Sixth Panzer Army[4] and the III Panzer Corps[5] of Balck's Sixth Army; and in the south, between the Drava river and the south-west corner of Lake Balaton, by the Second Panzer Army[6] (part of Army Group South-East and a 'Panzer' Army in name only).

Serious concerns were expressed by Sepp Dietrich and his senior staff officers that as the Sixth Panzer Army and III Panzer Corps moved south-east and east, they would become increasing vulnerable to any counter offensive launched by the Soviet forces already located north of Székes-fehérvar and west of the Danube. These comprised a Soviet Army of three Rifle Corps, backed by a Guards Mechanized Corps (Panzer Division).[7] Since, as will become evident, Balck's Sixth Army defences in this area[8] were woefully inadequate, these concerns were fully justified. Nevertheless, a proposal that these Soviet forces should be dealt first, or at least engaged, was rejected by Hitler and the date of the offensive confirmed as 6 March.

For its premier role in this final German offensive in WWII, Dietrich's Sixth Panzer Army was reinforced to a strength of six Divisions: I SS Panzer Corps with the Leibstandarte and Hitlerjugend; II SS Panzer Corps with the 2nd SS Das Reich and 9th SS Hohenstaufen Panzer Divisions; and I Cavalry Corps with the 3rd and 4th Cavalry Divisions.[9] The latter were genuine mounted troops and were a considerable asset in the conditions of the Eastern Front where the horse sometimes had advantages over motorized transport.

Whilst the Germans were preparing SPRING AWAKENING, the Soviets were planning their own offensive which was due to start on 15 March. It was designed to capture Vienna and be carried out by the Second and Third Ukrainian Fronts (Army Groups) with four Armies.[10] Although the Soviets learned of the impending German offensive during the Gran bridgehead fighting, STAVKA (the Supreme Soviet Headquarters) decreed that two of the Russian Armies[11] due to take part in the Vienna offensive were to continue their preparations and were not to be included in any defensive planning.

Since the main German threat was known to be in the Third Ukrainian Front sector, the Soviets concentrated the bulk of their forces between Lake Balaton and a point some 20km to the north of Székesfehérvar. Here Marshal Tolbukhin massed three Armies, together with two Tank Corps (Panzer Divisions) and a Guards Mechanized Corps (Panzer Division).[12] According to the Soviet Official History[13], his forces totalled 407,000 men, 6,890 guns and mortars, 407 tanks and self-propelled guns and 965 aircraft, but it is likely that many of his formations were much weaker than these figures suggest.

The Third Ukrainian Front commander reasoned that if and when the Germans attacked, they would be sufficiently weakened by the depth of his defences for him to be able to launch his own offensive as originally planned, using the STAVKA reserve Armies and any forces unaffected by the fighting.

German intelligence of the Soviet defences was good. Although it failed to identify the correct designation and exact positioning of every formation, it estimated the number of Armies, Corps and Divisions in the attack area with remarkable accuracy. Its only serious errors were in not detecting a Guards Mechanized Corps (Panzer Division) and a Guards Cavalry Corps in the path of the Sixth Panzer Army, and the positions of two of the three Corps of Tolbukhin's second echelon Army astride the Danube.[14]

To the north of the Third Ukrainian Front, Marshal Malinovsky's Second Ukrainian Front numbered some half a million men and another 600 tanks, but over 400 of these were in STAVKA reserve for the forthcoming offensive.

That part of the SPRING AWAKENING offensive in which we are interested can be narrowed down to the area between Lakes Balaton and Valencei. There the attack involved Sepp Dietrich's Sixth Panzer Army and the III Panzer Corps of the Sixth Army, with some 300 tanks and assault guns. These forces were opposed by over 1,200 guns and mortars and, in theory but in the event not in practice, by some 300 Russian tanks and SUs.

The state of the ground caused great anxiety in the German command. At the end of February the weather had become unexpectedly warm, +11° Celsius by day, and as the ground thawed all movement became difficult and cross-country movement, even by tracked vehicles, virtually impossible. The onset of what is called 'razputitza', a three to four week period of almost complete immobility in Spring and Autumn due to muddy conditions, did not augur well for Hitler's last offensive. Dietrich's Chief Operations Officer reported:

> In the constricted area between Lakes Balaton and Valencei the mud became alarming. The closer one came to the . . . assembly area, the more widespread the land that was under water – impassable for all kinds of vehicles. It looked the same . . . in the enemy area, as far as the terrain permitted observation . . . A Panzer attack in open terrain under these conditions is out of the question.

As a result of this report, a request was made to Headquarters Army Group South that the attack should be postponed for at least two days and Dietrich himself asked General Guderian at OKH to support the proposal – to no avail.

II SS Panzer Corps' final assembly area was just to the south of Székesfehérvar and its initial mission was to establish a bridgehead over the Danube between Dunaujvaros and Dunaföldvar (some 60km away). Das Reich and Hohenstaufen were to attack side by side on a 10km frontage, from a Start Line running due west from Seregélyes. The initial objectives were Sarkeresztur and Sarosd, both about 10km from the Start Line. III Panzer Corps was tasked with screening the Corps' left flank and its boundary with I SS Panzer Corps was the Sarviz canal, which together with the adjacent 15m-wide Sarviz river, formed a major obstacle. On the right of I SS was I Cavalry Corps. The objective of these two Corps was the Sio canal between Mezökomarom and Simontornya, 15km and 25km away respectively.

Units of Balck's Sixth Army[15] were manning the forward defences in front of these assault forces and would come under command as the attack developed. A Panzer Division, the armoured element of another and a motorized Brigade[16] were held in Army Group South Reserve. Readers may recall that during the campaign in the Ukraine, General Balck had proved himself no friend of either Willi Bittrich or the Waffen-SS.

(Map 29)

The area over which the Waffen-SS Divisions were to advance, although very open, is gently rolling country with a number of significant hill features and ridges.[17] There were, and still are, only two hard-surface roads running south-east from Székesfehérvar and even these had been turned into rivers of mud by the thaw. Had the ground been frozen at the time of the attack, the initial results might well have been very different.

The Soviet Defence

The Soviet defences between Lakes Balaton and Valencei were constructed in great depth – on average some 30km. Seven infantry divisions were holding the front line between the lakes and four more, one of which was in Army reserve, were sited in depth between Sarbogard, Mezökomarom and the south-east edge of Lake Balaton. Two of the front line divisions were to the east of Lake Balaton, immediately in front of I Cavalry Corps, two faced I SS Panzer Corps, two more were opposite II SS Panzer Corps[18] and a divisional equivalent[19] was to be found in front of III Panzer Corps. Most importantly from the point of view of this history, the XVIII Tank Corps (Panzer Division), with about seventy-five tanks and SUs, provided a mobile reserve in the area of Sarosd, directly in the path of II SS Panzer Corps, and four more Rifle Divisions[20] and a Guards Mechanized Corps[21] (Panzer Division) were situated just to the west of the Danube directly covering II SS Panzer Corps' objectives of Dunaujvaros and Dunaföldvar. As if all this was not enough to contend with, the Soviets had a further twelve Rifle Divisions[22] within 30km of the east bank of the Danube and three more between the west bank and Lake Valencei.[23] When one considers that the normal ratio expected for a successful attack is three to one in favour of the attacker, it becomes clear that the Sixth Panzer Army in general, and II SS Panzer Corps in particular, had been given formidable tasks.

We are fortunate in having the benefit of a very detailed Russian study[24] on the Lake Balaton offensive which gives full details of the strength and dispositions of one of the Divisions forming the Soviet defence in our area of interest – the 233rd Rifle Division. Although this particular Division was opposing the Hitlerjugend and part of the Leibstandarte, the Divisions facing Das Reich and the Hohenstaufen would have been very similar in strength and deployment. The study is particularly useful for this history, since it covers the actions of the Soviet Corps principally engaged against II SS Panzer Corps.

The study says the 233rd Rifle Division had dug, between 18 February and 5 March, 27km of trenches, 130 gun and mortar positions, 113 dug-outs, seventy command posts and observation points, and laid 4,249 anti-tank and 5,058 anti-personnel mines – all this on a frontage of 5km! It goes on to quote a figure of 114 guns and mortars, including six 122mm howitzers and thirty-three 120mm mortars for the Division, giving an average of twenty-two guns and mortars per kilometre of front, with up to sixty-seven being able to fire on the most important axes. Although there were no tanks in this defensive zone, there was an average of seventeen anti-tank guns per kilometre, forming twenty-three tank 'killing grounds'.

The Division was deployed with two Regiments forward and a third on a flank in depth. This latter Regiment was given counter-attack tasks into what the Divisional commander considered to be three areas of vital ground.

The defences were made up of three zones. The first, 1 to 1.5km deep, comprised two continuous trench lines and parts of a third. Some 1.5 to 2km farther back there was another position made up of one continuous and one intermittent trench and then, 3 to 5km from the front line, lay a final trench line and strongpoint. Sadly, at least from an historical point of view, nothing remains of these defences today.

In terms of personnel strengths, the study claims that on 6 March the Division was 70% below its authorised strength and that its Regiments, with an average strength of only 665 men each, had therefore been reduced to two instead of three Battalions. This may well be true, but just as we have seen the Germans exaggerate their losses in order that the actions of the survivors might appear more heroic, so it is more than likely that the real Divisional strength was in fact higher – at least in the region of 40% of authorised establishment, or in other words nearer 5,000 than the 3,500 quoted. The whole study is written in the 'heroic' style.

NOTES

1. Army Group South War Diary.
2. The original Feldherrnhalle Div was destroyed at Stalingrad in 1943. Reformed as a Pz-Gren Div, the bulk of the Div was trapped in Budapest at the end of 1944 but some of its armour escaped and gave the Corps its name.
3. Soviet figure.
4. The Sixth Pz Army is usually described as the Sixth SS Pz Army to distinguish it from the Sixth Army, but this was not its correct title.
5. 1 & 3 Pz Divs.
6. LXVIII Corps & XXII Mountain Corps with 16 SS Pz-Gren & 13 SS Mountain Divs & three inf divs.
7. The Forty-Sixth Army with three Rifle Corps & II Gds Mech Corps (Pz Div).
8. Astride and north of Székesfehérvar, the Sixth Army comprised the Third Hungarian Army with two Corps and Gille's depleted IV SS Pz Corps.
9. Each div comprised two regts, each of two bns, supported by partly motorized units including recce and a/tk bns, an arty regt & an engr coy.
10. Fourth & Ninth Gds Armies, Forty-Sixth Army & the Sixth Gds Tk Army.
11. Sixth Gds Tk Army with V Gds Tk Corps (Pz Div) & IX Gds Mech Corps (Pz Div) & Ninth Gds Army with nine Rifle Divs.
12. Twenty-Sixth Army with CIV, CXXXV & XXX Rifle Corps and XVIII Tk Corps

(Pz Div); Fourth Gds Army with XXI, XX & XXXI Gds Rifle Corps and XXIII Tk Corps (Pz Div); Twenty-Seventh Army with XXXIII, XXXV & XXXVII Rifle Corps; I Gds Mech Corps (Pz Div) in reserve.

13. *IVOVSS, Vol 5, Pt 1*, p. 195. But, as an example of reduced strengths, A I Radzievskiy in his *Army Operations* claims the XVIII Tk Corps (Pz Div) numbered only seventy-five tanks & SUs; the official establishments of the XVIII & XXIII Tk Corps & I Gds Mech Corps totalled 604 tanks and 166 SUs.
14. Three divs, each with an official strength of about 5,000 men & including SU, a/tk, mortar and AA bns.
15. 44 Gren & 356 Inf Divs (German), 25 & 26 Hungarian Inf Divs.
16. 23 Pz Div, the armd elements only of 6 Pz Div (some thirty tks & StuGs) & 92 Bde.
17. The area south-east of Székesfehérvar has few roads and it is difficult, even in a four -wheel drive vehicle, to visit some of the scenes of the fighting without trespassing and/or crossing agricultural land.
18. 36 Gds & 155 Rifle Divs.
19. 1 Gds Fortified Region; about the same size as a rifle div but stronger in MGs & arty.
20. 108 Gds, 84, 316 & 320 Rifle Divs.
21. I Gds Mech Corps.
22. XXXIII, XXXVIII, XXIX & CCCLXXVI Rifle Corps, each with three Divs.
23. XXXV Rifle Corps.
24. *The Frunze Military Academy Study of the Defence by Formations of XXX Rifle Corps of the Twenty-Sixth Army in the Balaton Defensive Operations* by Lt Col V F Yashin.

CHAPTER XXXIV

SPRING AWAKENING: 2 – 19 March

2 – 6 March

(Map 28)

On 2 March Das Reich and Hohenstaufen were placed on an alert status and told to be prepared to move. All training was immediately suspended. The following day the Divisions were ordered forward to their final assembly areas for the new offensive, south and south-east of Székesfehérvar. By first light on the 4th, Das Reich, after moving through Györ and Zirc, had reached the Varpalota area while the Hohenstaufen, following a route through Kisbér, was in the region of Mor. According to Otto Weidinger the curtailment of the planned training period by half and a lack of troop carrying transport meant that his own 1st SS Panzer-Grenadier Battalion and Wisliceny's 2nd had to be left behind.

(Map 29)

It seems that detailed orders for the attack were not received by either Ostendorff or Stadler until around midday on the 5th – only some sixteen hours before H-Hour and when their leading Grenadiers were still over 20km away from their final jumping off points. A lack of cover and clogged routes meant that most of the transport vehicles had to be left well to the north and the men had to complete this march carrying their full equipment and combat loads of ammunition. To compound this already desperate situation, the routes they had to take were a morass of mud, choked with other personnel and equipment and it snowed during the night of the 5th. There was no possibility of either Division's tanks or heavy equipment reaching the forward assembly areas in time for the attack. Otto Weidinger blames the 'high command' for failing to allow enough time for the troops to reach their jumping off points and says the Grenadiers, after their 20km march, were too exhausted to attack on 6 March.[1] It is not clear exactly who in the 'high command' he is criticising – Bittrich, Kraemer, Dietrich? And he ignores the fact that I SS Panzer Corps, which received the movement order at the same time and faced similar problems, reached its forward assembly area south-east of Polgardi in time for H-Hour.[2] It is, however, interesting to note the comments of Ralf Tiemann who became the Chief Operations officer of Das Reich a few days later. After the war he wrote: 'The misleading reports from Headquarters II SS Panzer Corps about delays resulting from movement problems led to considerable dissatisfaction amongst the forward commanders'.[3] In fairness though, it has to be pointed out that, whilst I SS Panzer Corps had the route through Polgardi to itself, II SS had to share its way through Székesfehérvar with another Corps – III Panzer.

Complaints by both Divisional commanders and the Corps Chief of Staff, SS Lieutenant Colonel Keller, that there was no possibility of II SS Panzer Corps being ready in time were to no avail. Bittrich was not empowered to authorise a delay or postponement and, as we have already heard, Dietrich's appeal to OKH had already been rejected. The attack order was a Führer Order and that was that.

As dawn broke on 6 March, snow was still falling from low cloud and the temperature hovered on either side of 0° Celsius. The ground was frozen near the surface and men and vehicles sank into thick cloying mud the moment they moved off the few roads available. Conditions were very similar to those experienced in the Ardennes only three months previously.

Whilst it is generally agreed that the thirty-minute artillery barrage heralding the beginning of SPRING AWAKENING began as planned at 0400

hours on 6 March, Tieke, Weidinger and the Chiefs of Staff of the Leibstandarte and Hitlerjugend Divisions differ on exactly when the II SS
Panzer Corps attack began. Weidinger says Wisliceny's 3rd Deutschland
SS Grenadiers could not advance at H-Hour since they were only then
beginning to arrive in the attack zone and claims that his Regiment did
not arrive until the following day. Tieke says the Hohenstaufen attacked
around noon and the two Chiefs of Staff say II SS Panzer Corps did not
advance until 1830 hours. From all the available evidence, it is clear that
II SS Panzer Corps did not launch any serious attacks on the 6th. This is
in fact confirmed by Tieke, who goes on to say that, in October 1973, he
discussed the whole matter with Bittrich. The latter told him that after
looking at the ground on the morning of 6 March, he came to the conclusion that the appalling conditions and difficult terrain between Aba
and Seregélyes demanded detailed reconnaissances by his commanders
and careful attack preparations. He therefore no longer had 'the intention
to attack immediately off the line of march'.[4] It is slightly ironic then that
Dietrich's orders to Bittrich for the following day read, '*Continue* (author's
italics) the attack along the Sarkeresztur–Sarosd road to the high ground
east of Sarkeresztur, exclusive Aba'.[5]

Elsewhere on the Sixth Panzer Army front, things were little better. I
SS Panzer Corps managed to launch its attack on time, but surprise
was not achieved and the gains were depressingly small, the deepest
penetration being a mere 4km. Farther to the west, the 3rd and 4th
Cavalry Divisions were forced back to their start-lines by Soviet counter-
attacks.

On the eastern flank there was some success. By midday units of the
3rd Panzer Division (III Panzer Corps) had advanced about 4km to the
east, south of Lake Valencei, and penetrated into Seregélyes. This not
only secured the Hohenstaufen part of the German Start Line, but it also
threatened the rear of the Soviet defence zone in the XXX Corps area,
causing alarm within the Soviet command. The reaction was swift. Marshal Tolbukhin reinforced Lieutenant General Gagyen, the Twenty-Sixth
Army commander, with two tank brigades (Panzer battalions) and three
anti-tank regiments from his reserve XVIII Tank Corps (Panzer Division)
and Gagyen ordered these units to take up positions confronting III
Panzer and II SS Panzer Corps. Gagyen also placed his reserve Rifle
Division[6] under the command of Major General Lazko, the XXX Corps
commander. Finally on this day, Tolbukhin ordered a Division[7] from his
reserve Army into a second defensive line opposite II SS Panzer Corps,
a complete Rifle Corps[8] from east of the Danube to move to a new position
to the south of Simontornya and two tank regiments (Panzer Battalions)
of I Guards Mechanized Corps (Panzer Division) to begin moving west
towards Sarbogard.

7 – 8 March

On the left wing of II SS Panzer Corps, the Hohenstaufen attacked towards Sarosd soon after first light on 7 March, in rain mixed with light snow. The entire landscape was a morass of mud and SS Lieutenant Colonel Telkamp, who personally accompanied the leading tank Company, soon realised that it would be impossible to commit the rest of his Regiment. After two tanks disappeared in mud up to their turrets, it was clear that the single tank Company would have to stay on the only hard-surface road in the attack zone and that the SS Panzer-Grenadiers, struggling forward on their feet, would be denied effective armoured support. To complicate matters further, long-range Soviet artillery was interdicting the bulk of the Hohenstaufen's armour still crossing the Sarviz canal at Szabadbattyan. The attack, which Stadler later claimed was clearly expected, reached a relatively high point about 5km north-west of Sarosd but then bogged down.

The attack by Das Reich was no more successful. Wisliceny's 3rd SS Panzer-Grenadier Regiment Deutschland attacked at 0500 hours but without, for reasons unknown, the benefit of a supporting artillery barrage. Again, the supporting tanks were mired and the Grenadiers could make only limited progress on their own against the well-prepared Soviet field fortifications. Weidinger's Der Führer Regiment, less its 1st Battalion, but with Knight's Cross holder SS Major Dieter Kesten's 2nd SS Panzer Battalion under command, was held in reserve ready to exploit a breakthrough that never occurred. Sadly for II SS Panzer Corps, the Russian XXX Corps commander had correctly identified the roads leading southeast out of Székesfehérvar as the most likely enemy axes and had deployed his strength accordingly. 'In this [10km] region, there were road junctions with usefully distributed villages containing stone buildings. Holding them created the conditions necessary for defeating the attackers by fire and restricting their movement'.[9]

On the right of II SS Panzer Corps' zone, the 44th Grenadier Division 'Hoch und Deutschmeister' managed to advance 4km to a hamlet northeast of Aba, but again Soviet counter-moves were decisive. Another Rifle Division[10] and a Tank Brigade (Panzer Battalion)[11] were allotted to XXX Corps and the Division which had come under command the previous day took up positions facing west along the Sarviz canal north of Sarbogard. One company of the Tank Brigade moved into the northern outskirts of Aba.

The Army Group South War Diary for 7 March reads:

II SS Panzer Corps, which did not get going yesterday because of a delayed arrival, today, primarily with infantry forces, drove a 6km deep wedge into the main enemy defences as far as the hills west of Sarosd.

On the 8th, despite bitter fighting, the Hohenstaufen failed to get beyond the Aba–Sarosd road. A motorized Rifle Brigade[12] had reinforced the hard-pressed infantry Division in this sector and the only real success for Stadler's men came just after dark when some fortified farmsteads were captured to the north-west of Sarosd.

According to Tieke, the 44th Division's Grenadiers, after knocking out seven T-34s, captured some relatively high ground west of Aba on the 8th, but 'numerous strong points, dug-in tanks and minefields formed the backbone of the Russian defence'.[13] The Soviets claim Das Reich made nine separate attacks on this day but again, 'anti-tank and artillery fire from concealed positions stopped the enemy attack'.[14]

I SS Panzer Corps was more successful during this period. The wider Soviet Study of the Balaton offensive[15] confirms that by 2000 hours on the 7th, the Leibstandarte had breached the second line defences of the 68th Guards Division on a 5km front, and this caused Major General Lazko to order the Division to withdraw behind the Sarviz canal where, it will be recalled, the Army's reserve Rifle Division[16] had already taken up defensive positions. This move began at 0100 hours on the 8th and, according to the study, despite German efforts to disrupt the withdrawal, the Division was dug in on the east bank by last light.

In addition, during the 7th, the leading units of the Rifle Corps[17], which Marshal Tolbukhin had ordered forward from the east side of the Danube, crossed the river at Dunaföldvar. Recall they had orders to take up positions behind the Sio canal at Simontornya, where the reserve Guards Cavalry Corps[18] had been deployed as an emergency measure.

On 8 March I SS Panzer Corps' attack began to gain momentum and by evening Nagy had been secured against minimal opposition, as had the Enying–Dég road about 3km west of Dég.

The failure of II SS Panzer Corps to make progress on the east side of the Sarviz canal was causing deep concern at Headquarters Army Group South and Sixth Panzer Army and this led, on the night of the 8th, to the release of the 23rd Panzer Division from the Army Group South reserve to I SS Panzer Corps. With some fifty tanks, Jagdpanzers and assault guns, the Division was ordered to follow behind the Leibstandarte and to be prepared to cross the Sarviz canal and attack the Soviet forces in the rear of the II SS Panzer Corps in the Sarkeresztur area.

9 – 10 March

On the left flank of Bittrich's Corps, the Hohenstaufen was unable to make any progress in this period. A strength return dated 10 March shows the Division with seventeen Panthers, only nine Mk IVs, fifteen StuGs, and thirteen Jagdpanzer IVs and Vs. Additional vehicles were certainly under repair but this is an alarming 37% reduction in the combat strength of the Division in less than a week.

In the Das Reich sector, Wisliceny's Grenadiers attacked again at first light on the 9th, this time with the benefit of an artillery barrage. They managed to secure two small hills and then Weidinger's armoured group, with tanks of Kesten's 2nd SS Panzer Battalion and SPW mounted Grenadiers of SS Major Werner's 3rd Battalion, was launched against Hill 159[19], deeper inside the Soviet defensive system. According to Weidinger, the group encountered anti-tank fire from a flank and after losing three tanks the advance ground to a halt. Soon after this, Ostendorff ordered Wisliceny to launch another attack to the right flank in order to make contact with I SS Panzer Corps on the other side of the Sarviz canal. This involved advancing through flooded, featureless and completely open terrain. A bitter argument followed between the two senior officers but Weidinger does not tell us the outcome.[20] On the way back to his Headquarters, Ostendorff's vehicle received a direct hit. His aide was killed and he was seriously wounded. SS Colonel Karl Kreutz again assumed command of the Division. Ostendorff died in hospital on 1 May and five days later, just before the war ended, he was posthumously awarded Oakleaves to his Knight's Cross.

Weidinger confirms Tieke's report that the appalling ground and weather conditions (it was raining and snowing), and stiff Soviet resistance prevented any further progress in the II SS Panzer Corps sector on the 10th. The Soviet Study says:

> Cruel fighting took place around Hill 159 where artillery played a significant role in the destruction of the enemy. Unable to achieve success with frontal attacks, the enemy tried to outflank the objective; however, this manoeuvre was frustrated by tanks and SP guns in enfiladed ambush positions. Fighting continued at night.

The lack of progress by Bittrich's Corps is hardly surprising. Apart from the adverse ground and weather conditions, II SS Panzer Corps was now up against the major part of six infantry Divisions[21] (with two more sited in depth farther east[22]), albeit most of them seriously understrength, and significant elements of two armoured formations.[23]

In the I SS Panzer Corps sector the situation began to change dramatically on 9 March. One KG of the Leibstandarte overcame well-defended positions covering the Nagy–Saregres road to the north of Saregres, before being brought to a halt by an anti-tank screen immediately north of the village; whilst another, in spite of the unfavourable ground conditions, reached the high ground 2.5km north of Simontornya before being halted by dug-in anti-tank guns and heavy artillery fire from positions south of the Sio canal. In the Hitlerjugend sector things also went reasonably well, particularly when one considers that there were no roads and few negotiable tracks in its area. Dég was soon captured, and by evening Hugo Kraas's men were immediately to the north of Mezöszilas.

On the right flank of Priess's Corps, one Division of I Cavalry Corps exploited the gap created by the Hitlerjugend and reached the main road between Enying and Mezökomarom, whilst the other attacked Enying.

The Russians viewed the events of 9 March with some alarm. As the Frunze Military Academy study describes it:

> From the morning of 9 March, the operational situation on the XXX Rifle Corps front [opposite II SS Panzer Corps] sharply deteriorated. The success of the enemy in breaking through the tactical defence zone of CXXXV Corps [on the I SS Panzer Corps front] created a serious threat to the rear of the Twenty-Sixth Army . . . Because of this breach, control between the two left hand Corps of the Army and XXX Rifle Corps became too complicated, so CinC Front [Tolbukhin] ordered XXX Rifle Corps transferred to the Twenty-Seventh Army.[24]

This transfer was part of an overall restructuring of the Third Ukrainian Front. From the night of the 9th Tolbukhin's reserve Twenty-Seventh Army became responsible for the sector between Lake Valencei and the Sarviz canal. Meanwhile, General Gagyen's Twenty-Sixth Army remained responsible for halting what Tolbukhin considered was the main threat – I SS Panzer Corps and I Cavalry Corps between the Sarviz canal and Lake Balaton. To this end Gagyen was reinforced with a tank regiment (Panzer battalion), a self-propelled artillery brigade and two anti-tank regiments, and the main weight of the Third Ukrainian Front's close air support effort was re-targeted to his sector.[25]

Whilst the 9th had been a good day for Priess's men on the west side of the Sarviz canal, Dietrich and his senior commanders were acutely aware that the left flank of I SS Panzer Corps was becoming dangerously exposed. II SS Panzer Corps had still not reached Sarkeresztur and only the difficulties of crossing the Sarviz river and canal were preventing the Russians from attacking the flank of the German penetration. Marshal Tolbukhin, however, was not slow to recognise the operational opportunities offered by this situation and on the same day he requested the release of one reserve Army to his control and the use of another.[26] STAVKA refused, saying that these Armies were earmarked for the forthcoming general offensive and that he would have to make do with what he had. In fact STAVKA went further and, on this same day, gave both Tolbukhin and Malinovsky revised missions. The Third Ukrainian Front was to continue to defend south of Lake Balaton with two Armies[27], but was to be prepared to launch a major attack north of Lake Valencei with two reserve Armies[28], one of which Tolbukhin had just requested. The aim of this attack was, as Dietrich had feared, to strike the rear of the Sixth Panzer Army. Malinovsky's Second Ukrainian Front was to join in the attack after one or two days, with two Armies attacking westwards along the south bank of the Danube. Later, the Armies north of the Danube and south of Lake Balaton were to join in the offensive. The initial attack by Tolbukhin was to be made as soon as the Sixth Panzer Army's offensive had been halted. This was expected to be on the 15th or 16th.

The strength of the Soviet position derived from their early knowledge of the forthcoming German offensive and their ability to formulate and develop an overall strategy to deal with it both before and during the fighting. The fact that they were facing reverses in one area did not distract them from their long-term aim and the, albeit serious, situation on the west side of the Sarviz was seen as an opportunity rather than as a setback. The similarities between the Balaton offensive, the Mortain counter-attack in Normandy and the Battle of the Bulge are obvious – the difference being that the Americans had no prior warning and had to react to events rather than pre-plan them.

On 10 March the terrible weather and ground conditions ensured that progress west of the Sarviz was slow. The Hitlerjugend continued its painful advance towards Ozora and, after capturing Mezöszilas by 2100 hours, moved on during the night to capture Igar, 4km to the north-west of Simontornya. In the sector of I Cavalry Corps, the 3rd Cavalry Division managed to seize a bridgehead over the Sio, 5km to the west of Mezökomarom, and the 4th Division encircled Enying.

On the same day the 23rd Panzer Division, despite heavy anti-tank and artillery fire from the east side of the Sarviz canal, closed up to Saregres. By nightfall it had taken over from the Leibstandarte on that flank and this allowed Kumm's Division to concentrate for its attack on Simontornya and subsequent crossing of the Sio canal. I SS Panzer Corps was now some 25km ahead of II SS Panzer Corps and the threat of a Soviet counter-attack into its exposed flank appeared ever more likely.

11 – 12 March

Das Reich made some progress on 11 March but there was stalemate on the Hohenstaufen front where it was the Soviets rather than the Germans who were doing the attacking. Sylvester Stadler wrote later:

> The Russians attacked all day long in battalion and regimental strength from their well-constructed positions. Since they knew the terrain well, support by artillery, heavy mortars and tanks was well targeted and effective. Scarcely was one attack repulsed when they appeared in another place. The Hohenstaufen kept up its high morale, as it was able to hold off all the attacks and make them extremely costly for the enemy. Unfortunately, our own losses were equally high.[29]

Das Reich was more successful. Kesten's 2nd SS Panzer Battalion and Werner's 3rd SS Panzer-Grenadier Battalion in SPWs, aided by good weather and support from the Luftwaffe and the Divisional self-propelled artillery Battalion, launched an attack described by Weidinger, the overall commander, as 'right out of the textbook'. It was successful and by mid-morning had reached an important hamlet lying 6km south-east of Sark-eresztur, known as 'Heinrich Major'. At the same time, Wisliceny's Deutschland Regiment, on the right flank, captured a vineyard immedi-ately north-east of Sarkeresztur, effectively cutting off Aba. Simul-taneously, in a further attempt to unhinge the Soviet defence in this area, Ernst Krag's 2nd SS Reconnaissance Battalion was moved across the Sarviz canal at Szabadbattyan and then south through Soponya to a road junction just to the north of Kaloz. There it turned east and re-crossed the canal to attack Sarkeresztur. The canal bridge was captured and a small bridgehead established on either side of it, but heavy defensive fire from the dyke on the east side of the canal and difficulties caused by the extensive marshy ground, where visibility was often reduced to just a few metres, forced Krag to abandon any further attempts to advance towards Sarkeresztur.

The 12th of March saw the status quo continue on the Hohenstaufen's front facing Sarosd and a similar situation develop on Das Reich's. The only real success seems to have occurred at Aba which was cleared by the 44th Grenadier Division.

Weidinger says the attack in the Heinrich Major area was continued but cost 'several tanks and SPWs'. Schulzer's 2nd SS Panzer-Grenadier Battalion was brought up to defend the flanks of the armoured group's penetration but, despite a claim of six Soviet tanks and four anti-tank guns destroyed, no further progress could be made. Later in the day two Soviets counter-attacks were repulsed, the second being supported by ten tanks, four of which were claimed destroyed. SS Senior Sergeant Major Emil Seibold, of the 2nd SS Panzer Battalion, knocked out his sixty-fifth enemy tank in this fighting for which he was later awarded the Knight's Cross. He ended the war as the Division's greatest tank ace with sixty-nine kills to his credit.

In conjunction with attacks from the north-west by the Deutschland Regiment and parts of the 44th Grenadier Division, Krag's Reconnaissance Battalion renewed its attack from the Kaloz bridgehead towards Sarkeresztur on this day. Although 'considerable territorial gains' (probably no more than a few hundred metres) were made, the Soviet reaction was violent and heavy artillery fire soon forced the 2nd and 3rd Companies to pull back to positions left and right of the canal bridge. That night they came under heavy attack but despite the difficulties of digging in the marshy ground, the positions were held:

> On top of the dyke were several dead Russians and directly in front of the dyke lay an even greater number of corpses. Stretching far out across the water-covered land lay many of the attackers, a large proportion of whom were partially or almost completely covered with water.[30]

The 12th of March saw important changes in the command structure of Das Reich. SS Colonel Rudolf Lehmann, the Chief of Staff of I SS Panzer Corps, assumed command of the Division and SS Major Ralf Tiemann became the Chief Operations officer. Both were Leibstandarte officers, the former a friend of Sepp Dietrich and holder of a Knight's Cross earned in Russia. Fortunately, they already knew most of the unit commanders so that the changeover did not, so we are told, adversely affect the Division.

I SS Panzer Corps had considerably more success than its Sixth Panzer Army partner on 11 March. Grenadiers of the Leibstandarte spent the day clearing the important ridge lying just to the north of Simontornya. At the same time, the Hitlerjugend captured the road junction 1,500m south of Igar. This secured the jumping off positions for the final attack on Simontornya, which was to be carried out the following day.

On I SS Panzer Corps' left flank, the 23rd Panzer Division penetrated into Saregres but was unable to clear it. Army Group South's hopes of launching an attack across the Sarviz in this area, in support of II SS Panzer Corps, were proving over-optimistic.

The Leibstandarte's attack on the town of Simontornya on 12 March was launched from the high ground north of the Sio canal. Fierce house-to-house fighting lasted all day but by last light Simontornya, north of the Sio, was largely in German hands with only a few pockets of resistance remaining.

Another somewhat surprising success on the 12th came in the I Cavalry Corps' sector, where the 3rd Cavalry Division managed to cross the Sio canal and secure a 6km-square bridgehead to the west of Mezökomarom while the 4th Cavalry Division closed up to Balatonszabadi. Nevertheless, despite these gains there was little doubt that the Sixth Panzer Army's offensive was losing its momentum. II SS Panzer Corps had been decisively halted and I SS Panzer Corps was now up against five infantry Divisions[31], backed by a Cavalry Corps. The fact that these Divisions were understrength was relatively unimportant, for the ground they were holding was ideal for defence and totally unsuitable for an attacking armoured formation.

Undetected by German intelligence, the build-up for the forthcoming Soviet offensive was proceeding rapidly on the 12th. The movement of the Sixth Guards Tank Army (Panzer Corps), with some 500 tanks, to an assembly area just west of Budapest was completed and a second attack Army[32] was in the process of moving in behind the Army[33] defending the sector immediately to the north of Lake Valencei. The scene was being set for the final destruction of the Sixth Panzer Army.

13 – 15 March

This period saw II SS Panzer Corps in a defensive posture with the Hohenstaufen still in front of Sarosd and Das Reich in a half circle around Sarkeresztur. The Deutschland Regiment and elements of the 44th Grenadier Division were just to the north of the small town, Krag's 2nd SS Reconnaissance Companies clung to their bridgehead north-east of Kaloz and Weidinger's armoured group continued to beat off repeated attacks on its positions at Heinrich Major. Numerous requests by both Weidinger and Lehmann to withdraw from this exposed salient, less than 3km wide, were rejected.

The 14th was mainly sunny and the temperature climbed to 13° Celsius, drying the ground. On the 15th, whilst the rest of Das Reich continued to beat off repeated Soviet counter-attacks, Krag was finally given permission to withdraw his Companies from the canal bridgehead near Kaloz.

Strength returns on this day show the Hohenstaufen with thirty-five Panthers, twenty Mk IVs, thirty-two Jagdpanzers, twenty-five StuGs and 220 SPWs and armoured cars. 42% of these vehicles were, however, under short or long term repair. Das Reich had twenty-seven Panthers, twenty-two Mk IVs, twenty-eight Jagdpanzers and twenty-six StuGs on hand. Figures for SPWs and armoured cars and vehicles under repair are not available. The most surprising thing about these figures is that the

Hohenstaufen had six Panthers and eight MK IVs more than when it started the offensive and was only two Jagdpanzers and one StuG worse off and Das Reich was down only seven Panthers, two Mk IVs, one Jagdpanzer, three StuGs and thirty-eight armoured cars and SPWs – the latter despite the fighting at Heinrich Major. Two things are clear from these figures: first, the repair and resupply system was working well and secondly, the appalling ground conditions, as already stated a number of times, had prevented the deployment of the majority of the armoured vehicles.

What of the more successful I SS Panzer Corps during this period? The Leibstandarte's small bridgehead across the Sio canal at Simontornya was successfully defended throughout the 13th. There were numerous Soviet counter-attacks, all supported by tanks and aircraft. Readers will probably have noticed that this is the first time there has been any mention of Soviet tanks being deployed against Priess's Corps. Meanwhile, the 23rd Panzer Division had managed to clear Saregres on the Sarviz river but a subsequent attempt to force a crossing of the canal near Cece failed in the face of tenacious resistance. This ended Army Group South's hopes of supporting II SS Panzer Corps' advance with attacks from west of the Sarviz.

Whilst the Sixth Panzer Army persisted in its efforts to implement the basic strategy of Operation SPRING AWAKENING, the Soviet preparations for their own offensive were nearing completion. In addition to the Sixth Guards Tank Army[34] (Panzer Corps) already assembled just to the west of Budapest, another twenty-four Rifle Divisions, a Tank Corps (Panzer Division) and a Guards Mechanized Corps[35] (Panzer Division) were being made ready for the strike across the rear of Sepp Dietrich's command.

On 14 March the bridge across the Sio in Simontornya, laid by the Leibstandarte's SS Pioneers, was badly damaged by Soviet artillery fire and the Corps' armour and heavy weapons were forced to remain on the north bank. Nevertheless, during the afternoon SS Panzer-Grenadiers manage to expand the Simontornya bridgehead to some five square kilometres.

Meanwhile, the Soviets were attempting to establish their own bridgehead across the Sarviz canal in the Saregres sector and at Ozora, and it was these Soviet counter-attacks that were seen by all the senior German commanders as ominous signs of things to come. At Army Group and Army level, German intelligence had detected part of the Soviet build-up on the 13th, but the moves had been misinterpreted as local reinforcements and it was not until the evening of the 14th that the Army Group South War Dairy recorded:

Today's movements leave no doubt of the enemy's intentions. Based on the results from aerial observation, motorized columns of at least 3,000 vehicles are moving out of the rear area from Budapest ... to the south-west, most of them in the direction of Zamoly. His objective will be to cut the rear connections of the German forces [Sixth Panzer Army and III Panzer Corps] which have advanced from the narrow passage of Székesfehérvar, by an attack in the direction of Lake Balaton.

During 15 March I SS Panzer Corps continued to hold its slender bridgehead across the Sio but it was now clear to most German commanders that SPRING AWAKENING had failed. Sepp Dietrich recommended an immediate withdrawal to a suitable defensive line in the north of his area but this was ruled out by his superior, General Otto Wöhler, the commander of Army Group South. At 1510 hours, the latter gave his assessment of the situation to OKH. He pointed out that any attempt to advance farther south in the I SS Panzer Corps area would be 'inexpedient' owing to the hilly terrain and the Corps' exposed left flank. This was a major understatement. The ground to the south was not only hilly; it was broken, wooded and bounded on both sides by waterways – something which should have been foreseen when the original plan was made. Wöhler proposed therefore to leave the 23rd Panzer Division where it was in the Saregres sector and, after relieving I SS Panzer Corps on the Sio with I Cavalry Corps and a Hungarian Division, to move it north to a position behind II SS Panzer Corps and III Panzer Corps. All three Panzer Corps would then attack east, between Sarkeresztur and Gardony, towards the Danube, before turning south in accordance with the original plan. He estimated it would take four days to complete the necessary regrouping. OKH approved this plan, which was hardly surprising since it was both strategically and tactically superior to the original concept, but demanded that it be put into effect in three days, not four.

Although this revised concept was considered impracticable by most of the field commanders involved, the necessary orders were issued at 2300 hours and during the night the first units of I SS Panzer Corps were withdrawn from the battle area.

16 – 19 March
(Map 30)

On 16 March, as I SS Panzer Corps made its first withdrawals from the Simontornya bridgehead, two Soviet Armies[36] launched a major attack on a 20km front in the IV SS Panzer Corps sector between Székesfehérvar and the Vertes hills. Behind them stood the Sixth Guards Tank Army (Panzer Corps) and on their northern flank another Army[37] waited to join in the offensive. The immediate Soviet objectives were Tatabanya and Györ in the north and Varpalota and Veszprem in the south. The southern thrust was of course designed to cut off and destroy Dietrich's Sixth Panzer Army. Unbelievably, as late as 2300 hours on the same day, General Wöhler still believed he could implement his plan to attack east with his three Panzer Corps, and that same night Headquarters Sixth Panzer Army issued orders for the relief of I SS Panzer Corps during the following two nights. At 0120 hours on the 17th, however, General Guderian, Chief of Staff at OKH, recommended to Wöhler's Chief of Staff that preparations be put in hand for I SS Panzer Corps to attack north rather than east! At 0145 hours, in spite of Hitler's refusal to allow any changes to his master plan or to allow any major redeployments without his personal permission, the Chief of Staff Army Group South, Lieutenant General von Grolmann, instructed Dietrich to prepare I SS Panzer Corps for just such an attack.

Dawn on 17 March brought rain and a consequent worsening of the ground conditions. The progress of the Soviet offensive will be described in the next Chapter; suffice it to say at this stage that the overall situation was becoming critical for the Germans, not least because Hitler still refused to authorise the necessary redeployments.

In view of the increasingly critical situation in the north, during the morning of the 17th General Wöhler finally requested permission from OKH to use I SS Panzer Corps for an attack from the Varpalota area towards Zamoly – into the flank of the Soviet advance. This was followed by another request at 2145 hours for authority to withdraw II SS Panzer Corps behind I SS Panzer Corps as soon as it arrived in the vicinity of Székesfehérvar. Bittrich's Corps had continued to defend its Aba–Sarkeresztur (Map 29) sector during this period and was now dangerously exposed. Hitler eventually gave his permission for these deployments at 0140 hours on 18 March, and at 0200 hours Wöhler ordered Dietrich to move I SS Panzer Corps to the area north of Varpalota and subordinate it to Army Group Balck.

At 1600 hours Bittrich received detailed orders. He was to retain command of Das Reich and the Hohenstaufen but he was to give up the 44th Grenadier Division to III Panzer Corps, which would continue to hold the front with that Division and its own 1st and 3rd Panzer Divisions. The 6th Panzer Division (originally from Army Group South's reserve) was to come under his command and was to move directly to an area to the south-east of Kisbér with the task of preventing any Soviet moves towards Komarom on the Danube. Das Reich was to be withdrawn at once, but the Hohenstaufen was to stay in position until the following night (19th/20th) when it was to pull back through III Panzer Corps and re-assemble, with Das Reich, behind I SS Panzer Corps to the south-west of Székesfehérvar. Both Divisions would then move to an area north of

Kisbér, from where they would launch a counter-attack to the east. At this time Das Reich still had the equivalent of a strong Panzer Battalion – twenty-three Panthers, twenty-two Mk IVs, twenty-six StuGs and twenty-eight Jagdpanzers. Only 26% these vehicles, however, were combat-ready. The Hohenstaufen too possessed the equivalent of a weak Panzer Battalion. On 17 March it had thirteen Panthers, sixteen Mk IVs, eleven StuGs and eighteen Jagdpanzers on strength. These figures indicate that over the period of SPRING AWAKENING II SS Panzer Corps lost twenty-seven tanks, eight StuGs and one Jagdpanzer.

So ended the last offensive action of the Sixth Panzer Army.

NOTES

1. Weidinger, *Comrades to the End*, p. 380.
2. The LAH & HJ moved via Papa and Varoslöd and Zirc and Vesprem respectively.
3. Tiemann, *The Leibstandarte IV/2*, p. 211.
4. Tieke, *In the Firestorm of the Last Years of the War*, p. 376.
5. Ibid.
6. 21 Rifle Div.
7. 316 Rifle Div.
8. XXXIII Rifle Corps.
9. *The Frunze Military Academy Study of the Defence by Formations of XXX Rifle Corps of the Twenty-Sixth Army in the Balaton Defensive Operations* by Lt Col V F Yashin.
10. 108 Gds Rifle Div.
11. 110 Tk Bde of XVIII Tk Corps.
12. 32 Rifle Bde from XVIII Tk Corps.
13. Tieke, op. cit., p. 378.
14. As Note 9.
15. Ibid.
16. 21 Rifle Div.
17. XXXIII Rifle Corps.
18. V Gds Cavalry Corps.
19. Hill 159 is the highest point in the entire attack zone.
20. Weidinger, *Division Das Reich, Vol V*, p. 444.
21. 36, 68 & 108 Gds and 21, 155 & 206 Inf Divs.
22. 316 & 320 Inf Divs.
23. I Gds Mech & XVIII Tk Corps.
24. Radzievskiy, *Army Operations*, p. 205.
25. Ibid., p. 206. As mentioned in Chap XXIV, Tolbukhin's 17th Air Army had 965 aircraft on 6 Mar, but after the German attack he was reinforced, on orders from STAVKA, with additional aircraft from Malinovsky's 5th Air Army.
26. Ninth Gds Army and Sixth Gds Tk Army (Pz Corps).
27. Twenty-Sixth and Twenty-Seventh Armies.
28. Fourth and Ninth Gds Armies.
29. Tieke, op. cit., pp. 378–9.
30. Ibid., p. 451.

31. 202, 209, 233, 236 & 337 Inf Divs.
32. Ninth Gds Army.
33. Fourth Gds Army.
34. XXIII Tk Corps.
35. II Gds Mech Corps.
36. Fourth & Ninth Gds Armies.
37. Forty-Sixth Army.

CHAPTER XXXV

The Soviet Offensive

Introduction

(Map 31)

The Red Army assault between the Danube and Lake Balaton area on 16 March was carried out, in accordance with its tactical doctrine, by two Combined Arms Armies – the Fourth and Ninth. The Germans talk of 'approximately twenty [Russian] tanks per kilometre of attack front'[1], but in fact these Armies had very little armour. The Ninth Guards had no mechanized or tank corps (Panzer divisions) allocated to it and most of the Tank Corps[2] (Panzer Division) in the Fourth Guards Army was already committed in the fighting to the south-east of Lake Valencei.

These two Armies which, even at half strength, numbered some 100,000 men and 4,000 guns, attacked between Székesfehérvar and the Vertes hills in the IV SS Panzer Corps sector. Their aim was to cause maximum attrition and to create a wide breach through which armour could debouch. Only after this breach had been made, and when Marshal Tolbukhin was convinced that the ground conditions were suitable for armoured forces, would the massed tanks[3] of the Sixth Guards Tank Army (Panzer Corps) be released for the exploitation phase – across the rear of Dietrich's Sixth Panzer Army.

Despite all the careful and secret preparations, the attack against Gille's IV SS Panzer Corps, which included a Hungarian tank Division, was not a success. After some early reverses, the Germans and Hungarians managed to hold their ground and at the end of the first day the Russians had made little or no progress.

The following day, 17 March, a third Soviet Army[4] from Malinovsky's Second Ukrainian Front opened a new attack in the sector between the Vertes hills and the Danube, with Tata, Komarom and Györ as its immediate objectives. This Army had a Guards Mechanized Corps[5] (Panzer

Division) in support; at full strength, which is unlikely, it would have amounted to some 200 tanks and SUs. This attack was successful. Although the 2nd Hungarian Panzer Division and 3rd SS Panzer Division Totenkopf held their ground around Mor and Söred respectively on the 18th, and the 5th SS Panzer Division Wiking remained firm in and around Székesfehérvar, the single Hungarian 1st Hussar Division defending a 20km sector in the wooded Vertes hills was overwhelmed. In the ensuing breakthrough, Dad fell to the Soviets.

(Map 30)

On the day of this breakthrough, General Wöhler, the commander Army Group South, reorganised his command and issued new orders. With effect from 1400 hours on 19 March, Balck's Sixth Army was to assume responsibility for the sector between Lakes Valencei and Balaton and Sepp Dietrich's Sixth Panzer Army from the south-west tip of Lake Valencei to the Danube. Dietrich would thus become responsible for the area of the breakthrough. He was to take command of IV SS Panzer Corps covering the front from Mor to Székesfehérvar and the 6th Panzer Division and Third Hungarian Army between Mor and the Danube. He was to retain command of I SS Panzer Corps, but II SS Panzer Corps would only revert to him after it had disengaged from the fighting south-east of Székesfehérvar. The WWI sergeant-major and Hitler's former personal bodyguard was thus to become an Army Group commander! General Balck took over I Cavalry and III Panzer Corps together with the Second Hungarian Army and, as just mentioned, he was to command II SS Panzer Corps until it could disengage.

This decision – to change the command structure in the face of the Soviet offensive – seems extraordinary and ill judged. It has been described as 'not having many parallels in military history'. After all, it meant extracting Dietrich's I and II SS Panzer Corps (four Panzer Divisions) from another commander's area of responsibility and condemning I SS Panzer Corps to the defence of the Bakony forest and the mountains between Varpalota and the Marcal canal – a region totally unsuitable for armour. The administrative difficulties caused by this change were no less serious; for example, the General commanding Balck's Communication Zone was required to move his Headquarters and administrative units over 60km to the south, from near Györ to the Sarvar area.[6] A glance at the map, however, shows why this decision was made. Between the Danube and Lake Balaton there were, and still are, only two major routes leading west – one runs through Komarom and Györ to Vienna, and the other from Székesfehérvar to Janoshaza and then on to Körmend in a generally south-westerly direction. Since this latter route led away from southern Germany, it was obviously of lesser importance. Therefore, despite the disruption and complications of switching forces in the middle of a battle, it made complete sense to Hitler to use his trusted and still relatively powerful Waffen-SS Panzer Divisions on the route leading directly to Vienna, Linz and Munich (München) (Map 27).

The new command arrangements proved unsatisfactory before the end of the first day. Dietrich requested the return of I Cavalry Corps to his Panzer Army for use in wooded mountains where he was desperately short of infantry, and Balck asked for armoured support from I and IV SS Panzer Corps. Dietrich's request was turned down but Balck managed to retain the 5th SS Panzer Division Wiking.

The Soviets were surprised by the tenacity of the German and Hungarian defence in the first three days of their offensive and, as a consequence, they were forced to commit the Sixth Guards Tank Army (Panzer Corps) to battle before a breakthrough on a wide frontage had been achieved.

Author's Note

In order to understand fully what happened to Das Reich and the Hohenstaufen in the period following SPRING AWAKENING, we have to look at the larger picture and include the actions of the other Panzer Corps in Dietrich's Sixth Panzer Army – I SS Panzer Corps. Only an outline of its activities will be given but for those interested in a full description, details can be found in the author's book *Men of Steel: I SS Panzer Corps The Ardennes and Eastern Front 1944–45.*

Basically, from 20 March the four Waffen-SS Panzer Divisions of I and II SS Panzer Corps were spread across the front, from the Danube in the north to Lake Balaton in the south. Facing east, from left to right we find: Das Reich, the Hitlerjugend, the Leibstandarte and then the Hohenstaufen. Alongside, in between and even attached to these Divisions, there were other formations, such as the 6th Panzer and 44th Grenadier Divisions and elements of Gille's IV SS Panzer Corps, but their actions will only be touched upon.

Readers will probably have been surprised to read that whilst Das Reich ended up on the left flank, the Hohenstaufen was many kilometres away on the right. In the event, however, the ferocity of the Soviet offensive and the new German command arrangements led very quickly to the separation of the latter from II Panzer Corps and, just as this made life difficult and unsatisfactory for Bittrich and Stadler, so it complicates this history. In an attempt therefore to make things as simple as possible, the German front will be described from north to south and then in reverse, in the order: Das Reich, I SS Panzer Corps (Hitlerjugend, Leibstandarte), Hohenstaufen. This will be done for each phase of the withdrawal back to the borders of the Greater German Reich.

It is also important to understand that in the last few chaotic weeks of the war, it was inevitable that many unit records and war diaries would be lost or destroyed, or in some cases not kept at all. So it was with Das Reich and the Hohenstaufen – their War Diaries for this period do not exist and with the beginning of the Soviet offensive, our picture becomes less clear. Fewer details of the fighting are available. Every effort has been made to produce a comprehensive image but much reliance has had to be placed on individual memories and accounts, particularly those of Wilhelm Tieke, Otto Weidinger, Hubert Meyer and Ralf Tiemann[7], which may or may not be wholly accurate.

Das Reich: 19 – 21 March
(Map 31)

In the early evening of 19 March, Rudolf Lehmann gave orders for the forward units of Das Reich to disengage and commence their withdrawal towards Szabadbattyan. The 3rd Deutschland Regiment and the 2nd Battalion of the 4th SS Panzer-Grenadier Regiment encountered no problems in doing so, but in the Heinrich Major salient (Map 29) Kesten's tanks and Werner's SPW Battalion found it more difficult. A platoon of Panthers, however, under the command of SS Senior Sergeant Barkmann managed to cover the withdrawal of the rest of the force and in an amazingly successful operation all the wounded men and disabled tanks and SPWs were extracted. During the night of the 19th, Das Reich, with virtually all its equipment, reached a staging area just to the south-west of Székesfehérvar between Szabadbattyan and Ösi. Then, in an amazing onward move, the tanks drove another 45km to Herend, to the west of Veszprem, where they were loaded onto railway flatcars for an 80km journey through Papa to Györ – all this with the Soviet spearheads only about 40km to the east. But then the whole idea of moving a Division some 200km from one flank of an active front to the other, in a crisis situation and across the path of your enemy, is beyond the comprehension of most soldiers – not least this author.

On 18 March, just before the beginning of the withdrawal, the armoured strength of Das Reich was ninety-nine tanks, Jagdpanzers and assault guns – twenty-three Panthers, twenty-two Mk IVs, ten Jagdpanzers, eighteen Jagdpanzer IVs and twenty-six StuGs. Twenty-six heavy anti-tank guns were also on strength. But not all the tanks made it. Eight Panthers of the 4th SS Panzer Company, including Barkmann's platoon, after taking part in a local counter-attack with an unknown army unit, ran out of fuel. They eventually managed to join a KG of the Leibstandarte with which they fought until 28 March when, after blowing up their last two Panthers, the surviving crews managed to rejoin the Division.[8]

The new defensive area for Das Reich lay between Nagyigmand and

Kisbér. An advance guard consisting of Krag's 2nd SS Reconnaissance Battalion and SS Captain Dreike's 2nd SS Flak Battalion, with eighteen 88mm and nine twin-37mm guns, was sent ahead, directly through the Bakony forest and behind the Hitlerjugend, to take up emergency positions there. Fortunately, the 2nd SS Panzer-Grenadier Battalion of the Deutschland under SS Captain Mattusch, which had been unfit for participation in the SPRING AWAKENING offensive, was already in position north of Kisbér and this provided a firm base. In addition, the whole force was soon to be joined by the Reconnaissance Battalions of both the Hohenstaufen and 6th Panzer Divisions. They had been detached from their parent formations on the orders of Headquarters II SS Panzer Corps in order to provide the extra 'punch' and mobility needed to hold the front until the rest of Das Reich could arrive. Bittrich's Headquarters had by this time withdrawn to a small hamlet 12km to the south-west of Györ.

Dreike recalled later that the advance elements of Das Reich had been fortunate not to come under attack from the air during this move and only the delay imposed on the Russians in the Bakony forest (by the Hitlerjugend) had enabled it to be completed satisfactorily. The rest of the Division, following on behind, had been forced to make a huge flanking march of some 160km, behind I SS Panzer Corps, via Veszprem, Papa, Tét and Györ.

Weidinger's 4th SS Panzer-Grenadiers arrived during the latter part of the night and, although the Deutschland and 2nd SS Panzer Regiments were still missing, by dawn on the 20th Das Reich 'had closed the gap in the front at Kisbér'. According to Weidinger, Wisliceny's Regiment was involved in an attack from the area north of Varpalota in the direction of the Vertes mountains and was delayed for another twenty-four hours. No further details are available.

The 6th Panzer Division, which readers will recall was now part of II SS Panzer Corps, had arrived to the south of Das Reich during the 20th; but the overall frontage was too great for the number of troops available and this probably accounted for the loss of Kisbér during the night. On the afternoon of the 21st, however, the Reconnaissance forces, with direct fire support from the guns of the 2nd SS Flak Battalion, managed to recapture the small town. Dreike reported that when he and his men saw the place the next day they witnessed the results of Soviet butchery on the civilian population and this did much to strengthen their resolve to fight on to the end.[9]

Little did he or the other members of the Sixth Panzer Army know that only two days earlier their Führer had ordered a 'scorched earth' policy in their own beloved Homeland:

The battle should be conducted without consideration for our own population . . . Everything . . . which could be of immediate use to the enemy for the continuation of the fight [was to be destroyed] ... all industrial plants, all important electrical facilities, waterworks, gasworks . . .all food and clothing stores . . . all bridges, all railway installations, the postal system . . . also the waterways, all ships, all freight cars and all locomotives.

When Albert Speer allegedly protested, Hitler is said to have replied:

If the war is lost, the German nation will also perish. This fate is inevitable. There is no need to take into consideration the basic requirements of the people for continuing even a most primitive existence . . . Those who remain after the battle are those who are inferior; for the good will have fallen.[10]

The 'good' would, of course, include many members of the Waffen-SS.

I SS Panzer Corps: 18 – 20 March

By 1800 hours on 18 March, the Leibstandarte had completed its withdrawal from the Simontornya sector and was concentrated around Dég (Map 29). From there it set out to join the Hitlerjugend which had moved, under the cover of darkness, to a new concentration area south of Mor. Both Divisions were under orders to take part in a I SS Panzer Corps counter-attack – the Hitlerjugend, supported by the 356th Infantry Division (from III Panzer Corps), were aimed at Zamoly and the Leibstandarte at Csor. This grandiose scheme had little chance of implementation on the scale envisaged. Soon after the Hitlerjugend moved into its new positions, the first Soviet attacks developed in its sector. Balinka was held but farther south, the enemy occupied Isztimer. More bad news came when stragglers from the 3rd SS Panzer Division Totenkopf began arriving at the Divisional Command Post at Balinka around midday on the 19th and aerial reconnaissance confirmed that the enemy had broken through that Division south of Mor. Meanwhile, the Leibstandarte, far from preparing for its part in the planned Corps counter-attack, was finding it difficult even to assemble in the Inota area and, during the evening of the 19th, it too found itself fighting off a heavy attack some 4km to the east of Varpalota. The need to prevent a Soviet advance along the Székesfehérvar–Varpalota–Veszprem road was obvious and Kumm's men were ordered to counter-attack before first light on the 20th and push the enemy away from this vital approach.

The Leibstandarte counter-attack towards Csor and the hills to its north on the 20th stalled in the face of intense Russian defensive fire. The enemy then counter-attacked along the Székesfehérvar–Varpalota road forcing the Division to withdraw to the eastern edge of Varpalota by evening.

Hitlerjugend: 20 – 21 March

The ground where the Hitlerjugend was fighting was forested and mountainous. This made it the most difficult axis for the Soviets in their advance westwards and, not surprisingly, they concentrated their main efforts on outflanking the German defence in the open rolling country to the north and south of the Balinka–Zirc road – the only major route through the area and the one being defended by the Hitlerjugend.

The Hitlerjugend's counter-attack began at 0500 hours on the 20th and initially made some progress. Unfortunately for Kraas, however, a coincidental Russian move along the Bodajk–Balinka road hit the flank of the advance and the German attack was brought to a halt. The Russians then continued to advance on the Division's left flank and, during the night of the 20th, a village 6km west of Mor was abandoned by Hungarian troops.

During the 21st the 2nd Hungarian Panzer Division defending the sector to the north of the Balinka–Szapar road in the Acsteszer area, was pushed back to the south-west. This exposed the Hitlerjugend's left flank. The resulting threat, combined with Russian attacks on both sides of the Balinka–Szapar–Zirc road westwards from Isztimer and from the north-east, caused a withdrawal that evening directly to Szapar and the important hill village of Bakonynana. The Hungarians abandoned Csatka at about the same time. Meanwhile, more Soviet troops advanced from Isztimer towards Tés, which fell during the afternoon. Three counter-attacks were launched in quick succession – the first at 1700 and the last at 2030 hours. They all failed.

During the late afternoon another Soviet group moved from the area north-east of Tés and approached Szapar. By the evening there was no longer a continuous German front in the Bakony region. The weakened Hitlerjugend was defending a frontage of some 16km running from just west of Tés, through Szapar, to a position 2km north-west of Csesznek.

Leibstandarte: 21 March

Meanwhile, on the 21st, the Leibstandarte came under heavy attack in the Varpalota sector. Its right flank was, as we shall hear, being covered by elements of the Hohenstaufen, in action near Pétfürdö and Ösi (Map 29), to the south-east of the town.

The first infantry and tank attacks, strongly supported by fighter-bombers, came soon after dawn and intensified throughout the day. Soon the Russians began to outflank the town to the north and it became obvious that Varpalota could not be held. The withdrawal to new defensive positions 2km east of Öskü and around Hajmaskér began at about

1800 hours. By now it was apparent that the other SS Corps under Dietrich's command, Gille's IV SS Panzer Corps, had lost its cohesion. Some sub-units of the Totenkopf were attached to the Hitlerjugend and others were fighting with the Leibstandarte. The 5th SS Panzer Division Wiking, which had been fighting a quite separate battle in Székesfehérvar, was forced to give up the town in the evening. It was clear that the southern part of the Sixth Panzer Army's front was beginning to disintegrate.

Hohenstaufen: 19 – 23 March
(Map 29)

The withdrawal of Stadler's Division did not go as planned. Owing to heavy Soviet pressure, particularly in the form of artillery and mortar fire, only Recke's 9th SS Reconnaissance Battalion and the 2nd Battalion of SS Lieutenant Colonel Seela's 19th SS Panzer-Grenadier Regiment managed to pull back during the night of the 19th. Then, with daylight, came an attack by '1,200 Red Army soldiers, supported by numerous tanks'[11], which had to be beaten off before any more units could be withdrawn. Ten T-34s were claimed in this fighting.

It was after dark on the 20th therefore before the Hohenstaufen was finally assembled in the Szabadbattyan area. By this time the situation pertaining when General Wöhler's original orders had been issued had changed drastically. The Soviets had bypassed Székesfehérvar and reached a line only just short of Varpalota and Nadasladany. The 5th SS Panzer Division Wiking in Székesfehérvar was therefore in danger of being cut off, as were a large number of German troops still to the south-east of the city and there was now no hope of the Hohenstaufen catching up with II SS Panzer Corps. Stadler was told that he was to come under the command of Gille's IV SS Panzer Corps and was to counter-attack north-east from a line running from Szabadbattyan through Nadasladany to Ösi. Readers will perhaps have noticed that this took the Hohenstaufen out of Dietrich's Sixth Panzer Army and placed it firmly under its old enemy – Hermann Balck.

The 9th SS Reconnaissance and 9th SS Flak Battalions were already in action around Ösi on the left wing of the designated start line for the counter-attack and, as we have heard, the Leibstandarte was under heavy attack in the Varpalota sector just to the north. When Soviet troops reached the railway yard to the south-east of Varpalota, the Hohenstaufen found itself defending the line rather than attacking from it. By midnight Telkamp's tanks, Jagdpanzers and StuGs, the 19th and most of the 20th SS Panzer-Grenadier Regiments were firmly in defence on the right flank of the Leibstandarte. Following the wounding of Geiger, SS Lieutenant Colonel Hofmann was now in command of the 20th Regiment.

The 21st of March saw the men of the Hohenstaufen struggling to hold open an escape route for their comrades still in Székesfehérvar and others of III Panzer Corps still south-east of that city and Lake Balaton. Ösi was lost after a costly battle, but fifteen giant IS (Stalin) tanks were knocked out by eight of Telkamp's Jagdpanthers in ambush positions just south of the village, and a total of seventy T-34 and IS tanks were claimed by the 9th SS Panzer Regiment during the day's fighting.[12] Möller's 9th SS Pioneer Battalion, one of the last of the Division's units to withdraw from the old defensive line at Sarosd, moved back through Polgardi, literally alongside advancing Soviets troops, and managed to reach and take up a position in Berhida. North of that village, Hofmann's 20th Grenadiers fought desperately to hold back Ivan, as the Russians were nicknamed, and SS Major Bergrath's 9th SS Flak guns took a heavy toll around Pétfürdö. At 1800 hours the Hohenstaufen was holding a line from Pétfürdö, through Berhida to a point somewhere north of Küngös. The Grenadiers of the Division had been forced to give ground and had suffered heavy losses, including the commander of the 20th Regiment, but their sacrifice had not been in vain. As the history of the 5th SS Panzer Division Wiking says:

> The Hohenstaufen, under its commander, Sylvester Stadler, played a decisive part in the fortunate breakout of Wiking. Contrary to orders, Stadler had pushed his front as far forward as possible to the northern part of Lake Balaton in order to hold the sector open for the Division.[13]

Wilhelm Tieke has described the actions of the Hohenstaufen in the period 22 to 23 March as 'worthy of any of the previous deeds of the Waffen-SS in the war'. The fighting took place initially around the areas of Pétfürdö and Berhida and then Vilonya and Papkeszi. In what was said to have been a 'murderous defensive battle with far superior Russian tank forces south of Pétfürdö', SS Captain Seiler's 1st SS Flak Battery lost all its guns except one on the 22nd and then fought on as an infantry KG. At the same time, SS Lieutenant Gropp's 2nd SS Flak Battery with four 88mm and three 37mm guns and some 200 Grenadiers of the 19th Regiment fought off no fewer than three separate Soviet 'massed' tank attacks, the first involving forty T-34s, and were subjected to an attack by twenty-two fighter-bombers. Gropp, of Arnhem fame, was wounded by mortar fire and his Battery, after losing two of its 88mm guns during the day, then found itself cut off. KG Seiler had by then joined him and in a scene reminiscent of a Hollywood Western, the combined group escaped by simply driving flat out through the sleeping Russians soldiers behind them.

Meanwhile, the surviving tanks of the 2nd SS Panzer Battalion and SPWs of the 3rd SS Panzer-Grenadier Battalion of the 20th Regiment held the high ground east of Berhida and linked up with units of the 23rd Panzer Division to the north of Polgardi, while other armoured sub-units of Telkamp's 9th SS Panzer Regiment covered the open flank north of Papkeszi. This allowed SS Lieutenant Colonel Seela to withdraw the remnants of the 19th and 20th SS Panzer-Grenadier Regiments to new positions on the forested high ground west of Berhida.

At 1600 hours on the 22nd, SS Colonel Karl Ullrich, commander of the Wiking, reached the Hohenstaufen's Headquarters at Papkeszi and told Stadler that not all his units had managed to get out of Székesfehérvar and that he was sure other units were still trapped inside the 'Pocket'. Stadler had just received orders from the commander of I Cavalry Corps, under whose command he was now operating, to withdraw to positions farther west at midnight. He decided to hold his present line. Flares were fired throughout the night to guide those attempting to escape, and by midday on the 23rd a complete Army artillery battalion, a 44th Grenadier Division KG and an estimated 1,700 men from the 1st and 3rd Panzer and Wiking Divisions had managed to reach friendly lines. Georg Maier, a former SS Lieutenant Colonel and Chief Operations officer of the Sixth Panzer Army, wrote in his book *Drama zwischen Budapest und Vienna*:

> The 9th SS Panzer Division fought to the point of self sacrifice . . . It held the line . . . together with elements of the 4th Cavalry Division and permitted troops . . . to escape destruction through a narrow, 2.5 to 3km, corridor. The corridor not only lay under strong enemy artillery fire, but also machine-gun fire.

As darkness fell, Viloyna and Papkeszi were abandoned and the Hohenstaufen began its withdrawal towards Veszprem (Map 31). Unfortunately, the Leibstandarte was already in the process of pulling out of the city towards Marko and the Hohenstaufen was about to be forced south-west and away from its comrades in the Sixth Panzer Army. The only good news was that during the withdrawal Telkamp discovered a fuel dump prepared for demolition. He allegedly took possession of it at pistol point and obtained enough fuel for all his vehicles and many others in the Division.

Leibstandarte: 22 – 23 March
(Map 31)

On 22 March the situation worsened considerably with a Soviet thrust by a tank brigade (Panzer Battalion) with infantry support down the main road from Varpalota towards Veszprem. Since substantial German groups were still trying to fight their way out from the south-east, it remained essential to keep the way open to and through this important communication centre. Thus, whilst the Leibstandarte fought on to the north-east of Veszprem, the 4th Division of I Cavalry Corps struggled to defend a 5km line running north-east from Balatonkenese to Küngös and, as we have just heard, the Hohenstaufen defended from there to north of Berhida. These actions allowed substantial elements of four German Divisions[14] to escape.

In the case of the Leibstandarte, the Soviet attack launched north of the main Veszprem road, through Hajmaskér, succeeded in splitting the defence and pushing part of the Division north-west towards Zirc, and encircling the southern part in the Öskü area. In the afternoon the Divisional commander gave orders for a breakout through Liter and the establishment of a new front on the eastern edge of Veszprem. This was completed under the cover of darkness by 2300 hours.

The Soviet assault on Veszprem on the 23rd was launched along three separate axes – from Balatonkenese, from Vilonya and from Hajmaskér. The Leibstandarte was responsible for the eastern and north-eastern approaches, while elements of the Hohenstaufen and 4th Cavalry Divisions covered those from the south and south-east. Twenty Russian tanks were claimed in the day's fighting, but as Otto Kumm, the Leibstandarte commander, later described it: 'The Division was thrown out of Veszprem by an armoured attack and pushed back to the eastern edge of Marko [7km to the north-west]'.[15]

Hitlerjugend: 22 – 23 March

The Soviet attack in the Hitlerjugend sector continued soon after dawn on the 22nd. Part of the Division was soon ordered to pull back to Zirc, whilst another part was pulled back to Dudar. Some of the Companies are said to have consisted of fewer than forty men. Towards evening Dudar came under heavy attack and another withdrawal was authorised.

The ever widening gap between the Hitlerjugend and the Leibstandarte was now causing serious concern and a force of the two Grenadier Battalions was sent on to Lokut to protect the southern flank.

On the northern flank sub-units of the Totenkopf Division were pushed back towards the Zirc–Csesznek road during the 22nd, but the 12th SS Reconnaissance Battalion is said to have restored the situation before dark.

The skies were clear on the 23rd, the weather warm and sunny and by now the ground had dried out, making cross-country movement much easier. The Hitlerjugend conducted a fighting withdrawal from Zirc back to Penzesgyör. On the left flank, however, the Russians broke through the Totenkopf blocking positions near Csesznek, threatening the Hitlerjugend's only remaining withdrawal route, Penzesgyör–Bakonykoppany–Beb, from the north-east.

Das Reich: 22 – 23 March
(Map 29)

On the 22nd Krag's 2nd and Recke's 9th SS Reconnaissance Battalions were detached to assist the 6th Panzer Division defending the sector south of Das Reich around Kisbér and Dreike's SS Flak Battalion assumed full responsibility for the right flank of the Division between Csép and Ete.

The intensity of the Soviet attacks on this day caused the 2nd SS Artillery Regiment to run short of ammunition and Dreike's Flak guns had to be called upon to fire final protective barrages. The Battalion also claimed that it shot down its 251st and last enemy aircraft. As Weidinger puts it: 'They are still waiting even today for their celebration'.

In the northern part of the sector, the 4th Der Führer Regiment, after beating off a strong attack supported by twenty-five tanks at Kisigmand, made a partial withdrawal in the late evening behind the Conco stream at Nagyigmand. Fortunately for Lehmann, the bulk of Wisliceny's 3rd SS Panzer-Grenadier Regiment caught up during the day and went into position alongside Mattusch's 2nd Battalion on the right of Der Führer, and Weidinger's 1st SS Panzer-Grenadier Battalion, which had also been unfit for SPRING AWAKENING, re-joined his Regiment. The Grenadier Regiments were holding frontages of some 14km each, which necessitated all Battalions being in the line and none in depth or reserve. The following day SS Captain Engelmann's 1st/4th SS Panzer-Grenadier Battalion suffered terrible casualties in its first action on the right flank of Der Führer but five Russian tanks were claimed and the line held.

The General Situation: 24 March
(Map 31)

Let us look for a moment at the whole German line from north to south as dawn broke on 24 March, a day that was to be unusually clear and warm with temperatures above 20° Celsius. The 356th Infantry Division, under command II SS Panzer Corps, had been brought right up to the left flank and was holding the sector between the Danube and the most northern units of Das Reich at Kisigmand. The rest of Lehmann's Division was deployed from Nagyigmand through Ete, to just north of Kisbér. Lieutenant General Freiherr von Waldenfels' 6th Panzer Division was holding the eastern part of the Kisbér–Gic road, and the Hungarians and the remnants of the Totenkopf were to the west of Csesznek with weak links to the Hitlerjugend in temporary positions at Penzesgyör and Lokut. The Leibstandarte had just been 'thrown out of Veszprem' towards Marko and the Hohenstaufen was attempting to establish some sort of defence immediately to the south and south-west of Veszprem.

(Map 30)

The 24th of March was to be the last day in the battle of the Bakony forest. From Lake Balaton, through Veszprem to Zirc, and then on to Kisbér and Komarom on the Danube, the Soviet Armies stood poised to break out into the great western Hungarian Plain. The Forty Sixth Army was attacking immediately south of the Danube, with Györ as its primary objective; it then planned to advance north-west, past Lake Neusiedler, towards Vienna. On the left flank, the Twenty Sixth Army had the mission of advancing from Veszprem to seize Szombathely on the far side of the Raba river. The main thrust, however, was in the centre. Here the Fourth and Ninth Guards Armies, strongly reinforced by the Sixth Guards Tank Army (Panzer Corps), were being directed through Papa towards Sopron and Wiener Neustadt. The Leibstandarte and Hitlerjugend, now Panzer Divisions in name only, were standing in their path and they had no chance of stopping them – indeed, as in Normandy the previous August, they were facing annihilation.

Das Reich: 24 – 27 March

(Map 31)

During the 24th the Forty-Sixth Army launched strong attacks with tanks and infantry across the Komarom–Nagyigmand–Ete road. The German line held until midday but then Kisigmand fell and a further break-through between Ete and Csép could only be held on the line of the Komarom–Kisbér railway and Conco stream(Map 29). On the right flank of II SS Panzer Corps front, the 6th Panzer Division was forced to give up all the ground to the south of the Kisbér–Papa railway line, and Gic and Bakonytamsi were lost. Similarly on the left flank, a Soviet force including forty tanks broke through the 356th Infantry Division's defences north-east of Kisigmand and were only prevented from reaching Komarom with the greatest difficulty.

Das Reich stood firm throughout the daylight hours of the 26th, but at 2100 hours it disengaged and withdrew to an area astride Rétalap. This withdrawal, and that of the 6th Panzer Division to positions due south of Györ, became necessary when Soviet armoured forces broke through farther south and, after advancing 20km and capturing Tét, ended the day threatening the Marcal and Raba crossings south-west of Györ and the withdrawal routes of II SS Panzer Corps.

It was during this period that the Divisional Escort Company, under the command of SS Lieutenant Tychsen, the brother of the famous commander of the 2nd SS Panzer Regiment killed in Normandy, was virtually annihilated. The remnants, amounting to no more than a platoon, joined up with Krag's 2nd SS Reconnaissance Battalion which was still with the 6th Panzer Division. One of Krag's officers, SS Lieutenant Auer, also died of wounds received from multiple rocket fire at this time.

According to Otto Weidinger, as Das Reich continued its withdrawal to the westwards on the 27th, it received a major reinforcement of about 2,800 men intended for, but unable to join, the Hitlerjugend Division.

Hitlerjugend: 24 – 27 March

By first light on the 24th, the combat elements of the Hitlerjugend had taken up new positions on a high wooded ridge just to the east of Penzesgyör, with orders to hold there for at least twenty-four hours in order to allow the administrative columns of the Division to escape. At 2000 hours, however, orders were received for a further withdrawal to Bakonykoppany. The sub-units of the Totenkopf on the left flank were to conform by pulling back to Papateszer. These moves were occasioned by a Soviet breakthrough between the Leibstandarte and Balck's Sixth Army which threatened Papa and the crossings of the Marcal canal at Marcaltö. The German front in Hungary was beginning to disintegrate.

On the 25th the situation in the Hitlerjugend sector went from bad to worse. By midday the Russians had taken Papateszer and Csot, and during the afternoon they attacked Vanyola. Thereafter they swung south and took Beb. Proposals that the Hitlerjugend should adopt a new front east of Papa or even try to defend the town itself were quickly rejected. On the flat, featureless ground between the Bakony forest and the Raba river there were no obstacles and few places suitable for defence. Furthermore, most of the tanks and other armoured vehicles that might have operated effectively in this area had by now been lost through enemy action or mechanical breakdown.

(Map 32)

By the morning of the 26th, the Organisation Todt[16] had prepared for demolition the bridges over the Marcal canal and Raba river at Marcaltö and Szany, and by midnight a new blocking line had been established on, and to the west of, the river. The Hitlerjugend was in the sector between Szany and Vag with a weak, so-called Panzer Division[17], holding a small bridgehead at Marcaltö. The next day, however, the Soviets penetrated into the bridgehead and by late afternoon the Germans had been forced to give up the east banks of both the canal and the Raba river. A similar situation was developing 9km to the north at Morichida where the 1st Hungarian Mountain Brigade was holding another bridgehead. By the evening it had been lost and the Russians were across the Raba in Arpas.

Leibstandarte: 24 – 27 March
(Map 31)

The bulk of the Leibstandarte was forced to evacuate Marko during the early hours of the 24th and moved back on the axis of the Varoslöd road. A smaller, but substantial element[18], separated from the rest of the Division by the Russian attacks, had already been pushed to the north-west and, by the end of the day, it was defending the south-eastern approaches to Papa in the Hitlerjugend sector.

Throughout the 24th the main body of the Leibstandarte tried to set up a series of delaying positions at, and between, Herend and Varoslöd; but each time they were bypassed. As darkness fell, and after repulsing a frontal attack east of Varoslöd, the Soviet advance was halted, 'albeit temporarily', in a blocking position running from Kislöd to east of Ajka.

Meanwhile, Soviet forces were able to pour through the widening gap between the Leibstandarte and the Hitlerjugend. Otto Kumm claimed afterwards that he met Hugo Kraas, the Hitlerjugend commander, during the day to discuss the dangerous gap between their two Divisions. With a combined frontage of over 40km, they agreed there was little they could do about it and that Soviet penetrations between their respective 'strongpoints' were inevitable. Kumm also said that advance parties of the 1st Volks Mountain Division had arrived on the 24th with the mission of taking over his part of the front.

The urgent need to close the gap in the Leibstandarte's sector between Kislöd and Tapolcafö was finally recognised on the 25th and Headquarters Army Group South gave permission for the Leibstandarte to be withdrawn to the Papa area as soon as it could be relieved by the 1st Volks Mountain Division. This was achieved during the day, and by 1600 hours the Division had assembled near Devecser. Unfortunately, at about this time a Soviet attack broke through the 1st Volks Mountain Division's slender defences and this led to accusations that the LAH had withdrawn before a proper relief had been completed. This was to have unfortunate repercussions. The Division was fortunate to get out of Devecser before it too fell in the early evening to Soviet forces moving rapidly north-west through the wide valley south of Ajka. The following day they advanced a further 16km to the west, before being halted by the 1st Volks Mountain Division on the Marcal canal just east of Janoshaza.

(Map 32)

The 26th was another bad day for the Leibstandarte. Its various KGs tried to hold the line of the road running from Devecser to Papa, but were soon outflanked to the south and in danger of being encircled; at midday they started to withdraw and by last light they, like their comrades in the Hitlerjugend, were west of the Marcal Canal. Once there, in the area north-west of Celldömolk, they were at least able to link up at last with the part of the Division which had become separated in the Papa area and was already in position south of Kenyeri.

By the morning of the 27th, the Soviets had closed up to the Marcal canal on a wide front and had achieved their first crossings near Celldömolk. At this point the German defence seems to have been powerless to stem their advance, and by midday on the 27th the Leibstandarte had been pushed back from the line of the Celldömolk–Kenyeri road to, and across, the Raba river.

Hohenstaufen: 24 – 27 March

(Map 30)

I Cavalry Corps with five badly depleted Divisions under its command (3rd and 4th Cavalry, the Hohenstaufen, 44th Grenadier and 23rd Panzer) was by this time attempting to hold the front between Veszprem and Lake Balaton on the approximate line of the Veszprem to Balatonfüred road. IV SS Corps was on its left.

During the morning of the 24th, the Soviets broke through the German defences to the south-east of Veszprem and those covering the Veszprem–Tapolca road. There are few details of the fighting but it seems that each time the Germans established any form of defence the Russians outflanked them. This is hardly surprising since the first 20km of the 10km-wide valley through which the Tapolca road runs is open rolling country with no obstacles.

A dramatic event at this time was the arrival of General Hermann Balck at Stadler's Headquarters. It is said that when the latter attempted to report the current situation of his Division, Balck cut him off and alleged that one of the Hohenstaufen's Pioneer companies had run away in the face of the enemy. He went on to demand that the Hohenstaufen should hold its line regardless of circumstances. Needless to say, Stadler defended his men, but when he pointed out that neither the Führer nor the Fatherland would be served by the senseless sacrifice of his Division, Balck lost his temper and threatened to court-martial him if he disobeyed 'a Führer Order'! The two men parted on the worst possible terms.

By dawn on the 26th, the Hohenstaufen was defending Nagyvaszony,

20km south-west of Veszprem and 12km north of Lake Balaton, but some forty Russian tanks broke its defensive line during the morning and by last light the Hohenstaufen had been forced back to Tapolca, with the 3rd Cavalry Division on its left flank and 44th Grenadiers on the right.

On the 27th the Soviets struck north-west in the open country astride Tapolca and, rather than be cut off, the Germans had to withdraw again. The Hohenstaufen pulled back to the hills north-east of Keszthely at the western end of Lake Balaton. The link with IV SS Panzer Corps and the Sixth Panzer Army was finally severed.

The Cuff Band Order

(Map 30)

Far away in his Berlin Bunker, Adolf Hitler was completely unaware of the real situation in the Army Group South operational area and had no idea that his prized Waffen-SS Panzer Divisions had already been decimated and were in the process of being routed. As far as he was concerned the front on 26 March, although under pressure, was holding on a line drawn from Komarom on the Danube, through the Bakony forest, to a point about midway on the north shore of Lake Balaton – his information was twenty-four hours out of date. It is hardly surprising therefore that when Army Group South asked OKH for permission to withdraw behind the Marcal canal and for II SS Panzer Corps to pull back into a smaller bridgehead around Györ, he refused and ordered that not one metre of ground was to be given up without a fight. The Führer's refusal reached General Wöhler at 1800 hours – by which time of course I SS Panzer Corps had already withdrawn across the canal! According to General Guderian:

> During the briefing, the Führer was horrified by the plan to occupy a front on the Marcal canal. The front would only become longer [this was true – 50% longer] and would not be able to be held [this was in fact what happened] ... The Führer was beside himself about the SS Panzer Divisions.[19]

Long after the war, SS Lieutenant Colonel Otto Günsche, a member of the Leibstandarte and Hitler's Adjutant in March 1945, gave his recollections of events at this extraordinary briefing:

> He [Hitler] expressed his bitterness against the leadership in harsh words – especially that of the Waffen-SS formations and even his own Leibstandarte. It was a horrible situation when ... the Führer revoked the right of the LAH to wear his name on their cuff bands. Everyone

present grew silent. Then Reichsmarschall Goering, who was not held in particular favour at that time, said something to the effect that the Waffen-SS, especially the LAH, had fought bravely on all fronts since the start of the war and had already lost several times its authorised strength. He regarded this measure as unjust and a betrayal of the men, officers and especially Sepp Dietrich ... Himmler [Head of the Waffen-SS] spoke no words in defence of the Divisions of the Sixth Panzer Army.[20]

Hitler's anger manifested itself early on the 27th in the form a teletyped message to Headquarters Sixty Panzer Army. It stated that the Führer did not believe that his troops had fought as the situation had demanded and that consequently he was stripping all Waffen-SS Divisions in the Sixth Panzer Army of their armbands.

SS Lieutenant Colonel Georg Maier, the officer who received the message at Dietrich's Headquarters, said later:

Filled with anger and indignation, I was on the verge of losing my self control ... when the door opened and Sepp Dietrich came in. I reported, briefed on the morning situation and handed over to him the shocking teletyped message ... He read, turned away slowly and bent over the map table, resting on it with both hands in such a way that I could not see his face. He was deeply shocked and moved, and it took him a long time to rally again. Then, after a long interval, still bent over the table, he said in an unusually quiet, almost fragile voice, which reflected deepest disappointment and bitterness: 'This is the thanks for everything.'

Finally he stood up, looked at me with moist eyes, pointed at his sleeve stripe and said briefly: 'This will be kept on. . . . You won't pass on the message to the Corps; inform Kraemer now; we will discuss it when I get back.' ... Shaking his head, he climbed into his car and drove to the front to his soldiers.[21]

Although Dietrich told his Corps commanders not to pass on or implement the Führer order, the message soon got out – according to Georg Maier, through Army Group South and Balck's Headquarters. In fact it had no practical significance since all cuff bands in the fighting units had been removed before the move to Hungary as part of the deception plan. In terms of morale, however, the veterans who had survived Russia, Normandy and the Ardennes were deeply shocked – in some cases it ended their loyalty to their Commander-in-Chief. On the other hand, their loyalty to one another and to their unit – their last Heimat, as some called it – became that much stronger.

After the war, a number of former senior members of the Leibstandarte branded General Balck, the commander of the Sixth Army, as the scape-goat for the infamous Order of 27 March. They claimed, probably with some justification, that it was Balck who had complained to General Wöhler that his Waffen-SS units suffered from weak command and control, lack of discipline and poor reporting, and that Wöhler had passed these comments on to Guderian, who in turn informed Hitler. It is interesting that, even after this shattering insult, these men could not bring themselves to wholly blame their Führer.

The General Situation: 28 – 29 March

By first light on 28 March, the Soviets had established a significant bridge-head across the Raba at Sarvar, and the following day elements of the Ninth Guards Army, supplemented by tanks of the Sixth Guards Tank Army (Panzer Corps), reached Acsad. Farther south, the Twenty-Sixth and Twenty-Seventh Armies had broken through at Szombathely, Kör-mend and Zalaegerszeg and were approaching the borders of the Third Reich itself. The separation of the Sixth and Sixth Panzer Armies was complete. The thrust to Zalaegerszeg threatened to encircle not only I Cavalry Corps (and the Hohenstaufen) but the whole of the Second Panzer Army[22], trapped between the south shore of Lake Balaton and the Drava and Mura rivers (Map 33). By the evening of the 29th, a fortnight after the start of the offensive, Soviet troops were beginning to reach designated German defensive positions before the Germans themselves – there was no longer an identifiable German front-line.

Then at last, at 1925 hours on the 29th, a 'Führer Decision' finally arrived at the Headquarters of Army Group authorising a phased withdrawal to what was called the Reichsschutzstellung – the Reich Guard Position. This followed the approximate line of Austria's eastern border. With it came also the alarming news that Hitler had replaced General Guderian as Chief of the OKH with General Krebs. As Georg Maier put it:

The news . . . was received with consternation by the front line troops, particularly the Panzer formations . . . who saw in the Panzer leader Guderian an illuminating example. Faith in the senior leadership dropped further.[23]

Hohenstaufen: 28 March – 7 April
(Map 33)

On 28 and 29 March, the Hohenstaufen, with the 3rd Cavalry and 23rd Panzer Divisions on its left flank and the 16th SS Panzer-Grenadier Division, part of the Second Panzer Army, defending south of Lake Balaton, was steadily forced back towards the Zala river. This river, running north–south just to the west of the Lake was a considerable obstacle and good defensive positions were available on the forested ridges immediately to its east and west. The Germans, however, were given no time to occupy them and on the night of the 30th the Soviets made a significant break-through and the withdrawal turned first into a retreat and then into a rout. The Russians were often in between and to the west of the German columns. Sylvester Stadler wrote later that as he looked for a new location for his Command Post in a village called Sarmellek, he was welcomed not by his own troops but by a group of T-34s with mounted infantry. Eight tanks of his 2nd SS Panzer Regiment and some SPW mounted SS Panzer-Grenadiers of the 20th Regiment, acting as a Divisional rearguard, were forced to fight their way through the village. They lost two unspeci-fied vehicles but claimed twelve T-34s. On the river line itself, the 9th SS Pioneer Battalion prepared hasty demolitions but lost a Company commander, SS Lieutenant Meier, and a Platoon commander in the fight-ing, both dying of their wounds.

At 1500 hours on the 31st, the Hohenstaufen began its final retreat to the Reich Guard Position, some 60km away. By 2 April it had withdrawn to another forested ridge just to the west of Söjtör, where it took up a temporary position. Meanwhile the 3rd Cavalry and 23rd Panzer Div-isions had been forced back to an east–west line running just a few kilometres south of Zalaegerszeg. Between the 3rd and the 6th, the now frantic withdrawal continued through thick forests and rolling country-side, to Paka and Lenti and then on to the flat plain at Murska Sobota (present-day Slovenia). On the 7th the Hohenstaufen was ordered to take up its final positions near Bad Radkersburg on the north bank of the Mura river. It was now part of the Second Panzer Army and over 150km away from its parent Corps – II SS Panzer (see Map 27).

According to Stadler:

> We were to occupy part of the Reich Guard Position, a concept new to us – permanent defensive positions, sited in depth with the Homeland behind us. The enemy no longer behind our backs, but in front. After the traumas of the retreat, this gave us impetus, strength and courage. Any further retreat was simply unthinkable. Here was where the final battle had to be fought, probably to the bitter end. These and similar thoughts stirred the men as the Division set out to occupy the final position.[24]

Unfortunately, his men were in for a shock – the Russians were already in some of the positions. Seela's weary and depleted SS Panzer-Grenadiers, his two Regiments amounting, according to Tieke, to little more than a normal Battalion each, cleared them out. Many drowned in the river as they fled and sixty or seventy were captured. It was the last attack of the Hohenstaufen. On the completion of its withdrawal, the Division had an armoured strength of just fifteen Panthers and eight Mk IVs.

I SS Panzer Corps: 28 March – 1 April
(Map 32)

By first light on 28 March, the Soviets, as we have heard, had established a significant bridgehead across the Raba at Sarvar. Inevitably, their tanks, cavalry and infantry pushed into the right flank of the Leibstandarte, causing it to pull back towards Vasegerszeg. In the afternoon and evening more Soviets forces were observed moving north-west from Hegyfalu and the danger of I SS Panzer Corps being outflanked became obvious. By the 29th the Corps was facing annihilation. Its only hope was to pull back as quickly as possible to the protection of the Reich Guard Position.

The Leibstandarte fought desperate battles all day as it fell back from Vasegerszeg towards Lövö, making maximum use of the extensive forests which lie to the south and south-west of the village of Ivan.

In the Hitlerjugend sector, Soviet troops captured Gyoro so that Kraas's men too were forced back into the woods area north-east of Ivan.

The withdrawal continued on 30 March – a day of sunshine and rain and temperatures of 16° Celsius. The bulk of the LAH ended the day around Nikitisch (for the first time it was fighting within the territory of the Third Reich), and during the afternoon a smaller element pulled back to Sopronkövesd.

The Hitlerjugend, lacking contact with both the LAH on its right flank and the Totenkopf on its left, tried to hold an 8km line running east from Lövö – a position which was nothing more than a line drawn on a map and which had no defensible features.

On the northern flank of I SS Panzer Corps, aerial reconnaissance reported 100 Soviet tanks near Kapuvar and, even more threatening, another forty around Csapod. By last light they had broken through and Priess's men found themselves manning a line with no defensible features running from Nikitsch to Pinnye and then north to Hegykö.

During the night of the 30th, I SS Panzer Corps, now a Corps in name only, received orders to move back to the Reich Guard Position at Sopron.

Early on 31st March, some sixty Soviet tanks of the Sixth Guards Tank Army (Panzer Corps), supported by infantry of the Fourth Guards Army, advanced along the axis of the Kapuvar–Sopron road. The reinforced Ninth Guards Army was on their left, heading towards Wiener Neustadt. The advance soon reached a line running from Lanzenkirchen to Mattersburg in the LAH sector and Fertöboz to Deutschkreutz in that of the HJ. Sopron, lying at the end of a wide valley stretching south from Vienna, lay at the mercy of the Soviets. In the evening they pushed into the city, but throughout the night small groups of Panzer-Grenadiers and tanks fought their way back to, and through, Sopron. On Easter Day, 1 April, the last pathetic remnants of the once proud and powerful Divisions of I SS Panzer Corps crossed the border of the Third Reich on the roads leading to Vienna.

Das Reich: 28 March – 5 April

OKW (Hitler) had declared Györ a 'Fortress'. This meant of course, that it had to be defended to the last man and, in a surprising move, Das Reich's 2nd SS Flak Battalion was detached to help defend the city. It went into action on the south-east side of Györ on the 28th but by the evening, when it was finally pulled out to rejoin its parent Division, the Russians were occupying most of the city and it had lost a third of its strength, including one of its battery commanders, SS Lieutenant Schmid. Meanwhile, as already described, the Soviets had advanced north-west from Tét, crossed the Marcal canal and Raba river and broken through the Hungarian Mountain Brigade defending Csorna. Stadler was ordered to counter-attack the Soviet penetration but, although some ground was gained, the leading elements of his Division were brought to a halt some 15km to the east of Csorna. Later in the day the Soviet advance threatened Kapuvar and it became obvious that the only viable escape route left for Das Reich, the 6th Panzer Division and the Hungarian Mountain Brigade lay between the northern end of Lake Neusiedler and the Danube. By 2300 hours most of Das Reich had pulled back across the Raba. Its armoured strength, according to Weidinger[25], was two Panthers, five Mk IVs, seven Jagdpanzers and three StuGs. Most of its artillery was intact, but the Panzer-Grenadier Regiments amounted to only 'five average battalions' and it had only 60% of its authorised motor transport.

The 29th was spent trying to establish delaying positions in the Csorna–Kapuvar sector, south of the Einser canal which runs east–west from the southern tip of Lake Neusiedler to the Danube. Despite this, by the morning of the 31st the Fourth Guards Army was pushing hard down the axis of the Kapuvar–Sopron road; the Forty-Sixth Guards Army was starting to strike north-west on the east side of Lake Neusiedler; Györ had fallen and II SS Panzer Corps had been forced back across the canal. At 2200 hours on 1 April, Das Reich began its withdrawal through Wallern (Map 30) towards the north end of the lake.

(Map 34)

The final retreat into what had inevitably been designated 'Fortress' Vienna took place in chaotic conditions over the period 2 to 4 April. The roads were totally jammed with German and Hungarian troops and hordes of civilians – all desperately trying to reach what they thought might be a place of safety.

Following the withdrawal of the LAH and HJ on 1 April, the Russians continued to advance north on the west side of Lake Neusiedler during the night. Das Reich, having successfully pulled back round the north end of the lake, was ordered to counter-attack and by midday on the 2nd had halted their enemy on line of the Piesting river just to the south-east of Münchendorf.

Some extraordinary events occurred at this time. A reinforcement unit under the command of an SS Major Hauser, made up of convalescents, leave personnel and replacement troops, all quite literally taken off trains passing through Vienna, found itself in action between the 3rd and 4th SS Panzer-Grenadier Regiments in the Piesting river sector. Not surprisingly, it was immediately taken under command. In the same way, individual replacements arriving on 3 April were quickly integrated into the Division but, according to Weidinger, it was no longer possible even to take down the names of these men. Losses were recorded in numbers rather than names.[26]

Perhaps the most extraordinary story of the period, however, concerns the Lipizzaner horses. Most of them were stabled in Schloss Laxenburg. Dreike, of the 2nd SS Flak Battalion, described how an army groom asked him for men to shoot the critically ill horses, a large number of which were resting or lying on the ground too weak to get up and covered in a dirty brown and green camouflage paint. The groom and stable staff had cared for the animals for weeks on end and could not bring themselves to do it. Neither could Dreike or his men so in the end they were handed over to the Russians in the care of their grooms.[27]

Otto Weidinger adds to this story by relating that his Divisional commander, Rudolf Lehmann, arranged, at the request of an old Austrian general by the name of Wessely, for about eight or ten of the stallions from the Spanish Riding School of Vienna to be evacuated in three of four Das Reich trucks late on the evening of 8 April. Despite the fact that this allegedly happened at the height of the battle of Vienna, they ended up in the St Polten area where they were handed into the care of General Patton's Third Army.[28] Carlo D'Este has a different version.[29] He relates that a former Austrian Olympic rider by the name of Colonel Alois Podhajsky smuggled the horses out of Vienna to a village near Linz, where

Patton, in order to save them being claimed as 'booty' by the Russians, made them 'wards of the US Army'.

By the 4th Das Reich, with a KG of the 3rd SS Totenkopf Division on its left flank in the area of the Vienna airport, had been forced back to a line running roughly from Mödling to Achau. It was now clear though that the Soviets[30] were beginning to push north-west towards the Danube valley in the area of Tulln with the intention of outflanking and isolating the Austrian capital. With I SS Panzer Corps being forced westwards into the mountains (the Vienna Woods), Stadler had little option other than to withdraw his KGs into the city itself.

Several important and experienced officers fell during the final withdrawal into Vienna. The commander of the 2nd SS Panzer Battalion, SS Major Kesten, was probably the most important, but the commander of Weidinger's 8th Company, SS Lieutenant Neumüller, was also killed and the entire Battalion staff of Schulzer's 2nd Battalion were lost when Russian tanks overran his Command Post. Schulzer himself was lucky to be away from his Headquarters at the time.

On 2 April Sepp Dietrich, still commander Sixth Panzer Army, had been presented to the people of Vienna as their 'defender', and on the 4th General Rudolf von Bünau was appointed Commandant of the City. The battle of Vienna was about to begin. On 5 April the commander of Das Reich, Rudolf Lehmann, received an order, said to have come from the Führer himself: 'From now on there is to be no more retreating.'

NOTES

1. Tiemann, *Die Leibstandarte IV/2*, p. 231.
2. XXIII Tk Corps.
3. Estimates of its strength vary widely. One Soviet source (IVMV, Vol 10) puts the figure as low as 197, while another (Zavizion, G T and Kornyushin, P A – 6 Gds Tk Army) gives a figure of 406 tanks and SP guns.
4. Forty-Sixth Army.
5. II Gds Mech Corps.
6. MS # B-139 – Interrogation of Lt Gen Walther Krause, commander Sixth Army Communications Zone, 13 Jun 52.
7. *In the Firestorm of the Last years of the War, Division Das Reich, Vol V, Comrades to the End, The History of the 12th SS Panzer Division Hitlerjugend* and *The Leibstandarte IV/2* respectively.
8. Weidinger, *Division Das Reich, Vol V*, p. 464.
9. Ibid., p. 468.
10. Wilmot, *The Struggle for Europe*, p. 679.
11. Tieke, *In the Firestorm of the Last Years of the War*, p. 382.
12. The number of Soviet tanks quoted as taking part in various attacks and/or being knocked out should always be treated with caution.
13. Strassner, *European Volunteers*, p. 207.
14. 5 SS Pz, 1 & 3 Pz & 44 Gren Divs.
15. Tiemann, op. cit., p. 256.

16. Units of civil labour, including men and women from the occupied countries, used throughout the industrial regions and communications system of the Third Reich. It took its name from the head of the Organisation – Dr Fritz Todt.
17. 262 Pz Div with two Pz-Gren Regts & just three armd vehicles.
18. 2 SS Pz-Gren Regt, a flak bty & elements of 1 SS Pnr Bn.
19. Tiemann, op. cit., p. 264.
20. Ibid., pp. 266–7.
21. Maier, *Drama zwischen Budapest und Wien*, p. 347.
22. 13 SS Mountain, 16 SS Pz-Gren & three army inf Divs.
23. Maier, op. cit., p. 373.
24. Tieke, op. cit., p. 395.
25. Weidinger, op. cit., p. 481.
26. Ibid., pp. 490–1.
27. Ibid.
28. Ibid., p. 508.
29. D'Este, *A Genius for War*, pp. 742–3.
30. XXXVIII Gds Rifle, IX Gds Mech (Pz Div) & V Gds Tk (Pz Div) Corps.

CHAPTER XXXVI

The Dream of Reich[1] is Shattered

Hohenstaufen: 8 April – 2 May

(Map 34)

Stadler and his officers had been led to believe that the Reich Guard Position was an 'Alpenfestung', or 'fortress'. In reality, only the forward trench line had been completed. Furthermore, the impression given by at least two German writers[2] that the new defence line was sited on hills to the west of the Mura river from which enemy movements could be observed is misleading. There *are* no hills to the west of the Mura – the nearest defensible high ground is some 12km north of the river. It is true, however, that whilst the fighting positions were sited to cover the roads leading west and north-west from Bad Radkersburg, observation posts were set up on a hill immediately west of the town on the south side of the river. Bad Radkersburg itself, lying in low ground beside the Mura, did not form part of the defensive system and was abandoned as soon as Möller's SS Pioneers had blown the iron bridge across the river – just as the first Soviet tank attempted to cross it.

Fortunately, apart from occupying Bad Radkersburg – with terrifying results for those civilians who ignored Stadler's advice to move out – 'the enemy remained completely quiet'.[3] This enabled the Todt Organisation and soldiers to work on the new positions without interruption. Its unfinished state had in fact one advantage – Stadler and his officers were able to decide for themselves the best positions for their few remaining armoured vehicles, heavy weapons and artillery pieces. On 10 April, however, the Division had only fifteen Panthers, eight Mk IVs, seven StuGs and Jagdpanzers and seven heavy anti-tank guns on strength.

Apart from recovering from the ordeals of SPRING AWAKENING and the retreat that followed it, the period between 10 and 26 April was spent receiving replacement personnel and new and repaired equipment. The only important officer reinforcement was SS Lieutenant Colonel Rohde, who arrived to take over the 20th SS Panzer-Grenadier Regiment. Amazingly, in less than three weeks, in an almost unbelievable feat of organisation, 'the Division again had its full authorized combat strength. The replacements came from all imaginable units and ranged in age from seventeen years to over sixty".[4] This meant that on the 26th, when the Hohenstaufen received orders to move to the Amstetten area in Lower Austria, it numbered some 18,500 men. Many of the replacements had, inevitably in this late stage of the war, received little or no serious military training. 'They were coming from schools and colleges and from all sorts of other institutions no longer considered important . . . Many had never even fired a shot on a rifle range'. The veteran officers and NCOs worked hard to rectify this situation but 'all gained a clear realization that the war could not last much longer'.[5]

The move to Lower Austria began on 27 April. The tracked vehicles, despite the dangers of air attack, were moved by rail and by 2 May the last units had arrived in the new location. There, they were joined by Recke's 9th SS Reconnaissance Battalion, which it will recalled had been operating with Das Reich and the 6th Panzer Division, and by the missing artillery batteries that had been left behind in the Györ area.

To the delight of Sylvester Stadler and his officers, the Hohenstaufen was subordinated directly to the Sixth Panzer Army. They were thus free of General Balck's control and back with their old master, Sepp Dietrich.

On 1 May Stadler received his new mission. He was to move his Division into a defensive position between Enns, on the Danube, and Steyr, and prevent the *Americans* crossing the Enns river. The previous day, the Americans and Soviets had agreed that the river would form the demarcation line in Austria. It had also been agreed that German troops would have to surrender to the opponent they had most recently been fighting. In the case of both I and II SS Panzer Corps, this was clearly the Russians.

Das Reich: 5 – 13 April
The Battle for Vienna
(Map 34)

Dawn on 5 April found Das Reich desperately trying to hold the line between the villages of Mödling and Achau in order to prevent a Soviet advance[6] along the main roads leading into Vienna from Wiener Neustadt and Sopron. Elements of the 3rd SS Panzer Division Totenkopf and the 6th Panzer Division were on its eastern flank. During the day the Soviets managed to occupy Mödling and, in intense fighting, force the Division back some 4km across flat, open ground to low ridge running from Vösendorf to Leopoldsdorf. There it occupied temporary positions on a reverse slope.

(Map 35)

At 2000 hours on 5 April, Lehmann gave orders for a further withdrawal to the high ground behind the Liesing river (today less than 2m wide), running from Mauer, through Altmannsdorf, to the area of Inzersdorf. This new position was within the city limits of Vienna itself and soon after occupying it the men, and particularly the officers of Das Reich, began to run into new problems. SS Captain Dreike, the commander of the 2nd SS Flak Battalion, said later that for the first time in the war he experienced a local Germanic population that was unfriendly and even treated his men with contempt and scorn. He found himself getting into arguments with the commanders of the local Viennese defence sectors over responsibilities and rank. He also described how the personnel of a fixed 88mm Luftwaffe flak battery joined him and stayed with his Battalion right to the end, displaying great bravery and apparently proud of the fact that they were suddenly part of the Waffen-SS.[7] Dreike was to receive a Knight's Cross for his leadership at this time.

At 0730 hours on 6 April, the Russians launched a major assault on the German positions. It has been said that this attack was due to coincide with an attempt by the Austrian Resistance Movement to hand over the city to the Soviets.[8] In any event, the attempt failed. The leaders of the movement had clearly not calculated on the presence of the men of the Waffen-SS and the 6th Panzer Division.

During the 6th, Ernst Krag's 2nd SS Reconnaissance Battalion pulled back through the Division's lines to the area around the Floridsdorf bridge across the Danube. This vital bridge, which was to become the focus of the fighting in the last hours of the battle, was already under observation from Soviet troops on the Kahlenberg feature in the north-western part of Vienna.

By the evening of the 6th, Das Reich, which was no longer fighting as a Division but in small unit groups, had been forced back to a line just south of the Schönbrunn Palace and extending west to the Hietzing sector of the city. Some of its tanks and certainly the 10th SS Heavy Battery had taken up positions in the Palace grounds. Another Battery, the 12th, was in position on the Prater Island between the Danube and the Danube canal. One of the 10th Battery officers, SS Second Lieutenant Möller, later described how they were shooting directly over the Gloriette towards the south and how one gun was positioned in the middle of the three main entrances into the Palace grounds, firing towards the Palace bridge to the north. He claimed the Palace suffered only slight damage, to the east side of the Gloriette.[9]

As darkness fell on the 6th and the Russians[10] began to threaten the Prater Island from the south-east, General von Bünau, who although still City Commandant had been placed under Bittrich's command, gave orders for the bridges across the Danube in the eastern part of Vienna to be blown. The same night saw the enemy trying to infiltrate towards the West Station but the deployment of a battalion of Hitlerjugend[11] put a temporary end to this threat. Nevertheless, by midnight parts of Weidinger's Der Führer Regiment had been pushed back into the streets just to the north of the Schönbrunn.

During the 6th the commander of the Third Ukrainian Front, Marshal Tolbukhin, arranged for a message on the following lines to be broadcast to the local population:

> The retreating German troops want to turn Vienna into a battlefield just as they did Budapest. Vienna and its inhabitants are under the threat of similar destruction and terror as was handed out there. Citizens of Vienna – help the Red Army to liberate the capital of Austria; play your part in liberating your country from the Fascist German yoke!

How much effect this broadcast had is unknown, but German morale was certainly not improved when it was learned from civilians and prisoners that in the sectors of the city already occupied by the Russians, men and women with red and white armbands were helping Soviet soldiers by carrying ammunition and equipment.

By the morning of 7 April there was no longer a German front-line in Vienna. Units defended positions considered by their officers to be tactically important, but they were often cut off from each other by Soviet troops. By the end of the day Lehmann's men had lost the West Station and withdrawn into the areas known as Mariahilf and Neubau, and

Krag's 2nd SS Reconnaissance Battalion had pulled back across the Danube to the Floridsdorf district.

In one of the more extraordinary stories of this day, SS Senior Sergeant Major Ernst Barkmann (of Manhay fame) related later how former prisoners of war – French, Belgians, Dutch and Slavs – were celebrating and waiting for the war to end with accordions and guitars playing in some of the local cafes and wine bars. There were even a few local people and German soldiers amongst them. He went on to point out that just a few hundred metres away, where the Soviets had broken through, men were dying.[12]

The important and famous Grinzing region of Vienna, only 4km from the Floridsdorf bridge, also fell to the Russians on the 7th, threatening all the Germans west of the Danube canal with encirclement. This led Lehmann to order the destruction of all the canal bridges except the Augarten and Aspern.

According to an Army Group South morning report, II SS Panzer Corps (Das Reich, Totenkopf and 6th Panzer Divisions) destroyed thirty-nine Soviet tanks in Vienna on 8 April. We have no details of fighting on this day, other than the fact that Das Reich's commander, Rudolf Lehmann, after being wounded in the hand whilst on a reconnaissance, set up an advanced Command Post near the Augarten bridge.

It appears that each day with the coming of darkness most of the fighting ceased and 'a deathly silence hung over the city'. The centre was apparently a sea of flames and Lehmann reported seeing looters dragging 'enormous sacks of plundered goods' along the streets.

By 9 April the German positions west of the Danube canal were no longer tenable. Das Reich was fighting in a rough semi-circle extending from the vicinity of the North bridge to just beyond the Aspern bridge. Elements of three Soviet Rifle Divisions and I Guards Mechanized Corps (Panzer Division) were attacking from the south-east towards the Prater, two Rifle Divisions and IX Guards Mechanized Corps (Panzer Division) from the south and west towards the Aspern and Augarten bridges, and V Guards Tank Corps (Panzer Division) was closing in towards the Floridsdorf bridge from the north-west.[13] Furthermore, Malinovsky's Forty-Sixth Army, having crossed to the east bank of the Danube with two Rifle Corps and II Guards Mechanized Corps (Panzer Division), was attacking north-west and west with the aim of sealing the escape routes of the Germans defending the city. It has to be pointed out, however, that none of the formations mentioned was anywhere near up to strength and by this stage of the war STAVKA was acutely aware of the Red Army's cumulative casualty figures. With Poland, Slovakia, Hungary and Rumania already occupied by Soviet troops and the desired 'buffer zone' between the western border of the Motherland and the fascist and capitalist enemies firmly established, there seemed little point in needlessly sacrificing more lives – except for Berlin.

In view of the rapidly deteriorating situation, and in spite of the Führer Order forbidding further retreat, Dietrich's Headquarters gave permission for II SS Panzer Corps to pull back across the Danube canal during the night of the 9th/10th and blow the remaining bridges. In true Waffen-SS fashion, and contrary to the normal tactics of the American and British Armies, tanks, StuGs and artillery pieces, rather than infantry, covered the final withdrawal. The guns of the 2nd SS Artillery Regiment went into direct firing positions at various intersections in order to seal off the streets. Their commander, SS Colonel Kreutz, received Oakleaves to his Knight's Cross for the achievements of his artillerymen and for his own leadership of both his Regiment and the Division during the battle of Vienna.

By first light on 10 April, all the bridges over the Danube and its canal except the Reichs and Floridsdorf had been blown.[14] The City Commandant, General von Bünau, had been the last man to cross the Aspern bridge. Das Reich was now behind the canal in the area of the Floridsdorf bridge with Der Führer on the right and Deutschland on the left. Each Regiment deployed two of its weak Battalions forward and kept one in reserve. The remnants of the Totenkopf and 6th Panzer Divisions were on the Division's left flank and Bitttrich's II SS Panzer Corps' advance Headquarters was now located on the east bank of the Danube near the Reichs bridge. Casualties continued to mount during the withdrawal and included SS Captain Engelmann, commander of the 1st/4th SS Panzer-Grenadier Battalion, who was killed with his whole crew when his command vehicle was shot up by a Russian tank on the south bank of the river. SS Major Hauser, of the convalescent reinforcement unit, took over command of the Battalion. The armoured strength of Das Reich on this day was still fifteen Panthers, eleven Mk IVs, four Jagdpanzer IVs, one Jagdpanzer V and eight Flakpanzer IVs.

The German front on the Prater Island held throughout the 11th, but on the 12th the Russians made a major incursion in the area of the Augarten canal bridge forcing the Germans back into two small perimeters – Das Reich's encompassing the North-West Station area and the Floridsdorf bridge and the Totenkopf's and 6th Panzer Division's the North Station and Reichs bridge.

At 2315 hours on 12 April, Bittrich, in what could be described as a convenient move, handed over command of all troops west of the Danube to General von Bünau. At the same time Das Reich's remaining armour was ordered back across the river and the remaining elements of the Totenkopf and 6th Panzer Divisions were withdrawn, or more probably forced back, to the east bank. This latter withdrawal resulted in the Reichs bridge falling into Soviet hands intact. The cause of this error is unknown but it has been alleged that it was due to a Führer Order expressly forbidding its demolition.[15] In any event, the surviving structure was covered with some anti-tank guns and at least six 37mm flak guns.

Das Reich was thus left holding the Floridsdorf bridge perimeter in isolation and with an open left flank.[16] Not surprisingly, it soon found itself having to abandon the area of the North-West Station and withdraw, on von Bünau's orders, into a close bridge garrison with a radius of only some 700 metres. Von Bünau saw the futility of holding on but knew that a further general withdrawal in daylight was out of the question since the bridge was under direct fire from Russian tanks and machine-guns. According to Otto Weidinger, he was also influenced by a 12 April Directive from OKW, signed by Keitel, Himmler and Martin Bormann, which demanded that important communication centres be defended and held to the bitter end. The appointed Commandant was to be personally responsible for carrying out this order and if any of them failed in, or acted in defiance of, their duties, they would be sentenced to death.[17]

This last day in the battle of Vienna found Rudolf Lehmann, the commander of Das Reich, together with his Chief Operations Officer, still in the tiny Floridsdorf bridgehead but with the main Divisional Headquarters back on the east side of the river. Von Bünau, the City Commandant, was also in the bridgehead, still refusing to give up and moving amongst the men in a simple forage cap with a stick grenade tucked in his belt. Lehmann called for all the available heavy weapons on the east side of the river, including an army 88mm flak battery, to keep up a wall of protective fire in front of his positions and for tanks to come forward again into the perimeter. An attempt by three Panther tanks of the 6th SS Panzer Company to do so was abandoned after the leading tank, commanded by SS Lieutenant Boska, the Company commander, was hit and set on fire.

Around midday von Bünau sent his Chief Operations Officer, Major Neumann, to brief Dietrich personally on the desperate situation in the bridgehead. Shortly after this Lehmann was wounded in the knee by a shell splinter and evacuated to the east bank. Yet again, SS Colonel Karl Kreutz took over command. Fifty-six men, too severely wounded to be evacuated without ambulances, were already sheltering under the arches of the bridge.

Major Neumann returned from Sixth Panzer Army Headquarters at around 1600 hours with the news that Dietrich had sanctioned a withdrawal. Von Bünau finally acquiesced and gave orders for it to begin as soon as possible after last light. Fortunately, as on the previous nights, the Soviet attacks ceased with the coming darkness and in almost total silence all the wounded were evacuated. Von Bünau and the last Grenadiers of SS Captain Bickel's 3rd/4th Battalion pulled back across the bridge at about midnight and shortly afterwards the order was given to blow it. The battle of Vienna was over. Willi Bittrich looked on the city for the last time as a serving officer – seven years earlier, at the time of the 'Anschluss', he had entered it as an SS major in command of the 1st Battalion, Der Führer Regiment.

Das Reich: 14 April – 7 May
(Map 34)

By first light on 14 April the surviving elements of Das Reich, including thirteen unspecified tanks and Jagdpanzers, together with the Totenkopf and 6th Panzer Divisions, were crowded into a wedge, roughly 2km wide and barely 10km long, running north-west from Aspern on the east bank of the Danube. The southern tip of this wedge was being held by the Führer Grenadier Division[18] and the Waffen-SS men found themselves sharing the limited space with army and local defence units, administrative units and baggage trains – all desperately trying to escape Soviet encirclement. This critical situation was exacerbated when units of the XXXI Guards Rifle Corps, which had crossed the Danube south of Klosterneuburg the previous night, began to advance towards Korneuburg. Only a successful counter-attack from Bisamberg by a reinforced Company of Krag's 2nd SS Reconnaissance Battalion, supported by two Tigers, and the fact that the Soviets made no attempt to cross the river in the vacated Floridsdorf–Reichs bridge sector of Vienna, saved the day.

During the 14th Kreutz's Headquarters set up in Stockerau and that night the rest of Das Reich broke out using an unsurfaced and forested road across the high ground north of Bisamberg.[19] Otto Weidinger described the breakout as one of the most strenuous night marches of the whole war. In the early hours of the morning the enemy attacked the flank of the marching columns. The Deutschland Regiment suffered losses from mortar fire and Der Führer from direct infantry attacks. Nevertheless, the march continued and during the morning the Division crossed a new line of resistance on the high ground between Loebendorf to Oberrohrbach.[20] The commander of the 3rd Battery of the 2nd SS Artillery Regiment told later how army units that could no longer move along the road beside the Danube because of enemy firing, converged from the south and south-east into the marching columns of the Division, causing violent arguments at the crossroads about who should take precedence. He went on to describe how just before they reached the exit from the forest into the open plain, they heard the rousing shouts of 'Hurrah, Hurrah'! Evidently Russian spearheads from the east and west had joined up in an encircling movement and many of the Germans were taken prisoner.[21]

By 16 April Günther Wisliceny's 3rd SS Panzer-Grenadier Regiment

Deutschland had reached Melk where, the following day, it received more reinforcements. Most of them, however, were inadequately trained and few had combat experience – they even included members of the Dresden fire brigade. In the meantime, Otto Weidinger's 4th Regiment Der Führer had moved back through Krems, recrossed the Danube at Melk and on the 18th taken up positions facing east astride Gansbach. St Pölten, only 15km away to the south-east, had fallen to the Soviets several days before and a scratch force known optimistically as 'Corps Shultz'[22] after the name of its commander, with I SS Panzer Corps on its right flank in the foothills of the Austrian Alps, was all that stood in the way of a renewed Russian advance. In fact, the situation was not as desperate as it seemed. STAVKA knew that the war on the southern front was almost at an end and that, even if it did order a major offensive towards Linz in the narrow valley between the Danube and the Alps, its troops were unlikely to get there before the Americans. It therefore made much more sense to go firm on the easily defensible line they had just reached, consolidate what had already been achieved by clearing up all resistance to the east of that line, and simply wait for the final German collapse. Accordingly, the Ninth Guards Army was placed in reserve and ordered to halt just to the west and south-west of Vienna while the badly depleted Sixth Guards Tank Army was transferred to Malinovsky's Second Ukrainian Front. There were no further Soviet attempts to advance west from the St Pölten area after the 14th and, on the 15th, Corps Schultz was able to close the 6km gap between it and I SS Panzer Corps in the Obergrafendorf area without difficulty.

(Map 27)

On 19 April Wisliceny's Deutschland Regiment, reinforced with Das Reich's 2nd SS Reconnaissance and 1st SS Artillery Battalions, the 1st SS Pioneer Company and a StuG Company took over the Gansbach sector and prepared to counter-attack towards St Pölten (Map 34). The following day the attack was cancelled and the KG ordered to move back and form a bridgehead at Passau with the aim of preventing American crossings of the Danube and Inn rivers from the north and west. The rest of Das Reich was due to follow by rail. Hardly had this order been issued than it was countermanded and Kreutz was told that his Division was to be transferred to the Dresden area, where it was to join General Wenck's Twelfth Army and take part in an operation to relieve Berlin.[23] Whilst all this was going on, Der Führer spent the period 19 to 24 April near St Margarethen (Map 34), in what was known as the 'Claudia' position. It saw no action there but continued to receive reinforcements which, although untrained, brought the Regiment back to almost full strength.

Author's Note

Most place names in the Czech Republic differ today from the German ones used in 1945. Czech place names will be shown in brackets where appropriate.

On 25 April Weidinger received orders for his Regiment to rejoin the rest of the Division (less the 3rd Deutschland Regimental KG which was still in the Passau bridgehead awaiting trains) in the Dresden area. The move of the 4th Der Führer Regiment took place by road and rail in chaotic conditions. Communications were lost with the train element which, it eventually transpired, had been diverted by a Führer Order towards Iglau (Jihlava) with a view to a possible redeployment in the area of Brünn (Brno). On the 27th the alleged Führer Order was cancelled and the original instruction taking the Regiment back to its parent Division north of Dresden re-issued. After moving through Leitmaritz (Litomerice) on the Elbe river and Dresden, Weidinger's men eventually arrived in the Grossröhrsdorf area on 30 April. Even then, Das Reich was not a complete Division. The Deutschland Regimental KG, without sufficient trains to move out of the Passau bridgehead, had withdrawn to a better position 20km west of Linz on 29 April and the 2nd SS Panzer Company, with twenty-two Panthers and a Tiger II, had been forced to remain in the Krems area because of fuel shortages. The 2nd SS Reconnaissance Battalion, which had been detached from the Deutschland KG and had moved north, was by this time some 50km to the east of Dresden. One of Krag's Company commanders reported seeing more and more signs of unrest during the journey. Just outside Prague, his men realised that the bolts had been removed on the stretch of railway track ahead of them. Engineers were able to avert the danger but they saw plenty of evidence of partisan activity, including trains adorned with Soviet stars. The Battalion eventually got through and unloaded in Schluckenau (Sluknov), but once there it received neither intelligence nor orders.[24]

During the evening of May Day the men of Kreutz's Division, scattered across an area stretching from Upper Austria through what is now the Czech Republic to Dresden and the Sudeten Highlands, heard a radio broadcast telling them of Adolf Hitler's death. Weidinger describes how his men were gripped by a mixture of shock that total defeat now seemed certain and relief that the unequal and hopeless struggle would soon end. At least no one could now be called upon to execute a 'Führer Order'. He went on to remind his officers, however, that they were still not released from their oaths of obedience since those oaths had also been made to the German people.[25]

The following day the plans and preparations, if they ever really existed, for the relief operation towards Berlin were cancelled; and then on the 3rd Günther Wisliceny, still without orders, decided to pull the Deutschland Regimental KG back behind the Enns river between Ernsthofen and Amstetten. On arrival, he found the Hohenstaufen Division already in position and was able to place his KG under Stadler's command.

During the early hours of 6 May, the day he was awarded Swords to his Knight's Cross and following ten days of order and counter-order, Otto Weidinger received clear instructions to move via Dresden and Leitmeritz into Prague. He was to help the German units there, some of which were already surrounded, to put down a popular, but apparently unexpected, uprising against the Germans and then to carry out any further orders he might receive from the City Commandant, General Toussaint. He was to be reinforced by two armoured car companies, one from Krag's 2nd SS Reconnaissance Battalion and the other from the Army, and Das Reich's 2nd SS Artillery Battalion.

Before they moved off at 0500 hours on the 6th, Weidinger's men were told of a broadcast by Admiral Dönitz in which he had ordered all divisions on the Eastern Front to continue resisting the Soviets with all their strength so as to allow the Western Allies time to occupy as much of the Greater German Reich as possible.

Approaching Prague from the north, Weidinger's men soon encountered stragglers from all branches of the Wehrmacht, many of whom had been relieved of their weapons by partisans. Then, as they got closer to the city, they came under fire from road blocks and anti-tank barriers that could not be easily bypassed because of the danger of mines. By last light the Grenadiers had fought their way to within 4km of the Troja (Svermuv) bridge over the Moldau (Vltava) river but then encountered a massive barrier of cobblestones torn up from the main roads. Spurred on by a message from the Army Group Commander, Field Marshal Schörner, which read: 'The honour and glory of the Der Führer Regiment is at stake if you fail to reach the inner city of Prague by 7 May', work continued throughout the night to clear a way. No further advance was ordered, however, because of the dangers of house-to-house fighting in the dark.

On the 7th SS Captain Schulzer's 2nd SS Panzer-Grenadier Battalion, supported by armoured cars and SP anti-aircraft guns, mounted a full-scale attack. The Troja bridge was reached at a cost of twenty-five dead and double that number wounded.[26] At this point, a Czech lieutenant from a partisan group attempted to negotiate a cease-fire. Weidinger agreed on the condition that his column was allowed to drive unmolested into the city centre. The Czech, not surprisingly, rejected this and demanded that Der Führer withdraw back to Leitmeritz. Weidinger replied that the purpose of the Czech rebels in the last days of the war was clearly to gain recognition from the Allies that they were a military power. The rebels therefore would bear sole responsibility for those who died in any forthcoming battle and for the destruction of Prague which meant as much to the Germans as to the Czechs. His soldiers did not wish to fight but they had their orders. He pointed out that Czech resistance was futile because they knew that they would achieve their national goal – liberation from the Germans – in a few days time without a fight.[27]

Hohenstaufen: 3 – 7 May
(Map 34)

Whilst the Hohenstaufen occupied its new positions east of the Enns river in the area of Amstetten–Enns–Steyr on 3 and 4 May, units of George Patton's Third US Army were rapidly closing up to the west bank. 'The advance to Steyr had been made through countless numbers of enemy troops, who threw down their weapons and attempted to surrender'.[28] The 65th Infantry Division occupied the city of Enns at 2245 hours on the 5th and the 71st Infantry Division, after reaching Steyr at 1000 hours, completed its occupation of the town by 1600 on the same day.[29] No fighting took place.

Between 4 and 6 May contact was established between American officers and the commanders of the Hohenstaufen Division and the 3rd Deutschland Regiment of Das Reich – Stadler and Wisliceny. Recall that the latter was now under Stadler's command. Major General Reinhart of the 65th Division demanded the Germans surrender unconditionally, to which Stadler replied that he was not authorised to take such a drastic step, and that anyway negotiations for a general capitulation were already in progress at a much higher level. 'It was only necessary to be patient for a few more days.'

On 7 May Sepp Dietrich, still commander of the Sixth Panzer Army, on his own initiative ordered the 12th SS Panzer Division Hitlerjugend to move into a new assembly area near the Hohenstaufen to the south-east of Amstetten and that night the remnants of the 1st SS Panzer Division Leibstandarte, which had been fighting a rearguard action in the Austrian Alps, were ordered to assemble south-east of Scheibbs and then move to the Enns river in the Steyr sector. We have, therefore, the extraordinary spectacle of four Waffen-SS Panzer Divisions, the 1st, 3rd, 9th and 12th, and a complete Regimental KG of another, the 2nd, all concentrated in a part of Lower Austria measuring only 50km by 40km.

It was on the 7th, at 0241 hours in the morning, that the document confirming the surrender of all German armed forces was signed on behalf of Admiral Dönitz at Eisenhower's Headquarters in Reims. Hostilities were to cease at midnight on 8 May, and by that time all troops had to be across the demarcation line between the Americans and the Soviets.

Anyone arriving late was to go into Russian captivity. In the case of the Waffen-SS in Lower Austria, the commander of the US XX Corps, Lieutenant General Walker, laid down further conditions: the Germans had to be across the Enns river on 8 May between 0800 hours and midnight; all weapons were to be unloaded 2km from the river and all small arms were to be removed; ammunition for tanks and artillery pieces was to follow behind them on trucks; tanks had to point their guns in the air; and all vehicles were to fly white flags. As a matter of interest, Stadler maintained that the Hohenstaufen still had thirty-five combat-ready tanks and StuGs on 7 May and that, if necessary, these were to be used to ensure that no members of his Division fell into Russian hands. He wrote later:

> Now followed for everyone the saddest day . . . We had indeed now lost everything. The German Reich was totally destroyed . . . However, no man could imagine what would actually happen to us – that they would deprive us of everything and simply stamp all of us, without exception, as a group of criminals and thus take the last thing that a man treasures – his honour. A terrible hate and revenge would determine our fate from now on.[30]

This was true. The members of the Waffen-SS were soon to discover that the Americans had no intention of extending to them the honours and courtesies applicable to normal prisoners of war. What Stadler and his comrades failed to appreciate was that, although they would constantly claim that they had never been anything more than combat soldiers and had no knowledge of extermination squads and concentration camps, their conquerors would never accept this. In the first place, the latter was simply not true and secondly, *anyone* who wore SS runes was seen as part of a diabolical machine that had caused endless misery and countless deaths – as a barbarian who deserved to be treated as such.

Headquarters II SS Panzer Corps: 14 April – 7 May

After Vienna fell to the Soviets on 13 April, Willi Bittrich's II SS Panzer Corps, shorn of its designated Divisions, was left holding a front north of the Danube in the region of Stockerau. The ground here is featureless, flat, open and virtually impossible to defend. He was still commanding what was left of the 3rd SS Totenkopf[31] and 6th Führer Grenadier Divisions and others caught up in events beyond their control. There were even some complete individual sub-units, such as the 2nd SS Panther Company of Das Reich, already mentioned, forced to stay behind because of fuel shortages.

Fortunately for Bittrich's men, the Soviets made no serious attempt to interfere with their 120km withdrawal to the Linz area. The main body of the Corps reached an area 25km to the north-east of that city on the 9th, with the Totenkopf attempting to surrender to elements of the US 11th Armored Division. The Americans, however, refused to allow the SS men to cross the demarcation line and most of the Totenkopf survivors ended up in Soviet captivity.

Few details of the withdrawal to the Linz area are available. One report from the 2nd SS Panzer Company Das Reich tells us that its Panthers were ordered to go into position about half way between Stockerau and Krems and hold the road open until the last German units had passed through. Once this had been achieved, the Company commander is said to have led his men in singing the Panzerwaffe march and national anthem, after which he thanked them for what they had done for their nation and formally released them from their oaths of allegiance. He then shook hands with each man, ordered them on to waiting trucks and then calmly shot up all the tanks before blowing up his own.

NOTES

1. German for Empire.
2. Tieke, *In the Firestorm of the Last Years of the War* and Fürbringer, *La Hohen-staufen*.
3. Tieke, op, cit., p. 396.
4. Ibid., p. 397.
5. Ibid..
6. XX, XXI, XXXIX Gds Rifle Corps & I Gds Mech Corps (Pz Div).
7. Weidinger, *Division Das Reich, Vol V*, pp. 493–4.
8. Ibid., p. 501.
9. Ibid., p. 502.
10. XX Gds Rifle Corps.
11. Not to be confused with troops of 12 SS Pz Div HJ, which by this time was fighting in the hills and mountains to the west of the city.
12. Weidinger, op. cit., p. 505.
13. Rauchensteiner, *Der Kampf um Wien 1945*, p. 516. These Corps were from the Fourth & Ninth Armies.
14. The Augarten bridge was only partly demolished.
15. Weidinger, *Comrades to the End*, p. 393.
16. Weidinger makes no mention of the 3rd Deutschland SS Pz-Gren Regt in the defensive actions around the Floridsdorf bridge. Not for the first time, he claims his own units did all the fighting.
17. Weidinger, *Division Das Reich, Vol V*, p. 517.
18. An under-strength Div comprising one tk bn, one SPW bn, two inf bns, recce bn, PzJg bn, three arty bns, Flak & Pnr bns.
19. 358m (1,175 ft).
20. Weidinger, *Division Das Reich, Vol V*, p. 529.
21. Ibid,, pp. 530–1.
22. Three reserve inf bns (two made up of SS replacements meant for the Sixth

Pz Army), two bns of an a/tk bde equipped only with Panzerfausts, the under-strength 1st Pz Recce Bn, three aslt gun & five arty bns.
23. Weidinger, *Division Das Reich, Vol V*, p. 539.
24. Ibid., p. 537.
25. Weidinger, *Comrades to the End*, p. 402.
26. Weidinger, *Division Das Reich, Vol V*, p. 552.
27. Ibid.
28. AAR 71 Inf Div dated 2 Jul 45.
29. Ibid. & AAR 65 Inf Div dated 11 Jul 45.
30. Tieke, op. cit., p. 440.
31. Said to have still numbered nearly 9,000 men.

CHAPTER XXXVII

The March into Captivity: 8 and 9 May

The Hohenstaufen

(Map 34)

The Americans had issued instructions that the Hohenstaufen Division should pass into captivity at Steyr on the Enns river. In spite of the conditions of their surrender, Sylvester Stadler was determined that his men should earn the respect of their enemies by their 'impeccable soldierly bearing, iron discipline and unbreakable comradeship'.[1] After inspecting his command for the last time on 8 May, he describes what happened next:

> I said my final words in front of the Divisional staff . . . and took my place at their head. Shortly before the meeting point with the Americans, we received rifle fire from grain fields on both sides of the road. Hundreds of armed former concentration camp inmates came up to the column and attempted, with armed threats, to force us to their camp. With the exception of a few pistols we were practically unarmed . . . [but] we simply drove on to the Enns bridge which was already in sight. Some of the camp inmates clung on to our vehicles.[2]

Trouble with concentration camp inmates was not restricted to the Hohenstaufen. The men of the Leibstandarte, the Hitlerjugend and the Deutschland Regiment all suffered the same treatment and it was perhaps ironic that so many members of the Waffen-SS were required to surrender in the vicinity of the Mauthausen Concentration Camp. Mauthausen was one of the first concentration camps in Nazi Germany and between 8

August 1938 and 5 May 1945 some 195,000 men and women were imprisoned there and in its sub-camps. Of these, more than 105,000 died. According to today's Austrian authorities, when the SS guards fled Mauthausen on 3 May there were 68,268 inmates including 1,734 women, four British and two American citizens. Another 81,000 prisoners were liberated by American troops from the sub-camps and other concentration camps in Upper Austria.

Stadler continues:

> To our amazement, the Americans who were waiting for us – a lieutenant colonel, other officers, soldiers and interpreters – immediately disarmed and arrested the camp inmates. Our request that care should be taken that the unarmed main body of the Division should not be fired on, was met by an order for an American company to secure the approach route. I was then led to the American Headquarters and there received by the general [Major General Wyman] and officers of the 71st Infantry Division . . .
>
> The camp site for the Division was discussed and agreed. A second point of discussion was armed guards to protect the camp from outside attack. Since all members of my Division had destroyed their weapons, it was agreed that my Military Police would be rearmed and that all officers would be re-issued with pistols . . .
>
> Now came the march past by the main body of the Division Hohenstaufen before me, their last commander and before the astounded Americans. The men realised its significance and in spite of all the bitterness, made an outstanding impression.[3]

To some extent, Stadler's report reflects wishful thinking rather than reality. First, the concentration camp inmates were restrained, not arrested; second, the Americans were astonished and angry rather than 'astounded' at the arrogance of their defeated enemies; and third, if the weapons were ever issued to Stadler's officers and men, they were very quickly withdrawn again.

It is not clear whether the camp designated for Stadler's men was a small Mauthausen sub-camp near Ternberg, 15km to the south, or another rather closer to Steyr. They probably went to both.

Das Reich

With one of its Panzer-Grenadier Regiments in Lower Austria and another in Prague, there was no possibility of Das Reich ever surrendering as a composite Division. On 8 May the rump of Kreutz's command was still around Dresden but the 2nd SS Reconnaissance Battalion, less a Company with Weidinger's Regiment in Prague, was isolated some 50km away to the east and it seems that some armoured elements had also become separated. No details of exactly how, when or to whom, these armoured sub units surrendered are available. In the case of Ernst Krag's 2nd SS Reconnaissance Battalion, however, we know that after reaching the Elbe and finding the crossings blocked by refugees, his men destroyed their weapons and equipment, pushed their vehicles into the river, and then dispersed westwards into the nearby forests in small groups.[4] All we know of Kreutz, his Headquarters and the other units is that 'they went west as prisoners of the Americans'.

The Deutschland Regimental KG

Günther Wisliceny's Regimental KG, including the 1st SS Artillery Battalion and 1st SS Pioneer company, was ordered to surrender to the American 65th Infantry Division at the main river bridge at Enns. The morning of the 8th was spent making weapons unserviceable and attending an award parade. Then, according to SS Captain Bastian of the 2nd Battalion, the Regiment moved off in motorised convoy, smartly turned out as if on parade, complete with field kitchens and supply wagons. They drove past the American commander and Wisliceny who jointly took the salute.[5]

Der Führer Regimental KG

Perhaps the most extraordinary thing about Otto Weidinger's command[6] on the day hostilities ended is that it was fully replenished, with all three Battalions up to strength, vehicles fully fuelled and all sub units well provided with rations and ammunition. Weidinger claims that at the end of the war, the Regiment in fact possessed more equipment and manpower than it had seen for years.[7] Although he omits the fact that most of the replacement personnel lacked proper training and that two complete Grenadier Companies had still to catch up with his KG, his claim goes some way to explaining his extraordinary attitude and arrogance on 8 May 1945.

Early that morning Der Führer, far from ceasing its military activities, launched a further attack in the Troja bridge sector and 'with support from all heavy weapons' established a bridgehead south of the river. Weidinger knew full well from radio broadcasts that at midnight all German forces were to surrender, but as far as he was concerned he was under orders to report in person to General Toussaint, the overall German commander in Prague, and until he had done so and personally received orders from him to surrender, his war would continue. Whilst he agreed that an Army liaison officer could accompany a rebel group to General Toussaint to discuss a permanent cease-fire, and that fighting should cease until 1500 hours, he insisted that in the end his Regimental KG should have 'peaceful and unhindered transit' to the General's Headquarters. When by 1600 hours the liaison officer had not returned, Weidinger gave orders for the attack to continue. Fortunately for those involved and the city of Prague, the attack had scarcely got under way when a message was received from the 2nd Battalion in the bridgehead saying that the German peace envoy had just returned and was requesting an immediate cease-fire. He had confirmed that an armistice had been signed between the overall German commander and the Czech rebels.[8]

At 1800 hours Weidinger led his triumphant KG into the centre of Prague. He claimed later that this was achieved because he made the Czechs fully aware that he was ready to continue the attack at any given moment.[9] At 1900 hours Weidinger radioed Headquarters Army Group Schörner, through Headquarters Fourth Panzer Army:

> Mission accomplished. Contact made with the Wehrmacht Commander of Prague. Following the cease-fire, Der Führer is marching towards Pilsen into American captivity. Der Führer is signing off. Long Live Germany!

It is unlikely that the message was ever received.

Weidinger then made arrangements to evacuate as many German nationals as possible from the Czech capital and at about 2100 hours a convoy of some 1,000 vehicles, over-flowing with military and civilian personnel, moved off, with private cars and trucks interspersed throughout the column.

The only major incident on the journey was at the city boundary where an unidentified German general and Czech colonel demanded that all weapons be handed over in accordance with the terms of the cease-fire. Weidinger claimed he knew nothing about this and, although a few weapons were rendered useless and thrown away, the column soon continued on its way unmolested. Weidinger's pride and arrogance, however, were about to be brought to an ignominious end. He told later how, at about 1000 hours on 9 May near a small village named Rokicany, 15km short of Pilsen, the leading vehicles of his Regiment were stopped at a sentry post by a member of the US 2nd Infantry Division and orders given for everyone to dismount. He and his staff then marched in step to a meadow where he claims the Americans shouted and swore at them and stole all their war decorations and personal valuables. They were even told they were to be shot. No American officers were to be seen and Weidinger's hopes that he would be able to surrender to a high-ranking officer were dashed. He goes on to say that the next few hours were the most depressing in the lives of his men. Czech civilians repeatedly attempted to attack and rob them and it was only after repeated requests that the Americans eventually took action to protect their prisoners of war.[10]

SS Senior Sergeant Winkler, of the Das Reich Medical Battalion, described how, after fighting their way through Czech rebels, his group came across the first American tanks. They were then escorted by US soldiers to a square where they were stripped of their weapons, watches, cameras and decorations. His attempt to hang on to his old Leica camera brought him his first blow from a rifle butt and he suddenly realised that he had no rights anymore. 'Unconditional surrender' meant what it said.[11]

To this author the only extraordinary thing about these events is that Weidinger and his men should have been so surprised and shocked by the treatment they received. Without gainsaying its military achievements, Der Führer, as one of the most infamous Regiments in the entire Waffen-SS, should have expected nothing less. Its members had, after all, treated the defeated soldiers of other nations in a very similar manner.

Not all Weidinger's men reached safety in formed sub units. The 3rd and 4th SS Panzer-Grenadier Companies of Hauser's 1st Battalion found themselves on 6 May without transport for the move to Prague and by the time sufficient trucks had been made available the roads to the south were blocked. They ended up, each Company some 600 men strong due to an infusion of stragglers, spending the 9th, 10th and 11th without orders and completely isolated in a defensive position in some woods half way between Dresden and Prague. On the evening of 12 May the overall commander, SS Lieutenant Schmager, gave orders for weapons to be made unusable, Waffen-SS emblems destroyed and for the men to disperse to the west. He described later how even veteran NCOs could not hide their tears, and his men's faces twitched as the precious emblems of years of combat were placed in a pile, soaked in petrol and set on fire.[12]

Once in their homeland the soldiers of the Waffen-SS hoped to find help in reaching their families. None suspected how forlorn this hope would be. A few days after the end of hostilities, posters appeared throughout the Allied occupation zones warning that anyone who took in, helped or failed to report soldiers of the Waffen-SS to the responsible authorities would be punished. It went on to threaten that forced labour awaited the soldiers of the Waffen-SS!

In fact, worse was to come. The men of Paul Hausser's once mighty Divisions were to suffer the worse of all possible indignities for a soldier – they were to be branded criminals. In December 1945 it was announced that the entire Waffen-SS was being charged before the International Military Tribunal with being a criminal organisation. This was followed in November 1946 by the removal of their prisoner of war status and the announcement that they were henceforth civilian internees in automatic arrest. Their demise was complete.

Headquarters II SS Panzer Corps

After the Headquarters staff and men of the Corps Escort Company and Army Signal Company 400 (permanently attached to Headquarters II SS Panzer Corps) reached the safety of Linz on 8 May, Willi Bittrich addressed them as follows:

> My comrades!
> We stand here today at the saddest of all moments for a soldier – surrender on orders from above. But we look each other in the eye once more at this time of farewell and however discouraging our inner world may be, we know we still have a duty to fulfil. The way ahead is uncertain, with the bitter lot of captivity and perhaps even exile stretching before us . . .
> I thank you for your military commitment and for your loyalty; and for your admirable discipline, which I ask you to maintain in the dark days ahead. For many long years, even decades, our national anthem will no longer be heard and the words Germany and Fatherland will not be spoken. But in our hearts we will keep them sacred for the coming generations, to whom God may grant freedom and a better fate.
> Long Live Germany and the Fatherland!

With that, Bittrich led his men into captivity.

NOTES

1. Tieke, *In the Firestorm of the Last Years of the War*, p. 440.
2. Ibid., pp. 440–1.
3. Ibid., p. 441.
4. Weidinger, *Division Das Reich, Vol V*, p. 554.
5. Ibid., p. 553.
6. Including 2 SS Arty Bn, a coy of 2 SS Recce Bn & an Army Recce coy.
7. Weidinger, op. cit., p. 556.
8. Ibid.
9. Ibid., p. 557.
10. Ibid., p. 566.
11. Ibid.
12. Wiedinger, *Comrades to the End*, p. 424.

Epilogue

The traumas faced by the veterans of the Waffen-SS in the immediate post-war years must be amongst the most unique and harrowing in modern history. From an intimate environment of comradeship and discipline, forged in a regime of racial and military supremacy and tempered in the exhilaration and terror of battle, these men were derided, degraded, abused and ultimately branded common criminals. Most were able to come through the initial months of captivity relatively unscathed by falling back on their own inner discipline and the support of their fellow prisoners. Allied attempts to break their morale, by separating them from other prisoners of war, severely restricting food, depriving them of mail and contacts with their families, breaking up units and segregating the officers and senior NCOs, failed. And it was soon clear that the men who had participated in undreamed of victories, endured crushing defeats and seen a new and, as far as they were concerned, idealistic Empire crumble to nothing, were not going to be defeated again within the confines of a prison camp. In fact, the treatment meted out by their captors caused them to draw ever closer together.[1]

Most of the Waffen-SS veterans felt they were deliberately maligned after the war and their efforts as soldiers misrepresented. Paradoxically, those efforts had prolonged the war and actually led to the total destruction of the very things for which they had been fighting. The men of II SS Panzer Corps failed to comprehend that through their membership of the SS, and by the fact that they had worn the same uniform and emblems as the SS doctors and guards in death camps like Auschwitz, they had, in the eyes of most people outside Germany and many inside, forfeited the right to be recognised as honourable men. Most of them had been so brainwashed by Nazi ideology and military jingoism that they had no understanding of the bitterness felt by their former enemies in the West. Even today they are puzzled that so few American, British, Canadian or Polish WWII veterans are prepared to 'forgive and forget'.

Yet, the pressures and degradation suffered in the late 1940s were to bring many veterans to the depths of despair. One of their most bitter shocks was to find their own countrymen, armed with rifles and dressed in green uniforms, guarding the very camps in which they were incarcerated. Soon they met comrades who had reached the sanctuary of their homes and villages, only to be betrayed to the occupying authorities. The loss of prisoner of war status upset them greatly, for after being re-graded as civilian internees in automatic arrest rather than prisoners of war, only those who had been 'denazified' could be released from the 'internment' camps. Special tribunals were established to carry out this 'denazification' and the former members of the 2nd, 9th and 10th SS Panzer Divisions were graded into one of three categories: 'major offender' (which automatically included all officers down to SS major), 'incriminated' or 'fellow-traveller'. The only exceptions were those who had been drafted into Waffen-SS, but even then if the draftee had been promoted to NCO rank, he too was 'incriminated'. The grading decided the 'sanction': labour service in an internment camp, monetary fine, prohibition of working in one's profession, or loss of right to vote or to be elected either for life or for a limited period after release.

Release itself often added to the traumas. Many veterans found that on returning home they were not only shunned by their neighbours but were able to obtain only manual work. Alone amongst the former members of the Wehrmacht they were denied any form of war or disablement pension.

Most of the veterans of I and II SS Panzer Corps had been released by the end of 1948 but for some, particularly the veterans of the Leibstandarte, Das Reich and Hitlerjugend Divisions, there were to be many more years of captivity. Quite apart from the overall charge of genocide laid against the Nazi regime, all the Allied armies had a particular horror or atrocity to lay at the doors of the Germans in general and Waffen-SS in particular – the Americans had the 'Malmédy Massacre', the British 'Wormhoudt', the Canadians the 'Ardenne Abbey' and the French had 'Oradour-sur-Glane'.

Military trials of those accused of war crimes began in late 1945, and on 25 December that year the former commander of the Hitlerjugend Division, Kurt Meyer, was sentenced to 'suffer death by being shot'. The sentence was never carried out but as late as January 1949 the British hanged two Hitlerjugend officers[2] for causing the death of three Canadian PWs in Normandy in June 1944.

The first major military trial was held in the former concentration camp at Dachau in May 1946 and concerned the events surrounding the 'Malmédy Massacre'. The details need not concern us but can be found in this author's book, *The Devil's Adjutant – Jochen Peiper, Panzer Leader*. Suffice to say here that on 16 July 1946 forty-three former members of I SS Panzer Corps were sentenced to death by hanging, twenty-two others, including Sepp Dietrich, the Sixth Army commander, received life and the remainder long terms of imprisonment – Hermann Priess, the Corps commander, got twenty years and Fritz Kraemer, Dietrich's Chief of Staff, ten. In the event, no one was hanged and all had been released by the end of December 1956.

More pertinent to our history is the trial held before a French Higher

Military Court in Bordeaux in early 1953, in which twenty-one former members of Das Reich were charged with participation in the Oradour-sur-Glane massacre. Forty-two others were indicted but could not be traced. As already mentioned in Chapter IV, of the two officers directly involved, one was dead and the other, Erich-Otto Kahn, had disappeared.[3] Fourteen of the defendants were French citizens – Alsatians who had been serving in Das Reich at the time. Twelve of them were not taken into custody until 1952 and their arrest caused fury throughout Alsace. Inevitably, the trial proved highly controversial and the verdicts satisfied no one. One Alsatian and one German were sentenced to death; the rest of the Alsatians got four to eight years' imprisonment and the Germans, except one who was cleared, eight to twelve. In Limoges, 50,000 marched in protest and the Bishop spoke out against the sentences. In Paris, the National deputies were accused of condoning the Oradour massacre. In the end a special amnesty law was rushed through the National Assembly, the death sentences commuted to imprisonment and all the Alsatians freed. The last Germans were released on 17 April 1959.

But what of some of the main characters in our history? Paul Hausser appeared as a witness rather than as a defendant at Nuremberg and was questioned about atrocities at Lidice, Oradour-sur-Glane, in Yugoslavia and in the Warsaw Ghetto. He denied personal responsibility for, or connection with, any of these events and said he had no knowledge of the Waffen-SS being involved in the destruction of the Warsaw Ghetto. He wrote two books about the Waffen-SS before dying, aged 92, in 1972.

Sepp Dietrich was paroled in October 1955, tried before a West German court in 1957 for his part in the 'Night of the Long Knives' and sentenced to another eighteen months in prison. He died in April 1966 and was given a hero's funeral by his 'boys'.

Willi Bittrich was handed over to the French who held him in custody until his trial for alleged atrocities before a Higher Military Court in Bordeaux in 1953. He was acquitted and returned to West Germany the following year. He died in April 1979.

Heinz Lammerding, the commander of Das Reich at the time of the Oradour-sur-Glane massacre, was indicted by the French in 1951 but the British refused to hand him over for trial. He was sentenced to death in absentia. He eventually returned to his original profession of engineering and died of cancer in Düsseldorf in 1971.

Sylvester Stadler settled in the Augsberg area and died in August 1995. Heinz Harmel worked as a manufacturer's representative in Duisburg. He died in September 2000 aged 94. Walther Harzer became a consulting engineer in the Stuttgart area. He died of heart failure in May 1982.

Rudolf Lehmann, after working as a senior officer in HIAG – the 'Society for the mutual help of members of the former Waffen-SS' – and writing four volumes of the History of the Leibstandarte, died of cancer in Bad Tölz in 1971. Ralf Tiemann completed the LAH history and is still alive.

Ernst Krag was released in January 1948 and worked as a construction engineer in Istanbul before returning to West Germany in the same capacity. He died in 1994.

Otto Weidinger died in 1990 after writing a complete history of the 2nd SS Panzer Division Das Reich (five volumes) as well as the story of the Regiment Der Führer.

Rudolf Enseling died in Karlsruhe in 1977, Hans-Peter Knaust of cancer in Kevelaer, only 50km from Arnhem, in 1983 and Günther Wisliceny in Hannover in August 1985.

It is difficult today to understand the awe, dread and terror that the mere mention of 'Waffen-SS' engendered fifty-five years ago. Initially no more than novices in the art of warfare and mocked by the rest of the Wehrmacht as bungling amateurs, its members soon earned the respect of friend and foe alike. Why was this? What made these men go on fighting when most others would have quit? And here we face a number of contradictions. That they were motivated by the supremacism of a thoroughly evil regime did not prevent them from being fine leaders and soldiers and the fact that they came almost exclusively from Christian homes and schools did not prevent them from acting brutally and sometimes without mercy. But then, the Waffen-SS did not believe that war was a 'game' to be played by 'rules'; it was a contest that had to be won and it was unthinkable that other contestants could or should be allowed to win. The Soviets were seen as inferior beings and the Americans, British and Canadians as inferior soldiers. Wounds were to be borne with pride and never used as a reason to leave the field of battle; mercy was seen as a sign of weakness and was normally neither offered nor expected.

Despite the short and often inadequate training received before being committed to battle, the motivation, discipline and intense comradeship of the men of the Waffen-SS enabled these men to achieve remarkable results. The combination of skilled officers and senior NCOs and brave, dedicated soldiers made for an extremely formidable military machine. Suggestions that the junior ranks acted out of blind obedience are completely erroneous. In fact, there was a very close relationship between officers, most of whom had served in the ranks, NCOs and men and there are countless examples of junior NCOs and even privates taking over positions of responsibility when those above them were killed or wounded – a rare occurrence in the Allied armies.

Finally, it has to be said that the fact that these men were part of an elite organisation within an elitist nation inevitably affected their outlook. They believed themselves to be superior to all others and this attitude, when coupled with excellent weaponry, attractive uniforms and symbols and an abundance of meaningful medals worn even in battle to single out the brave, made these men unique. It also has to be said that the men of the Waffen-SS Panzer Divisions were, and still are, proud of being soldiers and of being members of those Divisions. This pride, and a singular lack of culpability for the crimes of the Waffen-SS, is clearly evident in the German histories quoted in this book. Their comradeship is undiminished and for many, their unit remains their real 'home'.

NOTES

1. Weidinger, *Comrades to the End*, p. 427.
2. Bernard Siebken and Dietrich Schnabel.
3. In 1985 he was reported living in Sweden.

Appendix I

In order to complete this history, it is now time to look, if only briefly, at what happened to the 10th SS Panzer Division Frundsberg, and the 102nd SS Heavy Panzer Battalion.

Frundsberg: January – May 1945
(Map 27)

We left Heinz Harmel's 10th SS Panzer Division on 25 January in Upper Alsace. Much as Hitler might have wished it to join its fellow SS Panzer Divisions in Operation SPRING AWAKENING in Hungary, events elsewhere on the Eastern Front were dictating otherwise. Soviet offensives in the north had advanced over 150km; Warsaw, Lodz and Cracow had fallen, and by early February Soviet Armies had occupied much of East Prussia and reached Frankfurt am Oder, 60km due east of Berlin. The threat to the capital and the inner Reich was clear. It is not altogether surprising therefore that on 4 February the Frundsberg was summoned to help stem a Red tide which was threatening to overwhelm most of Germany before the Western Allies had even crossed its frontiers.

The first Frundsberg trains began arriving in Stettin on 10 February. Two days later a strength return shows the Division with fifty Panthers, thirty-seven Mk IVs, eight Flakpanzer IVs and twenty Jagdpanzer IVs and Vs. Even so, the Frundsberg was still incomplete on 16 February when, as part of XXXIX Panzer Corps[1], it was thrown into an unsuccessful counter-offensive code-named Operation SONNENWENDE.

The fighting on the east side of the Oder, opposite Stettin, was bitter and chaotic. Apart from a week in reserve, Harmel's men remained fully involved until 19 March when Hitler finally agreed to a withdrawal across the Oder. By this time the Frundsberg was part of III SS Panzer Corps.[2] Wilhelm Tieke describes the end of this phase of the Frundsberg's operations:

The last Panthers of the 10th SS Panzer Regiment passed over the railway bridge across the Oder. Then this bridge too went up in the air. With that, the battle in Eastern Pomerania found its conclusion – a conclusion that saw the virtual destruction of III SS Panzer Corps. It had stood in sacrificial combat to the last and its only concern was

327

to hold open a way across the Oder for streaming treks of refugees and stragglers.[3]

A strength return dated 15 March shows a surprisingly small reduction in armour – only five Mk IVs fewer than a month earlier. Personnel statistics, however, indicate losses, from all causes, of over 2,000 men between 1 February and 25 March. Amongst the leaders, the commander of the 10th SS Panzer Regiment, SS Lieutenant Colonel Otto Paetsch, was killed on 9 March. Ernst Tetsch of the 1st SS Panzer Battalion took over and was awarded a Knight's Cross for his actions in this period. After knocking out thirteen Soviet tanks, so bringing his total kills to forty, the commander of the 7th SS Panzer Company, SS Lieutenant Franz Riedel, also received this coveted award, as did another officer in the 1st SS Panzer Battalion, SS Lieutenant Franz Scherzer.

On 27 March Harmel received orders to move his Division to the Frankfurt am Oder sector. Two days later, whilst the bulk of the Frundsberg was still on the move, the destination was changed to an assembly area 20km to the east of Görlitz. This change probably occurred because Hitler was still convinced, wrongly, that the Soviets were more interested in linking up with the Americans in Saxony than in taking his capital. On arrival, the Frundsberg was allowed to spend a period of nearly two weeks 'refitting and training'. A strength return for this period shows the Division with a total of 15,067 men, forty-seven Panthers, thirty-five Mk IVs, eight Flak Panzer IVs, eighteen Jagdpanzers, ten Shermans, and 138 SPWs. It also had thirty-three howitzers and ten 100mm cannon ready for action.[4]

It was towards the end of March that Heinz Harmel developed severe neuritis in an arm and left for treatment in Berlin. Whilst in the capital, he personally briefed Hitler on the state of his Division and it was there, on 16 April, that he learned that the Soviets had broken out of their bridgeheads over the Oder and Niesse rivers in a final great offensive. As Harmel rushed back to his Division, he learned that his Führer had given orders that the Frundsberg was not to be committed but was to be placed in Army Group reserve and moved to a location between Dresden and Görlitz. But hardly had the first units started to arrive in this new area on the 17th, when the orders were changed again and the Division ordered to counter-attack a serious Russian penetration around Spremberg. This proved beyond its capability, and by the 19th the Russian onslaught had split the Division into three groups. Brinkmann's 10th SS Reconnaissance Battalion was separated somewhere to the north of the main fighting element, and some of the tanks and artillery pieces were stranded without fuel with the Divisional administrative units in the original assembly area. By last light on the 20th, a substantial part of the Frundsberg, together with the 344th Infantry Division and the Führer

Begleit Brigade, was surrounded to the north-west of Spremberg. It was at this critical moment that Harmel received orders direct from the Führerbunker. They were endorsed by the Army Group commander, Field Marshal Schörner, and read:

> The gap in the front existing in your sector between Spremberg and Cottbus is to be closed by immediate attacks to the north. You are held personally responsible for the completion of these orders. You must carry the attack to victory or fall with your Division.[5]

Harmel knew full well that such an attack was unlikely to achieve any-thing decisive and would almost certainly lead to the destruction of his command. His Division had suffered losses of 577 killed, 1,432 wounded and sixty-seven missing, including fifty-one officers, in the previous two weeks.[6] After consulting his staff and fellow formation commanders, Harmel decided to ignore the order. Whether he decided to do so for purely military reasons or because he had become aware of the true state of his leader's mental health during his recent visit to Berlin, we shall never know. Whatever the reason, the result was to be dramatic. Harmel, and Otto Remer of the Führer Begleit Brigade resolved, instead of attack-ing, to break out to the north-west and join up with the German forces south of Berlin.[7] These included the Frundsberg's 10th SS Reconnaissance Battalion. The commander of the 344th Infantry Division eventually agreed to cover their northern flank, and during the night of 20 April the withdrawal began.

Harmel's plan of moving north-west soon proved impracticable. The Russians were everywhere but clearly strongest in the sector between Spremberg and Berlin. As his already depleted force was forced to move, first west and then south-west, towards the Dresden sector of the Elbe, it became ever weaker and more dispersed. SS Major Brandt, the com-mander of the 10th SS Pioneer Battalion, was blinded whilst leading the column on the 21st, and the following day the 10th and 11th SS Artillery Batteries, after firing off their last rounds, were forced to destroy their guns. The only real success came on the 24th, when a Russian re-supply convoy was ambushed and 'rations, fuel and intact vehicles taken along as booty'.

On 26 April the remnants of the Frundsberg went into a 'hedgehog' position 20km north-west of Dresden. It desperately needed time to reor-ganise and it was fortunate that the units that had been stranded without fuel west of Görlitz on the 17th were able to rejoin during this short respite without too much difficulty. The Division then remained in its 'hedgehog' position awaiting orders.

On the 27th a Fiesler Storch light liaison aircraft, carrying an unidenti-fied Luftwaffe general arrived in the 'hedgehog'. He had come to find out which formation it was and to brief the commander. The following day the pilot returned with instructions that Harmel was to report personally to the commander of Army Group Mitte, Field Marshal Schörner. When he arrived at the Army Group Headquarters he was kept waiting until the following morning and then told that the Field Marshal was away at the front. Harmel was handed a letter. It accused his Division of refusing its duty at Spremberg and relieved him of his command. To Harmel's surprise he was not placed under arrest, and two days later the former commander of the 10th SS Panzer Division Frundsberg was commanding a hotchpotch of units in the Klagenfurt sector of southern Austria. There he fought a delaying action until surrendering to the British on 8 May.

Following Harmel's abrupt departure, SS Lieutenant Colonel Franz Roestel, the commander of the Division's SS Panzerjäger Battalion, became the last commander of the Frundsberg. On 3 May, in an attempt to form some sort of front against the advancing Russians, he ordered part of his force to make a limited move to the east, north of Dresden. But it was too late for heroic moves and on 6 May the Frundsberg cleared the Elbe in the Dresden area and headed south. On the same day the last survivors of Brinkmann's 10th SS Reconnaissance Battalion, which had become embroiled in the fighting on the south-eastern approaches to Berlin, managed to cross the Elbe due west of the capital and surrender to the American 102nd Infantry Division.

The last tank engagement of the Frundsberg took place on the 7th. Five T-34s were claimed but that night the German crews were forced to blow up their last remaining vehicles. During the 8th and 9th small columns and groups of the once powerful Division continued moving south-west but were:

> Fired on and scattered by Russian tanks. The cohesiveness was lost ... The remnants of the Division fought their way ... to the border at Klingenthal and arrived there between the 10th and 12th. Many Frundsbergers fought their way to their birthplaces where many were captured by the Russians or Czechs and many, all too many, died along the way. No stone or cross preserves their names.[8]

102nd SS Heavy Panzer Battalion

Re-numbered as the 502nd SS Heavy Panzer Battalion, the II SS Panzer Corps Tiger Battalion was reformed at the Sennelager Training Centre near Paderborn in November 1944 under the command of SS Major Kurt Hartrampf. By 8 March 1945, when it was ordered to the Eastern Front, it had thirty-one Tiger IIs, organised into three Companies. SS Captain Kalls was still commanding the 1st Company and SS Second Lieutenant

Schroif, another Normandy veteran, was one of the platoon commanders.

The Battalion went into action against the Soviet bridgehead over the Oder north of Frankfurt on 22 March as part of XXXIX Panzer Corps. Then, as part of XI SS Panzer Corps, it remained continuously in action to the east and south of Berlin until 28 April, when the final attempt was made to break out to the west with thirteen operational Tigers from what was known as the Halbe Pocket. The commander of the 1st Company, SS Captain Kalls was killed on 2 May; by then all the 502nd's Tigers had been put out of action. An unknown number of Hartrampf's crewmen, but certainly the majority, managed to cross the Elbe due west of Berlin and surrender to the Americans before the Russians finally sealed the demarcation line. The commanding officer, Kurt Hartrampf, despite coming under fierce criticism from some of his own officers for his performance during this period[9], was awarded the Knight's Cross on 28 April.

NOTES

1. 4 SS Pz-Gren Div Polizei, Pz Div Holstein & 28 SS Pz-Gren Div Wallonien.
2. 11 SS Pz-Gren Div Nordland, 23 SS Pz-Gren Div Nederland, 27 SS Gren Div Langemarck & FBB.
3. Tieke, *In the Firestorm of the Last Years of the War*, p. 362.
4. Ibid., p. 474.
5. Ibid., p. 402.
6. Ibid., pp. 474–6.
7. Ibid.
8. Ibid., pp, 410–1.
9. Schneider, *Tigers in Combat II*, p. 334.

Appendix II

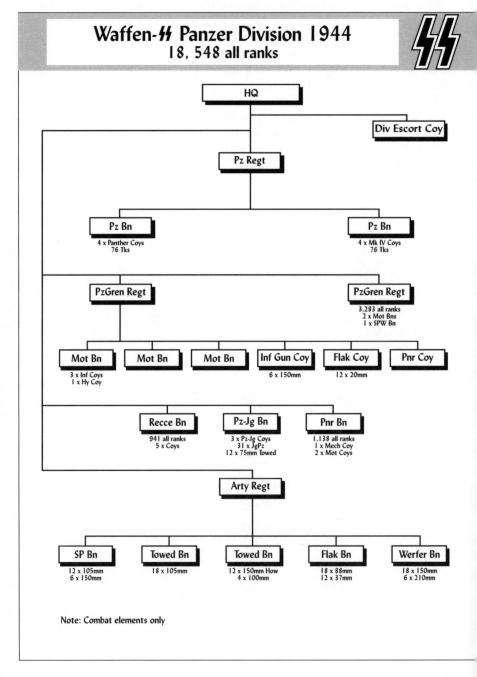

Waffen-**SS** Panzer Division 1944
18, 548 all ranks

HQ

Div Escort Coy

Pz Regt

Pz Bn
4 x Panther Coys
76 Tks

Pz Bn
4 x Mk IV Coys
76 Tks

PzGren Regt

PzGren Regt
3,283 all ranks
2 x Mot Bns
1 x SPW Bn

Mot Bn
3 x Inf Coys
1 x Hy Coy

Mot Bn

Mot Bn

Inf Gun Coy
6 x 150mm

Flak Coy
12 x 20mm

Pnr Coy

Recce Bn
941 all ranks
5 x Coys

Pz-Jg Bn
3 x Pz-Jg Coys
31 x JgPz
12 x 75mm Towed

Pnr Bn
1,138 all ranks
1 x Mech Coy
2 x Mot Coys

Arty Regt

SP Bn
12 x 105mm
6 x 150mm

Towed Bn
18 x 105mm

Towed Bn
12 x 150mm How
4 x 100mm

Flak Bn
18 x 88mm
12 x 37mm

Werfer Bn
18 x 150mm
6 x 210mm

Note: Combat elements only

Appendix III

Soviet Guards Mechanized Corps, 1945

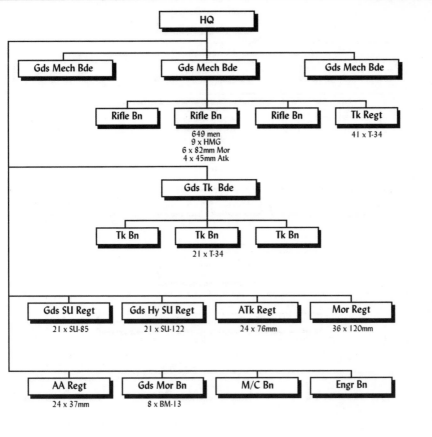

HQ

Gds Mech Bde Gds Mech Bde Gds Mech Bde

Rifle Bn Rifle Bn Rifle Bn Tk Regt

649 men
9 x HMG
6 x 82mm Mor
4 x 45mm Atk

41 x T-34

Gds Tk Bde

Tk Bn Tk Bn Tk Bn

21 x T-34

Gds SU Regt Gds Hy SU Regt ATk Regt Mor Regt

21 x SU-85 21 x SU-122 24 x 76mm 36 x 120mm

AA Regt Gds Mor Bn M/C Bn Engr Bn

24 x 37mm 8 x BM-13

Totals: 16,318 men
188 x T-34/85
21 x SU-85
21 x SU-122

Note: A Soviet Tank Corps was similarly organized but with three
Tank Brigades and one Motorized Rifle Brigade. It had
208 tanks and 62 SUs.

Appendix IV

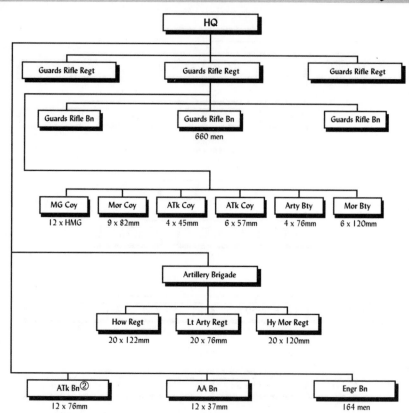

Soviet Guards Rifle Division, 1945
(11,706 men)[1]

HQ

Guards Rifle Regt — **Guards Rifle Regt** — **Guards Rifle Regt**

Guards Rifle Bn — **Guards Rifle Bn** — **Guards Rifle Bn**
660 men

MG Coy	Mor Coy	ATk Coy	ATk Coy	Arty Bty	Mor Bty
12 x HMG	9 x 82mm	4 x 45mm	6 x 57mm	4 x 76mm	6 x 120mm

Artillery Brigade

How Regt	Lt Arty Regt	Hy Mor Regt
20 x 122mm	20 x 76mm	20 x 120mm

ATk Bn[2]	AA Bn	Engr Bn
12 x 76mm	12 x 37mm	164 men

Notes:

① Normal Soviet Rifle Divisions were not as strong; they had
    2087 fewer men
      17 fewer 120mm mortars
      17 fewer 82mm mortars
       8 fewer 122mm howitzers
       6 fewer 37mm AA guns and about
    1500 fewer MGs of all calibers.

② Sometimes equipped with 16 x 76mm SP guns.

Appendix V

British/Canadian Infantry Division
June 1944

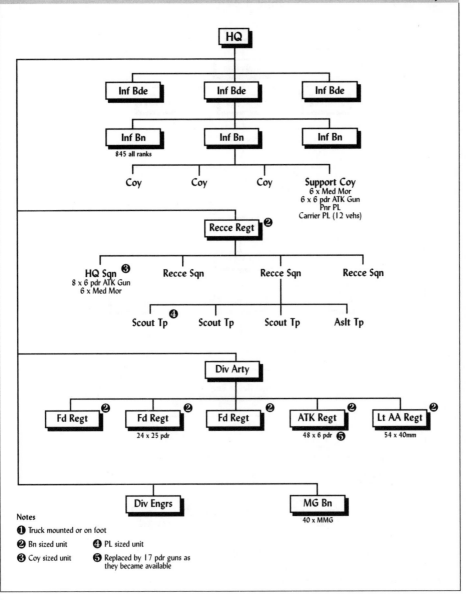

HQ

Inf Bde — Inf Bde — Inf Bde

Inf Bn — Inf Bn — Inf Bn
845 all ranks

Coy — Coy — Coy — Support Coy
6 x Med Mor
6 x 6 pdr ATK Gun
Pnr PL
Carrier PL (12 vehs)

Recce Regt ❷

HQ Sqn ❸ — Recce Sqn — Recce Sqn — Recce Sqn
8 x 6 pdr ATK Gun
6 x Med Mor

Scout Tp ❹ — Scout Tp — Scout Tp — Aslt Tp

Div Arty

Fd Regt ❷ — Fd Regt ❷ — Fd Regt ❷ — ATK Regt ❷ — Lt AA Regt ❷
24 x 25 pdr — 48 x 6 pdr ❺ — 54 x 40mm

Div Engrs — MG Bn
40 x MMG

Notes
❶ Truck mounted or on foot
❷ Bn sized unit   ❹ PL sized unit
❸ Coy sized unit   ❺ Replaced by 17 pdr guns as
they became available

Appendix VI

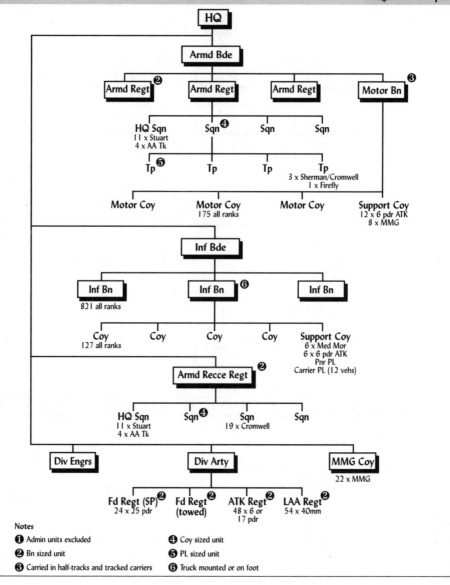

British/Canadian/Polish[1] Armoured Division June 1944

HQ

Armd Bde

Armd Regt[2] **Armd Regt** **Armd Regt** **Motor Bn**[3]

HQ Sqn
11 x Stuart
4 x AA Tk

Sqn[4] **Sqn** **Sqn**

Tp[5] **Tp** **Tp** **Tp**
3 x Sherman/Cromwell
1 x Firefly

Motor Coy **Motor Coy**
175 all ranks **Motor Coy** **Support Coy**
12 x 6 pdr ATK
8 x MMG

Inf Bde

Inf Bn **Inf Bn**[6] **Inf Bn**
821 all ranks

Coy **Coy** **Coy** **Coy** **Support Coy**
127 all ranks 6 x Med Mor
6 x 6 pdr ATK
Pnr PL
Carrier PL (12 vehs)

Armd Recce Regt[2]

HQ Sqn **Sqn**[4] **Sqn** **Sqn**
11 x Stuart 19 x Cromwell
4 x AA Tk

Div Engrs **Div Arty** **MMG Coy**
22 x MMG

Fd Regt (SP)[2] **Fd Regt**[2] **ATK Regt**[2] **LAA Regt**[2]
24 x 25 pdr (towed) 48 x 6 or 54 x 40mm
17 pdr

Notes

[1] Admin units excluded
[2] Bn sized unit
[3] Carried in half-tracks and tracked carriers
[4] Coy sized unit
[5] PL sized unit
[6] Truck mounted or on foot

Appendix VII

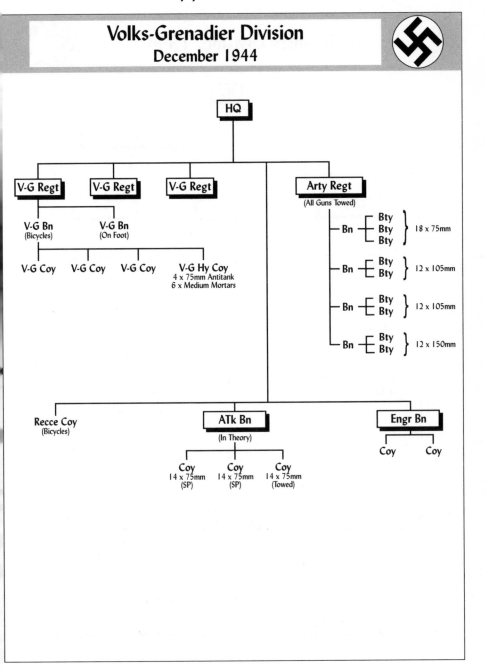

Volks-Grenadier Division
December 1944

HQ

V-G Regt

V-G Regt

V-G Regt

Arty Regt
(All Guns Towed)

V-G Bn
(Bicycles)

V-G Bn
(On Foot)

V-G Coy   **V-G Coy**   **V-G Coy**   **V-G Hy Coy**
4 x 75mm Antitank
6 x Medium Mortars

Bn — Bty Bty Bty } 18 x 75mm

Bn — Bty Bty } 12 x 105mm

Bn — Bty Bty } 12 x 105mm

Bn — Bty Bty } 12 x 150mm

Recce Coy
(Bicycles)

ATk Bn
(In Theory)

Engr Bn

Coy   Coy

Coy
14 x 75mm
(SP)

Coy
14 x 75mm
(SP)

Coy
14 x 75mm
(Towed)

Appendix VIII

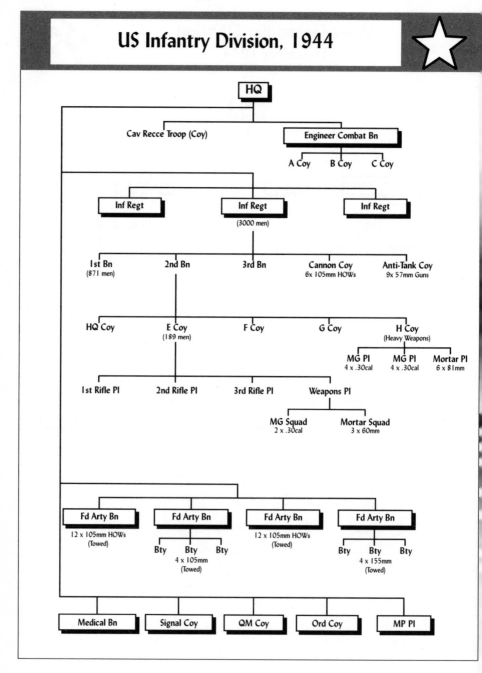

US Infantry Division, 1944

HQ

Cav Recce Troop (Coy)

Engineer Combat Bn
- A Coy
- B Coy
- C Coy

Inf Regt

Inf Regt (3000 men)

Inf Regt

1st Bn (871 men) — 2nd Bn — 3rd Bn — Cannon Coy (6x 105mm HOWs) — Anti-Tank Coy (9x 57mm Guns)

HQ Coy — E Coy (189 men) — F Coy — G Coy — H Coy (Heavy Weapons)

H Coy:
- MG Pl (4 x .30cal)
- MG Pl (4 x .30cal)
- Mortar Pl (6 x 81mm)

1st Rifle Pl — 2nd Rifle Pl — 3rd Rifle Pl — Weapons Pl

Weapons Pl:
- MG Squad (2 x .30cal)
- Mortar Squad (3 x 60mm)

Fd Arty Bn — 12 x 105mm HOWs (Towed)

Fd Arty Bn
- Bty
- Bty (4 x 105mm, Towed)
- Bty

Fd Arty Bn — 12 x 105mm HOWs (Towed)

Fd Arty Bn
- Bty
- Bty (4 x 155mm, Towed)
- Bty

Medical Bn — **Signal Coy** — **QM Coy** — **Ord Coy** — **MP Pl**

Appendix IX

US Armored Division, 1944[1]

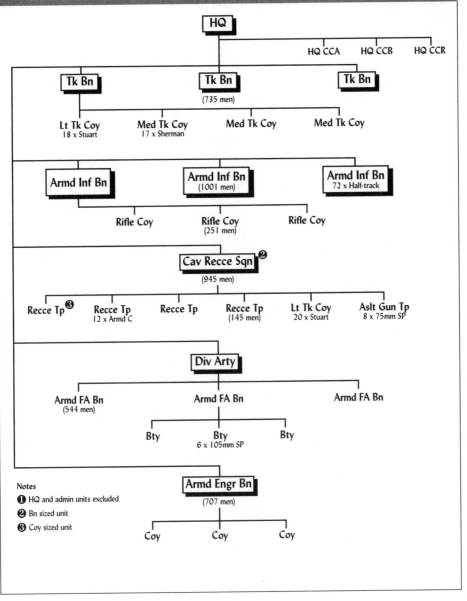

HQ

HQ CCA   HQ CCB   HQ CCR

Tk Bn

Tk Bn
(735 men)

Tk Bn

Lt Tk Coy
18 x Stuart

Med Tk Coy
17 x Sherman

Med Tk Coy

Med Tk Coy

Armd Inf Bn

Armd Inf Bn
(1001 men)

Armd Inf Bn
72 x Half-track

Rifle Coy

Rifle Coy
(251 men)

Rifle Coy

Cav Recce Sqn [2]
(945 men)

Recce Tp[3]

Recce Tp
12 x Armd C

Recce Tp

Recce Tp
(145 men)

Lt Tk Coy
20 x Stuart

Aslt Gun Tp
8 x 75mm SP

Div Arty

Armd FA Bn
(544 men)

Armd FA Bn

Armd FA Bn

Bty

Bty
6 x 105mm SP

Bty

Armd Engr Bn
(707 men)

Coy

Coy

Coy

Notes
[1] HQ and admin units excluded
[2] Bn sized unit
[3] Coy sized unit

Appendix X

Main Weapon Systems

Note: this short guide is not intended to be comprehensive in terms of total weapon systems or technical detail.

German

Mk IV tank – crew 5, 75mm high velocity gun, two MGs, 80mm frontal hull armour, range 210km, weight 25 tons.

Mk V Panther tank – crew 5, 75mm very high velocity gun, up to three MGs, 80mm frontal hull armour, range 200km, weight 45.5 tons.

Mk VI Tiger I tank – crew 5, 88mm high velocity gun, up to three MGs, 100mm frontal hull armour, range 140km, weight 56 tons.

Mk VI Tiger II tank – crew 5, 88mm very high velocity gun, up to three MGs, 150mm frontal hull armour, range 170km, weight 69 tons.

StuG III (assault gun) – crew 4, 75mm high velocity gun, up to two MGs, 80mm frontal hull armour, range 155km, weight 24 tons.

Jagdpanzer IV (anti-tank tank) – crew 4, 75mm high velocity gun, two MGs, 80mm frontal hull armour, range 210km, weight 24 tons.

SPW (armoured personnel carrier) – many types ranging from a basic infantry personnel carrier (12 men, including commander and driver) with two MGs, to engineer, AA, anti-tank and command vehicles, 14.5mm frontal armour, range 300km, weight 9 tons, open topped.

Hummel – 150mm SP heavy howitzer, crew six, gun maximum range about 14km, 30mm frontal armour, range 215km, weight 24 tons, open topped.

Wespe – 105mm SP light howitzer, gun maximum range about 12km, 20mm frontal armour, range 220km, weight 11.5 tons, open topped.

Bison (Grille) – 150mm SP infantry howitzer, crew four, maximum range 5km, range 190km, 12 tons, open topped.

Flak (AA) guns – 88mm towed, 37mm and 20mm towed and SP, single and multi barreled; all open topped.

Mortars – 80mm and 120mm with ranges of 2.4 and 6km respectively.

Nebelwerfers – 150mm, 210mm and 300mm with maximum ranges of 6.5km, 7.5km and 5km respectively.

Basic anti-tank gun – 75mm, towed, range out to 4.5km.
Panzerfaust – hand-held anti-tank weapon, range out to 100m.

Allied

M-4 American Sherman tank – crew 5, 75mm medium velocity gun, up
to three MGs, 50mm frontal hull armour, range 160km, weight 32 tons.
Cromwell British tank – crew 5, 75mm medium velocity gun, two MGs,
63 to 102mm frontal hull armour, range 240km, weight 29 tons.
M-5 (Stuart) American light tank – crew 4, 37mm high velocity gun, two
MGs, 38mm frontal hull armour, range 112km, weight 15 tons.
T-34/85 Soviet tank – crew 5, 85mm high velocity gun, two MGs, 90mm
frontal hull armour, range 300km, weight 35 tons.
SU-100 Soviet SP TD – crew 4, 100mm high velocity gun, two MGs, 45mm
frontal hull armour, range 240km, weight 36 tons, open topped.
M-10 American SP TD – crew 5, 76mm low velocity gun, one MG, 38mm
frontal armour, range 300km, weight 30 tons, open topped.
M-36 American SP TD – crew 5, 90mm high velocity gun, one MG, 38mm
frontal armour, range 240km, weight 28 tons, open topped.

Bibliography

In compiling this history, my primary sources of information are listed below. In addition, all relevant American After Action Reports and British War Diaries have been consulted, as well as numerous German Headquarters' Radio and Telephone Logs and Daily Reports. Further valuable information was obtained through personal interviews with veterans and from interviews carried out shortly after the war by various individuals on behalf of the US Army Historical Branch. The records of these latter interviews are held in the US National Archives. Information on German equipment holdings originated in the Bunbdesarchiv Germany (Reference RH 10). Various Soviet Official Histories and other relevant documents originated in the Frunze Military Academy, Moscow.

Books consulted and in some cases quoted, were:

Belfield, Eversley & Essame, H., *The Battle for Normandy*, Batsford Ltd, 1965.

Brereton, Lewis H, *The Brereton Diaries, The War in the Air in the Pacific, Middle East and Europe, October 1941–8 May 1945*, William Morrow & Co, New York 1946.

Cantlay, W G, *A Sapper's War*, unpublished.

Carver, Lt Col R.M.P., *Second to None*, Messrs McCorquodale & Co Ltd, 1954.

Cooper Derek, *Dangerous Liaison*, Michael Russell (Publishing) Ltd, 1997.

Danchev, Alex & Todman, Daniel, *War Diaries 1939–1945, Field Marshal Lord Alanbrooke*, Weidenfeld & Nicolson, London, 2001.

D'Este, Carlo, *A Genius for War*, HarperCollins Publishers, 1995.

Dugdale. J, *Panzer Divisions, Panzer Grenadier Divisions, Panzer Brigades of the Army and the Waffen SS in the West, Volume I [Part 1]*, Galago Publishing, 2000.

Eastwood, Gray & Green, *When Dragons Flew*, Silver Link Publishing Ltd, 1994.

Ellis, Major L F, *The Welsh Guards at War*, Gale and Polden, 1946.

Elstob, Peter, *Hitler's Last Offensive*, Macmillan, USA, 1971.

Fey, Will, *Armour battles of the Waffen-SS 1943–45*, J J Fedorowicz Publishing Inc, Manitoba, Canada, 1990.

Fitzgerald, Major J D L, *The History of the Irish Guards in the Second World War*, Gale and Polden Ltd, 1949.

Forbes, Patrick, *The Grenadier Guards in the War of 1939–45*, Gale and Polden Ltd, 1949.

Fürbringer, Herbert, *La Hohenstaufen*, Editions Heimdal, Bayeux, France.

Gavin, James M, *On to Berlin*, Leo Cooper Ltd, London, 1978.

Graham, John, *Ponder Anew*, Spellmount, 1999.

Harclerode, Peter, *Arnhem, A Tragedy of Errors*, Caxton Editions, 1994.

Hey, J A, *Roll of Honour Battle of Arnhem September 1944*, Society of Friends of the Airborne Museum Oosterbeek, The Netherlands, 1999.

Horrocks, Sir Brian, *A Full Life*, Collins, London, 1960, and *Corps Commander*, Sidgwick & Jackson, London, 1977.

Kershaw, Robert, *It Never Snows in September*, The Crowood Press, England, 1990.

Langdon, Allen, *Ready – A History of the 505th Parachute Infantry Regiment*, manuscript sent to the author by Allen Langdon in November, 1989.

Lehmann, Rudolf & Tiemann Ralf, *The Leibstandarte IV/1 and IV/2*, J J Fedorowicz Publishing Inc, Manitoba, Canada, 1993.

MacDonald, Charles B, *US Army in World War II, ETO, The Siegfried Line Campaign*, Washington, 1967

Maier, Georg, *Drama zwischen Budapest und Wien*, Munin Verlag, Osnabrück, 1985.

Marshall, S L A, *Bastogne – The First Eight Days*, US Army in Action Series, Center of Military History, US Army, Washington, DC, 1988.

Mawson, Stuart, *Arnhem Doctor*, Spellmount Classics, 2000.

Meyer, Hubert, *The History of the 12th SS Panzer Division Hitlerjugend*, J J Fedorowicz Publishing Inc, Manitoba, Canada, 1994.

Michels, Wilhelm & Sliepenbeek, Peter, *Niederrheinisches Land im Krieg*, Kleve, Boss-Druck und Verlag, 1975.

Middlebrook, Martin, *Arnhem 1944 The Airborne Battle*, Penguin Books, 1995.

Montgomery, Field Marshal The Viscount, *Memoirs*, Collins, 1958.

Munoz, Antonio J, *The Last Levy: SS Officer Roster March 1st, 1945*, Axis Europa Books, New York.

Powell, Geoffrey, *The Devil's Birthday*, Leo Cooper, London, 1992.

Radzievskiy, A I *Army Operations*, Voenizdat, Moscow, 1977.

Rauchensteiner, Dr. M, *Der Kampf um Wien 1945*, Österr. Milit. Zeitschrift, Heft 4/1970.

Reichelt, Walter E, *Phantom Nine*, Presidial Press, Austin, 1987.

Rosse, The Earl of, and Col E R Hill, *The Story of the Guards Armoured Division*, Geoffrey Bles Ltd, 1956.

Ryan, Cornelius, *A Bridge Too Far*, Hamish Hamilton, London, 1974.

Schneider, Wolfgang, *Tigers in Combat II*, J J Fedorowicz Publishing Inc, Manitoba, Canada, 1998

Sosabowski, Major General S, *Freely I Served*, William Kimber 1960.

Stacey, C P, Col, *Official History of the Canadian Army in the Second World*

War, Vol III, The Victory Campaign, Queen's Printer, Ottawa, Canada, 1960.

Strassner, Peter, *European Volunteers*, J J Fedorowicz Publishing Inc, Manitoba, Canada.

Swiecicki, Marek, *With the Red Devils at Arnhem*, Maxlove Publishing Ltd, 1945.

Taurus Pursuant, A History of the 11th Armoured Division. Germany, British Army of the Rhine, 1945

Tiemann, Ralf, *The Leibstandarte IV/2*, J J Fedorowicz Publishing Inc, Canada, 1998.

Toland, John, *Battle*, Severn House Publishers, 1977.

Urquhart, R E, *Arnhem*, Cassell 1958.

Weidinger, Otto, *Division Das Reich, Vol V*, Munin Verlag GmbH, Germany, 1982.

Weidinger, Otto, *Comrades to the End*, Schiffer Military History, Atglen, PA.

Wilson, B D, *The Ever Open Eye*, The Pentland Press Ltd, 1998.

Winter, George, *Manhay The Ardennes Christmas 1944*, J J Fedorowicz Publishing

Inc,1990 and *Freineux and Lamormenil – The Ardennes*, J J Fedorowicz Publishing Inc, Manitoba, Canada, 1994.

Yashin, Lt Col V F, *Study of the Defence by Formations of XXX Rifle Corps in the Balaton Defensive Operations*, Frunze Military Academy, Moscow, 1988.

Zavizion, G T and Kornyushin P A, *I na Tikhom okeane . . .*, Voenizdat, Moscow, 1967.

Zetterling, Niklas, *Normandy 1944*, J J Fedorowicz Publishing Inc, Manitoba, Canada, 2000.

Every effort has been made to obtain permission to quote from letters and specific books. In some case the authors are known to have passed away or could not be contacted and in others, publishing companies have ceased to exist or failed to reply to letters.

Index

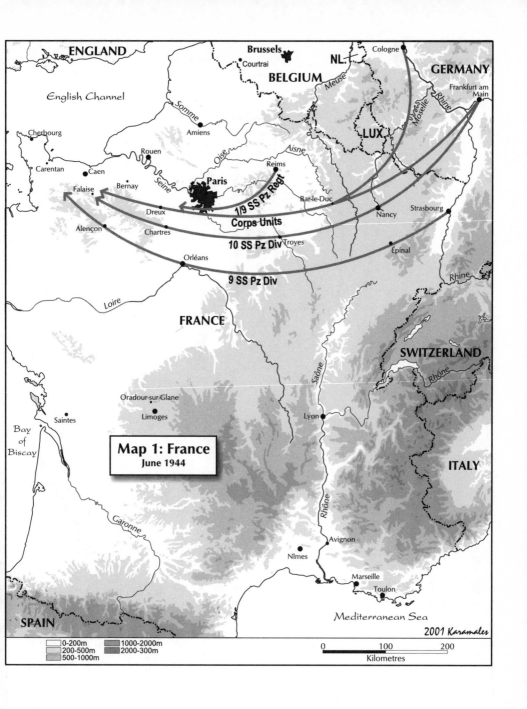

Map 1: France
June 1944

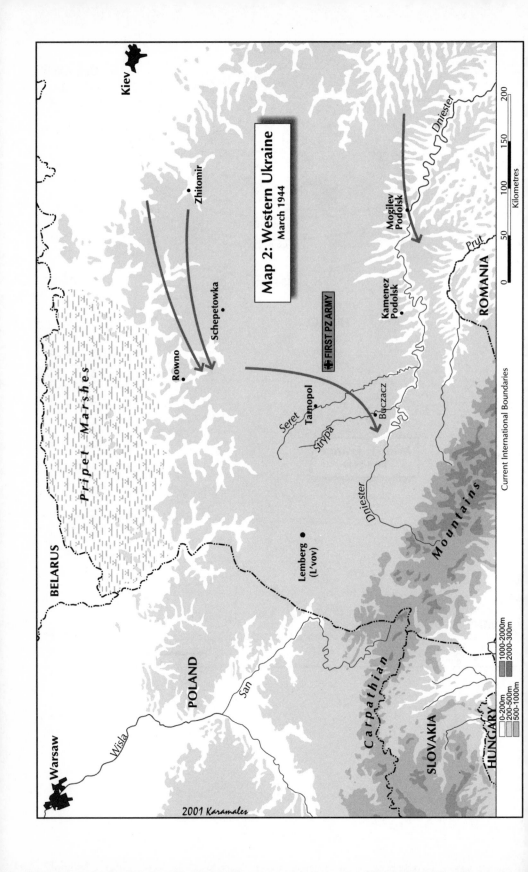

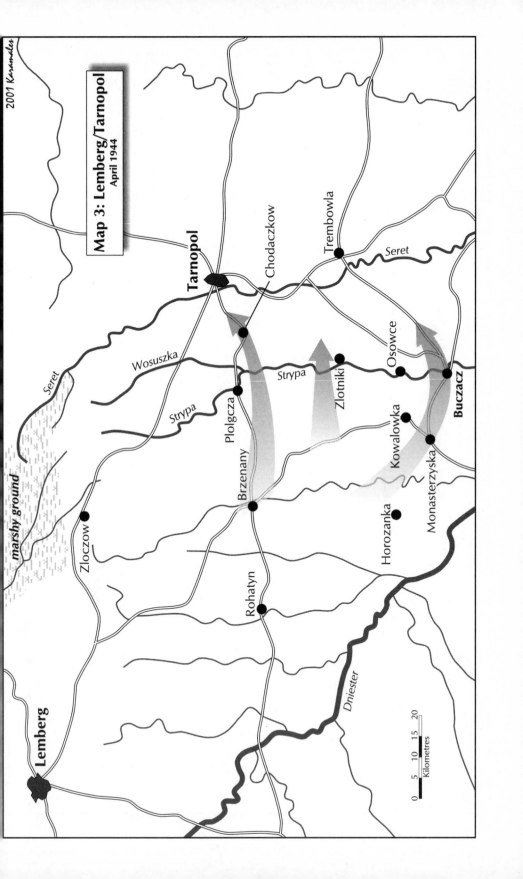

Map 3: Lemberg/Tarnopol
April 1944

2001 Karsander

Lemberg

marsh ground

Zloczow

Seret

Strypa

Wosuszka

Tarnopol

Chodaczkow

Trembowla

Seret

Plolgcza

Strypa

Zlotniki

Osowce

Brzenany

Buczacz

Kowalowka

Rohatyn

Horozanka

Monasterzyska

Dniester

0 5 10 15 20
Kilometres

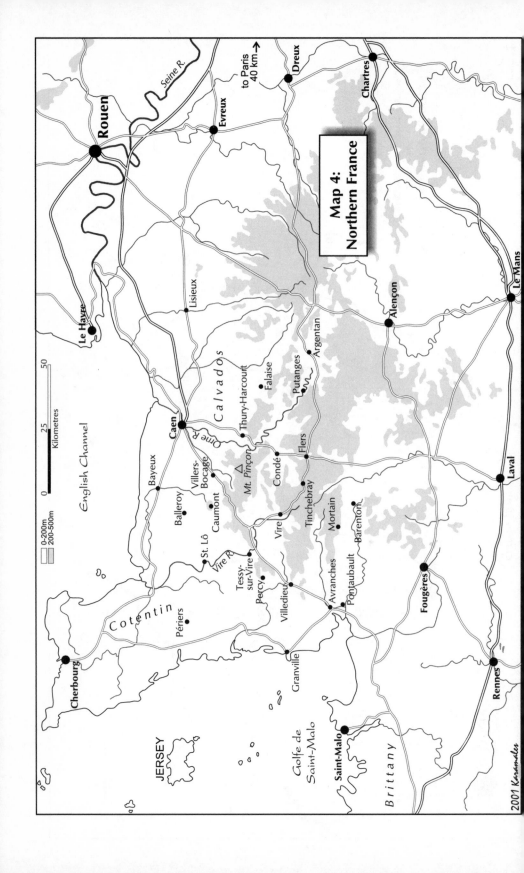

Map 4:
Northern France

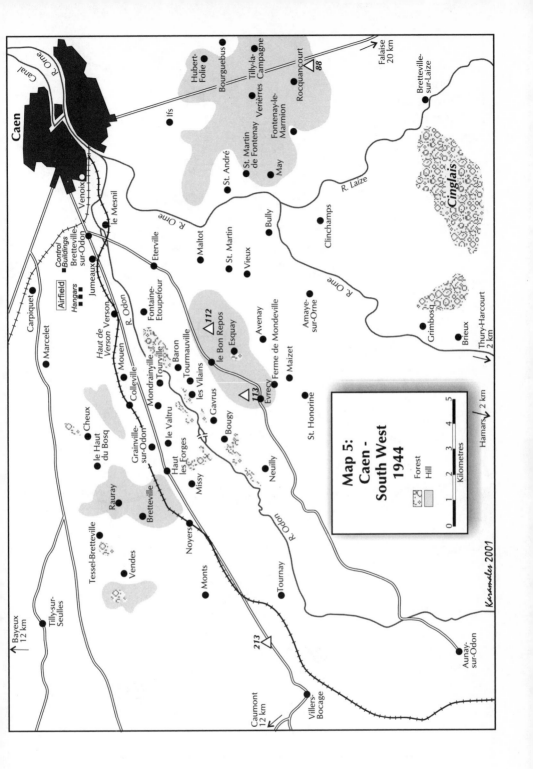

Map 5:
Caen –
South West
1944

Forest
Hill

Kilometres

0 1 2 3 4 5

Karamander 2001

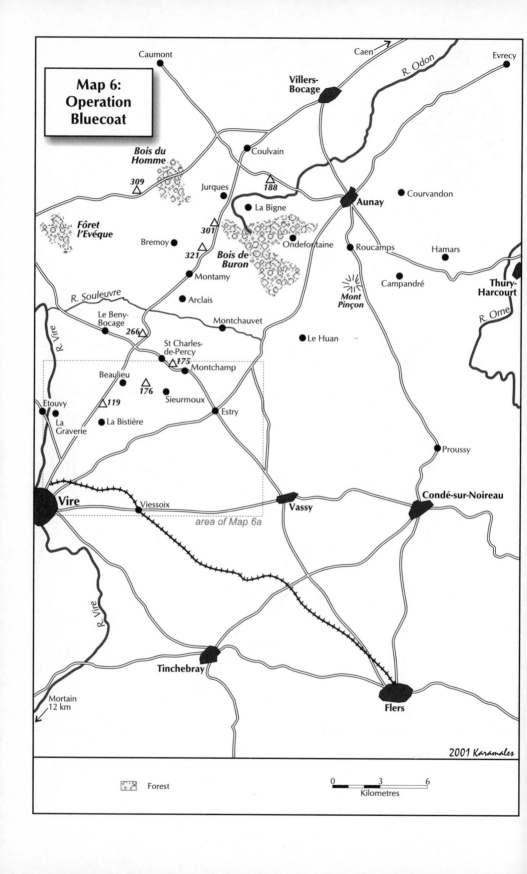

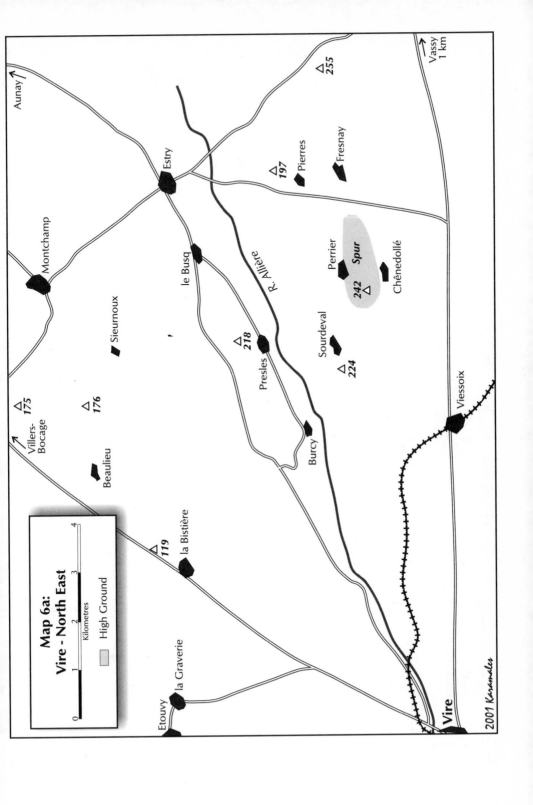

Map 6a:
Vire - North East

Kilometres
0 1 2 3 4

High Ground

Aunay

Montchamp

Estry

255

Villers-Bocage

175

176

Sieurnoux

le Busq

Pierres

197

Fresnay

Beaulieu

Presles

218

R. Allière

Perrier

Spur

242

Chênedollé

la Bistière

119

Burcy

Sourdeval

224

Vassy
1 km

Etouvy

la Graverie

Viessoix

Vire

2001 Kesmodes

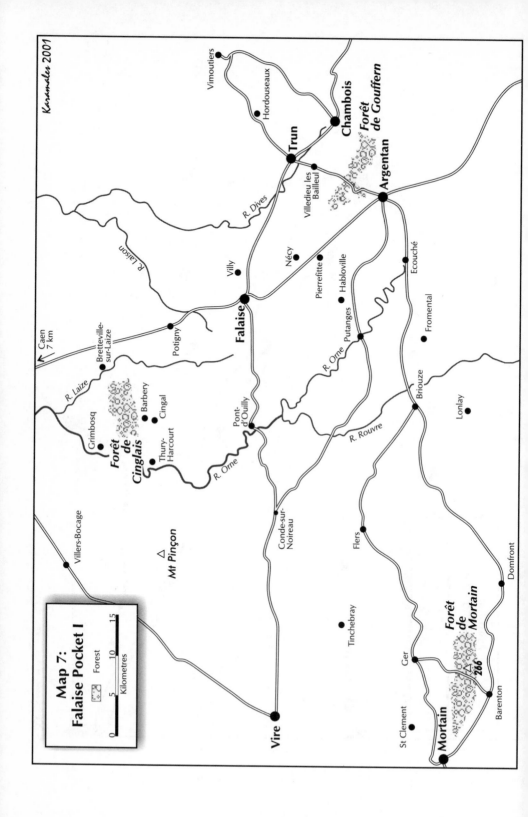

Map 7:
Falaise Pocket I

Forest

Kilometres
0   5   10   15

Caen
7 km

Villers-Bocage

Mt Pinçon

Vire

Conde-sur-Noireau

Tinchebray

Flers

St Clement

Mortain

Forêt de Mortain

266

Ger

Barenton

Domfront

Lonlay

Briouze

Fromental

Ecouché

Putanges

R. Orne

R. Rouvre

Pont-d'Ouilly

R. Orne

Thury-Harcourt

Grimbosq

Forêt de Cinglais

Barbery

Cingal

Potigny

Bretteville-sur-Laize

R. Laize

R. Laize

R. Laison

R. Dives

Falaise

Villy

Nécy

Pierrefitte

Habloville

Villedieu les Bailleul

Argentan

Forêt de Gouffern

Chambois

Trun

Hordouseaux

Vimoutiers

Karsander 2001

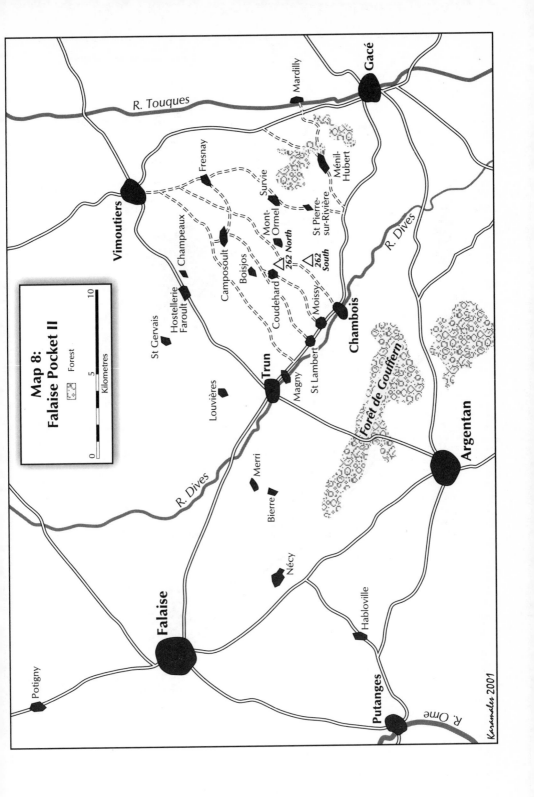

Map 8:
Falaise Pocket II

Forest

0   5   10
Kilometres

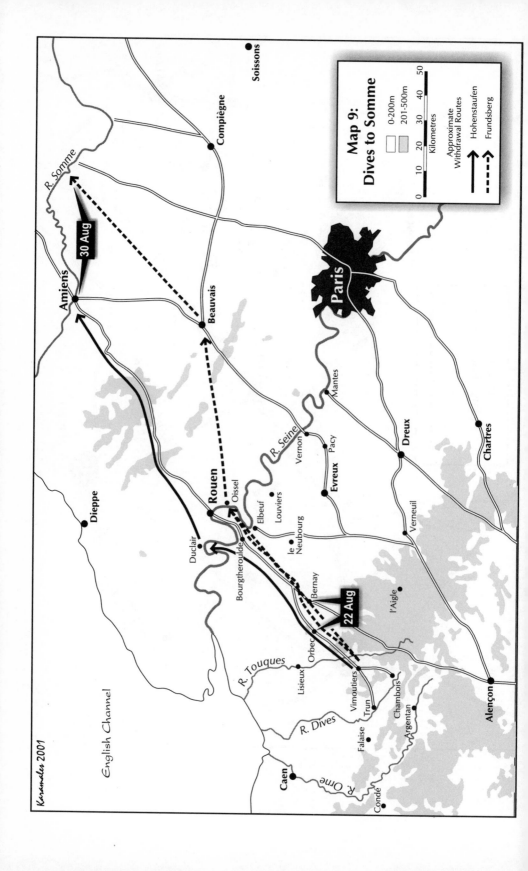

Map 9:
Dives to Somme

0-200m
201-500m

Kilometres

Approximate
Withdrawal Routes

Hohenstaufen
Frundsberg

Kerswoles 2001

English Channel

Soissons

Compiègne

R. Somme

30 Aug

Amiens

Beauvais

Paris

Dieppe

Duclair

Rouen

Oissel

Elbeuf

Louviers

le Neubourg

Bourgtheroulde

Bernay

22 Aug

Orbec

l'Aigle

Lisieux

Vimoutiers

Trun

Chambois

Falaise

Argentan

Alençon

R. Touques

R. Dives

R. Orne

Caen

Condé

Mantes

R. Seine

Vernon

Pacy

Evreux

Dreux

Verneuil

Chartres

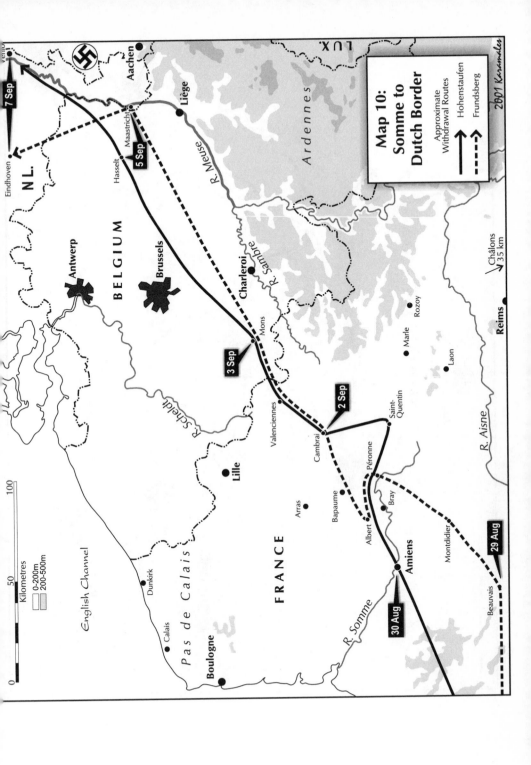

**Map 10:
Somme to
Dutch Border**

Approximate
Withdrawal Routes

Hohenstaufen

Frundsberg

LUX.

Aachen

7 Sep

Liège

Maastricht

5 Sep

Hasselt

Eindhoven

N.L.

Ardennes

R. Meuse

Antwerp

BELGIUM

Brussels

Charleroi

R. Sambre

Mons

3 Sep

Châlons
35 km

Rozoy

Marle

Reims

2 Sep

Saint-
Quentin

Valenciennes

Cambrai

Laon

Péronne

R. Aisne

Lille

Bray

Bapaume

Arras

Albert

Montdidier

29 Aug

Pas de Calais

Amiens

30 Aug

English Channel

Dunkirk

FRANCE

R. Somme

Beauvais

Calais

Boulogne

R. Scheldt

Kilometres
0   50   100

0-200m
200-500m

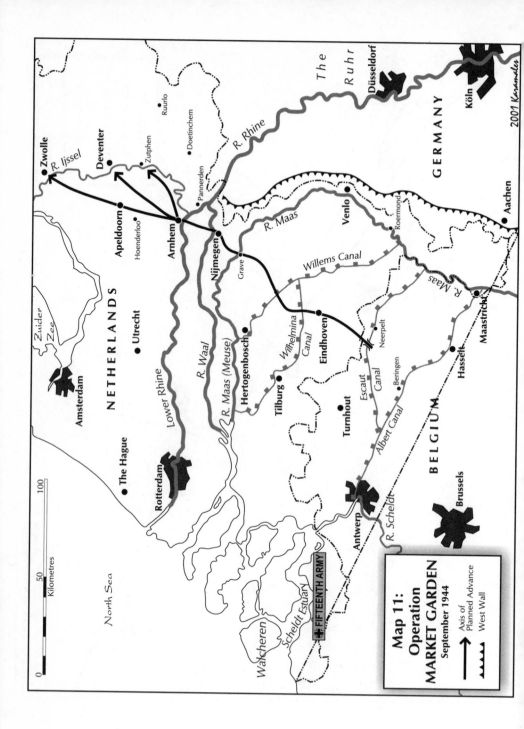

Map 11:
Operation
MARKET GARDEN
September 1944

Axis of
Planned Advance

West Wall

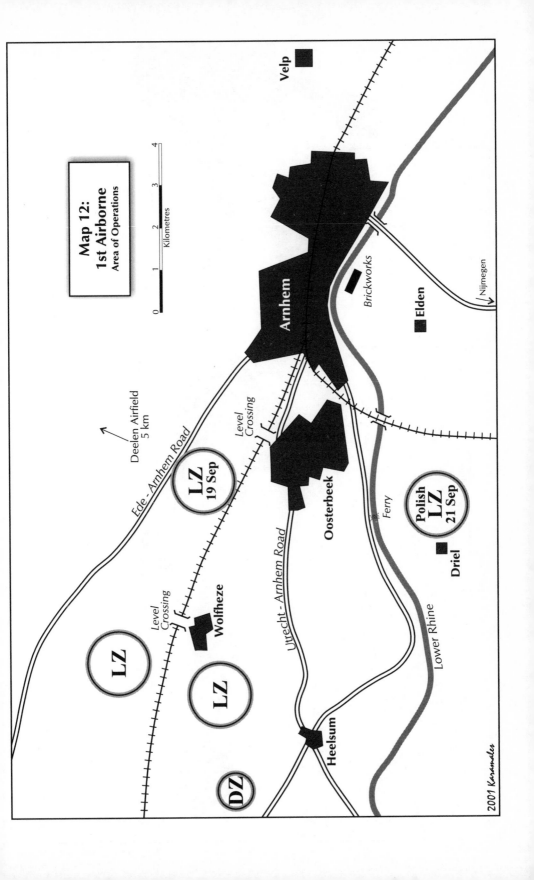

Map 12:
1st Airborne
Area of Operations

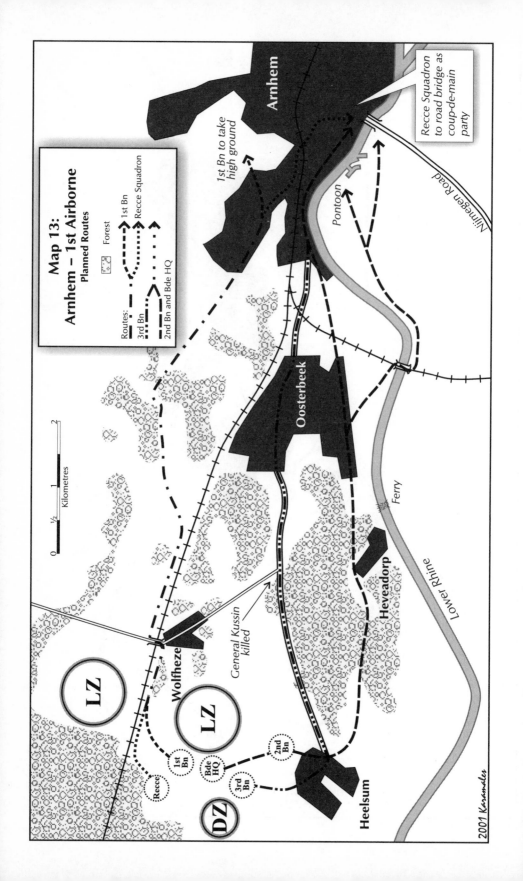

Map 13:
Arnhem – 1st Airborne
Planned Routes

Forest

Routes:
1st Bn
Recce Squadron
3rd Bn
2nd Bn and Bde HQ

Kilometres
0   ½   1   2

Arnhem

1st Bn to take high ground

Recce Squadron to road bridge as coup-de-main party

Pontoon

Nijmegen Road

Oosterbeek

Ferry

Lower Rhine

Heveadorp

General Kussin killed

Wolfheze

LZ

LZ

DZ

1st Bn

Bde HQ

Recce

3rd Bn

2nd Bn

Heelsum

2001 Karamler

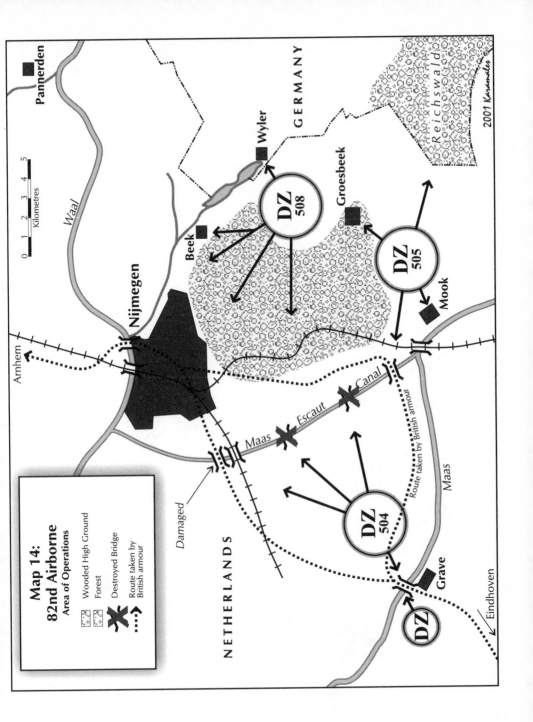

Map 14: 82nd Airborne
Area of Operations

	Wooded High Ground
	Forest
✖	Destroyed Bridge
┈	Route taken by British armour

Kilometres
0 1 2 3 4 5

NETHERLANDS

GERMANY

Reichswald

Pannerden

Waal

Arnhem

Nijmegen

Wyler

Beek

Groesbeek

Mook

DZ 508

DZ 505

DZ 504

DZ

Escaut

Canal

Maas

Maas

Damaged

Grave

Route taken by British armour

Eindhoven

2001 Kanander

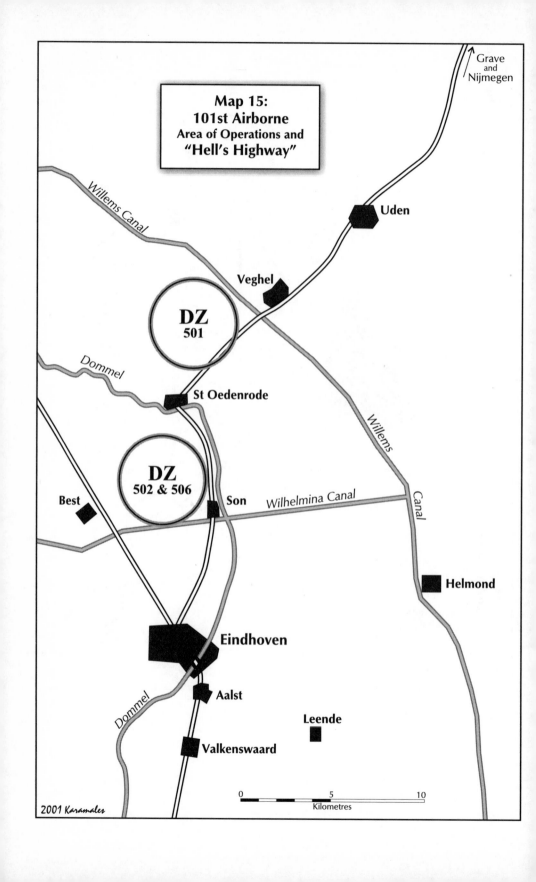

Map 15:
101st Airborne
Area of Operations and
"Hell's Highway"

Grave and Nijmegen

Willems Canal

Uden

Veghel

DZ 501

Dommel

St Oedenrode

Willems

DZ 502 & 506

Best

Son

Wilhelmina Canal

Canal

Helmond

Eindhoven

Dommel

Aalst

Leende

Valkenswaard

0   5   10
Kilometres

2001 Karamales

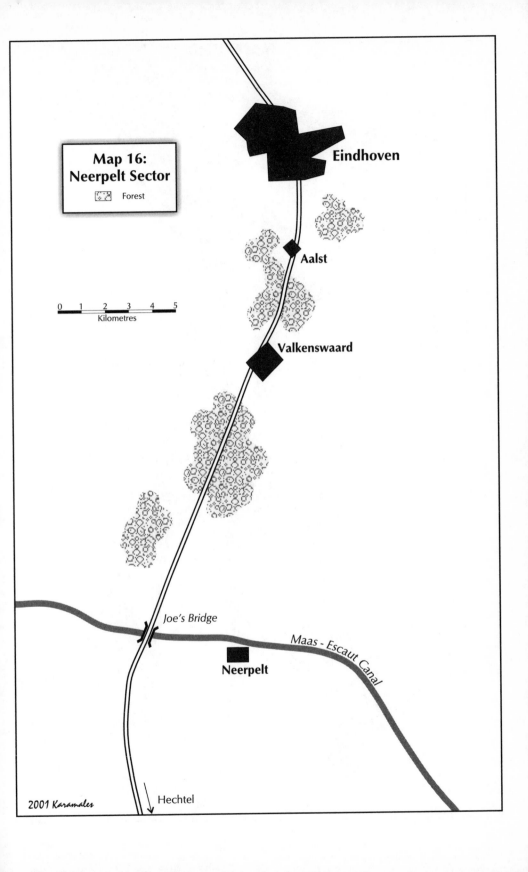

Map 16:
Neerpelt Sector

▨ Forest

0 1 2 3 4 5
Kilometres

Eindhoven

Aalst

Valkenswaard

Joe's Bridge

Maas - Escaut Canal

Neerpelt

Hechtel

2001 Karamales

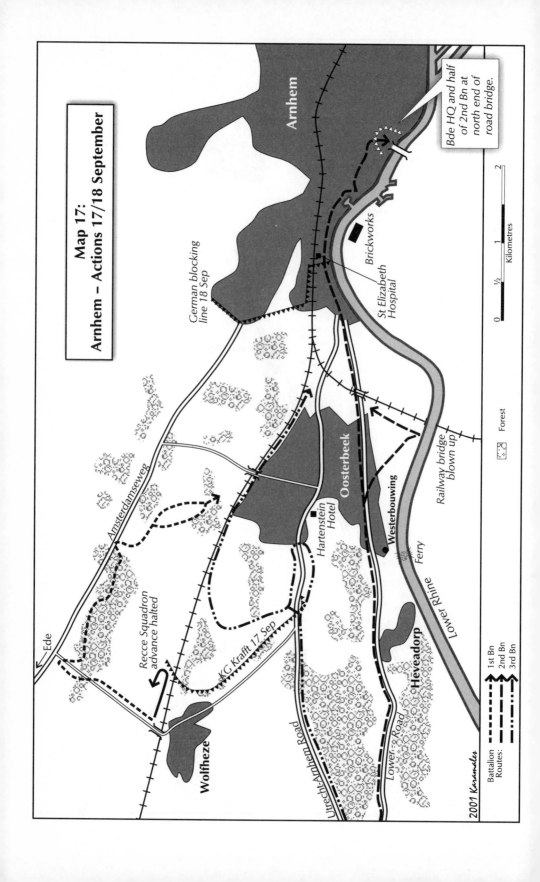

Map 17:
Arnhem – Actions 17/18 September

Arnhem

Bde HQ and half
of 2nd Bn at
north end of
road bridge.

Brickworks

St Elizabeth
Hospital

German blocking
line 18 Sep

Oosterbeek

Hartenstein
Hotel

Westerbouwing

Railway bridge
blown up

Amsterdamseweg

Recce Squadron
advance halted

Ede

KG Krafft 17 Sep

Ferry

Lower Rhine

Wolfheze

Utrecht-Arnhem Road

Lower Road

Heveadorp

2001 Karamdas

0   ½   1   2
Kilometres

Forest

Battalion
Routes: 1st Bn
               2nd Bn
               3rd Bn

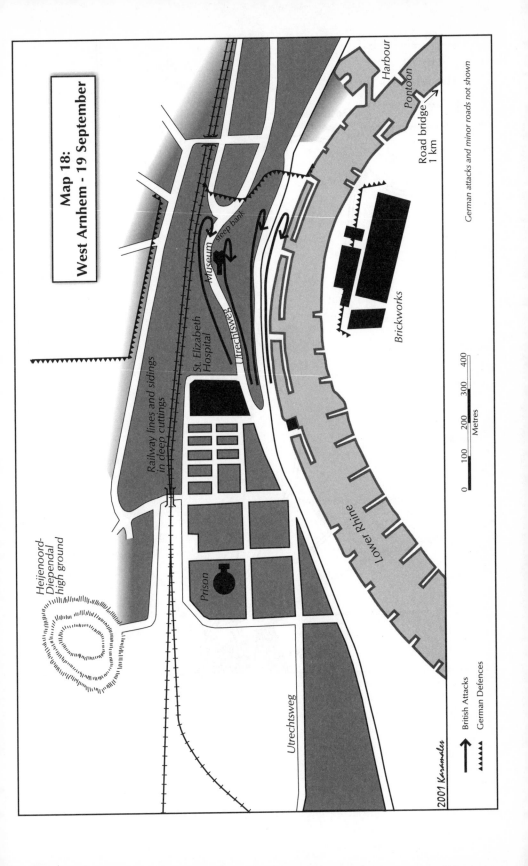

**Map 18:
West Arnhem - 19 September**

Heijenoord-
Diependal
high ground

Railway lines and sidings
in deep cuttings

Prison

St. Elizabeth
Hospital

Museum

steep bank

Utrechtsweg

Utrechtsweg

Brickworks

Harbour

Pontoon

Road bridge
1 km

Lower Rhine

0   100   200   300   400

Metres

German attacks and minor roads not shown

2001 Karssander

→ British Attacks

▲▲▲ German Defences

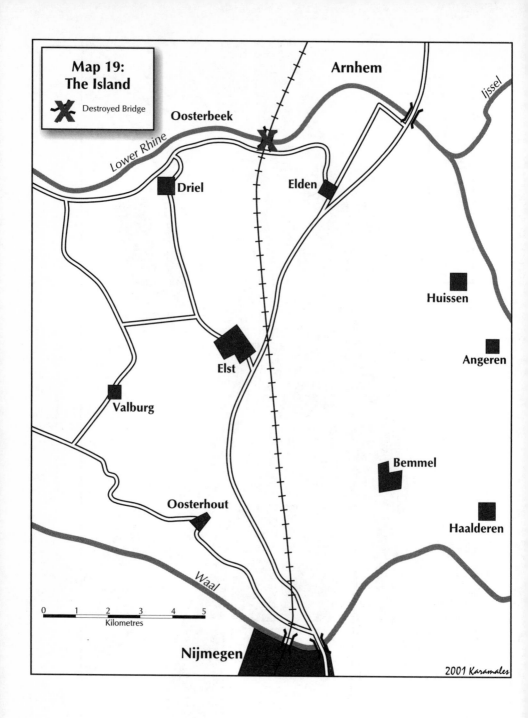

Map 19:
The Island

Destroyed Bridge

Arnhem

Oosterbeek

Ijssel

Lower Rhine

Driel

Elden

Huissen

Angeren

Elst

Valburg

Bemmel

Oosterhout

Haalderen

0 1 2 3 4 5
Kilometres

Waal

Nijmegen

2001 Karamales

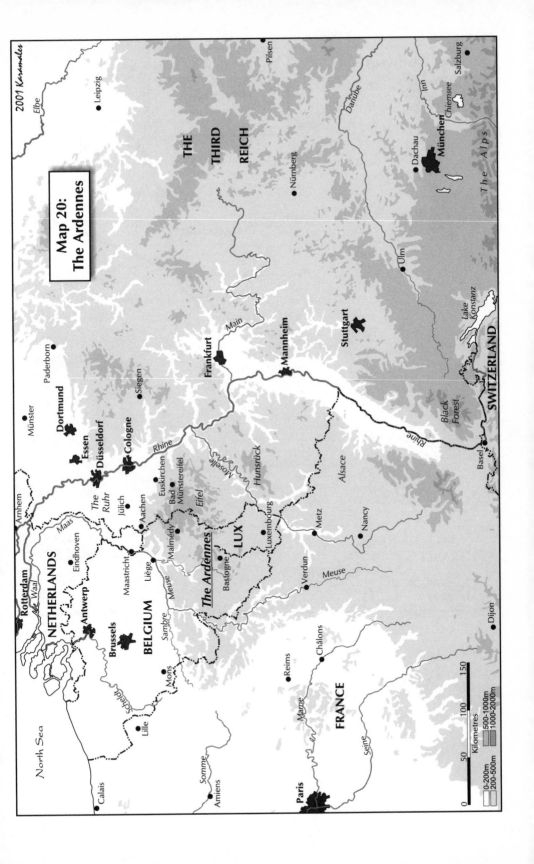

Map 20:
The Ardennes

2001 Kessander

North Sea

NETHERLANDS
Rotterdam
Arnhem
Eindhoven
Maas
Waal
Antwerp
Maastricht
BELGIUM
Brussels
Liège
The Ruhr
Jülich
Aachen
Essen
Düsseldorf
Dortmund
Münster
Paderborn
Cologne
Euskirchen
Bad Münstereifel
Eifel
Siegen
Rhine

THE
THIRD
REICH

Pilsen

Leipzig
Elbe

Salzburg

Münster

Mons
Lille
Calais

Somme
Amiens

FRANCE

Paris

Seine

Marne

Châlons

Reims

Verdun

Meuse

Metz

Nancy

Luxembourg
LUX
Bastogne
Malmédy
Meuse
Sambre
Scheldt
The Ardennes

Moselle
Hunsrück

Alsace

Frankfurt
Main

Mannheim

Stuttgart

Nürnberg

München
Dachau

Chiemsee
Inn

Danube

Ulm

Black
Forest

Rhine

Lake
Konstanz

Basel

SWITZERLAND

The Alps

0   50   100   150
Kilometres

0-200m
200-500m
500-1000m
1000-2000m

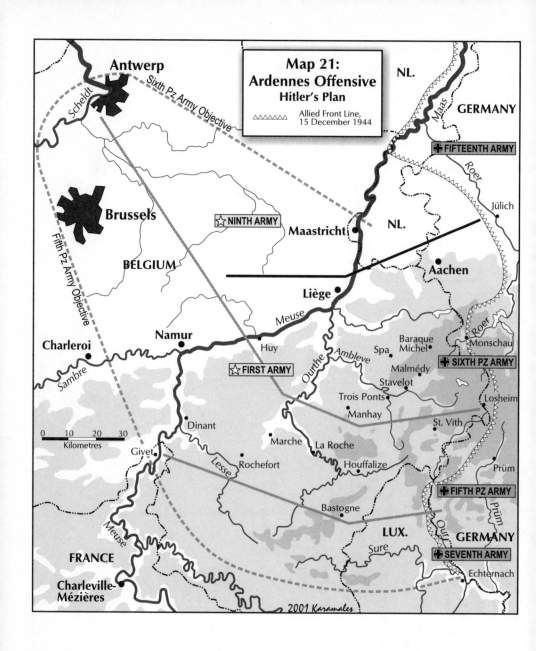

Map 21:
Ardennes Offensive
Hitler's Plan

ʌʌʌʌʌʌ Allied Front Line,
15 December 1944

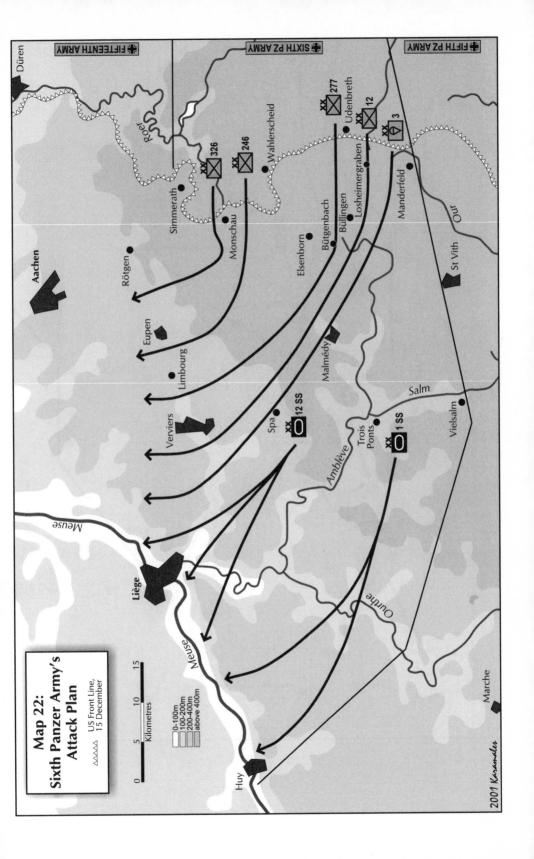

Map 22:
Sixth Panzer Army's
Attack Plan

△△△△ US Front Line,
15 December

0   5   10   15
Kilometres

0-100m
100-200m
200-400m
above 400m

2001 Korander

FIFTEENTH ARMY

SIXTH PZ ARMY

FIFTH PZ ARMY

Düren

Roer

Simmerath

Monschau

Wahlerscheid

XX 326

XX 246

XX 277

XX 12

3

Udenbreth

Losheimergraben

Büllingen

Bütgenbach

Elsenborn

Manderfeld

Rötgen

Aachen

Eupen

Limbourg

Verviers

Malmédy

Salm

St Vith

Out

Spa

XX 12 SS

Amblève

Trois
Ponts

XX 1 SS

Vielsalm

Meuse

Liège

Ourthe

Meuse

Huy

Marche

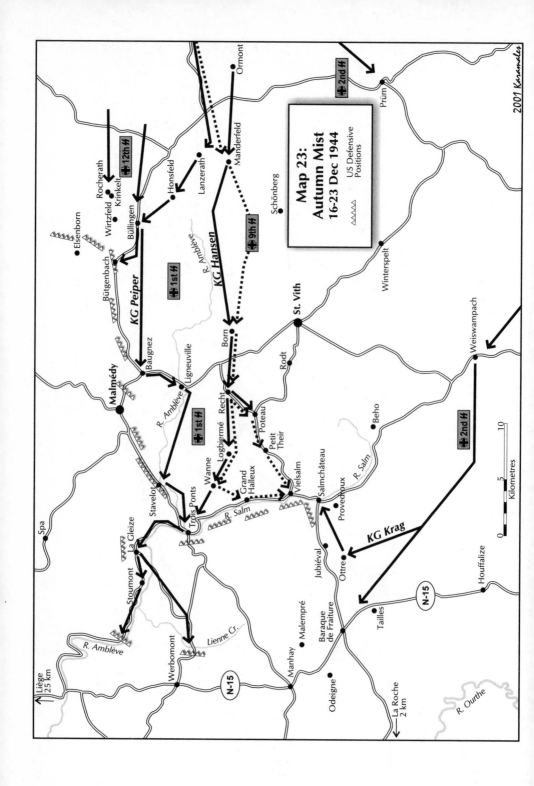

Map 23:
Autumn Mist
16-23 Dec 1944

US Defensive
Positions

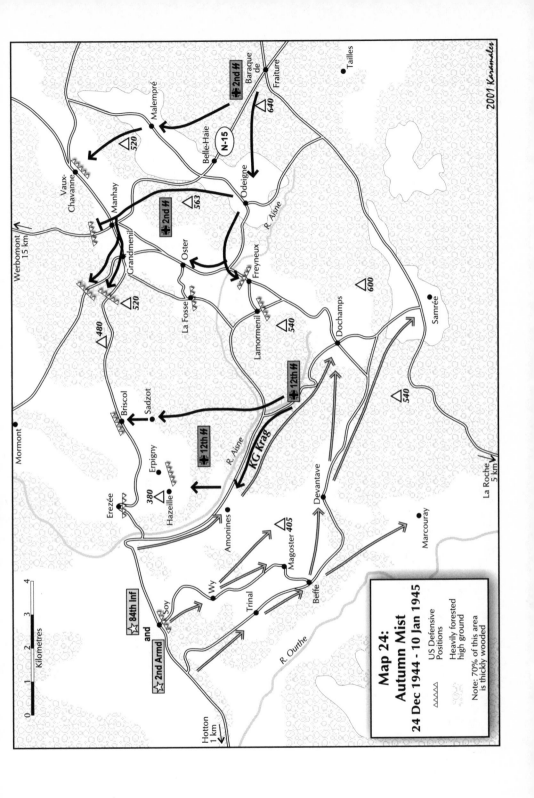

Map 24:
Autumn Mist
24 Dec 1944 - 10 Jan 1945

△△△△△ US Defensive
         Positions

         Heavily forested
         high ground

Note: 70% of this area
      is thickly wooded

Kilometres
0 1 2 3 4

2001 Kraemer

2nd ⚔
Baraque de Fraiture
Tailles
Malempré
△ 640
Belle-Haie
N-15
Odeigne
Vaux-Chavanne
Manhay
2nd ⚔
△ 563
R. Aisne
Werbomont
15 km
Grandmenil
Oster
Freyneux
△ 600
La Fosse
Lamormenil
△ 540
Dochamps
Samrée
△ 480
△ 520
Briscol
Sadzot
12th ⚔
△ 540
Mormont
Erpigny
12th ⚔
R. Aisne
KG Krag
La Roche
5 km
Erezée
380
Hazeille
Devantave
Amonines
△ 405
Marcouray
Wy
Magoster
84th Inf
and
Soy
Trinal
Beffe
2nd Armd
R. Ourthe
Hotton
1 km

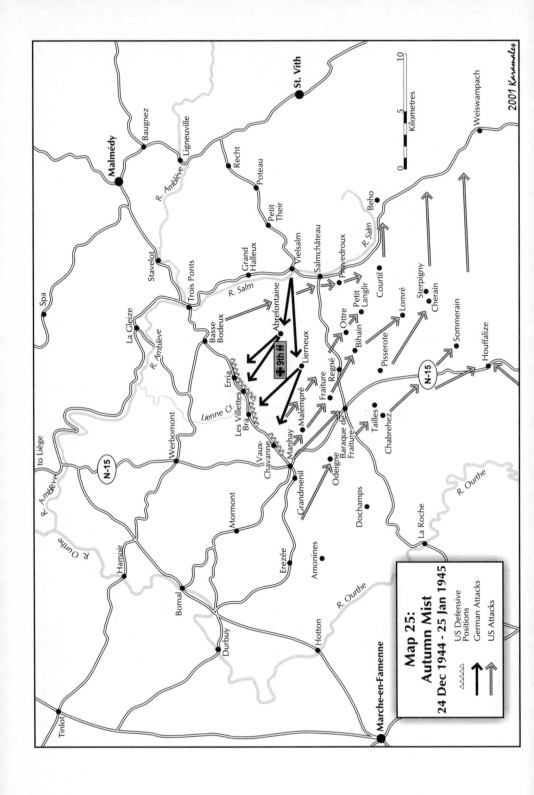

2001 Kransmiler

St. Vith

Malmédy

Baugnez

Ligneuville

Recht

Poteau

Petit Their

Spa

La Gleize

Stavelot

Trois Ponts

Grand
Halleux

Vielsalm

Salmchâteau

Provedroux

R. Salm

Beho

Weiswampach

R. Amblève

R. Amblève

Basse
Bodeux

Abrefontaine

Courtil

Sterpigny

✠ 9th ⚡⚡

Lierneux

Ottré

Petit
Langlir

Bihain

Lomré

Cherain

Sommerain

Erria

Regné

Fraiture

Pisserote

Houffalize

to Liège

Werbomont

Lienne C.

Les Villettes
Bra

Malempré

Tailles

N-15

N-15

Vaux-
Chavanne

Manhay

Baraque de
Fraiture

Chabrehez

R. Ourthe

Mormont

Grandmenil

Odeigne

Dochamps

La Roche

R. Ourthe

Hamoir

Bomal

Erezée

Amonines

R. Ourthe

Durbuy

Hotton

Tinlot

Marche-en-Famenne

Kilometres
0   5   10

**Map 25:
Autumn Mist
24 Dec 1944 - 25 Jan 1945**

◇◇◇◇◇   US Defensive
Positions

⬆   German Attacks

⬆   US Attacks

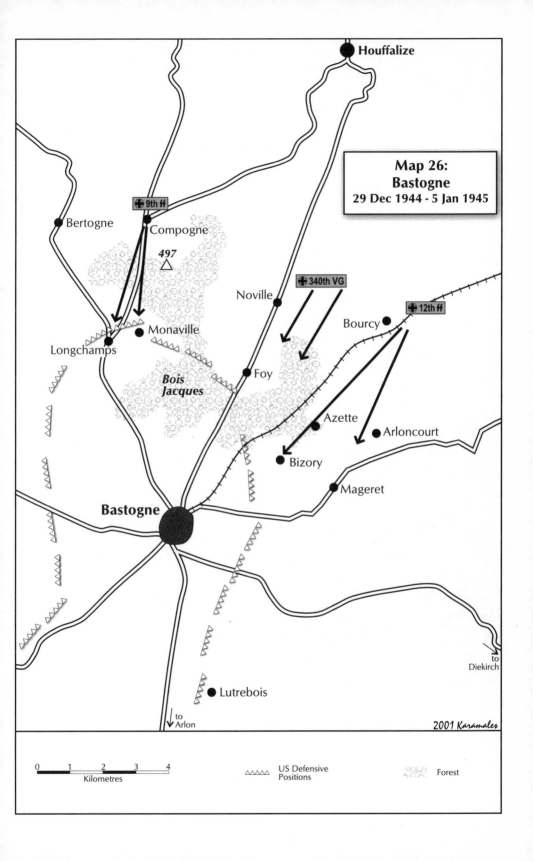

Houffalize

Map 26:
Bastogne
29 Dec 1944 - 5 Jan 1945

Bertogne

9th ✠

Compogne

497 △

Noville

340th VG

Bourcy

12th ✠

Monaville

Longchamps

Bois
Jacques

Foy

Azette

Arloncourt

Bizory

Bastogne

Mageret

to
Diekirch

Lutrebois

to
Arlon

2001 Karamales

0   1   2   3   4
Kilometres

∧∧∧∧∧ US Defensive
       Positions

       Forest

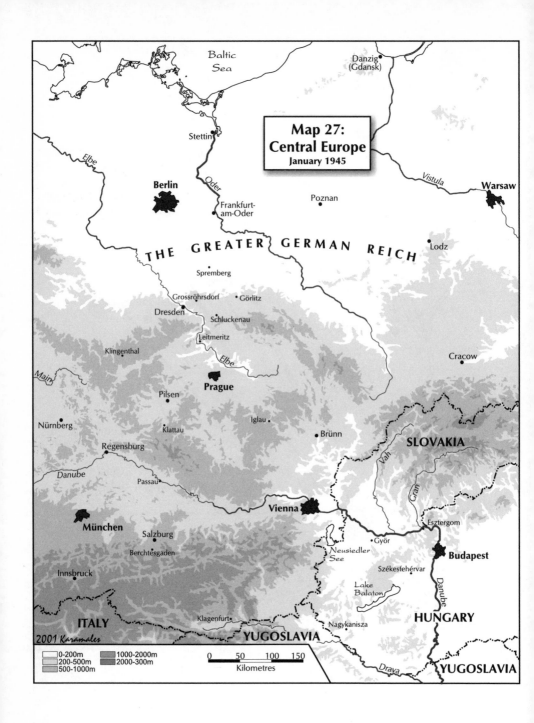

Map 27:
Central Europe
January 1945

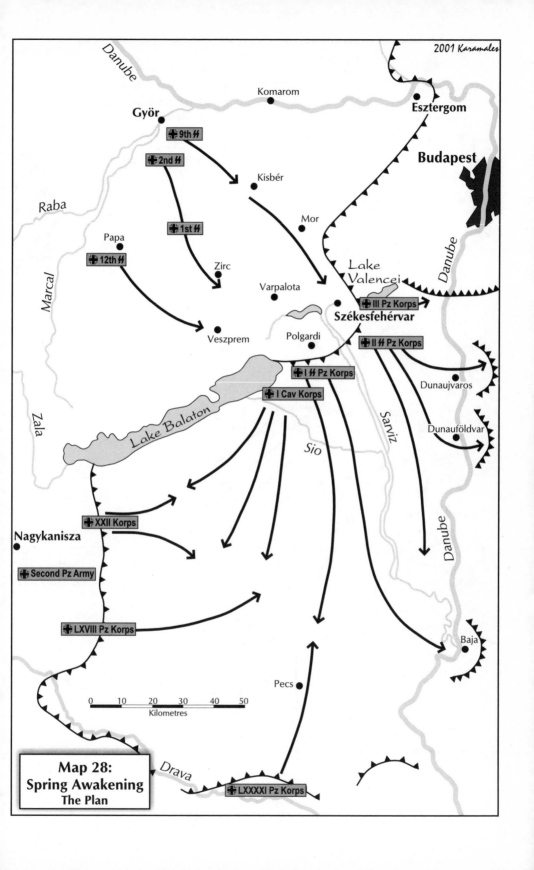

2001 Karamales

Danube

Komarom

Esztergom

Györ

9th ⚡

Budapest

2nd ⚡

Kisbér

Raba

1st ⚡

Mor

Papa

12th ⚡

Zirc

Lake Valencei

Danube

Varpalota

III Pz Korps

Székesfehérvar

Veszprem

Polgardi

II ⚡ Pz Korps

Marcal

I ⚡ Pz Korps

Dunaujvaros

I Cav Korps

Zala

Lake Balaton

Sio

Dunaföldvar

Sarviz

Danube

XXII Korps

Nagykanisza

Second Pz Army

LXVIII Pz Korps

Baja

0   10   20   30   40   50
Kilometres

Pecs

Map 28:
Spring Awakening
The Plan

Drava

LXXXXI Pz Korps

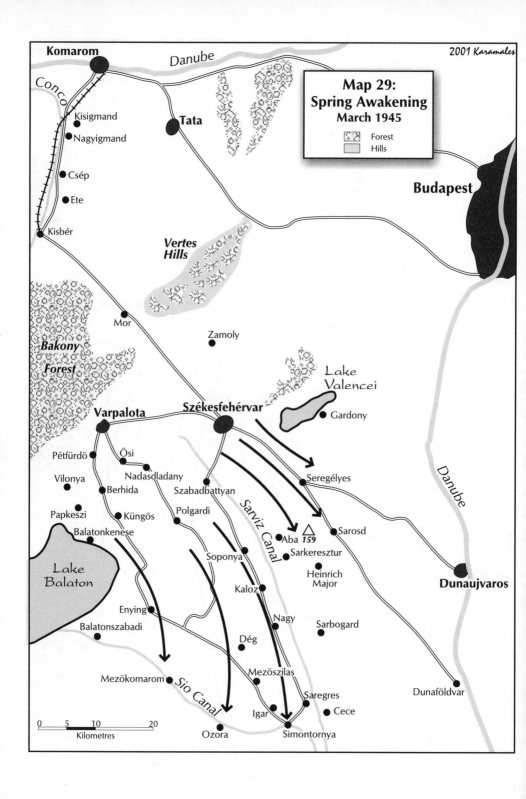

Map 29:
Spring Awakening
March 1945

Legend: Forest, Hills

2001 Karamales

Komarom, Danube, Conco, Kisigmand, Nagyigmand, Tata, Csép, Ete, Kisbér, Vertes Hills, Budapest, Mor, Zamoly, Bakony Forest, Lake Valencei, Varpalota, Székesfehérvar, Gardony, Pétfürdö, Ösi, Nadasdladany, Seregélyes, Vilonya, Berhida, Szabadbattyan, Papkeszi, Küngös, Polgardi, Sarviz Canal, Sarosd, Balatonkenese, Aba 159, Danube, Soponya, Sarkeresztur, Lake Balaton, Kaloz, Heinrich Major, Dunaujvaros, Enying, Nagy, Sarbogard, Balatonszabadi, Dég, Mezökomarom, Sio Canal, Mezöszilas, Saregres, Cece, Igar, Dunaföldvar, Ozora, Simontornya

0 5 10 20
Kilometres

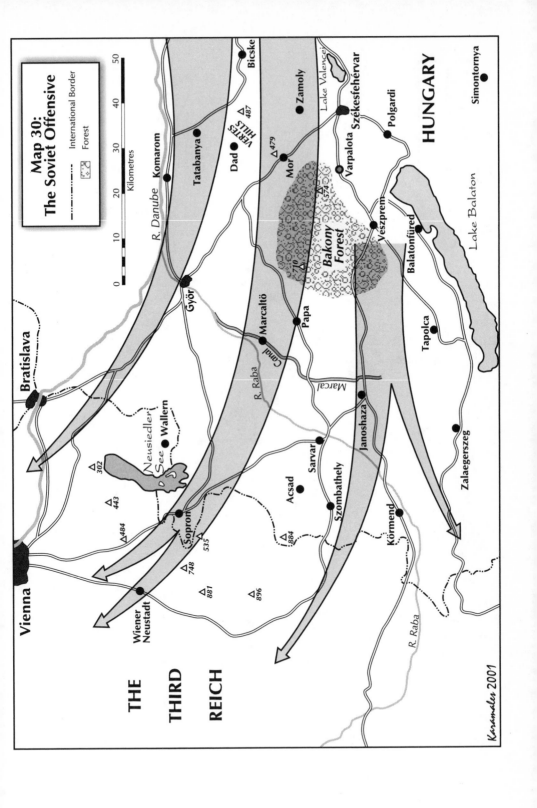

Map 30:
The Soviet Offensive

International Border
Forest

Kilometres
0 10 20 30 40 50

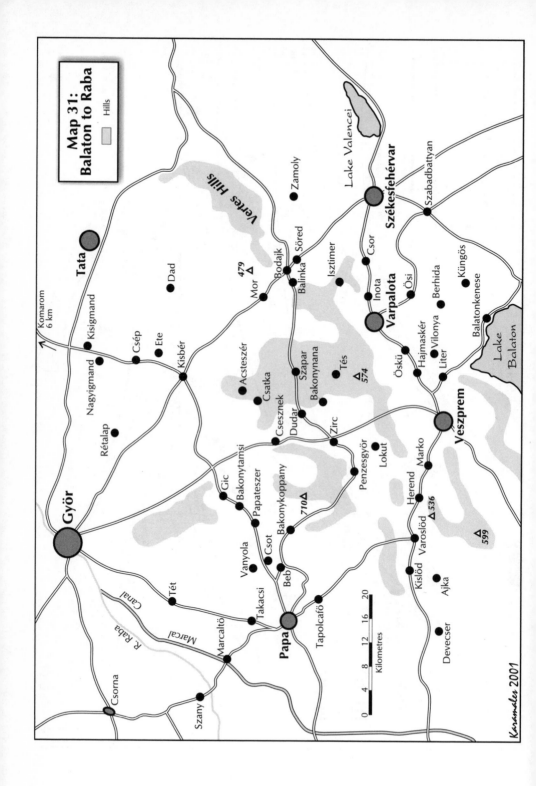

Map 31:
Balaton to Raba

Hills

Komarom
6 km

Tata

Nagyigmand
Kisigmand
Csép
Ete
Kisbér
Dad

Rétalap

Győr

Vértes Hills

479 △
Mor
Bodajk
Sőred
Balinka
Isztimer

Zamoly

Lake Valencei

Székesfehérvar

Szabadbattyan

Csor
Inota
Varpalota
Ösi
Küngös
Vilonya
Berhida
Hajmaskér
Liter
Balatonkenese

Acsteszér
Csatka
Csesznek
Dudar
Szapar
Bakonynana
Tés
574 △
Öskü

Lake
Balaton

Zirc

Penzesgyör
Lokut
Marko
Veszprem

Bakonytamsi
Gic
Papateszer
Bakonykoppany
710△
Csot
Beb

Vanyola

Herend
Varoslöd
536 △

599 △

R. Raba
Canal
Marcal
Canal

Tét
Takacsi
Marcaltö

Papa

Tapolcafö

Kislöd
Ajka

Devecser

Csorna
Szany

0   4   8   12 16 20
Kilometres

Karsmaler 2001

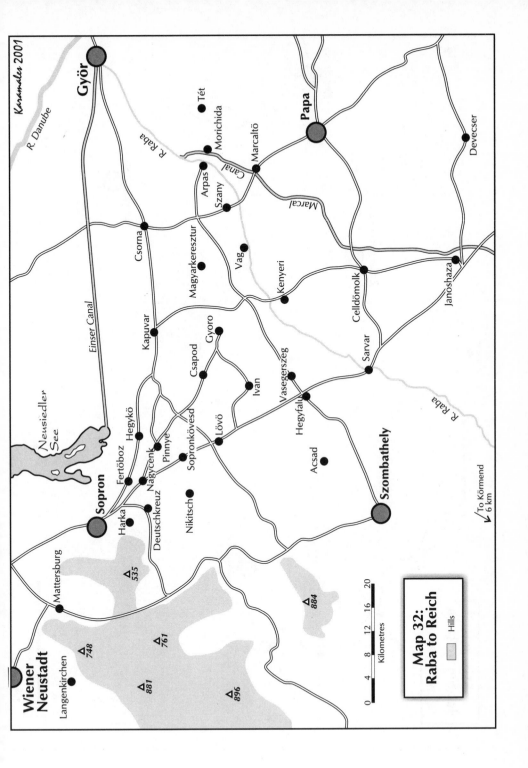

Kersmeier 2001

R. Danube

Neusiedler
See

Einser Canal

R. Raba

Canal

Marcal

R. Raba

**Wiener
Neustadt**

Langenkirchen

Mattersburg

△ 748

△ 881

△ 761

△ 896

△ 535

△ 884

Harka

Deutschkreuz

Nikitsch

Sopron

Fertöboz

Hegykö

Nagycenk

Pinnye

Sopronkövesd

Lövö

Csapod

Ivan

Gyoro

Kapuvar

Csorna

Magyarkeresztur

Vag

Kenyeri

Arpas

Szany

Magyarkeresztur

Tét

Morichida

Marcaltö

Papa

Devecser

Janoshaza

Celldömolk

Sarvar

Vasegerszeg

Hegyfalu

Acsad

Szombathely

Györ

To Körmend
6 km

0   4   8   12   16   20

Kilometres

**Map 32:
Raba to Reich**

☐ Hills

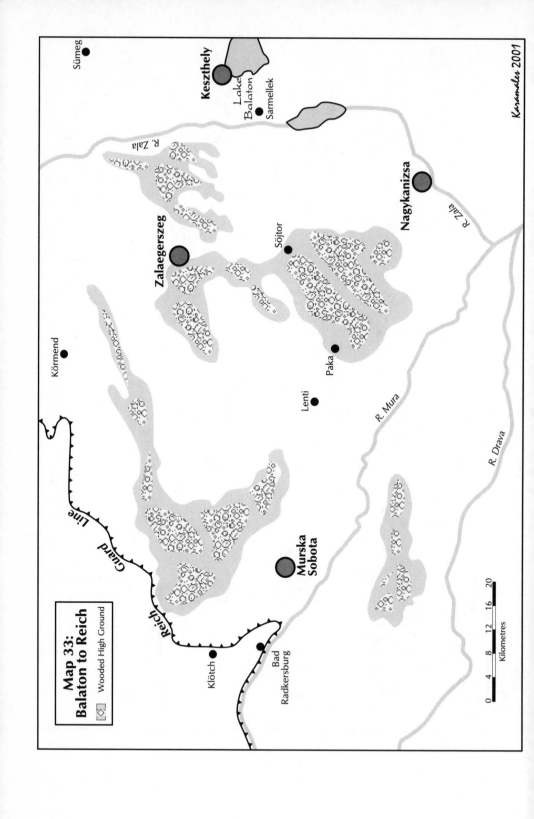

Map 33:
Balaton to Reich

Wooded High Ground

Sümeg

Keszthely

Lake Balaton

Sarmellek

R. Zala

R. Zala

Nagykanizsa

Zalaegerszeg

Söjtor

Körmend

Paka

Lenti

R. Mura

Murska Sobota

R. Drava

Klötch

Bad Radkersburg

Reich

Guard Line

Konsunder 2001

0   4   8   12   16   20
Kilometres

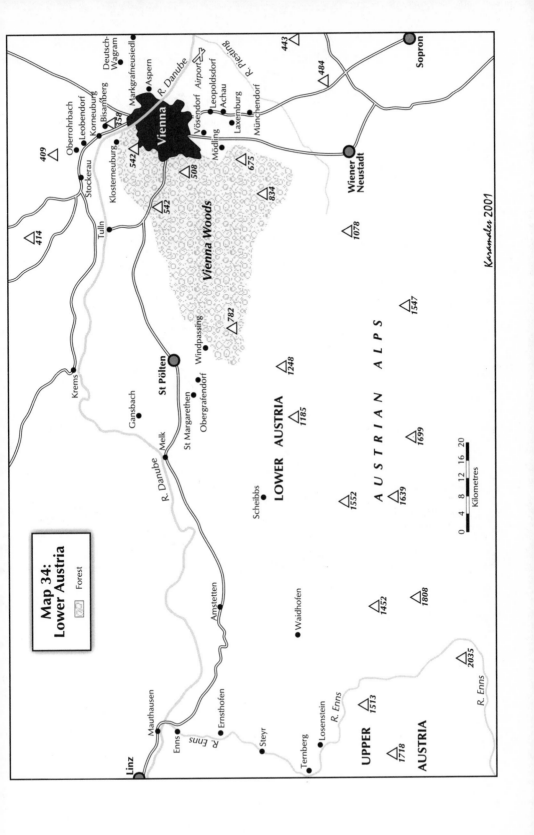

Map 34:
Lower Austria

Forest

Linz

Mauthausen

Enns

UPPER

AUSTRIA

Ternberg

Steyr

Losenstein

Ernsthofen

R. Enns

1513

1718

2035

R. Enns

R. Enns

Amstetten

Waidhofen

1452

1808

Scheibbs

1552

1639

LOWER   AUSTRIA

Melk

St Margarethen

Obergrafendorf

Gansbach

St Pölten

Krems

R. Danube

Windpassing

792

1185

1248

1699

1547

AUSTRIAN   ALPS

1078

0   4   8   12 16 20
Kilometres

Tulln

Stockerau

Klosterneuburg

542

542

508

834

675

Vienna Woods

Mödling

Korneuburg
Leobendorf

Oberrohrbach

409

414

Bisamberg

358

Markgrafneusiedl

Deutsch-
Wagram

Aspern

R. Danube

Vienna

Vösendorf
Airport

Leopoldsdorf

Achau

Laxemburg

Münchendorf

Wiener
Neustadt

443

484

Sopron

R. Piesting

Korsmeier 2001

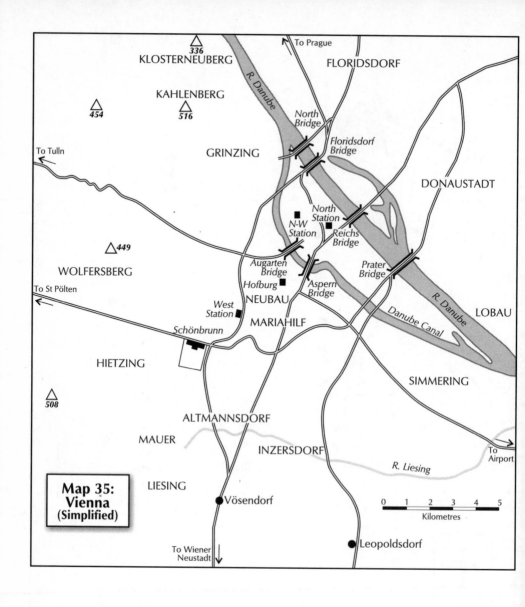

KLOSTERNEUBERG
△ 336

To Prague

FLORIDSDORF

KAHLENBERG
△ 516

R. Danube

North
Bridge

△ 454

To Tulln

GRINZING

Floridsdorf
Bridge

DONAUSTADT

△ 449

North
Station

N-W
Station

Reichs
Bridge

WOLFERSBERG

Augarten
Bridge

Prater
Bridge

To St Pölten

Hofburg

Aspern
Bridge

R. Danube

LOBAU

West
Station

NEUBAU

MARIAHILF

Danube Canal

Schönbrunn

HIETZING

SIMMERING

△ 508

ALTMANNSDORF

MAUER

INZERSDORF

To
Airport

R. Liesing

LIESING

Vösendorf

0   1   2   3   4   5
Kilometres

Map 35:
Vienna
(Simplified)

To Wiener
Neustadt

Leopoldsdorf